HOLLYWOOD:
The Golden Era

By **JACK SPEARS**

HOLLYWOOD:

The Golden Era

CASTLE BOOKS ★ **NEW YORK**

CONTENTS

ACKNOWLEDGMENTS

This book is a revised and updated collection of articles which appeared in their original form in *Films In Review,* official publication of the National Board of Review of Motion Pictures, Inc., between 1955 and 1968. For permission to reprint this material, I am indebted to Henry Hart, whose guidance, encouragement and friendship have been invaluable. I cannot adequately thank Robert Florey, who has taken long hours from his own career as a successful film director to share his enormous store of film history with me, and to open many doors that would otherwise have remained closed.

The material about Mary Pickford was obtained in a memorable visit with that gracious lady at Pickfair in 1962. Special thanks are due to Colleen Moore for interviews and assistance in the preparation of her career article. William K. Everson made it possible for me to see many of the films described. The late Sallie Marshall Chase, secretary to Marshall Neilan, was particularly helpful in filling in the details of Mickey's last tragic years, and a constant source of encouragement.

For their cooperation and patience in providing information and comment, I am indebted to Blanche Sweet, Frances Marion, Elia Kazan, Budd Schulberg, Henry R. Davis, Allan Dwan, Gertrude Bambrick Alicoate, Wesley Barry, Harold W. Grieve, Gloria Swanson, Charles Rosher, George Geltzer, Constance Talmadge, Ferde Grofe, Iron Eyes Cody, George J. Mitchell, Harold Lloyd, Francine Larrimore, Eleanor Boardman, Pinky Tomlin, Lillian St. Cyr (Red Wing), DeWitt Bodeen, Edward Wagenknecht and Francisco Rialp.

Death has claimed others who shared information and experiences, including Harry d'Arrast, William Beaudine, Adolphe Menjou, Chief John Big Tree, Sally O'Neil, Oliver LaFarge, Stanley Vestal (W. S. Campbell), Roy F. Overbaugh, Edward A. Wendel, and John L. Murphy.

For assistance in assembling the photographs, my deepest thanks to Rosendo Marinho, Charles Smith, Kenneth G. Lawrence, Maurice Bessy, Charles Ford, Kevin Brownlow, Paul Ivano, Nick Grinde, Roi A. Uselton and Leonard Maltin.

The quotation from *The Film Till Now* was used by permission of the author and copyright owner, Paul Rotha. The stills of Robert Florey are from his private collection. Permission for use of stills was kindly granted by Warner Brothers Pictures Corporation, United Artists Corporation, 20th Century-Fox Film Corporation, and Walt Disney Productions, Inc.

And for patience and understanding, my wife Helen, to whom this book is dedicated.

HOLLYWOOD:
The Golden Era

1
THE MOVIES OF
WORLD WAR I

*T*HE outbreak of World War I in Europe in 1914 came as the motion picture was emerging from the clumsiness of its formative years and standing hesitantly on the threshold of recognition as a new art form. Significantly, D. W. Griffith was at work in the same year on *The Birth of a Nation,* a monumental film which would boldly portray the enormities of an earlier war and reveal for the first time the tremendous propaganda potentials of the screen.

The events that began at Sarajevo were the impetus for a gradual but remarkable transition in film content. In the next three years the motion picture would become a major force in shaping public opinion, leading the United States from the trough of pacifism which had existed for a generation into a mounting war passion, culminating in America's entrance into the European conflict.

Pro-war sentiment, fed by disorganized propaganda, began growing in the United States soon after the German invasion of Belgium. For a time the neutrality policies of President Wilson kept these forces in check. It was not until late in 1916, with Wilson safely re-elected on the "he kept us out of war" platform, that peaceful idealism was abandoned for outright militarism. Nowhere is the transition from peace to preparedness to total war more vividly reflected than in the motion pictures of this turbulent era.

Hampered by growing pains in production and exhibition, and uneasily aware of strong national political pressures, the motion-picture industry steered a cautious course in the controversy. Peace was the keynote of the few war films released in the early months of the struggle abroad. Essanay's *The White Sister* ('15), a tragic story of a young woman (Viola Allen) who becomes a nun when she thinks her lover has been killed at the front, pointed up religious objections to war. The French-made *War Is Hell* ('14) had a similar plot and advocated a return to Christian teachings as the only antidote for war. *Be Neutral* ('14) reportedly filmed in forty-eight hours to support Wilson's neutrality proclamation, had an odd twist—two men argue neutrality so bitterly that a senseless murder follows. Francis Ford and Grace Cunard of serial fame had the leads.

Selig's *War O' Dreams* ('15) anticipated the atomic bomb by three decades. A young man (Edwin Wallock) invents a powerful explosive called "Trixite," triggered by nuclear elements, which wipes out thousands of civilians in an aggressive war. Aghast at the terrible consequences of his discovery, he carries the formula to a suicide's grave. A happy ending was tacked on by making it all a dream. *The Horrors of War*, produced in France in 1914 before the German onslaught, told of a Paris mother who watches her family die or degenerate one by one in the Prussian siege of 1870. Imported into the United States, it was widely shown but eventually withdrawn as the sentiment for preparedness mounted. Another import that met a similar fate was *Lay Down Your Arms* ('14), a Danish film produced for the projected Peace Convocation of Vienna, which never materialized. John Emerson's *Old Heidelberg* ('15), with Dorothy Gish and Wallace Reid (and Erich von Stroheim, as Lutz, the Prussian officer), attempted to perpetuate the operetta concept of Germans as quaint and harmless people. It was a fervent preachment against war, and its stunning battle scenes (which D. W. Griffith supervised) emphasized the suffering and futility of conflict. The exhibition of *Old Heidelberg* was also curtailed as the war fever grew. J. Searle Dawley's *One of Millions* ('14) was a blatant plea for peace in which the sight of a soldier's dead body drives his wife to madness.

The one distinctive anti-war film was Herbert Brenon's fine production of *War Brides* ('16), starring Alla Nazimova. Although based on a faulty premise—that the Germans were basically unwilling to participate in an aggressive war—it presented a boldly dramatic idea: the refusal of aroused women to bear children for slaughter. Nazimova was seen as the peasant wife whose husband and his brothers have been killed at the front. She organizes a demonstration against a government de-

Alla Nazimova (left) starred in Herbert Brenon's early peace picture, War Brides *(1916). Here her home is invaded by enemy soldiers of teutonic characteristics.*

cree that all single women must marry and produce children for the army. Told by a king there will always be war, she kills herself in protest. In a moving climax her body is borne aloft by the women, who vow there will be no children until men outlaw war forever.

Ostensibly laid in a mythical kingdom, *War Brides* clearly portrayed the Teutonic character of the invaders in physical characteristics and costuming. The film was deliberately suppressed, largely through the influence of William Fox, after the entrance of the United States into the war. Its producer, Lewis J. Selznick, was quoted as saying he "feared it might be misunderstood by unthinking people"—but in reality he feared it might be understood by thinking people.

Herbert Brenon, the sensitive director of *War Brides*, was said not to have been an active pacifist, but some of his later films—notably *The Side Show of Life, Beau Geste, Sorrell and*

Son, and *The Case of Sergeant Grischa*—contain pointed references to the futility of war. (However, in 1918, Brenon also made a pro-war propaganda picture for the British government although it was completed after the Armistice and never shown.) As a result of its limited release and unpopular theme, the superior production values and dramatic qualities of *War Brides* were generally overlooked. Nazimova gave a compelling performance in the best picture of her career—she had not yet embarked upon the neurotic heroines so disliked by American audiences—and a young Richard Barthelmess attracted attention in his first important acting assignment.

Thomas H. Ince's *Civilization* ('16) was an overpraised film whose role in the peace movement has been consistently magnified. Too much significance was attached to the recognition Woodrow Wilson gave it at the behest of the Democratic party. Naïve and shallow in conception, *Civilization* told of the spirit of Christ returning to earth in a war hero's body. Although persecuted and maligned for his efforts to restore peace, the inspired soldier finally triumphs. The picture suffered from an implausible setting—a Graustarkian kingdom—and was pseudo-religious, poorly motivated, and lacking in sincerity. Some of the film's uneven execution was due to a multiplicity of directors. Ince is usually credited with personally directing *Civilization,* but it was largely the work of Raymond B. West. Other directors engaged on it were Reginald H. Barker, Scott Sidney, and J. Parker Read (Ince's business manager and publicity director). Ince undoubtedly lacked any real enthusiasm for pacifism (his war films of '17-'18 were shockingly brutal), and he seized upon the peace motif of *Civilization* purely for its topical appeal at the box office. It cost $100,000 and returned a profit of $800,000. Ince had, in fact, turned out a pro-war film, *The Coward,* the previous year, in which the audience is led to admire a young man who overcomes his cowardice to serve the war cause.

D. W. Griffith's *Intolerance* ('16), which many consider to be the finest motion picture ever made, is not fundamentally concerned with war, although conflict is vividly enacted in the Babylonian and Huguenot sequences. Griffith probably did not set out to make an anti-war film of *Intolerance,* but its pacifism is obvious. He saw war as an inherent product of intolerant attitudes in nations, races, and individuals. Griffith protested the motivations of war, rather than the act itself, yet so stunning and magnificent are the battle scenes of *Intolerance* that they lend a frightening glamour to war. The moral was lost in an overemphasis upon spectacle. *Intolerance* was not a popular success, and it lost money—Griffith was still paying off its debts in 1923. (Most estimates place its loss at $1.9 million.) It is doubtful that it would have enjoyed greater success had it been released a year earlier, at the floodtide of pacifism. Audiences were simply bewildered by its excessive length, ponderous moralizing, and the confusing manner in which four separate stories were interwoven.

The mounting demands for preparedness in the United States were readily discernible by mid-1915, although public opinion continued to resist participation in the European war. The fighting was overseas and remote in any personal sense. The Wilson administration, with an eye to the presidential elections of the following year, was following a staunch neutrality policy. Preparedness and its eventual goal of a shooting war would obviously have to be sold to the American public.

The first impetus to the use of motion pictures for militaristic propaganda came with J. Stuart Blackton's *The Battle Cry of Peace* ('15), an account of an imaginary invasion of New York by a foreign power. This unabashed piece of cinematic flag-waving set in motion an insistent demand for increased armaments. It was, as Blackton admitted later, "a call to arms . . . propaganda for the United States to enter the war . . . made deliberately for that purpose." Theodore Roosevelt, Blackton's neighbor at Oyster Bay, encouraged its production.

The Battle Cry of Peace was bitterly attacked as a ruse to enrich munitions manufacturers (its author was Hudson Maxim, whose family developed the machine gun). Henry Ford spent thousands on full-page newspaper advertisements, trying ineffectually to combat the inflammatory spirit of the film. Blackton was assailed as a warmonger and professional patriot. Interestingly, the first instance of the movies being used for pro-war propaganda dated back to Blackton's pioneer production, *Tearing Down the Spanish Flag* ('98), filmed in a few hours on the roof of the Morse Building in New York the same day the United States declared war on Spain.

As directed by Wilfred North, *The Battle Cry of Peace* was a skillful and entertaining picture. Norma Talmadge and Charles Richman had the leads, and many scenes showed Woodrow Wilson and his Cabinet with prominent military and political figures. The most significant aspect of the film was the manner

Irene Castle was fetching in a low cut gown amid the horrible decor of the Hearst propaganda serial, Patria *(1916).*

in which the Germans—although not actually identified as such —were depicted as cruel aggressors. It created the prototype for the mustached Prussian villain, the lustful Hun bent upon rape, pillage, and murder. Scenes of rape by bestial soldiers, bayoneting of babies and young children, village-burning, and needless brutality were all purposely designed to create a universal feeling of hatred and loathing for the enemy. Blackton continued his vicious propaganda appeals to the very end of the war with such lurid films as *Wake Up, America* ('16), *The Glory of a Nation* ('17), *Womanhood* ('17), *Common Cause* ('18) and *Safe for Democracy* ('18).

The Battle Cry of Peace hastened a flood of pro-war pictures that grew in bitterness and patriotic hysteria as the weeks sped by. *Defense or Tribute?*, financed by a group of American businessmen and released in March, 1916, showed the Founding Fathers of the United States revisiting earth and considering the grave perils of the country. Flashbacks pictured the Jews suffering at the hands of their oppressors, the Roman conquest of Gaul, and the ferocity of the Italian Revolution and the French

Terror. The audience was then asked point blank if it wanted invasion and conquest, and President Wilson, Admiral Dewey, and Theodore Roosevelt were quoted. The film ended with, of all things, a re-creation of the Charge of the Light Brigade and the analogy of the United States blundering unprepared and ill-led into the Valley of Death!

Pacifists were openly ridiculed in many movies. In Lubin's *A Nation's Peril* ('16), Ormi Hawley was a bird-brained pacifist heroine who is made to realize war is inevitable. She becomes a militant advocate of preparedness, and at the close is seen herding young men into an Army recruiting office. Mutual's *Perkins' Peace Party* ('16) told of a bumbling professor and his feckless friends who go to Europe to stop the war by peaceful persuasion. After a series of absurdities and hardships they realize force is needed, and return home disenchanted with the peace movement. Douglas Fairbanks played a brash young man in *In Again, Out Again* who set out to convert his pacifist sweetheart (Arline Pretty) to preparedness. Opportunely released in early 1917, it attacked the hypocrisy of peace leaders who were secretly selling war materiel at fabulous profits. Mutual came out in 1916 with a whole series of two-reelers, entitled *Uncle Sam's Preparedness,* calling for intervention in the fighting abroad. Both fictional stories and documentary film were utilized.

The Fall of a Nation ('16) was a foolish and inept picture which likened pacifism to treason and openly criticized nationally known personalities, particularly William Jennings Bryan (as had *The Battle Cry of Peace*), for their anti-war stand. Written and produced by the Reverend Thomas A. Dixon, author of *The Birth of a Nation,* it was about a deluded politician who insists on peace at any price and eventually, by discouraging military preparedness, betrays the United States to enemy invaders. The impersonation of Bryan (by Percy Standing) was only thinly disguised—the make-up was identical—and quotations from Bryan's speeches and writings were used in endless aphoristic titles. Dixon also attacked the clergy for its adherence to neutrality, and a minister, sent out to reason with the invaders and welcome them with kind acts, was portrayed as little better than a moron. After a series of atrocities and humiliations the country's young men arise and drive out the enemy. (Dixon said the climactic battle scenes were filmed at a cost of $31,000 on the identical location used for the Confederate charge in Griffith's *The Birth of a Nation.*)

Most of the acting in *The Fall of a Nation* was amateurish, and the direction (by Bartley Cushing) mediocre. Dixon was immediately set upon by critics in Washington and many segments of the press. Less than two weeks after the picture opened in New York, he denied it was anti-German, despite the marked Teutonic character and uniforms of the enemy soldiers. Said Dixon: "I chose these men because they were out of work and hungry. Five hundred Germans applied to me for work in the battle scenes, and I was glad to give it to them." He went on to describe his own Prussian ancestry and said "this strain in my blood, as well as my inherent sense of fairness . . . would prevent me from singling out Teutons for attack." The only good thing about *The Fall of a Nation* was a musical score by Victor Herbert, who had invested money in the picture. Dixon claimed Herbert wrote 1,238 musical themes for the film, which was advertised as "a grand opera of the cinema"—but *Photoplay* Magazine called it "a symphony with pictorial fetters."

Spy stories, built around German and Japanese villains, made ideal vehicles to emphasize the need for preparedness. Many highly romanticized espionage dramas attacked the fallacy of insular security, pointed the finger of suspicion at enemy aliens, and questioned the loyalty of some highly placed government officials. Typical of these routine spy thrillers was Vitagraph's *The Hero of Submarine D-2* ('16), starring James Morrison and Zena Keefe, which dealt with attempts of German agents to destroy an American naval base. In Unity's *My Country First* ('16), a mustachioed Alfred Vosburgh, made up to resemble the Kaiser, tried to steal the formula for a powerful explosive from a young inventor (Tom Terriss). Kitty Gordon was a pretty double agent in World's *As In a Looking Glass* ('16), who foiled Prussian efforts to copy the fortification plans of New York Harbor. Kay-Bee's *Over Secret Wires* ('15) told of a U.S. Secret Service operator who discovered German spies sending messages to an enemy submarine off the coast of Oregon.

Serials were a particular source of preparedness propaganda. *Patria* ('16), financed by William Randolph Hearst, was described as "a cinematic editorial for preparedness." Irene Castle played an American heiress to the world's largest munitions factory and a secret fund of $100,000,000 to prepare the nation against attack. In keeping with Hearst's current hate policy, the film was rabidly anti-Japanese and anti-Mexican, and the Oriental villain (Warner Oland) who menaced Miss Castle and hero

Milton Sills was particularly offensive. *Patria* became something of a cause célèbre when President Wilson sent a note to the producers saying the picture was "extremely unfair to the Japanese . . . and is calculated to stir up a great deal of hostility which would be far from beneficial to this country." He suggested the serial be withdrawn from exhibition, and in a few areas *Patria* was banned outright. Oland's role was toned down, and shots of the Japanese and Mexican flags were eliminated.

In *Pearl of the Army* ('16), publicized as "the serial with a purpose," Pearl White combatted Oriental spies trying to destroy the Panama Canal. Other preparedness serials were *The Secret of the Submarine* ('16), with Juanita Hansen, in which Japanese and Russian agents tried to steal a device that enabled a submarine to remain submerged indefinitely; *Liberty, A Daughter of the U.S.A.* ('16), with Jack Holt and Marie Walcamp, which utilized the Pancho Villa disturbance on the Mexican border as a pretext for preparedness; and *Grant, Police Reporter* ('17)—actually a series instead of a serial—which traced a newspaperman's discovery of a secret German submarine base in New England.

Other films fanned the war fever by focusing upon the German atrocities in Belgium, France, and Russia. J. Searle Dawley's *In the Name of the Prince of Peace* ('15) was a shocking pro-war picture about a nun denouncing her father, an invading German soldier, and witnessing his execution upon a church altar. Fox's *The War Bride's Secret* ('16) attempted to capitalize on the Nazimova-Brenon film (Brenon was so incensed that he tried to get an injunction to stop its exhibition). It had none of the peace ideology of *War Brides,* but relied upon brutal scenes of rape and murder to create an anti-German feeling. Rupert Julian's *We French* ('16) reflected the patriotism and heroism of the French peasant in the face of repeated invasions from the east. Gale Kane played a young Normandy girl, tortured and humiliated by the Huns, who helped an American escape from occupied France in World's *On Dangerous Ground* ('17). In the same year that his anti-war and anti-German *Civilization* was released, Thomas H. Ince's *Bullets and Brown Eyes* ('16), starring William Desmond and Bessie Barriscale (and John Gilbert in his first role), pictured the brutality of the German horde as it marched through Poland to the Russian front in an earlier, imaginary war.

Many war pictures were imported from France between

1914 and 1917 to bolster the pro-war spirit in the United States. These patriotic dramas had two things in common—the unwavering heroism of the French and the barbarism of the Germans. The titles are self-illustrative—*La Marseillaise, The Avenging Poilu, The Second of August* (with Max Linder), *Christmas in Wartime, Wives of France, Heart of a Frenchwoman, Sweethearts of 1914,* etc.—all propaganda for domestic morale and foreign sympathy. Even the ailing Sarah Bernhardt made one of her rare screen appearances in Louis Mercanton's *Mothers of France* ('16), which included scenes actually photographed in the front-line trenches.

Less of a national spirit was seen in the relatively few war films which came from Great Britain. Most of these dramas had similar, almost plotless incidents set in Belgium or France, in which a child or a witless soldier, or even an animal hero, seemed to have no difficulty in outfoxing the Germans. The Huns were seen as rather foolish and stupid individuals, easily foiled and outfought. The atrocities were given little attention. After 1915 war pictures became poison at the British box office, and the government did not seem to object when they were almost totally discontinued. Some of the better English war films were *Serving the Colours* (in which a dissipated hero is regenerated by military service), *The Outrage, In the Clutches of the Hun, England's Menace* (about two boys who foil a German invasion by picking up coded wireless signals), Maurice Elvey's *Midshipman Easy,* and George Pearson's *The Better 'Ole,* a tongue-in-cheek comedy based on Bruce Bairnsfather's cartoon character, Old Bill.

The British made a more effective use of documentary and teaching films for propaganda purposes. They were not above "reconstructing" great events of the war on a studio stage, often using trick methods, and passing off the results as authentic, eyewitness pictures. Percy Smith's *The Strafer Strafed* ('16) was a trick film purporting to show a German Zeppelin being shot down over the village of Cuffley. Smith later did *Kinotank* ('16), using animated models to show the use of tanks in trench warfare. *The Battle of the Somme* ('17) was supposed to be an authentic newsreel of that bloody struggle, but was actually a trick reconstruction by Edgar Rogers, a studio technician who later re-created the Battle of Trafalgar in *Jack Ahoy!* ('34).

The Italians made few contemporary war films, but stimulated the national fervor by countless, generally well-made spec-

An aging Sarah Bernhardt was seen with Gabriel Signoret in the French war propaganda film, Mothers of France (Meres Française) *in 1916.*

tacles based on Roman history (*Cabiria, The Survivor, Atilla*). Some of these were imported into the United States, but made little impression upon the campaign for intervention. Motion-picture production in Russia during World War I was still primitive and handicapped by shortages of raw film stock and equipment. Several pictures depicted the Russian heritage of courage from past victories over many enemies, including two versions of Tolstoy's *War and Peace*. Few of these films found their way to America.

The shift of American public opinion from peace to pre-paredness was reflected in dozens of documentary films of the war abroad. Within a few weeks of the beginning of the hostilities in Europe, theaters were flooded with military and political imports graphically recounting both sides of the struggle. Old newsreels of the Kaiser, Franz Joseph, and King Albert were soon replaced with scenes of combat on the French, Austrian, and Russian fronts. As late as 1916, in keeping with President Wilson's plea for neutrality, these pictures were significantly devoid of deliberate anti-German sentiment. An official German war film, *Germany and Its Armies of Today,* premiered at the New York Strand as late as January, 1917.

Virtually all of these war documentaries were assembled and edited in Europe, and tended to reflect the country of origin in the most favorable light. *On the Firing Line with the Germans, Austria at War, The German Side of the War,* and *The Log of the U-35* stated the Entente position, while *The Great War in Europe, Behind the Battle Line in Russia, At the Front with the Allies,* and *The Italian Battle Front* were pro-Allies. Despite their timeliness, few of these documentaries were financially successful in the United States, and none was handled by a major distributor.

As the pro-war agitation grew, American producers began to piece together old newsreels and stock shots in a manner calculated to create anti-German feeling. Such a compilation was *Guarding Old Glory* ('16), which used atrocity shots as a plea for American preparedness. A group of Chicago businessmen sent photographer Merl LaVoy abroad to make *Heroic France* ('16), which featured many scenes of British and French military and political personalities. It was an ingeniously constructed, blatant demand for American entrance into the fighting.

The culmination of pro-war propaganda from Hollywood came in two pictures by Cecil B. De Mille, *Joan the Woman* and *The Little American.* An early advocate of military preparedness, De Mille was at first dissuaded, if not prohibited, by Adolph Zukor and other industry figures from making pro-war films. By 1916, when the agitation for the United States to enter the conflict neared its height, De Mille exposed his feelings in *Joan the Woman,* a spectacle of Joan of Arc with Geraldine Farrar as the Maid of Orleans.

"I knew when I played Joan of Arc in Mr. De Mille's picture that it would be . . . the greatest of pro-Ally propaganda," Miss Farrar said later. Few films so stimulated the mounting sentiment for war as *Joan the Woman,* despite De Mille's characteristic bad taste in introducing a mild romance between Joan and a young soldier (Wallace Reid) who betrays her when she spurns him. The exciting battle scenes and stunning pageantry, coupled with the emotional appeal of religion, created strong feelings of patriotism. The glory of womanhood in war was symbolized by the peasant girl who led an army against the enemies of France. Above all, the picture expressed the philosophy, however questionable, that the Anglo-Saxon peoples had a moral obligation to come to France's aid in expiation of their crime of having burned Joan at the stake. *Joan the Woman* was, as De Mille declared, "an age-old call to a modern crusade."

With the United States teetering on the brink of war, De Mille brought out *The Little American* ('17), starring Mary Pickford, an inflammatory film calculated to provoke Americans to seek vengeance on Germany. The story followed familiar patterns—Miss Pickford was an American girl, doing war relief in Belgium, who is captured by the Germans and held as a spy. The plot contained every known element of pro-war propaganda —the violation of Belgium neutrality, the sinking of the *Lusitania,* the atrocities against women and children, the Prussian goal of world conquest, and the conflicting loyalties of German-Americans. (The hero, played by Jack Holt, was a German-American who returns to become a Prussian army officer—but he is redeemed by Mary's love and helps her to escape.) The Hun, painted in blackest terms and without a saving grace, was made an object of fear and dread.

The significance of *The Little American* lay in the selection of Mary Pickford as its star. Incredibly popular with both men and women, she became, as "America's Sweetheart," the symbol of the nation's innocent womanhood. When the brutal German colonel (Walter Long) threatened Our Mary with rape and death, it was a personal affront to every American, an insult that called for Prussian blood and punishment. Miss Pickford's popularity assured *The Little American* would be seen by millions around the world. De Mille had forged, with Mary Pickford's aid, one of the most powerful weapons of World War I.

With the official declaration of war by the United States on April 6, 1917, the motion-picture industry was immediately conscripted for a wide variety of war services. George Creel, a young Midwestern newspaperman (and husband of actress Blanche Bates), was named Chairman of the Committee on Public Information, a hastily organized federal propaganda agency. The movies, Creel told the press, would play an important role in helping "sell the war" to the American public.

Creel did not get off to a good start with movie officialdom.

He offended many influential leaders by making the "mistake" of bringing in Charles S. Hart, a Hearst editor, to coordinate motion picture activities. Two other Hearst men, Edgar Sisson and E. B. Hatrick, were also given top administrative posts, and other key employees were drawn primarily from government and the publishing world. At first, not a single film figure of note was called upon.

Sensing his error, Creel quickly set up an advisory committee of industry executives, including Adolph Zukor, Lewis J. Selznick, Thomas H. Ince, William Fox, D. W. Griffith, and others. There was strong criticism at the inclusion of Jules E. Brulatour, who stood to make millions from the sale of Eastman film stock to the government. An exhibitors branch was established to utilize theaters, and in Hollywood and New York committees of performers were created to channel talent into the propaganda program. Members included such stars as Mary Pickford, Douglas Fairbanks, Gale Kane, Anita Stewart, June Elvidge, William S. Hart, Norma Talmadge, and William Farnum.

In retrospect, Creel does not appear to have been fully aware of the enormous propaganda potentials of the screen. Charles S. Hart had recommended a steady flow of documentary films tailored to the changing propaganda needs of the war, but fourteen months elapsed before the first of these pictures, *Pershing's Crusaders,* reached the nation's theaters. Hart encountered many difficulties. The Army Signal Corps, the only government agency making films, was found totally inadequate for the job, and even its scanty output was committed to the American Red Cross for distribution. The Army, for unexplained reasons, resisted the assignment of motion-picture photographers to both training and combat units, and eventually this impasse was solved only through White House pressure. Creel and Hart found the motion-picture industry split into highly competitive factions and suffering from a hangover of bitterness from the patents war. Any degree of cooperation in solving production problems was difficult to attain.

In March, 1918, the American Red Cross relinquished its pictorial functions, and the Division of Films of the Committee on Public Information was established, with Charles S. Hart as director. In addition to *Pershing's Crusaders,* the unit turned out two other feature-length documentaries, *America's Answer* and *Under Two Flags,* as well as a series of arresting short subjects, *The Official War Review.* The high quality of these films was largely due to Ray L. Hall, an official of the Hearst newsreel, and Charles Urban, the pioneer motion picture producer and distributor, whose connections with the British and French film industries were useful in securing valuable war footage from abroad. (Urban was one of the developers of the early Kinemacolor process of color photography.)

Somewhat to the industry's surprise, Hart resolved to sell these films to exhibitors, rather than distribute them for free showings. They were handled on a percentage basis by various companies, principally Associated First National, and returned $852,744.30 in rentals. Hart constantly badgered distributors to obtain more play dates and better local exploitation. Eventually, the government films were seen in about a third of U.S. theaters.

As the war progressed, the Signal Corps began to assign a growing number of experienced cameramen from newsreels and the studios to combat units in France. Some of the prominent Hollywood cinematographers to photograph the war, often at great personal risk, were J. Roy Hunt, Ira Morgan, Leonard Smith, Paul C. Vogel, Reginald Lyons, Gus C. Peterson, Harry Thorpe, William J. Craft and Victor Fleming (later director of *Gone With the Wind*). There was little pre-planning or coordination to these activities, and some of the earlier American campaigns were inadequately covered. Because of censorship, and because the realism of battle was not always compatible to the home-front propaganda, much of this footage was stored away in Army vaults and not given any extensive editing and showing until years after the war.

Through the industry advisory committee Creel was able to stimulate the production of theatrical pictures which served a specific purpose in a nation at war—such as conservation of food, military recruitment, increased industrial and agricultural productivity, and such outright propaganda objectives as creating a distrust of enemy nationalities in America. In all of these truth was frequently slighted or distorted to serve the purpose at hand. The real issues were avoided or obscured, and war was made to seem a glorious means to a necessary end. An Allied victory was seen as the key to a new era of peace and prosperity.

Near the end of the war the Division of Films of the C.P.I. began to supply a limited amount of direct assistance to the studios. It provided story ideas and even complete scenarios, soldiers for battle scenes, military facilities as locations, and

Charlie Chaplin impersonates a German officer in Shoulder Arms *(1918).
At right is Sydney Chaplin, and the girl is Edna Purviance.*

extensive free publicity and advertising. There was even some
financing with government money—repaid from rentals—but
the finished picture remained the property of the producers.
Pathé, Paramount, Universal, Hodkinson, and Chester Productions were some of the companies to receive subsidies. Hodkinson's *Made in America,* which came belatedly into release in
early 1919, was filmed from a C.P.I. script to illustrate the
operation of the draft, and received $40,000 in government
financing. Allegations of waste and graft in the production of
Universal's *The Yanks Are Coming* ('18) became the subject
of a Congressional investigation, but the charges were to prove
unfounded.

By controlling the sale of American films in neutral countries,
the Committee on Public Information was able to resist the
inroads of German propagandists. So popular were Pickford,
Chaplin, and Fairbanks that theaters in the Orient, Scandinavia,
Mexico, and South America were willing to accept American
propaganda films in order to secure the pictures of these and

other leading stars. As the war continued the C.P.I. used these movies to shut out propaganda pictures from Germany, eventually refusing outright to sell Chaplin, Pickford, and other box-office favorites to neutral countries doing business with German film distributors.

The C.P.I. sent mobile theaters into many politically questionable areas of the world, showing both regular and propaganda films as a means of creating pro-American sympathy. These pictures were shown in tents, schools, railway cars, and even outdoors. Among Army officers on loan to the C.P.I. to supervise these projects were Fiorello La Guardia, Walter Wanger, and Frederick Palmer, the publisher.

Peace pictures were forbidden by government decree. Robert Goldstein, a motion-picture costumer who had been associated with D. W. Griffith at one time, was charged in 1918 with violation of the Espionage Act for producing and exhibiting a feature entitled *The Spirit of '76*. The film, said to have been financed by German aliens at a cost of $120,000, was alleged to give aid and comfort to the enemy by encouraging disloyalty, mutiny, and insubordination in the Armed Forces. Goldstein was given ten years in prison.

One of the first propaganda objectives of the screen was to incite public opinion against men who failed to enlist or attempted to evade the draft. "Slacker" became a shameful term often indiscriminately applied to those not in uniform. Many movies, designed to inspire loyalty and speed up recruiting, were built around the slacker and the draft. The slacker was invariably seen as a misguided youth who is made to realize his patriotic duty to flag and country. In a moving climax he would enlist, and often become a battlefield hero, redeeming himself in the eyes of the girl back home.

Christy Cabanne's *The Slacker* ('17) set the pattern of such films with its story of a rich wastrel (Walter Miller) who marries a well-bred American girl (Emily Stevens) to escape the draft. She arouses his manhood through patriotic example rather than contempt, and the inspired husband is with the first troops to sail for France. Paul Revere's ride, the death of Nathan Hale, and Lee's surrender were introduced via flashbacks as brief incidents to emphasize the nation's heritage. Cabanne later did a similar picture, *Draft 258* ('18), in which Walter Miller is a slacker drafted into the Army. He comes to realize the necessity and the glory of fighting for his country. The film did propaganda duty by helping to explain the operation of the draft.

The complex story of *The Service Star* ('18) concerned a young woman (Madge Kennedy) who invents a fictitious husband who is also a war hero. A man of that name turns up, but it develops he is a slacker seeking to evade the draft. His mother excuses him by saying he has "inherited weakness." Madge shames him into enlisting. Hobart Henley's *Mrs. Slacker* ('18) had a similar theme with emphasis upon the effects of a slacker's conduct on his wife. John W. Noble's *Shame* ('17) also pictured the disgrace which a draft evader brought to his family.

Wives, sisters, and sweethearts were admonished not to show sympathy for the slacker, but to encourage him to do his duty. In *For Valour* ('17) Richard Barthelmess was a slacker who is finally brought around by his sister (Mabel Ballin), a Red Cross war worker. Other films which dealt harshly with the slacker included Essanay's *The Man Who Was Afraid* ('17), and Alan Crosland's *The Unbeliever* ('18), the last release of the Edison Company, which was produced with the cooperation of the U.S. Marine Corps. Universal's *The Man Without a Country* ('17) used Edward Everett Hale's famous story in flashback to convince a conscientious objector he should enlist.

In a lighter vein, *Bud's Recruit* ('18), one of King Vidor's first directorial efforts, was a two-reel comedy about a youngster (Wallis Brennan) who shames his brother into enlisting by attempting to enlist in his place. Fox's kiddie stars, Jane and Katherine Lee, performed a similar chore in *Smiles* (which did not come out until two months after the Armistice), except that the slacker turned out to be a Secret Service agent trying to capture a German spy. In *Dolly Does Her Bit* ('18) Baby Marie Osborne rounded up the kids in the neighborhood and told them to shame fathers and brothers not in uniform. Quite similar was *A Little Patriot* ('17), in which Baby Peggy, after dreaming she was Joan of Arc, harangued the children to spit on fathers who were slackers. Madge Evans was a child movie actress in *The Volunteer* ('17) who gives up her screen career to do war work. She is shown saying good-bye to popular stars at the World Studios at Fort Lee, and urging the men to enlist. (In real life the nine-year old Madge was given a special award by Secretary of the Treasury William Gibbs McAdoo for her record sales of Liberty Bonds.) Raoul Walsh's *18 to 45* ('18) was a propaganda film made expressly for the government to assure registrants of the impartiality of the draft, but it also encouraged older men with specialized talents to enlist, suggesting that their family and friends would be proud of them.

In *An Honest Man* ('18) William Desmond was a tramp who was rejected for service much against his wishes. It was one of the few films to sympathize with the plight of patriotic men who, because of physical reasons, were not permitted to serve. Another Triangle film, *The Gown of Destiny* ('17), starring Alma Rubens, was about a male dress designer who was too puny for the Army, but uses the profits of his modiste shop to buy ambulances for France. Hobart Henley's *Too Fat to Fight* ('18) showed how an overweight man, after a series of amusing incidents, got into physical shape for the A.E.F.

Concern over the loyalty of millions of Americans of German extraction was expressed in many World War I movies. An early inclination to condemn these people as disloyal, evidence of the depths of anti-German feeling, was soon replaced by more objective films which encouraged them to cast away their ties to the Fatherland—and even to develop hatred for relatives abroad. Raoul Walsh's *The Prussian Cur* ('18) was an inflammatory picture which advocated mob violence against disloyal German-Americans. The story concerned a hooded band—the Ku Klux Klan thinly disguised—which takes the law into its hands and lynches several men of German extraction suspected of being saboteurs. Coming on the heels of a plea by President Wilson for tolerance and understanding, *The Prussian Cur* was bitterly attacked in many quarters and its exhibition finally curtailed.

Chester Withey's *The Hun Within* ('18), starring Dorothy Gish and George Fawcett, was about a second-generation German-American who becomes a spy for Germany. His father remains loyal to the United States, his adopted country. Audiences cheered as the old man, encountering his son toasting a portrait of the Kaiser, kicked him in the seat of the pants. By contrast *Me Und Gott (When America Woke)*, a cheap film of 1918, had a second-generation German-American turning on his disloyal father by refusing to destroy an American munitions factory. In Goldwyn's *Fields of Honor* ('18) Mae and Marguerite Marsh were two French girls visiting in the United States. One falls in love with an American, the other with a German. The German couple returns to Berlin and, when war comes, suffer tragedy and death, while the American couple enjoys the fruits of liberty and victory.

Ruth Stonehouse played an immigrant Swedish maid in *Follow the Girl* ('17) who is taught she must assume new responsibilities as a citizen in wartime—including acting as a counterespionage agent. Florence La Badie was a girl of alien parentage in Pathé's *War and the Woman* ('17) who proved her loyalty by betraying her stepfather as a spy to the Secret Service. In *An Alien Enemy* ('18) Louise Glaum used her wiles to induce German-Americans to spy for the Fatherland. On the far-eastern front, Sessue Hayakawa was a Japanese-American in William C. de Mille's *The Secret Game* ('17) who helped ship American soldiers to the Russian front to fight the Japs. Fox's *The Spy* ('17), was typical of many movies which attempted to arouse suspicion and distrust of foreign-born elements ("Do you know your neighbor?" screamed the ads). In many areas naturalized German-American citizens were directed to attend showings of *The Immigrant,* a government documentary (not the Chaplin comedy) which taught allegiance to the Stars and Stripes.

The declaration of war stimulated a flood of espionage dramas, many exciting and suspenseful, others drearily routine. Ideally suited to propaganda purposes, they effectively demonstrated the superiority of American courage and cleverness. Our spies were seen as brave and resourceful operators for whom no risk, not even death, was too great to be taken in line of duty. Some of these dramas were laid in domestic settings, with ordinary citizens caught up in webs of intrigue, while others showed American agents in daring exploits behind the enemy lines.

Ince's *The Kaiser's Shadow* ('18) had a corking but thoroughly implausible story of two German spies, Dorothy Dalton and Thurston Hall, trying to steal the plans of a "ray rifle" from an American inventor (Edward Cecil). It developed Dorothy was actually a French intelligence agent, and Thurston a U.S. Secret Service operator, both trying to discover the real brains of a Prussian espionage ring—ironically, he was named "Kremlin." *Suspicion* ('18) told of a lonely wife neglected by her husband, an aircraft-factory superintendent. She takes up with another man, who is uncovered as an enemy agent trying to dynamite the plant. In *Luck and Pluck* ('19) George Walsh was a crook reformed by the call of patriotism. He uses his knowledge of the underworld to save the daughter of an American intelligence agent from marriage to a German spy. In *I'll Say So* ('18), directed by his brother Raoul, Walsh outwitted

Charlie Chaplin in the famous dugout scene in Shoulder Arms.

another foreign spy ring with his spectacular acrobatics.

Vitagraph's *The Highest Trump* ('18) was the old twin brother theme in a war setting. One brother, a German agent, is killed, and his twin, an American Secret Service operator, takes his place and captures the espionage ring. Earle Williams played dual roles, and Grace Darmond was the girl who thought her lover had sold out to the enemy. In *Love In a Hurry* ('18) Carlyle Blackwell was a New York millionaire who innocently sells scarce war metals to German saboteurs. He pursues them to England and rounds up the gang in a one-man commando operation. Billie Burke played a scatterbrain in *In Pursuit of Polly* ('18) who was mistaken for a German spy, but Thomas Meighan, both a handsome millionaire *and* a Secret Service agent, straightened things out and caught the real culprit. Bessie Barriscale in *Madam Who?* ('18) was also an innocent young woman branded an enemy spy. To save her reputation she tracks down the real spies and brings them to justice.

Fred Niblo's *The Marriage Ring* ('18) told how Prussian

agents tried to burn vital sugar-cane plantations in Hawaii owned by an American woman (Enid Bennett), but are thwarted by an Army officer (Jack Holt). Universal's *Who Was the Other Man?* ('17) starred Francis Ford as a Secret Service operator on the track of Germany's famous undercover sabotage unit, the "Black Legion." *Daughter Angele* ('17) had Pauline Starke and Philo McCullough as a young married couple who discover a German spy signalling U-boats off the New England coast. In *Madame Spy* ('18) Jack Mulhall was a government agent who donned women's clothes to lure Boche operators into a trap. *Love and the Law*, filmed in 1918 but not released until after the Armistice, had Glen White as a New York City policeman who stumbled upon a plot by railroad saboteurs to blow up an Army troop train.

Even westerns took on a topical appearance as Hun spies turned up in the traditional surroundings of the old West. Tom Mix was an Army undercover operator in *Mr. Logan, U.S.A.* ('18) who went to Arizona to keep enemy agents, masquerading as cowboys, from sabotaging tungsten mines. German villains also invaded such wartime serials as *Wolves of Kultur, A Daughter of Uncle Sam,* and *The Eagle's Eye,* all released in 1918. Supposedly "authorized" by George Creel and the C.I.P., *The Eagle's Eye* was unusually vicious in directing suspicion at German-Americans, so much so that the Loews' chain refused to book it.

American agents abroad encountered similar success in defeating the Germans at their own game. In *Berlin Via America* ('18) Francis Ford was a U.S. Secret Service operator who pretends to be disloyal. Winning the confidence of two Prussian spies, he is smuggled into Germany where he becomes an aviator with Baron von Richthofen's Flying Circus. Ford flies over the allied lines to drop messages of impending enemy attacks. At the end he escapes to America, unmasks his rival for the heroine's hand as a German spy, and regains his reputation as a loyal American!

Fox's *For Liberty* ('17) showed the sacrifices an American woman could be expected to make for her country. Gladys Brockwell was an artist living in Paris who becomes intimate with a German officer. She returns with him to Berlin, where he causes the death of an American boy in a brutal, senseless murder. She helps the brother of the victim avenge the killing, and the two, now in love, escape to France as the United States enters the war.

Henry King's *A Soul in Pawn* ('17) told of a beautiful woman (Gail Kane) who becomes a spy in order to exact vengeance upon the Germans who killed her husband. In Edwin Carewe's *The Greatest Power* ('17) Ethel Barrymore betrays her lover, a Prussian agent, when she learns of his disloyalty. Léonce Perret's *Lafayette, We Come* ('18) pulled all the stops of patriotic propaganda. E. K. Lincoln was an American composer whose sweetheart (Dolores Cassinelli) mysteriously disappears. Later, in a French army hospital, where he is recovering from war wounds, he discovers her spying for Germany. She is revealed to be a double agent secretly working for the United States, and the spy ring is apprehended. (This film had a scene re-creating the moment at Lafayette's tomb when a Pershing aide made the now famous greeting, "Lafayette, we are here!".)

In *For the Freedom of the East* ('18) an American diplomat matches wits with a German consular official who is trying to get China to join the Entente. Lady Tsen Mei, the Chinese actress, was a viceroy's daughter who becomes infatuated with the American (Robert Elliott) and threatens to use her influence against the United States when he jilts her. Audiences were astonished at the tiny Tsen Mei's judo in subduing the villain, an act she did in vaudeville for many years.

Among countless other spy movies of World War I were *The Claws of the Hun* ('18), with Charles Ray; *When Men Desire* ('19), starring Theda Bara; *Vive La France* ('18), another Ince drama with unnecessary brutality, with Dorothy Dalton; Paul Scardon's *The Stolen Treaty* ('17), teaming Corinne Griffith and Earle Williams; *Kultur* ('18), starring Gladys Brockwell; J. Stuart Blackton's *Life's Greatest Problem* ('19), a drama of sabotage in a shipyard; and Allan Dwan's *The Dark Star* ('19), a Marion Davies vehicle that did not get into release until several months after the Armistice.

Sparked by the success of *The Little American,* atrocity films now increased in number and intensity. All the suffering and death of the Belgian and French invasions became the focal point of distorted screen propaganda to create hatred of the enemy. Ella Hall was the star of *Bitter Sweet* ('17), a typical account of Belgium's distress, in which the heroine—a fourteen-year-old girl—is brought to America after suffering unbelievable hardships at the hands of the Huns. Sidney Olcott's *The Belgian* ('17), with Valentine Grant and Walker Whiteside, depicted the futile efforts of daring Belgian patriots to hinder the German advance. The heroic French were praised in Wesley Ruggles'

For France ('17). Mary Maurice was the peasant mother humbled by a corrupt Prussian commander (Arthur Davidson) and his aide (Erich von Stroheim). Her death is avenged by an American aviator (Frank Anderson).

Alice Brady was seen in *The Maid of Belgium* ('17) as a young Belgian wife who loses her memory from the shock of the atrocities she witnesses. She is found wandering in France and is brought to the United States by an American Consul. Cecil B. De Mille's *Till I Come Back to You* ('18) emphasized the mistreatment of children by the Prussians. An American engineer (Bryant Washburn) falls in love with the Belgian wife (Florence Vidor) of a German officer. When war comes her son is among Belgian children who are shipped to Germany as slave labor in munitions factories. The children are shown being whipped and starved—and brainwashed by the German propagandists. De Mille made a pointed appeal for vengeance in the

A mutilated veteran of World War I, Richard Barthelmess, finds happiness in his love for a plain woman, May McAvoy, in The Enchanted Cottage *(1924).*

name of all the world's innocent children.

In *Adele* ('18) Kitty Gordon was a nurse who goes to France with her father, an Army surgeon. She is captured by the Huns and raped. Marshall Neilan's *The Unpardonable Sin* had Blanche Sweet as an American girl who goes to Belgium to rescue a twin sister (also played by Miss Sweet) held hostage by the Boche. She is made to witness many brutal indignities against Belgian women and children, ordered by a sadistic enemy officer (Wallace Beery). Not released until mid-1919, *The Unpardonable Sin*'s propaganda message was dated and resented in some quarters.

The execution of the English nurse, Edith Cavell, by the Germans on a trumped-up charge of spying was the basis of such atrocity propaganda as *The Martyrdom of Nurse Cavell* ('16), a pioneer Australian production, John G. Adolfi's *The Woman the Germans Shot* ('18), with Julia Arthur, and *Why Germany Must Pay* ('19).

Joseph Kaufman's *Arms and the Girl* ('17) was in a lighter vein. Billie Burke was a mischievous American girl caught in the invasion near the French border. She uses a number of pranks and practical jokes, and some innocent sex appeal, to rescue a Texas engineer (Thomas Meighan) whom the Germans plan to execute. Although the Prussian officers were portrayed as fat, stupid, and lecherous clowns, the atrocities were astonishingly realistic.

My Four Years in Germany ('18), the first major film of the Warner Brothers, included many scenes of brutalities in German prison camps. These pictures purported to come from authentic captured enemy newsreels, but most of the shocking sequences were faked by director William Nigh in a tiny studio at Grantwood, New Jersey. Based on a series of sensational articles by James W. Gerard, former U.S. Ambassador to Berlin (actor Halbert Brown looked incredibly like Gerard), the picture was outright propaganda. Once again, German-Americans were incited to feel hatred and shame for their people abroad. The film earned $430,000 on an investment of $50,000.

The Kaiser became the symbol of German villainy in scores of propaganda movies. He was always seen as an arrogant, half-demented savage given to personal violence and cruelties. Some films depicted him as weak, lustful, greedy and uncouth—even as a victim of epilepsy and venereal disease—and always colossally conceited. His upturned mustache, insane leer, and pointed helmet gave him a Mephistophelian appearance, and the Kaiser was always the signal for spontaneous hissing and cat-calling by the audience.

The pinnacle of these inflammatory characterizations came in Universal's *The Kaiser, Beast of Berlin* ('18), in which director Rupert Julian played Wilhelm, a role he was to repeat many times in the next ten years. Lawrence Grant, a mild-mannered Englishman who made a study of the Hohenzollerns, was also frequently cast as the German ruler. His best performance was in *To Hell With the Kaiser* ('18), in which Satan (played by W. P. Lewis) is shown prompting the Kaiser to order the sinking of the *Lusitania,* the use of poison gas at the front, and air raids on Red Cross hospitals. Gustav von Seyffer-titz not only played the Kaiser but Uncle Sam as well (in Liberty Bond films); during the war he changed his name to G. Butler Clonebaugh because of public antagonism to everything German.

The sinking of the *Lusitania* in 1915 was used in many pictures to arouse indignation, most notably in Mary Pickford's *The Little American.* Léonce Perret's *Lest We Forget* ('18) made a personal impact because the star, Rita Jolivet, was one of the survivors of the *Lusitania* tragedy. The actress was so emotionally affected by the experience that she was unable to speak of it for many months. It was to Mlle. Jolivet that Broad-way producer Charles Frohman, one of the victims, said as the boat began to sink: "Why fear death? It is life's greatest adventure." His last words were widely quoted during the war for their inspirational value. A novelty film was Universal's *The Sinking of the Lusitania* ('18), a one-reel cartoon for which artist Winsor McCay did 25,000 drawings on a gelatin base. Even the Russians did a *Lusitania* movie—*An American Millionaire Perishes on the Lusitania* (15)—with N. Saltikov as "Vanderbilt," the wealthy American hero.

While in Great Britain in 1916 for the premiere of *Intolerance,* D. W. Griffith was invited by Prime Minister David Lloyd George and Lord Beaverbrook to make a propaganda picture for the Allies. He was taken on a tour of the battlefields and promised the use of soldiers and training camps—and financing, which never materialized. In his London hotel Griffith sketched out the plot of *Hearts of the World,* a simple story of a French girl whose village is overrun by the Germans.

After a hurried trip to California, where his Fine Arts Company had collapsed in bankruptcy, Griffith returned to England in March, 1917, accompanied by Lillian Gish and her mother. Two months later they were joined by cameraman G. W. Bitzer (whose German background was the subject of an exhaustive security check), Dorothy Gish, Robert Harron, and several other performers. Another passenger on their ship was General Pershing. *Hearts of the World* was partially filmed in Great Britain and France, but most of it was shot later in Hollywood. The Gish girls were terrified by the air raids in London and Cambridge, but were enormously heartened by the courage and determination of the British people. In France some scenes were made at Compiègne and Senlis, only a few miles from the front and within sound of enemy guns. The ruined villages, strewn with the debris of war and human suffering, made impressive backgrounds. Griffith and Bitzer waded the mud of the front-line trenches to shoot authentic scenes, but most of these were found to be unusable. The director was lectured by a British officer for exposing himself to enemy fire—or so the publicity releases said.

By the time of its premiere in New York on April 4, 1918, much of the propaganda value of *Hearts of the World* had been lost. Its now familiar plot was trite and sentimental, and much footage was given to a commonplace love story (there was even a mild triangle). The war scenes, although rather sketchy, were extremely realistic and well constructed—and also contained some stock shots from a German propaganda picture, for which Griffith had paid $16,000. A typical Griffith climax had a last-minute rescue of the girl from the Huns by her soldier sweetheart.

Lillian Gish scored a great personal triumph as the distraught heroine of *Hearts of the World*. She had an unforgettable scene in which, dazed and carrying her wedding dress, she wanders among the village ruins and shell-pocked fields. Robert Harron was fine as the sensitive American artist who is so stirred by the war that he enlists in the French army, and Dorothy Gish scored as "The Little Disturber," a comic role with many moments reminiscent of Mae Marsh in *The Birth of a Nation*. Erich von Stroheim was assistant director and technical director, and may be glimpsed in a few scenes as a German officer. George Siegmann, who had menaced Lillian Gish in *The Birth of a Nation*, was the loathsome Von Strohm, a prototype of the Hun propaganda beast.

Hearts of the World was originally shown in better theaters at increased admissions up to $1.50. It was not seen in smaller towns and theaters until mid-1919, six months after the Armistice, when war-weary audiences gave it an indifferent reception. By that time Griffith had reluctantly agreed, at Adolph Zukor's urging, to cut out four reels—mostly scenes that would arouse hatred for the Germans—which gave it an uneven tempo. On the basis of reconstructed prints of the original twelve-reel version, *Hearts of the World* has come to be recognized as a fine and sensitive, if unappreciated, Griffith picture.

Griffith shot 86,000 feet of film for *Hearts of the World*, and some of the unused footage was incorporated into three other war films which he made—*The Great Love* and *The Greatest Thing in Life*, both starring Lillian Gish and Robert Harron, and *The Girl Who Stayed at Home*, with Bobby Harron, Richard Barthelmess, Carol Dempster, and Clarine Seymour.

The Great Love ('18) was about a Canadian soldier who falls in love with an English girl. While he is at the front she marries a man who turns out to be a German spy. The picture also purported, as Griffith said, "to show the remarkable transition of the butterfly life of British society to that of stern, sincere, hard workers in the great cause of winning the war." He induced several members of royalty and nobility—including Queen Alexandra, Lady Diana Manners, Lady Elizabeth Asquith, and Countess Maserine—to make token appearances.

The Greatest Thing in Life ('18), which Lillian Gish believes to have been Griffith's best picture, showed how war brought together a conceited young soldier and an idealistic girl devoted to a worthless man. It contained a famous scene in which a white soldier kisses the cheek of a dying Negro soldier. Griffith was accused by cynical critics of an insincere attempt to offset the racial bigotry of *The Birth of a Nation*.

The Girl Who Stayed at Home ('19) was made by Griffith at the request of the government to help popularize the draft. A drama of two parallel romances in wartime, it showed how a young wastrel (Robert Harron), after trying to evade the draft, is made into a man at the training camps. Eventually he becomes a battlefield hero. Once again, Griffith's efforts at propaganda were belated, and the film was not released until the spring of 1919. As evidence of the need for a kindlier attitude toward the enemy, Griffith did insert several scenes showing David Butler as a "good German" who keeps a Hun officer from raping Carol Dempster.

There was a lot of horseplay in Raoul Walsh's What Price Glory? *(1926). Dolores Del Rio is Charmaine, Edmund Lowe (center) was Sergeant Quirt, and Victor McLaglen (second from right) played Captain Flagg.*

Griffith unquestionably brought the greatest authenticity to combat scenes of the wartime movies, probably because he was virtually the only director permitted to visit the trenches and war-torn areas in France. Most pictures about the war were made by persons without any firsthand knowledge of the fighting, other than what could be gleaned from the newsreels. Soldiers laughed aloud and ridiculed unreal war films which showed the hero performing incredible feats of bravery. These criticisms eventually led studios to engage returned soldiers as technical advisers. However, Lt. Q. A. O'Hara of the 24th Canadian Expeditionary Force, hired as technical director of Select's *Over There* ('17), complained that the producer would not accept his suggestions for authenticity in the battle scenes—they limited the action and robbed the war of its glamour, the producer said!

Although romance was an integral part of virtually all World War I films, it was seldom given emphasis (except in Griffith's pictures). Producers felt that highly emotional love stories, with the heartbreak of separation and tragedy for the lovers, were too downbeat for the patriotic spirit which film propagandists sought to create. A heroine often appeared postively radiant as her sweetheart or husband marched off to war. These emotions were not realistically explored until years later in such films as *Seventh Heaven, Waterloo Bridge,* and *A Farewell to Arms.* A few movies of 1917-18 were exceptions. Fox's *Bonnie Annie Laurie* ('18) was a moving account of a Scottish girl (Peggy Hyland) who must choose between a Highland officer and an American doughboy, both of whom she has learned to love. J. Stuart Blackton's *Missing* ('18), with Thomas Meighan and Sylvia Breamer, described the effect of a man missing in action upon his wife and her sister, who also loves him. Some other good love stories of the war included another J. Stuart Blackton production, *Whom the Gods Destroy* ('16), and *The Greatest Power* ('17), *The Mother's Secret* ('18), and *Patriotism* ('18), with Bessie Barriscale.

War conditions at home and the need for conserving food, strategic materials, and manpower were emphasized in many pictures. Mr. and Mrs. Sidney Drew engaged in a series of matrimonial battles over food conservation in *The Patriot* ('17), a comedy which won the official endorsement of U.S. Food Administrator Herbert Hoover. Jack Conway's *Doing Her Bit* ('17) was about a spunky youngster who organized the slums for the war effort—everything from saving a mountain of tinfoil to recruiting Bowery bums for the Army. *The Charmer* ('17) had Ella Hall as a Belgian refugee who preaches self-sacrifice as the war to win. *Boy Scouts to the Rescue* was a series of Universal two-reelers of 1918 which showed what Boy Scouts could do to help win the war—including collecting surplus clothing and catching the inevitable spy. Jane and Katherine Lee were two moppets in *Doing Our Bit* ('18) who shamed their elders into wartime sacrifices. Cecil B. De Mille's *We Can't Have Everything* ('18), some of whose scenes were laid in a movie studio, covered every form of self-denial as the way to win the war—even to charging Gold Star mothers to accept heroically the loss of a son.

J. Stuart Blackton's *Safe for Democracy* ('18) was one of many pictures to preach the doctrine of work or fight. In *Her Country's Call* ('17) Mary Miles Minter took a succession of new jobs to demonstrate the many ways in which a man could be released for military service. *Women Who Win* ('18) was a British-made documentary which showed the contributions working women could make to the home front. Profiteering in food and war materiel was likened to treason in Allan Dwan's *The Food Gamblers* ('17) and J. K. Holbrook's *The Profiteer* ('18). The much maligned Home Defense Corps, a World War I version of Civil Defense, was the subject of several movies, frequently in a humorous vein. In *Home Defense* ('17) Victor Moore and his pals pretend to serve in a Home Defense unit, but are really out playing poker. Child star Bobby Connelly in *Bobby of the Home Defenders* ('17) organized the neighborhood kids into a Home Defense unit and caught some German spies trying to blow up a factory. Their parents are ashamed that such responsibilities have been left to children and quickly assume their patriotic duties.

Morale building in the nation's military training camps was also seen in many movies as a primary responsibility of every citizen. George Loane Tucker's *Joan of Plattsburg* ('18) was about an impish young girl (Mabel Normand) who lived near a training camp. She delights the homesick doughboys with amateur entertainments, forges letters from sweethearts who have neglected to write, and slips them home-cooked goodies— and catches a German spy ring! The picture emphasized how espionage agents seeded anti-American propaganda in training camps, and also how mothers back home were led to believe their soldier boys were being mistreated. Many scenes were shot at the famous Plattsburg (N.Y.) Officers Training Camp.

In *Johanna Enlists* ('18) Mary Pickford was a lovesick girl who boosts Army morale when a training camp is built on her farm. Mary finds herself the belle of the brigade, so much so that she is driven to pray: "Oh Lord, when I asked you for a man, why did you send me a regiment?" Eventually she lands a major for a husband. Two other training camp comedies heavy on morale building were *Come On In* ('18), with Shirley Mason, and *Private Pettigrew's Girl* ('19), starring Monte Blue and Ethel Clayton. The latter picture, filmed at Camp Kearney in California, was another propaganda film made obsolete by the Armistice.

During World War I few comedies dared satirize the war —it was too serious business to be taken lightly. Poking fun at the Kaiser was all right, but the hardships of army life were no laughing matters. Charlie Chaplin's *Shoulder Arms* ('18), released three weeks before the Armistice with considerable doubt as to its reception, proved to be the tonic America needed. With the tensions of war suddenly laid aside, audiences could now laugh at the lighter side of a struggle that killed 8,500,000 persons and wounded 21,000,000.

Shoulder Arms skillfully blends superb slapstick with fantasy and satire—and a characteristic Chaplin irony—to point up in absurd terms the insanity of war. There are also moments of tenderness and pathos, a counterpoint of realism to the film's comedy and burlesque. All the rigors of war—from the bullying sergeant of the training camp to the water-logged, flea-bitten trenches of France—are grist for Chaplin's humor mill. The result is one of his finest films.

The highlights of *Shoulder Arms* include a desperate attempt by Chaplin, with his extraordinary feet, to keep in step with a marching column; a hilarious encounter between Charlie, camouflaged as a tree, and a hot-tempered German soldier (Henry Bergman); and Chaplin's attempt to sleep in a rain-filled dugout. Equally unforgettable is the poignant scene in which Chaplin is the only soldier not to receive mail from home; homesick, he finds pleasure in slyly reading a buddy's letter. He ridicules the propaganda films (a dejected peasant girl is seen in the ruins of her home), and at the end Charlie and Sydney Chaplin, with lovely Edna Purviance as the French girl, capture the Kaiser (also played by Syd Chaplin) in a riotous climax that brings the war to a summary close.

Mack Sennett made several gay war comedies. *An International Sneak* ('18) parodied the wartime spy dramas, with Chester Conklin and Ethel Teare as a zany pair of espionage agents. Ben Turpin made a hilarious cross-eyed Kaiser in *Yankee Doodle in Berlin* ('19), which was only slightly more absurd than some of the serious portrayals of the German leader. Universal kidded its own *The Kaiser, Beast of Berlin* with *The Geezer of Berlin* ('18). *Shades of Shakespeare* ('18) was a Christie comedy which satirized wartime propaganda films. Harold Lloyd played a rube spy in *Kicking the Germ Out of Germany* ('18), one of his early Rollin comedies. Bebe Daniels was a pretty Red Cross nurse. Larry Semon was a scrawny janitor who became a spy-catcher in *Huns and Hyphens* ('18). Many cartoons poked fun at the German militarists. In *Doing His Bit* ('17) Happy Hooligan dropped a bomb on the Kaiser, while Mutt & Jeff captured the Big Bertha in *The 75-Mile Gun*

Richard Barthelmess was the prizefighter who went to war in The Patent Leather Kid.

('18) and trained it on von Hindenburg with amusing results. Mutt & Jeff also had a sadistic encounter with the German emperor in *The Kaiser's New Dentist* ('18) when they attempted to pull his aching tooth!

The Hollywood stars were quick to come to the aid of the war effort at home. Mary Pickford, Douglas Fairbanks, Charlie Chaplin, and William S. Hart were among many favorites who traveled from coast to coast selling Liberty Bonds and raising money for the American Red Cross. Miss Pickford promoted the sale of five million dollars in war bonds in Pittsburgh on a single afternoon, and in May, 1918, raised two million at Chicago in less than an hour.

Numerous war-relief balls and benefit entertainments gave fans opportunities to see their idols in person. One such event was a mock prizefight between Douglas Fairbanks and Charlie

Chaplin, with Mary Pickford as referee, at the Los Angeles Mason Opera House on September 8, 1917. Other stars who performed were Mae Murray, Wallace Reid, Jack Pickford, Olive Thomas, Raymond Hatton, and female impersonator Julian Eltinge. Programs were sold by Edna Purviance, Dorothy Dalton, Lottie Pickford, Anna Luther, Teddy Sampson, and others.

Patriotic tableaux featuring prominent players were part of recruiting campaigns in major cities. Many stars were sponsors for military regiments, not only building morale but greatly stimulating enlistments. Mary Pickford was mascot of the 143rd California Field Artillery and saw it off to France. Dressed in a private's khaki uniform, she met it upon its return in January, 1919, and marched twelve exhausting miles as the regiment paraded through the streets of Oakland and San Francisco. William S. Hart sponsored the 159th California Infantry, and Dustin Farnum was tireless in raising money and gifts for the 115th Army Sanitary Train at Camp Kearney. Entertainments at Army and Navy installations were frequently brightened by personal appearances of popular stars, but the embarrassing fact was that many silent screen favorites had no talent for singing or dancing. But for a lonely doughboy it was enough just to be reminded of the girl back home by the sight of Bessie Love, Mary Miles Minter, or Billie Burke.

Stars exhorted the public to save food (even Fatty Arbuckle went on a diet) and to knit for the boys in service. The fan magazines were filled with photos of stalwart screen heroes trying to knit—and looking completely befuddled! It was hard to believe that William Farnum, Earle Williams, Elliott Dexter, or William Russell spent much time with the knitting needles, but it made good propaganda. Writer June Mathis organized a campaign to collect old shirts for making clothing for refugee children abroad. Viola Dana and Helen Holmes were among Hollywood stars who publicized war gardens, and Harry Carey and Elsie Ferguson helped spark a nationwide drive to collect tobacco for free distribution to the A.E.F.

Fans were shocked to learn that many screen heroes, actually in their late thirties and forties, were considered too old for military service, including Douglas Fairbanks, William S. Hart, Arnold Daly, and William Farnum. There was considerable criticism of actors who sought deferment from the draft as married men.

Charlie Chaplin, a British subject, was bitterly attacked for not enlisting. A widely repeated rumor accused him of circulating petitions to women's clubs asking that he be exempted from the draft. This charge was hotly denied by Chaplin, who said he had registered with Selective Service as required by law and "had never claimed exemption nor . . . sought it . . . and will willingly respond when called." These criticisms were still being revived against the comedian nearly fifty years later. Chaplin made several war bond tours and also entertained at training camps, where his experience in the English music halls proved invaluable. In all fairness, Chaplin's value to the war effort through the morale building of his comedies probably exceeded any paltry contribution he might have made as a foot soldier.

Cecil B. De Mille's Lasky Home Guard, composed of studio employees, was the butt of many jokes and much ridicule for its play drills around the Lasky lot—it met for two hours every other Sunday! De Mille was named captain, with William C. de Mille as sergeant and Wallace Reid as corporal. The unit was eventually made part of the California State Militia, and De Mille claimed that all of the 105 men who went into the regular army after rudimentary training with the Home Guard were made noncommissioned officers.

Numerous stars served with distinction in Army and Navy units, and among those cited for their military records were Robert Warwick, Eugene Pallette, Earl Metcalfe, Jack Levering, Richard Travers, Wheeler Oakman, and Tom Forman, as well as producer Robert T. Kane and cameramen Harry Thorpe, Larry Darmour, and Ernest B. Schoedsack (later co-director of *Grass* and *King Kong*). Even Maciste, the Italian piano mover so popular in Roman strong-man spectacles, was seriously wounded on the Austrian front.

The quality of documentary war films released in the United States during 1917-18 improved considerably, although all were liberally sprinkled with the official "sell the war" propaganda.

With millions of husbands, sons, and sweethearts overseas, audiences had a more personal interest in military activities. Universal Newsreel turned out an excellent series entitled *The Boys From Your State,* which followed local units from each state through training camp, embarcation and arrival in France, and occasionally into combat. Given regional showings, these one- and two-reelers attracted huge crowds hopeful of a glimpse

Molly O'Day comforts Richard Barthelmess, the embittered soldier of World War I, in The Patent Leather Kid.

of a loved one on the screen.

To aid recruitment military life was always pictured in the most attractive terms. Pathé's *Under the Stars and Stripes in France* and Universal's *On to Victory* exploited the glorious rewards of the Army, while the exciting inducements of the Navy were seen in *Your Fighting Navy at Work and Play* and in Selig's *Uncle Sam Afloat and Ashore. The American Ambulance Boys at the Front* was a study of the U.S. Ambulance Corps in France. *Horses of War* praised the Cavalry, while *War Dogs* showed how canine recruits were utilized.

Our Bridge of Ships extolled the Merchant Marine and emphasized the growing safety of convoyed troop transports in the North Atlantic. *Our Colored Fighters* pictured the training of Negro troops (invariably on a segregated basis) and was designed to stimulate enlistments by Negroes. *Over Here* was a two-reeler which showed how a model training camp was constructed, staffed and supplied—but it did not show any of the many shoddy camps, poorly built and short of training equipment, and often beset by epidemics of influenza, pneumonia, and malaria. *War Bibles* stressed that religion was not neglected in the services, and chaplains of all faiths were seen at work with the troops. The volunteer services of the American Red Cross overseas was the subject of *The Spirit of the Red Cross,* an inspiring documentary written and produced by artist James Montgomery Flagg. One well-intentioned documentary that went awry was *When Your Soldier Is Hit,* which was intended to reassure the family back home that a battlefield casualty was quickly removed to a hospital for prompt medical attention. The film upset women because of its pictorial realism and their realization of the dangers faced by the doughboy, and it was soon withdrawn from exhibition.

Major studios in Hollywood and the East turned out dozens of short propaganda pictures, many at their own expense, to which leading stars and directors contributed their services. These were particularly effective in promoting the sale of Liberty Bonds. *War Relief,* directed by Marshall Neilan, was an elaborate effort with Mary Pickford, Douglas Fairbanks, William S. Hart, Julian Eltinge, and Theodore Roberts. Fairbanks was also seen in *Sic 'Em Sam,* directed by Joseph E. Henabery, in which he had a boxing match with the Kaiser. *The Bond* had Charlie Chaplin and Edna Purviance in a series of skits, which ended with Charlie using a sledgehammer labeled "Bonds" to batter down the Kaiser. Another such film was directed by D. W. Griffith and had Lillian Gish as a carefree young girl who wants to spend her money on clothes. Her mother (Kate Bruce) urges her to buy war bonds instead. Lillian dreams of the atrocities abroad, and upon awakening eagerly puts her money into bonds.

Motion pictures were also used for indoctrination and training of troops during World War I. These educational subjects were produced by the Signal Corps and also by private studios on contract. The lack of sound limited their effectiveness, although some of these films were accompanied by a script, which was read aloud as the picture unfolded. One of the best was the inevitable treatise on venereal diseases, *Fit to Fight,* directed by Edward H. Griffith and starring Paul Kelly. *Loyalty* was about the effects of narcotics on the country's manhood and called for an end to drug addiction as a step toward victory. Both of these pictures were later given public showings in re-edited versions. In addition to training pictures, soldiers were purposely shown the more vitrolic theatrical films, such as *The Kaiser, Beast of Berlin,* and *To Hell With the Kaiser,* to create hatred of the enemy.

Independent distributors released a number of imported documentaries about the fighting abroad. Most of these were poorly edited and organized, and did not always contain authentic scenes. Some of the better efforts were *The Italian Battle Front, With the Drifters and Minesweepers in the Danger Zone, Behind the Lines in Italy, With the Polish Army in France,* and excellent *British Bulwarks* series turned out by the official war propaganda agency in Great Britain. Pro-Ally values were exploited, but box-office returns were poor, and only those films showing American troops seemed to enjoy any popularity.

Anticipating an early Allied victory, Hollywood embarked in the summer of 1918 upon a series of films calling for a bitter revenge upon Germany and Austria. These pictures often demanded personal vengeance upon the Kaiser and the Hohenzollerns (who went largely unpunished). Many of these movies were not released until after the Armistice, inopportunely confusing American sentiment and failing to reflect the constructive peace program which Woodrow Wilson was advocating at Versailles.

Allen Holubar's *The Heart of Humanity* ('19) foresaw the need of "a world of nations dedicated to peace," as one of its characters said, but campaigned for vengeance upon the Hun because of inhuman invasion atrocities. Charles Miller's *Why Germany Must Pay* ('19), built around the Nurse Cavell incident, suggested portions of the German borderland be evacuated and given to the Belgians as war reparations. Miller's *The Great Victory* ('18) had Wilson as a character and wrongfully implied that the President favored a bloody vengeance.

General Pershing's life was traced in Fox's *The Land of the Free* ('19), which demanded war guilt be fixed in individual terms. *Why America Will Win* ('18) also contained a stodgy impersonation of Pershing and urged the demilitarization of Germany, heavy reparations, and continuous occupation by an Allied police force. William Nigh's *Beware!* ('19), a sequel to *My Four Years in Germany,* had Ambassador Gerard warning of Prussian deception and calling for safeguards to prevent Germany from ever rising again to a position of international power.

John J. Harvey's *The Kaiser's Finish* ('18) proposed the German emperor be publicly hanged in New York City's Times Square! (It was seriously suggested in America that Kaiser Wilhelm be caged and sent on a theatrical tour, the profits from admissions to go to war relief.) *America Must Conquer (The King of the Huns)* ('18) boldly advocated sterilizing German warlords who did not qualify for the firing squad, while George Irving's *Daughter of Destiny* ('17), starring Olga Petrova, had a subtitle calling for the extermination of *all* members of the

Richard Barthelmess as the worthless soldier who returned from World War I to take another man's place in Henry King's Sonny.

imperial family, women included. Universal's *After the War* ('18), laid in an imaginary postwar Berlin, showed German military leaders being tried and executed for war crimes. In this tear-jerker, released just as the war ended, a French soldier seeks out a Prussian colonel to thank him for sparing his life in a German prison camp. He learns that his sweetheart, a beautiful opera singer (Grace Cunard), had married the officer in exchange for her lover's life. The film preached that Germans could never be trusted, and that even a simple act of kindness was dictated by hidden motives.

In the midst of a relentless influenza epidemic which closed down thousands of theaters in the United States, World War I came to an end on November 11, 1918. Except for the classic Chaplin comedies, Hollywood had failed to produce a single noteworthy or significant motion picture during the barren war years.

War-weary audiences had long since tired of war and propaganda pictures, and with the signing of the Armistice this type of film became unsalable. Exhibitors hastened to advise that such movies as *Red, White and Blue Blood* and *Break the News to Mother* were *not* war stories despite their titles. Marshall Neilan, caught with his expensive war drama *The Unpardonable Sin,* had no scruples about advertising it as containing "no horrible atrocities, no sinking of the *Lusitania,* no bloody fighting" and just as "a sweet love story." Producers were urged by *The Moving Picture World* to use "after-the-war characters . . . avoid harrowing scenes of human destruction . . . carry our thoughts brightly and encouragingly forward."

World War I was virtually forgotten by the movies until the release of King Vidor's phenomenally popular *The Big Parade* in 1925 triggered off a tremendous resurgence of pictures with war themes. In the intervening seven years there were only a few routine and generally unsuccessful war films. The major exception was Rex Ingram's masterpiece, *The Four Horsemen of the Apocalypse* ('21), which launched Rudolph Valentino on his fabulous career. This technically magnificent motion picture concerned a wealthy young Argentinian of French extraction who goes to Paris during the war. He falls in love with a lonely married woman (Alice Terry) whose husband is in the trenches. When the husband returns blinded, the horrified young man awakens to his duty, enlists in the French army, and meets his death as his unit moves up to the front.

The Four Horsemen of the Apocalypse was strongly pro-war and reflected the bitter feeling which still prevailed toward the Germans, who were again portrayed as barbarians killing for the love of killing. It was, in short, the popular conception of the war. Ingram's spectacular battle scenes were extremely realistic (he had been an aviator in the war) and were heightened by striking pictorial compositions, the use of symbolism, and intelligent editing. War was seen in a more intimate relationship with the protagonist, foreshadowing the dramas of personal conflict to come later in such films as *The Big Parade* and *All Quiet on the Western Front*.

The impact of Valentino's exotic personality and his over-night success obscured both the good and bad features of *The Four Horsemen*. Without him the picture would probably not have earned such financial rewards—a four-million-dollar profit —nor gained such public acceptance. Valentino helped sharpen the recognition of Ingram's exciting direction, which derived from Griffith and the rising German artists. Some of the credit was unquestionably due to June Mathis, the film's brilliant scenarist, and John F. Seitz, whose photography was among the best in screen history. Less distinguished as a portrayal of war, *The Four Horsemen of the Apocalypse* was an uncommon work of motion-picture art.

Abel Gance's *J'Accuse* ('19) was a French film which many critics consider to be a minor classic among war movies—and others as an absurd and overpraised melodrama. In it German soldiers rape a peasant wife and leave her with child. Her soldier husband, demented by the tragedy, suspects it is the child of his best friend. The two men find themselves together at the front, each seeking death. As night comes the now com-pletely insane husband commands the dead to arise from their graves and fight again. The two men die in an enemy attack. Although planned as part of the war propaganda and made with the cooperation of the French Army Photographic Service, *J'Accuse* was significant as the first evidence of a return to pacifism in motion-picture content. Its pacifist spirit aroused much criticism of Gance. The picture fared better in the United States, probably because it was not imported until 1921, when the war hysteria had begun to abate.

World War I was otherwise relegated to an occasional pro-gram picture during this period. Irvin V. Willat's *Behind the*

A scene in the dugout in James Whale's Journey's End *(1930). Left to right: Anthony Bushell, Colin Clive, Ian McLaren.*

Door ('19) was notable as the first authentic account of submarine warfare. It had an unpleasant theme of personal vengeance, and showed an American Navy officer torturing a German U-boat commander to death. The torture, administered because the German had killed the Navyman's wife, consisted of *skinning* him with a sharp razor! Of lesser merit was Jerome Storm's *Honor Bright* ('22), a story of twin brothers in the trenches. John Gilbert had dual roles. Hoot Gibson, as a brash cowboy in the A.E.F., had several action-filled encounters with the Germans (*Blinky, Shooting for Love, The Gentleman from America*), all played strictly for laughs. The romanticized espionage dramas, which had been so overworked during the war, virtually disappeared from the screen for several years. Mary Pickford's *The Love Light* ('21), a melodrama of a young Italian girl married unknowingly to a German spy, was a serious mistake for the popular actress.

Several pictures attempted to deal with the postwar problems of the returned doughboy, although frequently in a humorous fashion. Henry King's *This Hero Business* ('19) was about a war hero (William Russell) who returns from France laden with decorations. He tries to evade further adulation and become an ordinary citizen, but a series of amusing situations forces him to perform more heroics. In Paramount's *Civilian Clothes* ('20) Thomas Meighan found he lost his wartime glamour for his wife when he doffed his army uniform. She restored it by making him a butler! In *Dangerous Business* ('21) Constance Talmadge pretends to have married her father's male secretary who is away at the front. War makes a man of the pipsqueak (Kenneth Harlan), and he returns to win her hand in a whirlwind courtship.

In a more serious vein, Louis Gasnier's *The Hero* ('23) was a minor classic about a war hero (Gaston Glass) who lost the respect of his wife and friends when he failed to live up to his battlefield reputation. War ruins his life, but in a perverse way. Herbert Brenon's *The Side Show of Life* ('24) told of an English circus clown (Ernest Torrence) who becomes a general in World War I. After the Armistice he is unable to adjust to his old job and resents being laughed at. In Frank Borzage's *Humoresque* ('20) a concert violinist (Gaston Glass) is so emotionally upset by the war that he has difficulty in resuming his artistic career. Richard Barthelmess played dual roles in Henry King's *Sonny* ('22), a rich boy and a poolroom loafer. When the wealthy youth is killed in the trenches, the bum attempts to take his place, but cannot bring himself to deceive the dead boy's blinded mother. Both the physiological and psychological effects of battle injuries were explored in John S. Robertson's *The Enchanted Cottage* ('24). The young soldier (Barthelmess) was embittered by war wounds which mutilated his face and left him crippled. He finds love with an unattractive schoolteacher (May McAvoy), and they become handsome and beautiful in each other's eyes. Robert Florey's *Face Value* ('27) told of a war hero (Jack Mower) who thought his fiancée no longer loved him because of his shell-shattered face.

In retrospect, war tends to become obscured with a nostalgic glamour as the years pass, and its hardships and sufferings fade in intensity. America had reached this stage by 1925, when it could look back upon World War I as a glorious adventure. This sentimental state of mind was largely responsible for the success of a long series of war movies that continued into the

1930s. A more realistic presentation of war was seen in several notable pictures, due·in part to a small group of gifted writers (Laurence Stallings, John Monk Saunders) and directors (William A. Wellman, James Whale) with firsthand combat experience.

The first significant motion picture about World War I was King Vidor's *The Big Parade* ('25). Its simple story, by Laurence Stallings (a Marine officer who lost a leg at Belleau Wood), concerned an American playboy (John Gilbert) caught up in a war not of his making. In France he comes to appreciate the companionship of men in war with two fellow doughboys (Tom O'Brien and Karl Dane), falls in love with a peasant girl (Renee Adoree), and is initiated into the horrors of combat. Produced for $245,000, it ran for two years at the Astor in New York City, grossed fifteen million dollars worldwide (Vidor was misled into selling his percentage of the profits for a paltry sum). John Gilbert, previously confined to romantic leads, was revealed as a sensitive dramatic actor, and Vidor was catapulted into the top rank of directors.

The realism of the battle scenes was a major asset of *The Big Parade*. Vidor familiarized himself with the appearance of combat by viewing a hundred reels of Signal Corps footage made under fire. He achieved a remarkable sense of timing which accentuated the emotional pace of battle and gave it an intense personal quality. Unlike most directors, whose war scenes had a single frenzied tempo, Vidor effectively suggested a *changing* pace to successive phases of combat action.

This rhythm was carried over to other sequences, each of which was given an individual tempo—which Vidor intended to have a subliminal effect upon the viewer by contrasting the pace of parallel action. As the lumbering trucks, motorcycles, and caissons depart for the front, there is a sense of hurry and urgency. Later, the troops move at a decided cadence which transmits a sense of impending disaster and death—audiences were impressed and vaguely disturbed without really knowing why. It was enormously impressive.

Vidor effected this rhythm by matching every movement of his players—each step, gesture, turn of the head, or other motion of the soldiers—to the beat of a metronome (magnified on the set by a bass drum). Aided by sharp editing, these scenes acquired a distinctive symphonic quality. (Eugene O'Neill attempted a similar effect on the stage in *The Emperor Jones* by imperceptibly increasing the tempo of a drumbeat heard throughout the play as the climax neared. One theory is that the drumbeats increased the heartbeat of the viewer.)

The Big Parade is gimmicked with appealing, well-remembered bits of business—John Gilbert teaching Renee Adoree to chew gum, Karl Dane extinguishing a burning candle with a well-aimed wad of tobacco juice. The scene of Melisande (Adoree) attempting to hold back the heavy lorry which is carrying her lover to the front is now screen history. Gilbert throws her one of his army shoes, which she holds tenderly as the trucks recede into the distance.

Not all critics share the estimate of *The Big Parade* as an important screen work. Paul Rotha, in particular, considers it an insincere film which carried little of the real meaning of war. He is more impressed by the early sequences in which the spectator develops "an immense feeling that hundreds of thousands of people are being howled into war, none of them knowing its

Gladden James, Richard Barthelmess, and Douglas Fairbanks, Jr. were the World War I fliers in Howard Hawks' first version of The Dawn Patrol *(1930).*

meaning, the women regarding it as a thing of romance, and the young men a chance for gallant heroism . . ." Rotha was undoubtedly influenced by criticism which arose in England calling *The Big Parade* propaganda to minimize the British contribution to the war and attempting to picture America's role as that of a savior force.

A great many false reports have sprung up about *The Big Parade* and Vidor's attitude toward it. One is that he was indifferent to the assignment, being miffed that a pet project for a film about steel had been discouraged by Irving Thalberg, the boy mogul of Metro-Goldwyn-Mayer. Vidor maintains he had long thought of doing a war picture built around the emotional responses of an average American who has no strong feelings for or against a war whose motives he does not understand, but who is willing to go along and face each situation as it develops. (This concept is not entirely carried out in *The Big Parade*.) Another rumor is that *The Big Parade* was originally completed as an ordinary program picture, and that Thalberg fought with the M-G-M home office for several hundred thousand dollars to expand it to epic proportions. Vidor has denied this (in *Films in Review,* March '64), saying that only a few night battle scenes were added at a cost of $40,000. (In a more recent interview, Vidor said that these additional night battle scenes were directed by George W. Hill.)

As a Broadway play, *What Price Glory?* by Laurence Stallings and Maxwell Anderson was a barbed commentary on the futility of war. Brought to the screen by Fox in 1926, its "war is hell" message was considerably watered down by heavy comedy values and elaborate battle scenes. Much of the footage centered around the endless bickering of two tough Marine regulars, Captain Flagg (Victor McLaglen) and Sergeant Quirt (Edmund Lowe), usually over a woman. The film moved from Shanghai to Belleau Wood in France, where the spectacular and costly American attack was grimly re-created. The scenes in the dressing station after the battle were highly compelling, particularly the famous moment when the dying Barry Norton cries out, "Stop the blood! Stop the blood!"

As directed by Raoul Walsh, who had been responsible for many of Fox's blatant propaganda pictures of 1917-18, *What Price Glory?* lacked the depth and inventiveness of *The Big Parade*. Designed to cash in on the success of the Vidor film, it made little pretense of being more than popular entertainment.

It was a huge box-office hit, encouraging Fox to continue the Flagg-Quirt rivalry in several bawdy sequels (*The Cockeyed World, Women of All Nations*).

William A. Wellman's fine production of *Wings* ('27), with its exciting aerial dogfights, bombing raids, and spectacular plane crashes, popularized the air war picture. Except for a smattering of routine films released near the Armistice (*A Romance of the Air, The Zeppelin's Last Raid*), this aspect of the war had been generally neglected.

Wings was sheer spectacle, given breathless pace by Wellman's superlative direction of the combat sequences, the brilliant stunt flying (by Dick Grace and other ex-World War I pilots), and the beautiful aerial photography by Harry Perry. The effective land battles had an arty composition that showed the influence of the style of the German directors of the 1920s. Much of the authenticity of the picture stemmed from Wellman's wartime experience as a flying officer of the Lafayette Flying Corps, and from the cooperation of the United States Air Service (many scenes were filmed at Kelly Field in San Antonio, Texas).

The deficiencies of *Wings* lay in its occasional moments of "message" and in a trite story built around the inevitable triangle. Two young aviators (Buddy Rogers and Richard Arlen) are in love with the same girl (Jobyna Ralston). Clara Bow was the girl from back home, in love with Rogers, who follows him to France as a Red Cross worker. Arlen crashes in enemy territory, steals a German Fokker and flies back to his own lines, where Rogers unknowingly shoots him down. He realizes it is Miss Bow that he loves. Clara Bow was too sophisticated as the tomboy, and Paramount could not resist a hotel bedroom scene exploiting her flapper personality. The real hit of the show, in a scene lasting less than ninety seconds, was Gary Cooper as an ill-fated flier. Released at the end of the silent era, *Wings* was reissued in 1928 with added sound effects of roaring airplane motors and sputtering machine guns. It was a box-office bonanza.

The following year Wellman brought out *The Legion of the Condemned* ('28), starring Gary Cooper, which attempted to do for the Lafayette Escadrille what *Wings* had done for the American Army Air Force. The downbeat script was by John Monk Saunders, author of *Wings*, and Jean de Limur, who had shot down seven enemy planes as an Escadrille pilot. The reckless heroes were seen as being motivated by a desire to forget

Mary Astor and Richard Dix in the World War I drama of combat flyers,
Ace of Aces *(1933).*

their past, rather than by any sense of loyalty and patriotism,
and the Germans were pictured as heartless brutes with the
execution of the heroine (Fay Wray) by a firing squad. The
film was a pale imitation of Wellman's earlier success. Another
film about Americans in the French air service was *Captain
Swagger* ('28), with Rod LaRocque. George Fitzmaurice's *Lilac
Time* ('28) was pure hokum, blending cute comedy and a poignant love story with scenes of exciting aerial combat. Colleen
Moore was a French peasant girl who loved a British flying
officer (Gary Cooper). Despite the maudlin plot and use of
special effects to create part of the climactic air battle, *Lilac Time*
scored heavily at the box office. It was also released with added
sound effects and a theme song ("Jeanine, I Dream of Lilac
Time"). Universal's *The Lone Eagle* ('28) was typical of several quickies with an Air Service setting. Raymond Keane was
the hero who, yellow at first, redeems himself as a fearless ace
and wins his French sweetheart (Barbara Kent). *Hard-Boiled*

Haggerty ('27) stressed the romantic adventures of an American flyer (Milton Sills) with a French prostitute (Molly O'Day).

Two of the best air dramas of World War I, *Hell's Angels* and *The Dawn Patrol,* were released in 1930. A project of the eccentric young millionaire Howard Hughes, *Hell's Angels* had been in work since 1927. Dissatisfied with Luther Reed's silent version, Hughes scrapped it, replaced star Greta Nissen with an unknown named Jean Harlow, and began directing a sound version himself (aided by dialogue director James Whale). More than $4,000,000, then a phenomenal sum for a motion picture, was spent on production costs. *Hell's Angels* emerged as a mammoth spectacle with brilliantly staged aerial battles, a Zeppelin raid on London, and an attack on an enemy munitions dump. *Hell's Angels* failed only when it came down to earth. Its trite story of two brothers—one a weakling (Ben Lyon) who is protected and finally killed by the stronger (James Hall) to save him from cowardice before a German firing squad—intruded upon the drama in the sky. Both audiences and critics tended to evaluate the film in terms of its overpublicized costs, causing it to meet a disappointing reception.

Howard Hawks' *The Dawn Patrol* shifted the emphasis from spectacle to an examination of the personal motives and emotions of the combatants. The anguish of a sensitive commander (Richard Barthelmess), faced with repeatedly ordering inexperienced fliers to certain death, was clearly etched. Combat pilots were shown as gallant, devil-may-care individuals, but it was made clear this was only a veneer to hide their fears. *The Dawn Patrol* was essentially a pacifist picture, its anti-war message brought out in perceptive but overlong dialogue. The flying scenes featured many spectacular crashes, and some of these were used eight years later when Warner Brothers brought out a slick, superficial new version of *The Dawn Patrol,* starring Errol Flynn. This time the film was larded with pro-war overtones, part of a propaganda build-up that helped lead the United States into a new world conflict.

After 1930 aviation dramas of World War I became increasingly routine and eventually disappeared. Some of these uninspired efforts were *The Sky Hawk* ('29), *Young Eagles* ('30), *Sky Devils* ('32), *Body and Soul* ('31), *Cock of the Air* ('32), Richard Dix's *Ace of Aces* ('33), *Today We Live* ('33), *Crimson Romance* ('34), *Hell in the Heavens* ('34) and *Suzy* ('36). Somewhat better were Stuart Walker's *The Eagle and the Hawk* ('33), a drama of an American pilot (Fredric March) who cannot stand the strain of aerial combat and commits suicide, and Anatole Litvak's *The Woman I Love* ('37), with Paul Muni and Miriam Hopkins. The latter, a drama of a wartime pilot and his observer who are both in love with the same woman, was a remake of *L'Equipage,* a French silent of 1924 (which was also done in France in 1934 as a talkie under the title *Flight Into Darkness*).

One of the best of World War I aviation films is the unappreciated *The Blue Max* ('66), directed by John Guillermin. A harsh account of a cold and ruthless German pilot who is determined to win the Kaiser's highest medal, the Pour le Merite, nicknamed "The Blue Max," it presents a stunning display in aerial combat photographed in Cinemascope and color. These scenes, largely filmed against lush Irish backgrounds by Skeets Kelly, have a breathtaking quality that is emphasized by Jerry Goldsmith's exceptional musical score. The plot is somewhat hampered by the hero's class conflict with his aristocratic fellow officers, and also by the explicit love scenes with a German countess (Ursula Andress). *The Blue Max* is marred only by the miscasting of George Peppard in the lead. It creates a coldly compelling account of aerial warfare without injecting a single note of sympathy for its protagonists. Much of its realism may be attributed to the accurate reconstructions of World War I aircraft.

Despite the success of Chaplin's *Shoulder Arms,* Hollywood made few comedies about World War I until the mid-1920s. The studios feared the public would consider it bad taste to ridicule the soldier and his hardships, but the warm reception of the comedy scenes of *The Big Parade* and *What Price Glory?* brought a flood of broad burlesques of army life. Most were heavy with slapstick and lacked the satire of the Chaplin classic. The plots of these service comedies usually followed a routine pattern. A bumbling draftee is sent to a training camp, where he has a succession of misadventures with a belligerent sergeant or a pompous colonel, symbols of authority and regimentation. Shipped to France, he comes to grips with the Germans, who were more broadly caricatured than in the propaganda films of the war years. A comedy chase follows in which the hapless private inadvertently captures dozens of the enemy and becomes a hero. A shy French girl or a jazzy Red Cross nurse was always around for love interest.

While none of these films had any particular distinction, most major comedians—Harold Lloyd excepted—attempted a service comedy. Buster Keaton, ill at ease in the talkies, was seen in *Doughboys* ('30), which relied on a series of tired gags. Larry Semon was the wistful soldier clown of *Spuds* ('27), and Wheeler and Woolsey cavorted with the A.E.F. in *Half-Shot at Sunrise* ('30). Karl Dane and George K. Arthur did *Rookies* ('27), a cute comedy of the civilian training camps. Deserting their Cohen and Kelly roles, George Sidney and Charlie Murray were two unlikely elderly doughboys in *Lost at the Front* ('27). George Jessel was the Jewish lad constantly in hot water with the Irish Fighting 69th in *Private Izzy Murphy* ('27), and a Navy sequel, *Sailor Izzy Murphy* ('27), was equally appalling.

In Mack Sennett's *Soldier Boy* ('26), Harry Langdon was a bewildered doughboy who did not know the war was over. The opening scenes of *The Strong Man* ('27) were laid at the front, where Harry captured a giant German soldier whom he

Fredric March, as a French officer, has his wounds dressed in this scene from The Road to Glory *(1936). June Lang in center.*

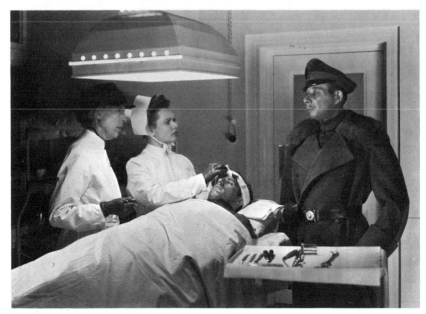

Anna Neagle (center) was the martyred Edith Cavell, a nurse who cared for an Allied soldier during the German occupation of Belgium. Edna Mae Oliver at left, Lucien Prival at right. Nurse Edith Cavell *(1939).*

brings to the United States. Langdon was later the comedy relief in a curious mishmash of military hijinks, *A Soldier's Plaything,* a semi-musical which Michael Curtiz directed for Warner Brothers in 1930.

Wallace Beery and Raymond Hatton had a superb war comedy in *Behind the Front* ('26), whose humor was tinged with uncommon irony as two reluctant soldiers philosophically accept the hardships of war. In a more slapstick vein were two Beery-Hatton sequels, *We're in the Navy Now* and *Now We're in the Air,* both released in 1927. The latter used some leftover flying scenes from *Wings* (of which there were plenty, Wellman having shot 200 reels of film) and had some zany airplane acrobatics. Much of the fun revolved around Louise Brooks in a dual role as twin wives whom the boys could not tell apart. Monty Banks' *Flying Luck* ('28) also featured many aerial comedy stunts, but its best asset was Jean Arthur as a colonel's pretty daughter.

The humor of the British Tommy was recorded by Sydney

Chaplin in *The Better 'Ole* ('26), based on the popular war cartoons of Bruce Bairnsfather. Two sanguine cockney soldiers are trapped in a French town recaptured by the Germans. Bill and Alf are hilarious as they attempt to escape costumed as a comedy horse. This American version, directed by Charles F. Riesner, was far superior to George Pearson's British-made original of 1918, but it did little to help the talented Sydney Chaplin overcome the handicap of his half-brother's genius.

For sheer absurdity, Laurel and Hardy in *Pack Up Your Troubles* ('32) were unmatched. They try to evade the draft by posing as one-armed panhandlers, but are caught by the M.P.s and forcibly conscripted. A highlight is the scene where the boys, dressed in flannel nightgowns, are asleep in a dugout at the front. Awakened by a shellburst, Hardy sends Laurel to see what has caused the noise. Stan's bewildered expression as he holds a candle aloft and peers into the darkness of No Man's Land is followed by a bedlam of explosions. In a typical climax Stan and Ollie, in a runaway tank, capture an entire German regiment. The last half of the picture is laid back in America, where the boys search for the parents of a buddy killed at the front.

Ham and Eggs at the Front ('27), authored by Darryl F. Zanuck, was a tasteless travesty of the colored troops played by an all-white cast in blackface (including Myrna Loy as a dusky vamp). All the clichés of the Negro were present—including the inevitable poker game in which every player has four aces and a razor! In the same vein was *Anybody's War* ('30), with Moran & Mack, the Two Black Crows of vaudeville fame.

One of the best training camp comedies was Henry King's *23½ Hours Leave* ('19), in which Douglas MacLean was a breezy young private who goes A.W.O.L. to capture a spy ring —and win the general's daughter. Eighteen years later MacLean produced a talkie version with James Ellison, but it was dated and no longer funny. In *Riley of the Rainbow Division* ('28) Pauline Garon, masquerading in an oversize army uniform, was smuggled into a barracks to search for her soldier sweetheart. Equally unlikely was *Top Sergeant Milligan* ('28), in which Wesley Barry and Wade Boteler were two comic rookies who fall for a French girl—but she turns out to be a male German spy!

World War I got a musical comedy background in *Marianne* ('29). Hampered by a French accent, Marion Davies sang, danced, gave imitations, and burlesqued Renee Adoree. Ukulele Ike (Cliff Edwards) and Benny Rubin frequently interrupted the shot and shrapnel for a song and dance. Even Mack Sennett tried a war comedy with his personally directed *The Goodbye Kiss* ('28). Photoplay hailed it for its "Griffith touches," but it was just an inept tale of a timid doughboy, with none of Sennett's Keystone inventiveness. Sally Eilers was cute as the girl, displaying a comedy talent which Hollywood inexplicably never utilized again.

Two comedies about the Army of Occupation in conquered Germany were MGM's *Tin Hats* ('27) and Universal's *Buck Privates* ('28). In the former Conrad Nagel and two buddies, separated from their unit, take over a sleepy Rhine town. Nagel abandons an elaborate plot to loot the treasury when he falls for a local princess (Claire Windsor). *Buck Privates* had some clever touches in the attempts of Malcolm McGregor and Eddie Gribbon to Americanize the German village where they are billeted. Lya de Putti, the faithless wife of *Variety,* had little to do as a wide-eyed fraulein. As a comic postscript to World War I, *Legionnaires in Paris* ('28) was about the horseplay that went on in the French capital when the American Legion held its tenth anniversary convention there in 1927.

Most of the war dramas which followed *The Big Parade* had little or nothing to recommend them. Plots were trite, action sequences sparse and often fleshed out with stock shots from old newsreels and features. *The Patent Leather Kid* ('27) was about a prizefighter (Richard Barthelmess) who becomes a coward in combat. Barthelmess was also seen as an army officer in *Out of the Ruins* ('28) who deserts to save his girl from a forced marriage. He is shot by a firing squad. *Closed Gates* ('27) was a silly quickie about a disgraced young millionaire (John Harron) who goes to war, loses his memory, and is rehabilitated by a Red Cross nurse (Jane Novak). *Comrades* ('28) concerned a brave lad who goes to war in place of a weakling. *Dugan of the Dugouts* ('28) told of a slacker who joins the Army to find his girl—an inevitable Red Cross nurse (Pauline Garon)—and becomes a man. Gary Cooper was peaceful cowboy who goes to war in *The Man from Wyoming* ('30), while Buck Jones, in *The War Horse* ('27) played a cowboy who went to France in search of his horse, which had been commandeered by the Cavalry.

World War I spy melodramas returned to the screen in

such pictures as *Three Faces East* ('26), with director Rupert Julian again filling in as the Kaiser; Mauritz Stiller's *Hotel Imperial* ('27), starring Pola Negri as a fetching double agent; and *I Was a Spy* ('33), which had Madeleine Carroll as the famous Belgian spy, Marthe Crachaert. Greta Garbo was a Russian operator in *The Mysterious Lady* ('28), and the notorious spy-dancer in the title role of *Mata Hari* ('32). (Jeanne Moreau also played Mata Hari in a French remake in 1965). The modern sequences of *Noah's Ark* ('28) came to a rousing climax as doughboy George O'Brien saved Dolores Costello from a German firing squad. Herbert Wilcox revived the Nurse Cavell incident in two films, the silent *Dawn* ('28), with Dame Sybil Thorndike, and *Nurse Edith Cavell* ('39), starring Anna Neagle as the martyred nurse. The latter was used as anti-German propaganda in the early stages of World War II.

Submarine warfare of 1917-18 was realistically portrayed in *Convoy* ('27), Rex Ingram's *Mare Nostrum* ('26), John Ford's *The Seas Beneath* ('31), and in three fine German productions, *Cruiser Emden* ('26), *U-9 Weddigen* ('27) and *Mor-*

George Brent and James Cagney starred in Warner Brothers' drama of World War I, The Fighting 69th *(1940).*

genrot ('33). The latter was remarkable for its absence hostility toward the United States and Great Britain. Despite its peaceful tendencies, *Morgenrot* was good propaganda for Prussian nationalism, with its depiction of the bravery of the German submarine fleet, and its exhibition was encouraged by the Nazis. The role of women in war was covered in such tearjerkers as *Corporal Kate* ('26), *She Goes to War* ('29), *War Nurse* ('30) and *The Mad Parade* ('31). Routine battlefield heroics were seen in *Havoc, Into No Man's Land, Fallen Angels, Beyond Victory, Under the Black Eagle, Find Your Man* (with Rin-Tin-Tin), *Surrender,* and many other films released between 1925 and 1933.

A resurgence of love stories with World War I settings also began in the mid-1920s. Most were maudlin and contrived, but their appeal for women made them strong box-office attractions. Some of the more popular included *Seventh Heaven, The White Sister, The Dark Angel, Waterloo Bridge, Shopworn Angel,* and *A Farewell to Arms,* all of which were filmed twice (*Waterloo*

Gary Cooper was the hillbilly sharpshooter, Alvin York, who became a World War I hero, in Sergeant York *(1941).*

Bridge was even updated for a third time in a World War II setting as *Gaby*). War was always seen as a pretext for the parting and misunderstanding of the lovers.

Surprisingly few documentaries about World War I have been seen since the close of hostilities, and these did not prove popular. The best have been Laurence Stallings' *The First World War* ('34), produced by Fox Movietone News, and Albert L. Rule's *The Big Drive* ('33). Both utilized combat footage long stored in Signal Corps vaults. Several collections of old newsreels and authentic battle scenes assembled in Germany, such as *Fighting for the Fatherland* ('26) and *Behind the German Lines* ('28), tried unsuccessfully to present the Prussian side of the war in a more favorable light.

A wave of sympathy for defeated Germany swept the United States in the mid-1920s, and this softening of American bitterness was reflected in several pro-German, essentially pacifist motion pictures.

Perhaps in retribution for his violent *Hearts of the World*, D. W. Griffith brought out a touching story of postwar Germany in *Isn't Life Wonderful* ('24). This minor masterpiece was actually shot on location—in Berlin, the shipyard of Cöpenick, and the forests of Crampnitz and Sacrow—and mirrored the economic chaos, food shortages, and political unrest which prevailed in Central Europe. Its spare plot concerned an impoverished family of Polish refugees who settle in Germany after the war. The heroine (Carol Dempster) is in love with a young German (Neil Hamilton), whom she finds to be a decent, sensitive person. For the first time in a generation the Germans were seen on the screen in a favorable light, as ordinary men and women caught up in the tragedy of defeat and hunger. There was no escaping the moral of *Isn't Life Wonderful*—that Germany was paying the price of its aggressive war, but its tone of forgiveness and the suggestion that the German people had suffered enough were apparent. A similar point was made with greater realism and much less sentimentality by G. W. Pabst's *The Joyless Street* ('25), a fine drama of postwar Vienna, in which Greta Garbo had a small role.

Because of the lingering effects of anti-German propaganda in America, these films were not entirely successful. They helped pave the way for John Ford's *Four Sons* ('28), which aroused pro-German sympathy with its story of a Rhine mother who sacrifices three of four sons to Ludendorff's war machine, and Fred Niblo's *The Enemy* ('28), in which Lillian Gish played a young Austrian bride to whom the war brings tragedy and intolerable hardships. Sympathy for the Germans was also reflected in such lesser pictures as *Young Eagles* ('30), in which a German ace was depicted as an honorable enemy who kills only through patriotic motives, and *Dog of the Regiment* ('27), in which a German girl and an American boy are sweethearts before the war. Later, he becomes a flying officer and is shot down near her farm. The girl (and Rin-Tin-Tin) help him to escape, and the lovers are reunited after the Armistice.

The culmination of a growing anti-war sentiment came in a series of militantly pacifistic motion pictures released in the early 1930s (*All Quiet on the Western Front, Journey's End, Westfront 1918, The Case of Sergeant Grischa, The Man I Killed, Road to Glory, Grand Illusion*). War was exposed as a horrible and futile destruction of humanity which served no useful purpose. The façade of glory and patriotism were replaced by a bitter cynicism. This questioning attitude prevailed until the aggressions by Hitler and Mussolini began anew the propaganda to condition the public to a second world holocaust.

Lewis Milestone's *All Quiet on the Western Front* ('30) is generally acknowledged as the best film about World War I ever produced. Much of its power derives from the striking battle scenes staged with ruthless realism. Milestone's fluid camera, staccato cutting, and effective use of sound create a devastating picture of trench warfare. The counterpoint to these overwhelming action sequences is an intimate account of a group of bewildered German schoolboys drawn into war by visions of glory. Their sudden disillusionment, the horrors of combat, and the final intimacy with death emphasizes the utter futility of war. Although marred by oversentimentality and Milestone's excessive use of symbolism, *All Quiet on the Western Front* is a film of tremendous impact, both visually and intellectually.

The peace message of *All Quiet on the Western Front*, like Erich Maria Remarque's novel, has a relentless repetitiveness. The callow youths are prompted to enlist by an older, militant generation—it is the Kaiser's war. A meek village postman (John Griffith Wray) becomes a domineering sergeant on the drillfields. The first encounter with combat is a shattering, sickening experience. The young soldiers are soon hardened to death, even of close friends, and the tragedy of the maimed and blinded is emphasized. In a famous scene the hero (Lew Ayres) suffers remorse as he shares a shellhole with a French poilu (Raymond Griffith) whom he has knifed; his promises to the dying soldier are forgotten as he escapes to his own lines. Back home on leave, Ayres is ridiculed when he speaks of the horrors of the trenches, and is called a coward. Subconsciously seeking death, he finds release in a sniper's bullet (in the famous ending, suggested by Karl Freund, as he reaches for an errant butterfly on the battlefield).

Although *All Quiet* aroused sympathy for the Germans, its anti-war message was intended to be so objective as to favor neither Germany nor the Allies. However, many countries were not yet ready to accept this concept and forgive Germany's war guilt. When first shown *All Quiet on the Western Front* incited riots in many parts of Europe. It was banned in France and not shown there until 1962, forty-four years after the Armistice, when it was booed by angry audiences. *All Quiet* was also prohibited in Germany after Hitler's rise to power as being in-

Alexander Knox played Woodrow Wilson in 20th Century-Fox's Wilson *(1944), with Geraldine Fitzgerald as Wilson's second wife.*

consistent with the goals of Nazi militarism. It got a good reception in the United States, where an economic depression and other political elements were conditioning public opinion to peace. Carl Laemmle, president of Universal Pictures, was seriously suggested for a Nobel peace prize for *All Quiet.*

G. W. Pabst's *Westfront 1918* ('30), which appeared simultaneously with *All Quiet,* bore many similarities in theme and construction to the Milestone film. An open indictment of war, it concerned a German unit trying to hold its position against repeated French assaults. As in *All Quiet,* compelling battle scenes are interspersed with an episodic plot. A young soldier is followed on leave to his village, where he surprises his wife with a butcher who has bought her favors with extra food. Disillusioned, he returns to his comrades and seeks death in a massive tank attack. In a contrived ending a French soldier and German officer, both dying, clasp hands on the battlefield and gasp out expressions of forgiveness.

Still partly under the influence of silent-picture techniques, Pabst relied heavily on pictorial values, but with less of the symbolism seen in *All Quiet.* Like Milestone, he used long traveling shots to give pace to the battle scenes, and effective sound to create the cacophony of battle. The editing was static and uninspired. The controversy as to the superiority of *All Quiet on the Western Front* or *Westfront 1918* is still raging. Both are distinguished movies, but Pabst's is probably the better. It has more sustained realism, less sentimentality, and (except for the hospital scenes and the forced climax) none of the obvious peace propaganda which marred *All Quiet.* The same goal was subtly achieved through a photographic reality which betrays the cruel truths of war.

A third anti-war film which came out at the same time was Tiffany's *Journey's End* ('30). As a play it was the surprise hit of the 1929 season in London's West End, and was produced through the influence of George Bernard Shaw. The author, Robert C. Sheriff, an insurance clerk who had served in France, originally wrote it for an amateur theatrical. Set in a frontline dugout in the British sector, the play revolved around a sensitive officer whom three years of relentless war had reduced to a whiskey-soaked brute. Only the love of a woman keeps him from giving way to a growing fear of death.

The motion picture version of *Journey's End* was a joint venture of British and American companies, filmed in Hollywood because no satisfactory sound-recording equipment was available in England. James Whale, director of the London play (and a former prisoner of war in Germany) was engaged to direct. An all-male cast was sparked by Colin Clive in his original role of Captain Stanhope (Laurence Olivier played it during the tryouts), and Keystone comic Billy Bevan was a delight as the sanguine Lieutenant Trotter.

In many respects *Journey's End* was a notable motion picture, largely because it remained faithful to Sheriff's powerful play. It was praised by critics and appeared on most Ten Best lists of the year—but audiences neither liked nor appreciated it. The film was talky and short on action—only a brief sequence of a raid on the German lines had been added—and women complained at the absence of love interest. Despite Whale's inventive use of the camera, the single set became tiresome, and some of the significant dialogue was lost in a harsh recording of the British accents. *Journey's End* was essentially a filmed play lacking in cinematic qualities. Its anti-war message, readily discernible in Stanhope's beautiful speeches, was lost on all but a minority of perceptive viewers. For all its limitations *Journey's End* remains a minor classic, a *succès d'estime* that is almost forgotten today.

Pacifism was the dominant theme of Ernst Lubitsch's *The Man I Killed* ('32), also known as *Broken Lullaby*. A sensitive French soldier (Phillips Holmes) is tormented by the memory of the German he killed on the battlefield. After the Armistice he goes to seek out the dead man's family. At first he hides his identity and is accepted as a friend by the parents. His guilt grows as he falls in love with the dead man's fiancée (Nancy Carroll), and finally he faces up to the ordeal of revealing his horrible secret. The picture was marred by ponderous moralizing, and American audiences resented the depths of its pro-German sympathy. The thesis of individual war guilt was explored in unreal, hysterical terms, and the peace propaganda of *The Man I Killed* was of an embittered, negative quality for which Lubitsch was strongly criticized in some quarters. He unwisely let his cast overact, although Nancy Carroll gave a surprisingly restrained performance as the fraulein. It was a confused and depressing picture which failed badly at the box office.

A few other pacifist films of the 1930s are worthy of mention. Herbert Brenon's *The Case of Sergeant Grischa* ('30) was a disturbing movie which failed to fully grasp the meaning of Arnold Zweig's powerful novel. The story was about a Russian deserter (Chester Morris) who is mistaken for another man and executed because of the inefficiency and indifference of military justice. Brenon's ingrained sentimentalism made him a poor choice to direct. Victor Trivas' German-made *Hell on Earth* ('31) was a fantasy of five soldiers of different nationalities who are trapped together in an abandoned trench. The film preaches that tolerance and fraternal spirit will outlaw war as enemies come to respect and understand each other.

Howard Hawks' *The Road to Glory* ('36) was a glossy melodrama of a French unit ordered to hold its position in face of certain annihilation—German sappers are heard mining the ground underneath. The needless sacrifice of men because of lack of personal integrity in ambitious commanding officers is emphasized. A poignant point is made as an aged veteran of the Prussian siege of 1870 (Lionel Barrymore) appears in the ranks, stressing the depletion of France's young manhood. Russell Mack's *Private Jones* ('33) was a biting satire on war in which a reluctant draftee (Lee Tracy) cannot understand the personal motivations which lead a man to kill in battle.

A more subtle pacifism was present in several movies in which postwar conditions, and their link to World War I, are explored. Most of these films were keyed to the social and economic injustices inflicted upon the returning soldier. In *The Last Parade* ('31) Tom Moore was a policeman who could not get back his old job and drifts into a life of crime. W. S. Van Dyke's *They Gave Him a Gun* ('37) showed how a decent man, trained to kill in war, becomes a professional murderer. The mistreatment of hungry veterans in the Depression was the theme of *Heroes for Sale* ('34), and was musically emphasized when Joan Blondell sang "Remember My Forgotten Man" in a lavish production number in *The Gold Diggers of 1933*. Disillusioned aces of the Lafayette Escadrille were seen earning a living as movie stunt pilots in *The Lost Squadron* ('32) and *Lucky Devils* ('33). John Ford's *Pilgrimage* ('33) was about a Gold Star mother who goes to France to visit her son's grave. She returns with a willingness to accept her dead son's sweetheart and their illegitimate child. Postwar conditions as they affected the German veteran were reviewed in James Whale's *The Road Back* ('37), a continuation of *All Quiet on the Western Front* by the same author, Erich Maria Remarque. Whale's opening battle scenes were of excellent quality, but the picture quickly bogged down in unrealistic melodrama. A more sympathetic approach, conveyed by a touching love story, motivated Frank Borzage's *Three Comrades* ('38), also by Remarque, in which three soldiers try unsuccessfully to adjust to changing political and economic conditions in Germany.

With the clouds of a second world conflict gathering in Europe, Jean Renoir's *Grand Illusion* ('37) was a last but hopeless appeal to Germany not to go to war again. Set in a German prisoner-of-war camp during World War I, it traced a growing respect and understanding between the aristocratic commandant (Erich von Stroheim) and a sensitive French officer (Pierre Fresnay). A parallel story concerns the common bond of sympathy which springs up between private soldiers of both sides. But intense national loyalties cannot be forgotten, and the French prisoners engineer a mass escape during which the German commandant deliberately shoots the French officer. At the end Stroheim, filled with remorse for his hasty act, places a flower on Fresnay's coffin.

Despite its beauty of theme and construction, *Grand Illusion*'s message of peace and appeasement was not well received. It had become clear that a European war could not be averted, and the French feared the picture would be interpreted as a sign of weakness. *Grand Illusion* was banned in the Third Reich by propaganda minister Joseph Goebbels and was given only limited showings in Italy, reportedly on personal orders of Mussolini. Recognition of the Renoir classic was not fully achieved until after World War II, when it could be viewed without nationalistic pressures and politics.

The outbreak of World War II brought a virtual end of films about the earlier conflict of 1917-18. So immense was the scope of the new struggle, set on a global basis, that it dwarfed the fighting which had been largely confined to Normandy and Flanders. (Pictures about World War I in areas other than France have included *Tell England,* about British operations at Gallipoli; *40,000 Horsemen,* John Ford's *The Lost Patrol; Lawrence of Arabia;* and *A Farewell to Arms.*) The First World War became something quaint and insignificant, except to the millions who had suffered through it.

Just prior to Pearl Harbor, when militaristic movies were being used to condition America to its entrance into the European war, the settings of World War I were used in *The Fighting*

Fred MacMurray impersonated World War I flying ace Eddie Ricken-
backer in 20th Century-Fox's Captain Eddie *(1945). Lynn Bari was his*
wife.

69th ('40), an account of the famous New York infantry regiment. It was a typical James Cagney-Pat O'Brien vehicle painted
red, white and blue, with an inspiring ending in which Cagney
saves his buddies by falling on a live grenade.

An important contribution to the pro-war propaganda was
Howard Hawks' *Sergeant York* ('41), a screen biography of
one of World War I's most colorful heroes. The story of Alvin
York, a Tennessee hillbilly and crackshot—and originally a
conscientious objector to war—was told with simplicity, dignity,
and understanding. The appeal of patriotism and religion,
coupled with exciting battle scenes and natural humor, made
it a timely and entertaining motion picture. Gary Cooper won
an Academy Award for his performance in the title role.

A less successful biography, also designed to strengthen the
war spirit, was *Captain Eddie* ('45), which was about World
War I ace Eddie Rickenbacker. It was muddied by an oversentimental plot that leaned more to comedy than to an authentic
account of Rickenbacker's life. Fred MacMurray was a poor

choice for the flier. (Germany's aerial hero was also the subject of a screen biography in the 1925 film, *Richthofen—The Red Knight of Germany.*)

Darryl F. Zanuck's *Wilson* ('44) traced the career of the World War I President from the early days at Princeton to his futile efforts to bring the United States into the League of Nations. Released at the height of the war, it was bitterly assailed as propaganda for internationalism and a fourth term for Franklin D. Roosevelt. Its political ideas, although thinly expressed, provoked a controversy which obscured much of the film's merit. Essentially a sincere and challenging movie, *Wilson* was dramatically faulted by its failure to realize the complexity of Wilson's character—despite a perceptive performance by Alexander Knox in the title role. The brutal struggle between Wilson and Senator Henry Cabot Lodge over American participation in the League of Nations was played down, and Wilson's last agonizing trip around the country to drum up public support—in itself material for a single movie—was compressed into a few technicolored train montages. Produced at a cost of $5,200,000, *Wilson* was carefully authenticated—160,000 feet of newsreels of the President were viewed by director Henry King. Despite its unfortunate release at a politically inopportune time, *Wilson* was nevertheless a significant attempt at maturity in motion-picture content.

World War I went into even greater eclipse after the Japanese surrender in 1945. John Ford's absurd remake of *What Price Glory?* ('52), with James Cagney and Dan Dailey as Captain Flagg and Sergeant Quirt, is best forgotten. Its vivid and unreal Technicolor, phony sets, pratfall comedy and the aging Cagney's ludicrous posturing made it a travesty of the original. William A. Wellman, director of the monumental *Wings,* ended his career with *Lafayette Escadrille* ('58), a subject he had always wanted to bring to the screen. Instead of an exciting and dramatic account of the Americans who flew for the French, it was a confused drama intended to show off the teenage idol Tab Hunter. The best World War I film to appear since *Wilson* has been Stanley Kubrick's *Paths of Glory* ('57). When a French attack against an impregnable enemy position fails, five private soldiers are selected at random and executed for "cowardice" as an example to their comrades. The heartlessness of ambitious general staff officers is brutally underlined. Kubrick's battle sequences in the early moments of the picture bear many similarities to Milestone's in *All Quiet on the Western Front*. Of lesser merit is the provocative British film, Joseph Losey's *King and Country* ('65), which discusses the court-martial and execution of a stupid, shell-shocked deserter (Tom Courtenay). The film questions that anything is to be gained by this ritual killing, but fails because it never satisfactorily answers this question. Its pictorial realism of the hardships of the trenches is physically sickening.

Richard Attenborough's first picture as a director, *Oh! What a Lovely War* ('69), spells out the utter lunacy of war in a sort of British music hall variety show. Based on Joan Littlewood's intimate stage play, it has been transferred to the screen as a sprawling satire on the false patriotism and jingoism of World War I. It is a message film to music, expensively conceived (at a cost of $3,000,000) and brilliantly executed, which has had limited appeal to American audiences, except perhaps those who can identify with its anti-war theme. Attenborough has executed *Oh! What a Lovely War* with taste and creativity, but it fails from its sheer physical size.

In 1964, on the fiftieth anniversary of the beginning of the war that was "to make the world safe for democracy," the Columbia Broadcasting System brought out an exceptional series of documentary films entitled *World War I* for television viewing. There is not a single staged scene (nor an added sound effect), and these archaic pictures are mute evidence of the horror and suffering and futility of war.

2

MAX LINDER, COMEDY'S TRAGIC GENIUS

*T*HE motion picture's first *great* comedian, and its first *genuine* star—in the sense of a screen actor who became a public idol—was a dapper Frenchman named Max Linder.

His friends called him "Joyous Max," so infectious was his bubbling personality. Between 1907 and 1914 his gay, often brilliant comedies made him internationally famous, and a fortune at a time when other film favorites were working in anonymity for $5 a day.

Linder was a major inspiration to Charlie Chaplin—"He was my teacher," Chaplin has written—and traces of his influence can be found in the whole school of American comedians, including Harold Lloyd, Buster Keaton, Laurel & Hardy, the sophisticates Adolphe Menjou and Raymond Griffith, and possibly Cantinflas of Mexico. Mack Sennett said Linder's "poursuites" inspired the Keystone chases, and Linder's early use of trick photography in comedy contributed to the Sennett technique. Many famous gags credited to Chaplin, Sennett, the Marx Brothers, and others were first seen in Linder's pictures.

He was the first to create a *distinctive* film character—that of an impeccably dressed Parisian dandy involved in the most absurd situations—and to bring *style* to screen comedy. While his contemporaries in the United States and elsewhere were still relying upon crude slapstick, Linder was utilizing the subtleties of humor and experimenting with satire.

Max Linder was born Gabriel Leuvielle on December 16, 1883, at Saint Loubes, near Bordeaux, in the rich wine district of Gironde. His wealthy parents owned vineyards, to which

Max Linder as the debonair boulevardier of the "Max" comedies (Circa 1915).

Linder took an early dislike. "Nothing was more distasteful to me than the thought of a life among the grapes," he said later.

Even as a child he was a precocious mimic, fascinated with the circuses and traveling shows which toured France, and he resolved early to be a vaudeville actor. At sixteen he entered the Bordeaux Conservatoire, a dramatic academy, and won first prize for comedy and second prize for tragedy in a competition among students. This led to a three-year engagement at the Theatre des Arts, a Bordeaux repertory company, where he acted under the name of Lacerda in the classics of Molière, Musset, and Corneille, as well as in more modern plays. He then went to Paris in hopes of being admitted to the Paris Conservatoire, but was rejected, possibly because of his impertinence with M. LeLoir, the Directeur.

Linder soon got a job playing minor roles at the famous Theatre de l'Ambigu, a comique theater dating back to 1812, which specialized in lurid melodramas. He also worked as an entertainer in such popular music halls, or café-concerts, as l'Alhambra, Le Cigale, the Olympia, and le Petit Casino. He adopted the name of Max Linder upon his arrival in Paris. Two of his close friends were the stage performers *Max* Dearly and Marcelle *Lender,* and it is possible his new name was a combination of their names. A help to his career was his friendship with Charles le Bargy, a distinguished member of the Comédie Française. Linder was a champion swordsman, having trained at the Paris Salle d'Armes, and he met le Bargy at Biarritz, where he had gone to participate in a fencing contest. Attracted by the witty young man, le Bargy offered to coach him for more important roles in exchange for fencing lessons.

Linder began appearing on the screen in July, 1905. A publicity story has it that Charles Pathé, the French movie mogul, saw him at l'Ambigu and sent an enthusiastic note backstage, promising to make him rich as a film comedian. The actual circumstances were much less dramatic. Linder simply applied for work at the Pathé Studio in suburban Vincennes at the suggestion of two Pathé directors, Lucien Nonguet and Louis J. Gasnier (formerly the "chef de claque" at l'Ambigu). For two years he acted at Pathé by day, and on the stage or in the music halls at night. The studio paid him twenty francs a day, whether he worked a few minutes or several hours, plus an additional fifteen francs if his wardrobe was damaged.

His first picture, in which he played a rakish student, was called *The Collegian's First Outing* and was probably shot in two or three hours, although it ran less than ten minutes. He was soon appearing in five to ten pictures a week, although in many he was only an extra.

Linder's most important role in this early period was in Ferdinand Zecca's *The Legend of Polichinelle* ('07), an elaborate version of the French fairy tale. He appeared in many dramas and costume adventures (*The Death of a Toreador, The Contrabanders, Poison, The Whim of an Apache*), but he felt most at ease in Pathé's comedies—*An Unexpected Meeting, The Collegian's First Cigar, Before and After the Wedding, A*

Graduation Celebration, An Evening at the Cinema (whose ideas were later borrowed by Sennett for *Mabel's Dramatic Moment*), and other comedies.

As his screen roles grew in importance, Linder's stage career also flourished, and in 1906 he achieved a long-cherished ambition by joining the Theatre des Varieties, a famous Paris vaudeville house. Audiences were captivated by his breezy personality, impudent pantomime and gifted sense of timing, particularly in two broad comedy sketches, "Miquette and Her Mother" and "The King."

France had taken a commanding lead in screen comedy soon after 1900, exporting hundreds of amusing and clever films with such versatile comedians as Dranem, Polycarpe, Little Moritz, Charles Prince (known as Rigadin), Boucot, and the incredible Bout-de-Zan, a child terror (who was not a midget nor an old man, as has been reported in some film texts).

Pathé's reigning comic was André Deed, a pantomimist and acrobat at the Folies Bergère, who appeared in various countries under a variety of pseudonyms (Boireau, Gribouille, Cretinetti, Foolshead, and Bilboquet). He got himself up as a pasty-faced simpleton clown, and his pictures combined chases and knockabout slapstick to good effect. When he quarreled with Pathé over money in 1907 and left to make movies in Italy, Linder was given the opportunity of starring in a new series of comedies.

Linder did not immediately hit upon the screen character which made him famous. Ignoring Charles Pathé's suggestion for another clown a la Deed, he tried being a bellboy, a railroad conductor, a gendarme, a rustic, a harassed schoolmaster, and even a lively, near-sighted old man in a white wig (in *The Duel of Monsieur Myope*), a blood brother to Mister Magoo.

But it was as Max, a well-tailored man-about-town usually dressed in morning clothes or a tuxedo, that Linder found lasting success. The screen Max was invariably the spoiled son of a wealthy family. He lived in a lavish bachelor apartment on a fashionable boulevard, and was pampered by attentive servants. He frequented bars, was inclined to drink too much, and never worked. Max adored women, and his troubles usually stemmed from some heartless lady-love putting him to some incredible test or ordeal. His small height and dandyish mustache added to the fun, and Max could provoke laughter by teetering on his heels while threatening an outsized villain. A modern d'Artagnan, he was always ready to defend his honor or that of a beautiful woman. In its day Linder's Max was as popular as Chaplin's tramp became a decade later.

His first big screen success was in *The Skater's Debut*, released in December, 1907, in which he cavorted on frozen Lake Daumesnil, flirted with a lovely skater, and outsmarted an egotistical bully. Chaplin's *The Rink* ('16) was straight out of this uninhibited comedy, which, incidentally, was a remake of an André Deed film. Unlike Chaplin, whose grace as a roller skater added to *The Rink* and later to *Modern Times*, Linder was hilarious by his skating ineptness. Max said later he ruined a new suit and lost a pair of gold cufflinks while making *The Skater's Debut*.

Pathé's new comedian soon caught the public fancy, and within a year exhibitors were clamoring for the "Max" comedies. Almost all were one-reelers, and were released at the rate of one each week. While no accurate count is now possible, Linder starred in at least 360 comedies for Pathé between 1907 and 1914. The first twenty or so were directed by Louis J. Gasnier, later director of such celebrated serials as *The Perils of Pauline*. Linder then worked with such directors as Lucien Nonguet, Georges Monca, Ferdinand Zecca, Albert Capellani and Rene Leprince, but after 1910 he directed most of his own pictures.

The variety of Linder's comedy is suggested by the titles of his early film successes: *Max Takes a Bath, Max in a Museum, Max and His Mother-in-Law's False Teeth, Max's Hanging* (a dream fantasy in which all sorts of ridiculous happenings save Max from the executioner), *Max—Aeronaut, Max's New Landlord, Max—Photographer*. Linder wrote most of his scripts with occasional assists from Pathé writers and vaudeville gagmen. He would begin with nothing but a title or bare idea, and build gag upon gag, measuring out the ingredients of laughter in carefully plotted comedy.

Max in a Dilemma ('10) ran eleven weeks at a Paris theater. Despondent when his girl rejects him for a wealthy suitor, Max makes several hilarious attempts at suicide, and finally negotiates with a gang of thugs to have himself killed. When a letter informs him an uncle has left him a large legacy, Max outwits his hired killers, and is reunited with his mercenary sweetheart.

Three other comedies in 1910-11 were particularly successful. *Max Is Absent-Minded* ran the gamut of gags about absentmindedness. Max was in constant hot water with a choleric

Max Linder (Circa 1917).

prospective father-in-law he was trying to impress. An imperious Grand Duke is mistaken for a butler, to whom Max hands his coat and hat. A mix-up in letters sends Max's wager on a horse race to the girl's father, and an R.S.V.P. for dinner to his bookie. In *Max's Astigmatism* the fun is built around his poor eyesight. Unable to see, Max apologizes to a lamppost, kisses the wrong lady's hand, and is challenged to a duel, and meanders through the frightening Paris traffic (speeded up with trick photography). *How Max Went Around the World* is a domestic comedy in which, to escape a nagging wife, Max pretends to leave on a round-the-world business trip, but drinks too much and is brought home drunk to his furious spouse.

The best of Linder's Pathé comedies was the inventive *Max, Victim of Quinquina* ('11), which is often used as a basis of comparison with Chaplin's later techniques. The story is a tissue of amusing misunderstandings. Linder, ill, is advised by his doctor to drink Quinquina, a popular appetizer, with his meals. At a café it is served in an enormous glass marked "Souvenir of Bordeaux," and Max becomes intoxicated. He quarrels with a pompous general over a taxicab, and the two exchange cards for a duel. At a nightclub Max flirts outrageously with a pretty girl, and returns the card of his first adversary when her escort challenges him to another duel. Max proceeds to provoke more duels, each time returning the wrong card. Picked up drunk by the police, he is mistakenly identified and taken to the general's home and put to bed. Everything winds up in a state of total confusion with angry duelists fighting each other, and the befuddled Max being solaced by the general's wife.

Most of Linder's comedies involved lady-loves who were essentially hard-hearted, demanding creatures given to whims and pettishness—and a sadistic talent for torturing the fawning Max. In *Max in the Alps* a rich widow demands edelweiss from an Alpine peak. After several hair-raising attempts at mountaineering Max buys the elusive blossom from a street vendor. In *Max Takes Up Boxing* he wins a boxing match on a fluke, only to have the girl whom he was trying to impress feel sorry for his defeated opponent. He pretends to be a ski champion in *Max on Skis*, fights an unruly bull in *Max—Toreador*, races an unmanageable horse in *Max, Jockey for Love*, flirts with the woman next door in *Max's Neighborly Neighbor* (and is soon exhausted running her incessant errands), and courts two sisters in *Max Embarrassed*—unable to make up his mind between them, he decides to remain a bachelor.

Max was willing to go to any lengths to win his sweetheart. In *Max Is Forced to Work*, his disgusted parents cut him off without a sou. Possessing only a dress suit, he wangles a job as a waiter at a fancy soirée. His girl shows up unexpectedly and Linder attempts to be both waiter and guest without the girl or his boss finding out. In *An Escape of Gas* he disguises himself as a gas repairman to gain entrance to his beloved's home. His "repairs" flood the house with water and virtually demolish it—but he gets the girl. Some of Linder's other early successes were *Max in the Movies, An American Marriage, Max Hypnotized, Marriage Is a Puzzle, Max Searches for a Sweetheart,*

*All's Well That Ends Well, I Want a Baby, The Cross-Country
Original, Max Is Distraught.*

His leading ladies were eye-catching beauties who made
Max's ordeals seem worth the effort. Stacia de Napierkowska,
Jane Renouardt (later Mme. Fernand Gravet), and Gaby Mor-
lay were among the most popular. Occasional performers in the
Linder films included Maurice Chevalier, Charles de Rochefort
(later Pharaoh in Cecil De Mille's silent *Ten Commandments*),
and Abel Gance, one of France's most distinguished directors
(*J'Accuse, Napoleon*).

Except for the photography, which was sharp and clear,
the technical values of Linder's Pathé comedies were not always
good. A scene was rehearsed once and photographed—there
were no retakes or matching shots from different angles. The
editing was primitive, and the final picture, particularly those
from earlier years, was shown much the same way the negative
came from the camera. Scenes were usually taken in a chronological story order. Interestingly, many Linder movies were labo-
riously hand-colored.

Nor were the comedy values *always* good. Many Linder films
were merely sets of repetitious gags revolving around single
incidents or situations. In *Max Is Almost Married,* for instance,
Max is kept from his own wedding by his fiancée's dog; *Max
Wears Tight Shoes* consists of Linder's attempts to retrieve his
shoes from another savage canine; *Max Is Stuck Up* is simply
ten minutes of Linder's encounter with a persistent piece of fly-
paper. Occasionally, but not often, his movies lapsed from good
taste. *Max—Pedicurist* was particularly offensive with a series
of disgusting gags centered around corn-cutting and odorous
feet.

In 1910 Linder was offered $12,000, an incredible fee at the
time, for a month of personal appearances with his films at
the Berlin Wintergarten. He had not realized the extent of his
popularity in Germany. A special detachment of police was
called out to handle the crowds of admirers, and even the Kaiser
and Crown Prince came to see him and afterward went backstage
for an informal visit.

While in Berlin he continued to make his weekly comedies
for Pathé, working in a tiny studio near the theater with a French
cameraman and two German assistants. One of these pictures,
Max Teaches the Tango (later released in America as *Too
Much Mustard*) was an enormous success. In it Max becomes

slightly drunk and is mistaken for a dancing teacher by a snobbish family seeking to learn the tango. To be near the pretty daughter, Max puts his awkward pupils through some hilarious gyrations before being exposed. Accompanied by his cameraman, Linder would scout the famous Berlin landmarks for interesting settings that had comedy opportunities. Many routines were devised on the spot and photographed before a curious crowd could form. These improvised bits of fun kept turning up in Max's movies for more than a year.

In the spring of 1911 Linder suffered a ruptured appendix and was hospitalized with peritonitis. Daily bulletins on his condition were published on the front pages of the Paris newspapers. While he was recuperating in his native Gironde, Pathé patched together several comedies from bits and pieces of earlier pictures and discarded shots (enterprising producers would later do the same thing with Charlie Chaplin). When a newspaper reported that Linder had died, Pathé dispatched a camera crew to Saint Loubes to make *Max in the Arms of His Family*, a semi-documentary which showed the comedian alive and well on the Leuvielle family estate.

Max Linder clowned with a trained lion in Seven Years Bad Luck.

In 1912, accompanied by his leading lady, Stacia de Napierkowska, Linder went to Spain for more personal appearances
and drew huge crowds. In Barcelona he did a comedy routine
in the bull ring, working with a large and vicious animal. These
hilarious antics were used in *Max, Toreador,* one of his best
films, and became the model for dozens of comic bullfight scenes
in Hollywood movies—including Eddie Cantor's *The Kid from
Spain,* Abbott & Costello's *Mexican Hayride,* Laurel & Hardy's
The Bullfighters, and *Around the World in 80 Days* with
Cantinflas.

Linder's films were so profitable that Pathé signed him to
a new three-year contract at around $85,000 annually, and his
personal appearance tours were even more lucrative. A two-
month tour of Russia in 1913 (during which he made several
pictures) netted him $600 a day. On his arrival in St. Petersburg
he was mobbed by a crowd of thousands, and enthusiastic admirers unhitched the horses and drew his coach through the
streets, an ovation previously reserved for Adelina Patti and
Sarah Bernhardt. Newspaper accounts said 30,000 persons
turned out to greet him in Moscow. The following year Linder
paid a return visit to St. Petersburg and got international publicity by boarding an antique airplane at the railway station and
flying in it to a field near his hotel. This time he earned $24,000
for a month of personal appearances in major Russian cities.

Linder's pianist at St. Petersburg was a gifted but unknown
young musician named Dimitri Tiomkin, later a distinguished
composer of film scores. In *Films In Review* (November, 1951)
Tiomkin wrote: "I sat at the piano and improvised all through
his act. He was brilliant and unpredictable, and ad-libbed frequently. He never did the act the same way twice. I watched
him and listened to him and learned to divine intuitively what
he would do. Linder was one of the truly great comedians of
our time . . . his pantomime and appeal were eloquent. He had
an inspired comedy sense, and he had an analytical, ingenious
mind.

"Except for Chaplin, I have never known another comedian
who had such an objective view of his art. Linder was sensitive
and responsive to any audience, and could talk audience psy-
chology with the intellectual perception of a professor. On stage
he would introduce a new bit suddenly and without previous
thought, and later he would give a profound and apposite reason
for having done what he did spontaneously."

When the St. Petersburg critic Brechko Brechkowski wrote that Linder had used a double for the bullfight scenes in *Max, Toreador,* Max challenged him to a duel, and Brechkowski apologized. A papier-mâché bull's head with artificial horns had been used in the studio close-ups, but the corrida sequences were genuine and had been filmed at great personal risk to Linder. He was quite fearless and performed many other dangerous stunts in his films—shooting river rapids in Italy, allowing a balloon to drop 4,000 feet, piloting a hydroplane for aquabatic stunts.

Linder's comedies were minor masterpieces by 1912, and were put together with much more care than in the early stages of his career. *Max, Virtuoso* is the source of many gags that are still used by film and television comedians. In it Linder is again a Parisian dandy in love with a demanding woman. To impress her family he pretends to be a great concert pianist. Called upon to demonstrate his technique at a party, he pretends to play a mechanical piano, and is exposed when it gets out of kilter. This gag, with various refinements, has been used by Sennett, Harry Langdon, Laurel & Hardy, and Abbott & Costello, was a stock item in vaudeville, and was widely used by the French clown Grock. Another classic gag in *Max, Virtuoso* occurs when Linder loses his eyeglasses in the piano's interior and demolishes the instrument trying to retrieve them. This routine has also been widely copied, and was used in a modified form by Laurel & Hardy in their Academy Award winning *The Music Box* ('32).

In *Max Gets the Reward,* Linder played a professional thief who uses his personal charm to purloin ladies' purses. When a pompous detective gets hot on his trail, Max humiliates the officer by delivering him to the police station in a sack. *Max's Vacation* brings to mind Jacques Tati's holiday frustrations as Mr. Hulot forty years later. In *Max's Marriage,* Linder was a sentimental husband who could not bear to be separated from his new bride, keeping her shut in a trunk so his wealthy uncle will not disinherit him for marrying. *Max's Honeymoon* was a surprisingly sophisticated comedy about the difficulties of young newlyweds getting into bed. *Never Kiss the Maid* and *Max Makes a Conquest* showed the results of an innocent flirtation, while *Max Is Jealous* and *Max's Mother-in-Law* milked humor from offensive relatives. A masterpiece of pantomime is *Max Does Not Speak English,* which depicted Linder's difficulties in

Max Linder in Seven Years Bad Luck *(1921). This extraordinary scene was photographed at a Los Angeles mansion.*

communicating with a pretty London miss and her pompous papa.

Max Makes Music is a curious comedy-fantasy in which Linder is a modern Pied Piper whose magic flute makes all who hear it want to dance. In *Max's Double* he is pestered by an obnoxious look-alike, while *Max, Magician* relied on interesting camera tricks in the Melies manner. *Max's Duel* was a series of absurdities as he tried to avoid a duel. *Boxing Match on Skates*, reportedly based on an idea by Charles Pathé, played on the silly notion of having Max box while on roller skates—but it ran thirteen weeks at a Paris cinema.

Who Killed Max? consisted in part of a hilarious encounter between Linder and a crusty landlord in which an entire house was demolished, reminiscent of Laurel & Hardy's later classic battles with James Finlayson. For pure charm Linder seldom exceeded his delightful *Max Creates a Fashion*, which satirized society's mania for keeping abreast of the latest modes. Max ruins his shoes in a mudpuddle as he is about to enter a stylish reception. He buys a frightful pair of boots from a street vendor and attempts to hide them under the ladies' skirts. Max convinces the guests they are the latest in fashion, and at the end everyone is seen happily wearing the horrible footwear.

Other Linder hits of 1912-14 included *Max and Jane Go to the Theatre, A Paris Original, Painter for Love, One Exciting Night, Entente Cordiale, Max Does Not Like Cats, My Dog Dick, The Little Roman, Max Attends an Inauguration, Marriage by Telephone, Flying by Hydroplane, The Billet Doux, Max's Hat, Max Is Decorated.*

Linder's comedy style was essentially one of *restraint*, in contrast to the frenzied antics of his contemporaries. He suggested humor rather than provoked it. "I prefer the subtle comedy," he once said, "but it is a mistake to say that I do not use slapstick. I do not make it the object, I do not force it, but I use it when it comes naturally. For slapstick to bring laughter there must be sudden action, a quick turn of events, something unexpected." However, Linder used a variation of the custard-pie gag in *Max and Jane Make a Dessert* years before Mabel Normand heaved a custard pie into Fred Mace's unsuspecting face.

Contrary to what has often been written, Linder's style did not derive from French vaudeville, although it did profit from his early vaudeville associations. "Stage and screen comedy are entirely different," he told an interviewer in 1916. "To be successful on the screen a comedian must think more." Linder felt the intimacy of the camera demanded more intimate forms of comedy, in which shrewdly planned expressions and gestures can achieve just as humorous effects as gags or slapstick. His films were rarely freed of some slapstick or chase, but the beginnings of an entirely new concept of screen comedy are to be seen in them.

His chases—the "poursuites" Mack Sennett found so stimulating—were often funny, and were carefully and cleverly plotted. Linder did not really like them, however, and as his comedies grew more sophisticated he virtually abandoned them. But he returned to them in his Hollywood-made movies of the '20s, when he was trying to create a maximum of appeal to American audiences. Another Linder contribution to screen comedy was the effective use of anachronisms, contrasts, and other unexpected, amorphous absurdities. In *Max and Jane Make a Dessert*, for instance, a stubborn cow is introduced into an ornate bedroom with hilarious results. Similar incongruities deriving from Linder's comedy devices were to appear later in the films of Harry Langdon, Buster Keaton, Laurel & Hardy (the classic example is in *Swiss Miss* when the boys are moving a piano across a swinging bridge over a deep chasm—and meet a ferocious gorilla coming toward them), and even by Jean Cocteau in some of his odd experiments in movie-making.

In 1914 Linder was again incapacitated by abdominal surgery. He was deeply disturbed at the possibility of a European war, and experienced the first of a series of mental depressions which would plague the remainder of his life. When the Germans violated Belgian neutrality and crossed into France, Linder remained in Paris only long enough to star in a patriotic semi-documentary, *The Second of August,* filmed by Pathé at the request of the French government. He used his comedy talents to ridicule the enemy, but audiences could not laugh in face of the sobering news from the front. Gaby Morlay was the leading lady.

Linder attempted to enlist in the French Army as a private (at the recruiting station he encountered the Parisian matinee idol, Charles de Rochefort), but was deemed physically unfit for general combat duty. He was permitted to serve as a chauffeur, using his expensive automobile, which he had offered to the government, to deliver military dispatches between Paris and the front. During the First Battle of the Marne the car was hit by shellfire and demolished. Linder, his right hand injured, hid in icy water beneath a bridge in constant use by the Germans. Rescued the next morning by a French patrol, he developed pneumonia from exposure and lay ill in a Paris hospital for weeks. A mysterious cable dispatch from Berlin, received in Rome, reported that Linder had been killed in action and his body recovered by the Germans. Pathé's offices were deluged with telegrams at the news, and it was nearly a week later when it was announced the comedian was alive in a French hospital. The origin of the cable was never explained.

In later years Linder's war record was inexplicably magnified, and a great many unfounded stories about it were widely repeated. The most persistent is that he was wounded in the right lung by machine-gun fire during the First Battle of the Aisne. Another is that he was the victim of poison gas. Many published accounts tell of his serving in a light artillery unit with the 13th French Regiment, and engaging in hand-to-hand combat. Yet another story is that he was a pilot in the French Air Force, making many dangerous missions over the enemy lines. These reports were particularly prevalent in America, and much of it can be traced to overzealous film publicity departments. However limited his military service, Linder was fiercely proud of it and brooded that he was not permitted to do more for his country.

Because of the damage to his lungs, Linder was excused from further military service. In the spring of 1915 he was booked for an extensive personal appearance tour in Italy and Switzerland. Another part of the Linder wartime legend is that he was sent to Rome by the French government on a diplomatic mission. With others he is supposed to have played an important role in helping persuade Italy to come into the war with the Allies. The details are vague, and there is little evidence that the story is anything more than manufactured publicity. The comedian did have at least one long private audience with Prime Minister Sallandra. At any rate, Linder did interrupt his performance at the Rome Opera House to announce from the stage that Italy had declared war on Austria! A tumultous ovation greeted the news, and "The Marseillaise" was sung.

Later in 1915 Linder suffered his first nervous breakdown, reportedly from brooding over the war. He went to Switzerland for rest and psychiatric treatment and gradually recovered. Friends persuaded him that he could make a contribution to wartime morale by resuming his films. In and around his hotel in Lausanne he turned out *Max Between Two Women* (frequently referred to by error as *Max Between Two Fires*) and *Max and the Clutching Hand,* both in the Linder tradition. They were produced by a company which he set up and were released by Pathé.

Max and the Clutching Hand was a glorious spoof of the bizarre American serials of the day, particularly of Pearl White's *The Exploits of Elaine,* directed by Linder's old mentor, Louis J. Gasnier. Linder nonchalantly extricated himself from dozens of impossible situations, outwitted a gang of masked villains, and calmly resisted the advances of a glamorous vampire. Charles Pathé said later that he tried to team Pearl White and Max Linder in a semi-comedy serial, but that neither of the actors was agreeable to the idea.

Linder discovered that a great many French soldiers had been interned in Switzerland—most had escaped from German prison camps—and one was his old friend, Charles de Rochefort. With the cooperation of the International Red Cross, Linder organized a series of lavish entertainments for the internees, as well as public performances to raise money for their needs. Most of these featured the comedian in his famous music-hall routines, and were given in the gardens of the Hotel Beau Rivage.

Exhausted by these activities and worried over the poor financial returns of his films—the war had closed many markets —Linder began to experience anew periods of deep depression. His health broke down completely in the summer of 1916, and he was admitted to the French Army hospital at Contrexeville. A surprise visitor to Contrexeville was the American movie magnate George K. Spoor, president of Essanay. Spoor laid his cards on the table: Essanay had lost Charlie Chaplin and was seeking a comedian to take his place. He offered Linder $5,000 a week to write, direct, and star in twelve three-reel comedies to be made at the company's Chicago studios. Spoor assured him a free hand and a generous budget. Intrigued by Spoor's glowing promises, Linder accepted the offer almost immediately—but not until he had made one last fruitless attempt to get back into the army. Doctors told him his military career was over. His ties with Pathé were at an' end—the war had virtually wrecked French film production, and Charles Pathé had offered him only a fraction of the attractive sum Spoor was dangling.

Max Linder's American debut was highly publicized. Much was made of his sartorial elegance, including the fact that he arrived with forty-six pieces of luggage. Spoor made the mistake of comparing Linder to Charlie Chaplin, and asserted the French comic would replace him in public favor. Essanay's publicity described Chaplin as "sloppy, unclean and sordid," appealing only to the lower classes, and Linder as a Beau Brummell of sophisticated comedy more suited to American tastes. There were even newspaper stories, all planted by Essanay, that Linder had challenged Chaplin to a duel because of the latter's failure to enlist for war service.

Linder's first Essanay picture, *Max Comes Across,* went into production in January, 1917, under difficult conditions. As Chaplin had discovered two years earlier, the Essanay studios in Chicago were uninviting, poorly equipped, and hamstrung by petty economies. Linder could speak little English, and two interpreters were required to assist him in the direction. Moreover, Chicago was in the throes of a severe winter, and some scenes of

Robert Florey (left) with Max Linder on the set of The Three Must-Get-Theres *(1922), Linder's last American film.*

Max Comes Across were filmed on the deck of a Lake Michigan steamer in below-zero temperatures. The picture, obviously inspired by Linder's trip to the United States on the *S.S. Espagne*, was about two shipmates who love a pretty passenger. A pretended shipwreck turns into a real disaster, giving Max a chance to best his rival by real heroics. *Max Comes Across* proved only mildly amusing, and critics were quick to refute Essanay's claim that Linder was another Chaplin.

Linder seemed more at ease in his second Essanay film, *Max Wants a Divorce*. It was a charming domestic comedy more in keeping with his traditional style—and allowing him to return to his tuxedo and morning clothes. Francine Larrimore had a bit in it.

But Linder was now quarreling with Spoor and his underlings, who were alarmed by the poor returns on *Max Comes Across* and *Max Wants a Divorce*. The Chicago winter was hard on Linder's lungs; he suffered from sleeplessness and indigestion, ate mostly soups, and was jittery because he was no longer allowed to smoke.

At the comedian's insistence, Spoor finally agreed to transfer the Linder unit to California, in the hope the milder climate would improve the health of his temperamental star. Although Essanay owned a studio at Niles, where most of the Broncho Billy Anderson films had been made, space was rented at the Thomas H. Ince studios in Culver City. Linder left Chicago on March 6, 1917, accompanied by a retinue of fourteen persons— including a number of his countrymen who went along for the ride (probably at Max's expense), two cameramen, and his leading lady, Martha Mansfield, who had appeared in musicals at the Winter Garden on Broadway. Two baggage cars were necessary to accommodate Linder's enormous wardrobe and the other properties. In a farewell speech to reporters at the station, Max diplomatically emphasized he loved Chicago and its friendly people, and was leaving only because of his health.

Soon after his arrival in California, Linder paid an official call on Charlie Chaplin at the old Lone Star Studios, where Chaplin had just completed *The Cure*. The two comedians were closeted for some time, and emerged smiling to have their photograph taken in a nearby lemon grove. Apparently, Chaplin had no bitterness over the Essanay publicity or the remarks about him attributed to Linder. The two men were attracted to each other, and were often seen together at social functions.

For some curious and unexplained reason Linder would deny in later years that he had been in California in 1917. He repeatedly told reporters and friends that his visit to Hollywood in the early '20s was the first time he had been West. His private secretary, Albert Petit, who was with him from the Lausanne days to Linder's death, also denied the 1917 trip. That it did take place is well documented in numerous articles in contemporary newspapers and magazines.

Linder's third Essanay picture, *Max and His Taxi,* filmed in California, contains many delightful things, including some cheerful-drunk antics which were copied by Chaplin and Harry Myers in *City Lights;* a horse harnessed the wrong way round; an obstinate taxi that becomes a mechanical monster; and the inventive dance of the telegraph wires, a charming bit of business that reflects Linder's ingenuity.

Soon after the release of *Max and His Taxi* in May, 1917, Spoor arranged with Linder to cancel the balance of his contract. It was announced that Linder was still suffering from his war wounds and after a stopover in the dry air of the Arizona desert would return to France for a long rest. The Essanay experiment ended in much bitterness, and Spoor said later the company lost $87,000 on the fiasco. Linder felt that Spoor had jeopardized his prospects with American audiences by the irresponsible publicity comparing him with Chaplin. A remarkable story circulated in film circles at the time alleged that Spoor had imported Linder knowing he would not succeed in the United States, and hoping the losses would force down the price of Essanay stock so Spoor could buy out his partner, Broncho Billy Anderson, at a low figure! For his part Spoor felt the French comedian had lost much of his inventiveness and originality. He asserted Linder behaved unreasonably and irrationally, and privately expressed the opinion that Linder needed psychiatric attention.

Shortly after his return to Paris in mid-1917 Linder opened the Ciné Max Linder, a lavish theater near the Champs Elysees. Furnished in the exquisite period of Louis XVI and decorated with paintings by the French masters, it featured new American movies and occasional revivals of Linder's better comedies. Unkind critics accused him of being jealous of Sarah Bernhardt, who had recently had a theater named in her honor. (Several years earlier Linder had built a smaller theater at 24 Boulevard Poissonière.)

His health improved, but he was unable to settle down emotionally. The war was on his mind, and he emotionally told an interviewer: "When you hold the hand of a dying comrade, you know the grim tragedy of life." Finally, Linder spent several months in a Swiss sanitarium near Leysin, in the shadow of Mont Blanc. He tried and failed to get back in the army, and occasionally he would entertain for the troops, including the green American doughboys now pouring through the Channel ports. Despite reports he would make movies in Paris and Rome, he did not resume his film work. A curious advertisement in a motion picture publication early in 1918 said Linder had recovered from his illness and would return to the United States in April—and was "open to offers." The trip did not materialize when his American agent, T. E. Letendre, was unable to interest producers (including Spoor, who was aghast at the idea). The advertisement incorrectly asserted Linder had appeared in *five* Essanay comedies, including two entitled *Max, Heartbreaker* and *Max Plays Detective,* but no such films had been made.

The end of World War I raised Linder's spirits, and in

Max Linder (Circa 1923).

1919 he returned to the screen in a feature comedy, *The Little Café,* produced in France under the direction of the promising young Raymond Bernard (later known for *The Miracle of the Wolves* and other historical spectacles). *The Little Café* was based on an enormously popular play by Tristan Bernard, father of the director, which had a long run at the Palais Royale. Its frothy plot was about an impatient waiter in a bistro who becomes a gay man-about-town after dark. It had many fresh gags and routines, but some critics said Linder was now imitating

Chaplin! *The Little Café* was very successful in Europe, but did not do well when Pathé imported it into the United States in 1920. A decade later Maurice Chevalier remade it for Paramount as *Playboy of Paris* ('30).

Despite the Essanay disaster, Linder resolved to try his luck again in America—reportedly with some encouragement from Charlie Chaplin. He made a quick trip to New York late in 1919 to discuss distribution details, and returned the following year with a large entourage. In a shipboard interview in New York harbor Linder said the Essanay comedies had been "over the head" of American moviegoers. He was still talking about the war and told reporters: "The horror of the battlefield is terrible . . . ghastly! To brood upon it drives men mad."

With his own money he formed an independent company in Hollywood and arranged to release through the Robertson-Cole organization. His comeback began auspiciously with *Seven Years Bad Luck* ('21), which he directed from his own script. In this delightful feature-length comedy Linder was again his typical wealthy playboy—but in an American setting. As the film opens, his butler is trying to kiss the maid and they fall against an expensive full-length mirror and break it. Max, hungover, is awakened by the noise, and the butler, fearful of losing his job, persuades the cook, who greatly resembles Max, to stand behind the frame and pretend to be Linder's reflection. The classic gag which follows—Max's every movement being anticipated by the cook, with Linder too befuddled to realize what is happening—has been frequently used in vaudeville and in movies. For many years it was a stock routine of the Marx Brothers and was used in *Duck Soup* ('33), later reappearing in films of Abbott & Costello, Red Skelton, and others. The gag originated with Chaplin, who used it briefly in *The Floorwalker* ('16), but never was it done so expertly as in Linder's *Seven Years Bad Luck,* where it accounts for almost a third of the picture. In the rest of the film Linder follows a pretty girl on a train, loses his wallet to a thief, disguises himself as a Negro porter by pulling a silk stocking over his head, and is later mistaken for a crook. A Keystone chase evolves, and the fun continues in a zoo with all sorts of animal antics. Max is saved from prison at the last moment, marries the girl, and in the final scene is out for a stroll with his wife, followed by four young sons dressed in the typical Linder morning clothes and top hats. *Seven Years Bad Luck* was only a moderate success in the United States, but earned a good profit abroad.

Linder followed it with *Be My Wife* ('21), a quasi-mystery comedy, in which he is put through many ordeals by his fiancée. The Goldwyn Company agreed to distribute it, but Max felt it did a poor job of selling and exploitation. The reviews were mild and the returns poor.

Soon after his arrival in Hollywood Linder purchased an expensive, beautifully landscaped house on fashionable Argyle Avenue. Charlie Chaplin lived next door in an ugly home built in the hybrid Spanish-Californian-Mauresque architecture first popularized about 1910. The two comedians resumed their friendship and were often seen at the boxing matches in suburban Vernon or the auto races in Culver City. Noting Chaplin had a black limousine driven by a Japanese valet, Linder bought a yellow limousine and hired a Negro chauffeur. Chaplin was vastly amused by this subtle joke.

Linder entertained lavishly. He drank little himself but served fine wines and liquors for his guests, and his gourmet dinners were often prepared by Georges Jomier, an amateur chef famous for his "poulet à la Jomier" and other dishes from the Bourgogne. Jomier was a brilliant linguist who taught French to dozens of Hollywood stars over a period of thirty-five years, and was also a great favorite of William Randolph Hearst. Among the guests at Linder's memorable Christmas party of 1921 were Chaplin, Rudolph Valentino, John Gilbert, Leatrice Joy, Thomas H. Ince, Ora Carew, Gaston Glass, Renee Adoree, Marguerite de la Motte, C. Gardner Sullivan, and Robert Florey. The trained lion used in *Seven Years Bad Luck,* a favorite Linder pet, was chained near the swimming pool and guarded by two giant Negroes in Nubian slave costumes.

While working on a picture Linder would go next door to Chaplin's home and discuss the day's shooting. The two often sat up until dawn, developing and refining the gags. Chaplin's suggestions were invaluable, Linder said.

Linder's influence upon Chaplin's comedy was first remarked by Chaplin himself. In several interviews in 1915 and 1916, and again in the early '20s, Chaplin freely acknowledged his indebtedness to the French comedian. Linder sometimes referred to himself as Chaplin's "professor" and prized a photograph Charlie had autographed "To Max, the Professor, from his disciple, Charlie Chaplin." Said Linder on one occasion: "Chaplin was good enough to tell me my films led him to make pictures" and "Chaplin called me his teacher, but I am glad enough myself to take lessons from him."

Essentially, Chaplin and Linder had different comedy styles, and it is a mistake to attribute too much to Linder's influence. Chaplin's comedy is uniquely his own, although certainly many of Linder's ideas and devices were utilized and refined by Chaplin.

The similarities are most apparent in the *content* of the films. The opening scenes of *City Lights,* in which the tramp is discovered asleep under a statue that is being unveiled, is identical with the beginning of *Max Attends an Inauguration.* Chaplin's *Tango Tangles* contains many bits of business reminiscent of *Max Teaches the Tango.* Linder's unsuccessful attempts at suicide in *Max in a Dilemma* apparently inspired some of Chaplin's comedy in *Cruel, Cruel Love.* *The Rink* was clearly derived from Linder's first starring hit, *The Skater's Debut.*

Linder and Chaplin used similar techniques in playing the drunk—as in Chaplin's *One A.M., A Night Out,* or *City Lights,* and Linder's *Max, Victim of Quinquina* or *How Max Went Around the World.* The Chaplin technique of flirtation owes much to Linder, as a comparison with *Getting Acquainted* or *Those Love Pangs,* or almost any Chaplin film, with Linder's *Max Embarrassed* or *Max's Neighborly Neighbor* will illustrate. *A Rustic Idyll,* one of Linder's more delightful comedies, has been mistakenly compared to Chaplin's *Sunnyside,* possibly because both films were given almost identical titles for their European showings. Both films have a farm background, but the resemblance ends there.

Linder played an arrogant waiter in several films (*Max Is Forced to Work, Max-Headwaiter*), and several of his comedy devices in this role reappeared with refreshing modifications in Chaplin's waiter in *The Rink, Dough and Dynamite* and *Modern Times.* And who can say it was not a remembrance of the elegant Max that prompted Chaplin's seedy dandy in his first movie, *Making a Living?* (In his first acting job with D. W. Griffith at Biograph, Mack Sennett admittedly patterned his character and costume on Max Linder.)

Chaplin drew heavily on comic gestures first used effectively in Linder movies. In *Max, Victim of Quinquina,* for instance, Linder becomes involved with a tablecloth and deftly flourishes it at a policeman in the manner of a toreador before a charging bull. This type of expressive, symbolic gesture became part of

Chaplin's stock-in-trade. Linder and Chaplin were equally re-markable for the way they used facial expressions to provoke laughter—particularly the quick nervous movements of the mouth and eyes, and the gingerly, testing smiles.

In later years Chaplin became less tolerant of attempts to draw parallels between his comedy and Linder's. He is said to have resented Linder's references to being his teacher, and to have felt that Max borrowed from him in the later Linder comedies. The autographed portrait, he told a friend, was given to Linder "in a weak moment." There is no mention of Linder in Chaplin's autobiography.

Linder's attempted comeback did not go well, and he was depressed at the mild reception accorded his first two Hollywood pictures. He evolved the idea of burlesquing Dumas' *The Three Musketeers*. For *The Three Must-Get-Theres* he abandoned his man-about-town character to play d'Artagnan (renamed Dart-In-Again). Chaplin attempted to dissuade him from doing the film, but Linder was convinced, perhaps rightly, that the "continental" Max would never succeed with American audiences.

The Three Must-Get-Theres, which premiered at the Dome Theatre in Ocean Park, California, in August, 1922, was a gay and colorful comedy unlike any other Linder had ever done. The broad humor was replete with anachronisms—Cardinal Richelieu used a telephone, the three musketeers slide down a firehouse pole to their horses, slow motion satirizes the wild ride from Calais to Paris (Linder had used this ruse in his early Pathé chases). The exciting duels gave Linder an opportunity to display his brilliant swordsmanship, and some of the casting was delightfully offbeat—Bull Montana played an esthetic Cardinal Richelieu! The film was an almost frame-by-frame parody of Douglas Fairbanks' *The Three Musketeers*, which had been released the previous year, and Fairbanks was greatly amused by it.

Despite his earlier pessimism, Chaplin was enthusiastic about *The Three Must-Get-Theres*, and helped arrange its release through Allied Producers and Distributors Corporation, a short-lived United Artists subsidary originally set up to handle the independent productions of Jack Pickford, Nazimova, Charles Ray, and J. Stuart Blackton. Despite a sumptuous mounting, *The Three Must-Get-Theres* is slow in spots and has some unbelievably archaic slapstick. The reviews were mixed. It did poorly at the box office, and Linder is said to have lost considerable money.

Max Linder poses with his bride, Helene Peters, after their marriage on August 2, 1923.

Although his early Max comedies for Pathé were moderately successful here, Linder never really caught on with American audiences. The inevitable comparisons with Chaplin, which came later, were not in his favor. As Louis Delluc, the director, once observed: "Charlie is international—Max is French; his sense of humor was not understood in America." While this is not entirely true, many critics felt that Linder lacked the skill to deeply touch the human emotions, as most great comedians are able to do.

Linder's Parisian playboy vis-à-vis Chaplin's tramp is relatively unsympathetic, and pre-World War I audiences could not identify with the misfortunes of a wealthy wastrel who took his problems so lightly. Linder's comedy, and certainly his screen character, might have been better understood and appreciated a few years later when Adolphe Menjou and Raymond Griffith were finding success in suave, sophisticated continental comedies of manners and morals. After 1915 and *Max and the Clutching Hand,* Linder seems less inspired—or does this appear so because of the tendency to compare him with Chaplin?

Linder's personal problems were partly at fault. His neurasthenia, stemming from the war, became progressively worse, and he worried constantly about his health. His periods of depression deepened, lengthened, and destroyed his will for creative work. The war, he maintained, "added a new element to my comedy . . . and taught me to inject a whimsical humor into tragedy—to bring laughter at the verge of tears." But he seemed unable to realize this concept on film.

Discouraged by the poor reception of his three postwar American productions, Linder abruptly sold his home and returned to France in the fall of 1922. His compartment on the Santa Fe was filled with bottles of medicine and pills, blankets, religious articles, candy, and leather cases containing a magnificent collection of Spanish engravings and popular caricatures. Prophetically, Linder told friends who had come to see him off that he did not expect ever to return to Hollywood.

Linder made little effort to get back into films for more than a year. In 1924 he starred in *Au Secours!* (*Help!*), directed by Abel Gance, whom Linder had badgered into the assignment by asserting he could not direct comedy. *Help!* was a fantasy, with some tragic episodes, in which Max has hair-raising experiences in a haunted castle. The story, written by Linder and Gance, was half Grand Guignol, half Mack Sennett, and the suspenseful gags were clever and fast-paced. Under Gance's gifted direction, Linder revealed himself as an excellent dramatic actor, and Gina Palerme made a lovely leading lady. *Help!* was to become Linder's "lost" picture—because of litigation over distribution rights it was not shown in either France or the United States. A print has reposed in the vaults of the Cinemathèque Française in Paris for many years, but has been seen by only a few film historians.

Linder's last picture, *The King of the Circus,* was shot in Vienna early in 1925. Linder co-directed with E. E. Violet, an established French director best known for *The Danger Line* ('24), with Sessue Hayakawa. The trite story was about a roisterous young nobleman, Count Max, who falls in love with a circus rider (Vilma Banky). Concealing his identity, he pretends to be an animal trainer to be near the girl. The comedy highlights centered about Max's furious arguments with a choleric uncle, a bored and recalcitrant lion, and a hilarious scene in which he awakens, after a night of heavy drinking, in a bed in a department store window (a gag later used in several Hollywood films). The humor of *The King of the Circus* was labored, and it was not particularly successful; Linder made some money from the picture, but lost it in a series of poor investments.

Chaplin's *The Circus,* which came out three years later, has some minor similarities to Linder's *The King of the Circus.* Chaplin and Linder had discussed a plot and gags for a circus comedy, and Linder had first become enthused about a circus picture while filming scenes for *Seven Years Bad Luck* at the Universal City zoo in 1921. A year later Chaplin was reported by the trade press to be planning a circus picture to be called *The Clown.*

On August 2, 1923, Linder married Helene Peters, the eighteen-year-old daughter of a wealthy Belgian. She had done some modeling and acting, and they had met at the Swiss resort of Chamonix. A daughter, Maud Max Linder, was born to them on June 27, 1925. Linder's friends thought him a jealous and possessive husband.

Linder's mental condition worsened, and he talked more and more of suicide. In February, 1924, he denied that he and his wife had deliberately taken an overdose of sleeping powders while in Switzerland, and assured the press it had been an accident. A few months later, while he was making *The King of the Circus* in Vienna, there were persistent reports of another suicide attempt.

Death had become an obsession, and worried friends took a revolver away from him. "Never mind," he shouted, "I know a better way!" A few days before the final tragedy his wife wrote her mother of her fear that Linder would kill her. She added that she would die rather than be parted.

Linder was described as irrational after he saw a stage performance of *Quo Vadis,* in which Petronius and Eunice bleed themselves to death. He told friends he had nothing to live for, more money than he could spend, and no ambition but to die. Director Roger Lion, with whom he was planning a new picture (*Le Chasseur de Chez Maxim's*) could not get him to work on the script.

On the evening of October 30, 1925, Linder and his wife

were heard quarreling in their Paris hotel suite. It appeared later that Linder was trying to persuade his wife to join him in a suicide pact. Exhausted and distraught, she apparently agreed, and both wrote several notes of farewell. Around nine the next morning they swallowed veronal. Linder then gave his wife and himself injections of morphine to deaden the pain of what followed. As the drugs took effect he slit her veins and slashed his own wrists. Later that morning Mrs. Linder's mother, when she got no answer to her knocking, had the door broken in. Linder and his wife were in a blood-soaked bed, alive, but in a coma. Their infant daughter was crying in her crib. Helene Linder died at noon, soon after being removed to the Piccini Clinique, and Max Linder died at 5:00 P.M. the same afternoon. He was forty-three, she twenty-one.

In Hollywood, visibly upset at the news, Charlie Chaplin spoke a few words in tribute to Linder before his co-workers at the Chaplin studio and dismissed them for the day. The double suicide provided a field day for the sensational press, and for years many bizarre and false stories were published about Linder and his wife.

In 1963 Linder's daughter, Maud Max Linder, brought out a compilation of her father's films entitled *En Compagnie de Max Linder*. It largely consists of the best portions of *Seven Years Bad Luck, Be My Wife,* and *The Three Must-Get-Theres,* the three feature films Linder made in Hollywood in the early '20s. "I wanted Max Linder to take his place in the history of the cinema," she says, "and not remain merely a name in the books, but a figure living forever on the screen." Mlle. Linder has spent many years, and much money, in collecting the old films of her father. Some have been found in South America and in the Orient. Max's old friends have helped to locate them, although Charlie Chaplin has never replied to her inquiries. While Linder is known to have had copies of most of his pictures at one time, most have been lost or have deteriorated for lack of care. The old Pathé negatives and prints were sold long ago for the chemicals which could be salvaged. Today, only a few of Linder's films, mostly in Paris and London movie museums, remain to remind us of this strange genius and the important contributions he made to motion picture comedy.

3

NORMA TALMADGE

NORMA TALMADGE once said she liked to play "women who have some definite meaning in their lives . . . with fire in their souls and true, wholesome romance in their hearts . . . not the last word in nobility, nor steeped in scarlet sins, but good enough to be real."

If her weepy heroines were not always so passionate or virtuous, they moved against the lavish settings of the bored rich or a king's court, from innocent youth to tired old age in a series of incredible hardships and sacrifices. It was inevitable that she would play a modern Camille, Balzac's fickle Duchesse de Langeais, Countess du Barry—and even a pseudo Madame Butterfly. She was, as a New York critic called her, "the lady of the great indoors."

By her own admission, her career, and a multimillion-dollar fortune, were built upon sobs and smiles. If enough suffering could not be compressed into a single lifetime, it spilled into a second generation of tragic heroines—as in *The Forbidden City* and *Smilin' Through*—with Norma playing dual roles. Even when her tribulations were set against the exotic backgrounds of the Middle East, India, or the Orient, she never ceased to be the woman who gave and paid, brave and defiant against the world. Her fans were aghast when, in *Kiki*, she made the disastrous mistake of trying to play comedy as a teenage hoyden.

Norma's popularity in the silents was second only to that of Mary Pickford. At the height of her success in the '20s she received 3,000 letters a week from admiring fans, many from beset women who felt a kindred spirit with her troubled heroines. Her beauty and poise gave her an enormous appeal, and she had an innate ability to convey the impression of being a lady, even though she might be portraying a jaded courtesan, a shop-

Norma Talmadge and L. Roger Lytton in Panthea *(1917).*

lifter, or a native dancing girl. Her career, begun twenty years earlier when the movies were emerging from their primitive beginnings, ended with the advent of talking pictures, a medium for which she was no longer suitable or adaptable. In a sense, an era began and ended with this gifted actress.

According to her mother, Norma Talmadge was born on May 26, 1897, at Niagara Falls, New York. After she became a famous star Norma admitted her birthplace was actually Jersey City, New Jersey, and that she and her mother thought Niagara Falls sounded more romantic for the fan-magazine biographies.

Her father, Fred Talmadge, was born in Connecticut to Presbyterian parents of British ancestry. Somewhat flashy and fond of drink, he earned a mediocre living as a traveling sales-man of advertising novelties. He was away from the four-room house on Fenimore Street in Brooklyn for weeks at a time, and eventually abandoned his family for a drifter's life.

The task of raising Norma and two younger sisters, Constance and Natalie, fell to their remarkable mother, Margaret Talmadge, who was born in Spain of Irish-Catholic parents. Affectionately known to her girls as Peg, she was a frustrated artist who added to the family income by painting sunsets on porcelain china. Disappointed in her own marriage, she was intensely ambitious for her children and never ceased to believe that better days were ahead. Witty and possessed of extraordinary self-confidence and determination, Peg Talmadge would become the prototype of the aggressive screen mother and a major factor in her daughters' success.

Except for the chronic absence of their father, the Talmadge girls had a normal childhood. They played the piano and mandolin, were fond of birds and pets, athletic to the point of being tomboys, indifferent scholars, and hopelessly movie-struck. At thirteen, in her first brush with show business, Norma earned a few dollars posing for stereopticon song slides then used in film and vaudeville theaters. She got three dollars for a hundred poses, and one of her slide sets, for Irving Berlin's "Stop, Stop, Stop," became quite popular.

In November, 1910, a family friend gave her a letter of introduction to Harry Mayo, casting director at the Vitagraph Studios, then located in the poor Midwood section of Flatbush. Accompanied by her mother, she filled out an application, left two photographs, and was told she would be called if needed. When three weeks elapsed without any word from the studio, Norma and Constance played hookey from Erasmus Hall High School and spent their lunch money for a trolley ride to Midwood. Norma wore a long russet gown and a large hat, which she thought made her look older. At the studio she attracted the attention of Beta Breuil, Vitagraph's scenario chief, who removed the hat and unpinned her long hair. Mrs. Breuil was impressed by her beauty and promised to see that she got work.

Soon afterward Norma made her screen debut in *The Household Pest*—but her face was never seen. She played a young girl kissing a photographer under a camera cloth. The cloth was removed by a trained horse, and Norma worried that it would nip her scalp. She got $2.50 for her bit in this one-reeler. As the story goes—probably emanating later from Vitagraph's publicity department—Norma ruined a scene on an adjoining set by dashing impulsively before the grinding cameras to gush over her idol, Florence Turner.

Norma's second film was *The Dixie Mother* ('10), a one-reeler starring Miss Turner as a patriotic Southern mother who sent her six sons to fight in the Civil War. The youngest (Carlyle Blackwell) was a coward who did not want to go, but finally accedes to her wishes. When he is killed the mother goes insane. Norma played the young daughter who elopes with a Northerner. Years later she returns to visit the impoverished family, and helps her grieving mother regain her sanity. Norma was paralyzed by stage fright and failed to make her first entrance on cue, and was unceremoniously shoved before the camera by director Charles Kent. She was not very good, being totally inexperienced, but her part was mercifully small.

With her mother's consent, Norma quit school to accept steady work at Vitagraph. After *The Dixie Mother* she played everything from a pickaninny to a seventy-year-old grandmother —even a painted prostitute—and filled in as an extra if nothing better was available. Her pay varied. She got fifty cents a day if called and not used, $1.50 if ready in costume but not used, and $2.50 for an on-camera bit. A larger role brought up to $5, plus a box lunch. After several weeks, Norma got up enough nerve to ask J. Stuart Blackton, Vitagraph's flamboyant production chief, for a stock contract. Blackton had some reservations about her acting ability, but finally hired her at $25 a week.

At the time the Vitagraph studios covered two city blocks, having grown from a crude shed which Blackton first used in 1903. There was a three-story administration building, several smaller structures housing shops, stables, and storerooms, and five large stages glassed in to catch the natural light. After 1912 the hot, blinding Aristo arc lamps were used for illumination. The sets were a standard 9x15 feet with scenery painted on canvas, and were photographed by a single stationary camera with a fixed focus. Exteriors were shot at The Cedars, a wooded area near Coney Island.

The Vitagraph stock company then comprised about eighty performers, each paid $25 to $50 a week. A few stars, like Florence Turner, Maurice Costello, and comedian John Bunny, got slightly more. Some of the players were Anita Stewart, Mabel Normand, Earle Williams, Dorothy Kelly, Zena Keefe, Leah Baird, James Morrison, Tom Powers, Leo Delaney,

Gladden James, Rose Tapley, and Lillian "Dimples" Walker (whom the company called "Buggs"). Everyone came to work on a horse-drawn trolley, and only the studio chiefs, Blackton and Albert Smith, had automobiles. Smith was a motorcar fanatic who later designed and built his own machine.

The salaried players were expected to help with odd jobs about the studio when not acting. Florence Turner, the top feminine star, was in charge of paying the performers and also helped her mother, who was Vitagraph's wardrobe mistress. Norma was assigned to sew costumes, and later to make up extras (a dead-white make-up was used). The men moved scenery and wielded paintbrushes—all except Maurice Costello, who flatly refused any non-acting tasks. Relatives were hired as extras, and Norma's mother and sisters soon began to earn money in this way.

Vitagraph's production was divided between a dozen or so units, each headed by a contract director. Some of the direc-

A scene on the set of Panthea *(1917). (Left to right): Director Allan Dwan, Frank Currier, Norma Talmadge, L. Roger Lytton, Earle Foxe.*

tors were Van Dyke Brooke, Charles Kent, Albert Angeles, John G. Adolfi, Albert W. Hale, Ralph Ince, Jay Williams, Larry Trimble (already doing the dog dramas—with Jean, the Vitagraph dog—for which he became famous), George D. Baker, William Humphrey, and the early film pioneer William Ranous. Many were experienced actors and often appeared in their own pictures.

Norma's first role as a contract actress was in *In Neighboring Kingdoms* ('11), an expensive two-reeler that took two weeks to film (most Vitagraph pictures were shot in one to three days). Beta Breuil had written the story of a prince whose parents arrange for his marriage, sight unseen, to a princess of an adjoining kingdom. Both are upset and run away, the prince to work as a miller, the princess as a shepherdess. They meet and fall in love for a predictable happy ending. John Bunny, later Vitagraph's $200-a-week comedian, played a straight dramatic role. Norma was lovely as the girl, but director William Humphrey told Blackton she "wasn't much of an actress." The question of keeping her on came up, and once again Mrs. Breuil intervened and persuaded Blackton to give her another chance. While her future was being debated, Norma burst into tears and was surprised when Blackton asked her why she couldn't show as much emotion on the screen.

Her work improved when Maurice Costello, whom she called "Mr. Dimples," began to give her pointers on acting, and through his help she got a good part as a saucy English maid in his *Mrs. 'Enery 'Awkins* ('11). Some of her early films with Costello were *Her Hero, The Thumb Print, A Broken Spell, The Convict's Child,* and *Her Sister's Children.* Costello's two daughters, Helene and Dolores, appeared in child roles at Vitagraph.

Norma Talmadge's first success came in *A Tale of Two Cities* ('11), an elaborate picturization of Charles Dickens' somber drama of the French Revolution. Although a three-reeler, it was originally released in weekly one-reel segments. Norma played Mimi, the seamstress who rode in the tumbril to the guillotine with Sydney Carton (Maurice Costello), clutching his hand. In the print which survives today, she is barely seen, and apparently most of her footage has been lost. Although she now appears much too young for the role, her performance was praised by several trade reviewers. Director William Humphrey had not wanted her for the part, but Cos-

Norma Talmadge in Passion Flower *(1921)*.

tello was sure she could do it. Costello teased her about "losing her head" and sternly told her she could never bring off the role until she laid aside her little-girl ways and displayed more maturity. *A Tale of Two Cities* was personally supervised by J. Stuart Blackton, and the remarkable cast contained most of Vitagraph's stalwarts—Maurice Costello, Florence Turner, John Bunny, Ralph Ince, James Morrison, Julia Swayne (Gordon), Leo Delaney, Tefft Johnson, Charles Kent, and William Shea. During the filming Florence Turner, who played the fragile Lucy Manet, became ill, and Norma doubled for her in several scenes, in which she is seen only from the back.

For another year Norma continued in bit roles—she did nearly a hundred pictures in 1911-12—and only occasionally, as in Maurice Costello's *The First Violin* ('12), was she given an opportunity to do any serious acting. Some of her best work was as a spunky slavey in the *Belinda* comedies (*Plot and Counterplot, Sleuthing, Omens and Oracles, A Lady and Her Maid*), directed by Albert Angeles. Mostly she played light comedy roles—a comic bellhop, a Sis Hopkins, a belligerent suffragette, a colored mammy, a clumsy waitress, a reckless young modern who liked to drive fast cars, and frequently as a mischievous brat who plagued John Bunny (as in *The Troublesome Stepdaughters* and *Mr. Bolter's Sweetheart*). In more dramatic moments she was a gun moll, a wild girl of the forest, a thieving gypsy, and an Oriental spy.

Norma was beginning to be noticed by the public; by mid-1912 she was receiving several dozen fan letters each week, although the studio did not bill her name until the following year. In an opinion survey conducted by Albert Dorris in early 1913, exhibitors named her Vitagraph's most promising young player. She ranked 42nd in *Photoplay* Magazine's popularity poll that year.

Miss Talmadge soon lost her chubby cheeks, discarded the long curls, and matured into a poised young woman. But Vitagraph's directors complained that she was difficult to direct and slow to learn her acting. Norma seemed to do best under Van Dyke Brooke, a genial old gentleman who could not shake off the exaggerated acting styles of a lifetime in stock and traveling tent theatres. In 1913 she was permanently assigned to Brooke's unit, and for the next three years appeared almost exclusively under his direction. Her leading man was the moody and unpredictable Leo Delaney, although she was occasionally teamed with handsome James Morrison (on whom she had a crush), Carlyle Blackwell, Harry Morey, or Wallace Reid.

One of her best performances was in *His Official Appointment* ('13), which was filmed on location in Washington, D.C.— her first trip away from home. It had authentic scenes of the White House and the Capitol, and Norma played the daughter of a Secretary of the Treasury who is involved in scandal. She learned to ride horseback for the picture, and was very fetching in her riding habit. Florence Turner and James Morrison had the leads. When *His Official Appointment* opened at a Brooklyn theater, Norma was paid $15 to make a personal appearance— but the manager complained that she was too nervous and could not be heard in the balcony.

The first picture written especially for her was *Under the Daisies,* released in September, 1913, which also marked the first time Vitagraph billed her by name. In this tear-jerker, a crude forerunner of the type of film which made her famous a decade later, Norma was a country girl who goes to the big city and is seduced by a ruthless scoundrel (Harry Northrup),

who promises to marry her but doesn't. She becomes ill and
returns to her home. As she approaches the cabin in which
she spent a happy childhood, she collapses and dies in a field
of beautiful daisies. Her faithful sweetheart buries her "under
the daisies." This immensely popular two-reeler brought Norma
a $10-a-week raise.

Norma Talmadge's films of 1913-14 provided her with a
variety of more mature roles. In *Sawdust and Salome* (one of
her few Vitagraph films which has survived) she played a clean-
hearted circus acrobat who marries a rich young man, only to
be rejected by his snobbish family. She returns to the circus,
and is soon joined by her husband, who decides he prefers his
bride to an inheritance. *Old Reliable* was a weepy drama about
a man (Van Dyke Brooke) who suffers ten years in prison
for a crime he did not commit. Norma played the daughter who
does not know that the old servant who defends her is in reality
her father. She gave a striking performance in the best Mary
Pickford tradition as the slavey in *The Sacrifices of Kathleen,*
and in *Officer John Donovan* she was an orphaned waif who
helped reform a young thief. In *The Vavasour Ball* she was a
headstrong wife who deceived her husband at a gay society
masquerade, and in *A Helpful Sisterhood* she played a sorority
girl who stole from a department store in order to keep up with
her wealthy college chums.

Vitagraph continued to cast her in many comedy parts. In
The Hero she was just a foil for comedian Hughie Mack (Hugh
McGowan). Audiences could not understand why she preferred
the fat, vulgar Mack to handsome James Morrison, whose
attentions she spurned. In *His Little Page,* Leo Delaney dressed
his wife (Norma) as a page boy to mislead a rich uncle (Van
Dyke Brooke) who opposed matrimony. In *Cupid Versus Money*
Norma married for money, but found her supposedly wealthy
catch was a penniless cad who had mistaken her for an heiress—
but all ended well when they fell in love and he reformed.

In 1914 Norma began to appear in longer features, some
of which ran to five reels. She was frequently teamed with a
handsome young Spaniard, Antonio Moreno, whom Vitagraph
had discovered acting on Broadway opposite Constance Collier
and Mrs. Leslie Carter. They made an engaging duo in such
melodramas as *The Hidden Letters, Fogg's Millions, Sunshine
and Shadows, Under False Colors, John Rance-Gentleman,* and
Goodbye Summer (in which Rex Ingram, later the brilliant

Norma Talmadge in Smilin' Through *(1922)*.

director of Valentino's *The Four Horsemen of the Apocalypse*, played a bit). She had a narrow escape in the prophetically titled *A Pillar of Flame* ('15) when her flimsy costume caught fire. Harry T. Morey, her leading man, threw her to the floor and smothered the flames.

Constance Talmadge, three years younger than Norma, was also working regularly at Vitagraph as a $2-a-day extra. She attracted the attention of director Ralph Ince with her amusing imitations of Flora Finch, John Bunny's angular co-star, and comedian Lee Beggs. Norma was chagrined when Vitagraph signed Constance to a stock contract at $30 per week, five dollars more than she had received to start, although Norma was by then making considerably more.

Constance's first picture was *The Maid From Sweden* ('14), directed by Lee Beggs. She was also slow to develop and appeared mostly in comedy bits, although occasionally, as in *The Moonstone of Fez, The Mysterious Lodger* and *In the Latin Quarter* (opposite Antonio Moreno), she essayed more dramatic roles. She had a gawky, adolescent charm that led the fan magazines to call her "the Vitagraph tomboy." Norma and Constance rarely played together at Vitagraph, but were seen to good advantage in *The Peacemaker* ('14), with Maurice Costello. As their incomes grew, the Talmadges moved to a larger house on Nostrand Avenue.

An important break for Norma came in the spring of 1915 when J. Stuart Blackton gave her the lead in an elaborate nine-reeler, *The Battle Cry of Peace,* an account of an imaginary invasion of New York by a foreign power. This vicious militaristic propaganda was intended to deliberately inflame pro-war sentiment and excite public demand for American intervention in the European struggle.

Anita Stewart had originally been cast for *The Battle Cry of Peace,* but at the last minute was reassigned to another picture. When Albert E. Smith suggested Norma as a replacement, Blackton was cool to his partner's suggestion, remembering her difficulties with several Vitagraph directors. Partly at Smith's urging, and partly because other top stars were unavailable—and possibly because of reports of Norma's growing dissatisfaction at Vitagraph—Blackton entrusted her with the difficult role of a young girl abused by enemy soldiers. His doubts were dispelled when she gave an intensely dramatic performance that marked a new high in her career.

By the time *The Battle Cry of Peace* opened on Broadway on September 6, 1915, Norma had left Vitagraph. Although she complained that she was indiscriminately assigned to any part that was open, money was the major factor in her departure. Vitagraph was notorious for its penuriousness, and the company's eventual downfall was largely due to its failure to pay enough to keep the many stars it developed. Norma had been refused a raise in June after scoring strongly in a dramatic three-reeler, *The Criminal,* in which she played the adopted daughter of a crook being prosecuted by a district attorney (Maurice Costello), who turns out to be her real father.

Soon afterward Norma signed to star in eight features to be made in Hollywood by National Pictures Corporation, an independent company organized by William L. Parsons and a group of Los Angeles businessmen. Parsons was a Chicago life insurance salesman who later became a minor screen comedian known as "Smiling Billy" Parsons. The two-year contract, negotiated by Margaret Talmadge, called for Norma to receive $400 a week. National also promised to develop Constance into a star. On August 2, Norma, her mother, and two sisters left for California. A few days earlier she had completed her last picture at Vitagraph, *The Crown Prince's Double,* a costume drama with a Prisoner-of-Zenda theme which turned out to be one of her best. In her five years at Vitagraph she made over 250 films. It was little consolation that Blackton belatedly offered to match her salary at National if she would stay.

The National Pictures contract quickly turned into a fiasco. Norma made only one five-reel feature, *Captivating Mary Carstairs,* a slight comedy drama. The company was underfinanced and cut costs with cheap sets and hurried shooting. The director, Bruce Mitchell, also played one of the leads, and Constance had a bit. Space had been rented at the old Oz Film Company studio on Santa Monica Boulevard, and in contrast to Vitagraph, it was little more than a roomy barn.

Norma was much discouraged and talked of returning to New York, but her mother would not hear of their crawling back to Blackton. Parsons was now pouring his limited resources into a series of two-reel comedies starring himself (and Constance as the girl), and could not finance a second Talmadge feature. Norma asked for and received her release from the contract. *Captivating Mary Carstairs* got poor reviews, although Norma was praised, and few bookings. Years later it was reissued to cash in on her phenomenal popularity (as were several of her longer Vitagraph features). Two years later Parsons struck pay dirt with the first version of *Tarzan of the Apes,* starring Elmo Lincoln. The screen adventures of the ape man made him a millionaire. On the strength of her excellent notices in *The Battle Cry of Peace,* which was just going into release in the East, D. W. Griffith signed Norma to a substantial contract—at three times her salary at Vitagraph. During the next eight months she starred in seven features for his Fine Arts Company, although—contrary to Peg Talmadge's biography of her daughters—none were directed by Griffith himself. The first, *Missing Links* ('16), was a murder mystery in a small-town setting, written by Griffith under his familiar pseudonym of Granville Warwick. Robert Harron and Elmer Clifton were her handsome leading men, and Constance had a bit (most of which was edited out).

Edwin Stevens, Norma Talmadge and Eugene O'Brien in The Voice from the Minaret *(1923).*

Norma was tremendously impressed by D. W. Griffith, and in spare moments would visit his set to watch him at work on *Intolerance.* She thought his voice had "a mesmeric quality of a well-tuned instrument" and wondered why he had not had greater success as an actor. "Griffith was extraordinarily self-confident," Norma recalled later, "but he never raised his voice on the set. His manner was easy and never obtrusive . . . he seemed like a kindly dean of a college, instructing his classes, yet firing them with his own enthusiasm. We were all in awe of him—all except Constance and Dorothy Gish."

D. W. Griffith was captivated with the naïve charm of Constance Talmadge and laughed at her pranks. She was quickly signed by Fine Arts, and Griffith cast her as the coltish mountain girl in *Intolerance,* a role that opened the gates of stardom to her.

Norma's Fine Arts pictures of 1916, all dramas laced with bits of comedy, brought a continued upsurge in her popularity. In *Martha's Vindication* she played a woman slandered by gossip, while *The Children in the House* was a domestic triangle enlivened by the antics of a group of talented child performers. In *Going Straight* she and Ralph Lewis were two reformed crooks being blackmailed by a member of their old gang (Eugene Pallette). The husband strangles the blackmailer and makes it

Eileen Percy and Norma Talmadge in Within the Law *(1923).*

appear as self-defense. Norma was a scheming artist's model in *The Devil's Needle,* a drama about drug addiction. She drags her lover (Tully Marshall) to the depths of vice, but in a change of heart nurses him through his misery, and both are rehabilitated by love. *The Social Secretary,* probably the best and most popular of her Fine Arts films, was a charming comedy drama written by the youthful Anita Loos, soon to become a lifelong friend of the Talmadge family. Erich von Stroheim had a bit as an unscrupulous newspaper reporter.

After the completion of *Fifty-Fifty,* her last picture for the Griffith organization, Norma and her mother came East to discuss several film offers. Peg Talmadge felt the time had come for her daughters to have their own company. At a lavish dinner party on Long Island, Norma met Joseph M. Schenck, an official of the Marcus Loew theater chain. The Russian-born Schenck, fifteen years her senior, had already made a fortune in two New Jersey amusement parks, and some of the profits had gone into a none-too-successful flyer in independent film production (with vaudeville headliner Josie Collins as star).

Schenck was much taken with Norma, and a few weeks later followed her to California with two proposals—one for an independent company with herself as star, and one of marriage. She accepted both. Schenck negotiated a releasing arrangement with Lewis J. Selznick's Select Pictures—but not until he tried, and failed, to interest Samuel Goldwyn at Famous Players-Lasky. Schenck, a novice in production, offered Goldwyn 25 percent of the profits to supervise Norma's pictures. "She's not a big name," Goldwyn told Schenck. It was, as Goldwyn admitted later, "a monumental blunder." Norma's films were to be made in New York, first at Selznick's studio in the Bronx, and later at her own studio at 318 East 48th Street, in the heart of Manhattan.

Miss Talmadge and Schenck were married on October 20, 1916, just two months after their first meeting. They had a brief honeymoon on the West Coast and were back in New York for a lavish New Year's Eve party attended by dozens of celebrities. At twenty, Norma found herself a famous movie star, head of her own company, and married to a millionaire.

The Norma Talmadge Film Company made an auspicious debut with *Panthea* ('17), based on Monckton Hoffe's hit play in which Olga Petrova had scored on Broadway. It had all the ingredients of the typical Norma Talmadge picture which would

Norma Talmadge and Eugene O'Brien in The Only Woman *(1924)*

propel her to great success in the next dozen years—a brave, tragic, and sacrificing heroine, lavish settings and beautiful clothes, and buckets of tears before the eventual redemption at the final fadeout. Allan Dwan, director of *Fifty-Fifty,* was engaged to direct. His two assistants, Erich von Stroheim and Arthur Rosson, would later become directors in their own right. The beautiful photography was the work of Roy F. Overbaugh, later a favorite cameraman of the Gish sisters and Richard Barthelmess.

Norma played the title role in *Panthea,* a beautiful Russian political exile who is brought into an English home after a shipwreck. She falls in love with a gifted composer (Earle Foxe) and breaks up his marriage. They flee to Paris, where he composes an opera but cannot get it performed. To help her husband, Panthea becomes the mistress of a wealthy nobleman (L. Roger Lytton), who finances the opera. When the husband learns the truth, Panthea kills the Count and escapes to Russia, where she is arrested and sentenced to Siberia as a political enemy. The composer, realizing that he loves Panthea, follows her into exile. Stroheim played a Russian officer, and Norma made the most of a stunning wardrobe, later wearing the costumes in personal appearances with the film at packed East Coast theaters. Schenck gave it a big play on the Loew circuit, and so successful was *Panthea* that it was reissued six years later to remarkable business.

Norma's second picture for her own company, *The Law of Compensation* ('17), a domestic tear-jerker, was disappointing, but she came back strong in *Poppy* ('17), set against the exciting South African veldt. For the first time her leading man was the handsome Eugene O'Brien, who had come to movies from Broadway dramas and musical comedies with Ethel Barrymore, Fritzi Scheff, Elsie Janis, and others. Miss Talmadge and O'Brien caught the public fancy and became enormously popular as screen lovers (despite the fact that O'Brien was fourteen years her senior). During the next several years they teamed in ten highly profitable films.

After *The Moth* ('17), with O'Brien and Adolphe Menjou, Norma did *The Secret of the Storm Country* ('17), described as a sequel to Mary Pickford's *Tess of the Storm Country*. Many of the beautiful exteriors were shot on location at Ithaca, New York, and Niles Welch, who photographed like an immature teenager, was her leading man. Although *The Moving Picture News* called it "a distinct triumph," audiences did not like Norma in the rags of a fisherman's daughter.

She was more sophisticated in dual roles in *Ghosts of Yesterday* ('18), based on a 1910 play of Mrs. Leslie Carter. It was all sobs and smiles. Eugene O'Brien played an impoverished artist who uses his wife (Norma) as a model. Her portrait is left unfinished when she dies from lack of food and care. The artist, burdened with guilt, meets another woman (also Norma) who greatly resembles his dead wife. She consents to sit for the portrait, but resents his affection as an expression of love for the first wife, and leaves him. Later, she returns when she learns he has gone blind.

In *By Right of Purchase* ('18) Norma played a mothlike young wife who flits from one frivolity to another. It gave her another opportunity to wear beautiful clothes and make love to Eugene O'Brien. One of the big scenes was a reproduction of

Hero Land, the lavish charity bazaar conducted by New York society for World War I relief. Hedda Hopper had a bit.

Another Talmadge hit of 1918 was the melodramatic *De-Luxe Annie,* in which Norma was a respectable married woman who loses her memory from a blow on the head. She becomes the confederate of a cheap crook in a badger game, but is restored to her husband and baby after a brain operation. In a change of characterization, O'Brien played the blackmailer. Roland West, Schenck's partner in the Josie Collins venture, was the director.

In 1918 Miss Talmadge renewed her association with the promising young director, Sidney A. Franklin, who brought a much-needed restraint and greater depth of emotion to her portrayals. She had been much impressed with him at Fine Arts, where he and an older brother, Chester M. Franklin, directed three of her Griffith films (*Martha's Vindication, The Children in the House, Going Straight*). Sidney Franklin had a flair for extracting sensitive performances from actresses, a talent he later used to good advantage with Mary Pickford, Constance Talmadge, Marion Davies, Greta Garbo, Norma Shearer, Luise Rainer, and Jennifer Jones. He was convinced success for Miss Talmadge lay in making her saccharine heroines credible.

Franklin directed her next five pictures—*The Safety Curtain, Her Only Way, The Forbidden City, The Heart of Wetona,* and *The Probation Wife.* Norma had an offbeat role in *The Forbidden City* ('18) as San-San, the beautiful daughter of a deposed mandarin. To regain his position her father betroths her to the Emperor, but she has secretly married an assistant U.S. Consul (Thomas Meighan) and is pregnant. The Emperor loses face and has her killed. Her baby, Toy, is raised at court and becomes a beautiful half-caste (Norma again). She falls in love with the Consul's ward, but Meighan, remembering his own tragedy, will not let them wed. When the Consul becomes ill and deliriously calls for his dead wife, Toy dresses in her mother's clothes and nurses him back to health. In gratitude he gives permission for the marriage. Set against the exotic Orient, it all seemed quite plausible, and Norma was stunning in both Western and Chinese costumes.

Much less successful was *The Heart of Wetona* ('18), which cast her as the half-breed daughter of a Comanche chief. She falls in love with a young engineer (Gladden James), who promises to marry her but doesn't. In her plight she turns to a white Indian agent (Thomas Meighan) who has always loved her. They marry, but find new problems with the vengeful Comanches, who believe him her seducer. Norma was unconvincing as Wetona, and appeared overly stupid in many scenes. Her drab and dirty buckskins robbed her role of glamour. *The Probation Wife* ('19) wisely took her back to the sophisticated world of the wealthy. Norma played three characterizations—a cabaret entertainer, a reformatory drudge, and an attractive, loving wife who fights to keep another woman from stealing her husband. Thomas Meighan was a rich philanderer. Norma's wardrobe was created by leading Paris designers.

The New Moon ('19) was a melodrama of a Russian noblewoman who escapes her captors by dressing as a peasant. An old friend from Fine Arts, Chester Withey, was the director, and Stuart Holmes made a sinister villain. While filming the lovely snow scenes at Saranac Lake, Norma had a narrow escape when her horses became frightened and bolted with the light sleigh in which she was riding.

Some of her other films of 1919-20 were *The Way of a Woman* and *She Loves and Lies,* the first of several appearances

Marc McDermott and Norma Talmadge in Graustark *(1925).*

A scene from Graustark *(1925). Left to right: Marc McDermott, Norma Talmadge, Eugene O'Brien.*

opposite the popular Conway Tearle; *A Daughter of Two Worlds*; *The Woman Gives*; and *Isle of Conquest*. The latter was a bromidic story of an unhappy wife shipwrecked with a brawny stoker, whom she at first despises and then comes to love. They are about to celebrate their wilderness-witnessed nuptials when rescue comes. Fortunately, her husband conveniently dies, and the lovers are married!

In 1920, Norma—with Constance, Natalie and Peg, and Dorothy Gish and her mother—made her first trip to Europe. She was fascinated with London, where government officials gave the famous girls a conducted tour of Buckingham Palace and Westminster Abbey. In Paris they were joined by John Emerson and Anita Loos, who had been married at the Schenck's Bayshore home the previous year, and later by Mary Pickford and Douglas Fairbanks. They explored the World War I battlefields, still grisly with live grenades and staring skeletons, and then went on to Switzerland, Italy—Norma was enchanted with Venice—and Spain. Two years later the Talmadges were back for a longer visit in Holland and Germany.

Joseph M. Schenck had remained behind, occupied with film

and theatrical ventures and his extensive real estate holdings. Soon after the expiration of Constance Talmadge's contract at Fine Arts, Schenck also set her up in her own company. Not to be outdone by her sister, Constance even had her own studio, next door to Norma's on East 48th Street. Constance wisely kept to light comedies which best suited her pixie personality, and while her films did well at the box office, she never approached Norma's huge popularity.

Schenck also was profitably partnered with Roscoe (Fatty) Arbuckle in the Comique Film Company, whose slapstick two-reelers were made on the top floor—actually little more than a loft—of the Talmadge Studios. For a time Natalie Talmadge worked as secretary and bookkeeper for Comique, where she met the frozen-faced Buster Keaton, then playing supporting roles. Keaton fell madly in love with Natalie, whom he described as "a meek, mild girl . . . with great feminine sweetness." The romance was interrupted by World War I, but flourished anew after Keaton's return from France. Although it may have been obvious that Keaton was destined to be his brother-in-law, Schenck wisely recognized the potentials of the young comedian, and in 1920 began to star him in a series of two-reelers. Keaton was an immediate success and soon graduated to features. Buster and Natalie were married at Norma's country home on Long Island on May 31, 1921. Schenck gave them a fine automobile for a wedding present.

Buster Keaton's association with the Talmadge family left an emotional scar from which he never recovered. He said later that he liked the Talmadges very much, and felt that they liked him, but he did not understand their intense family spirit. He felt it was like being married to the whole family, which seemed to think and act as one. Keaton appears to have resented the "corporation aspect" of the Talmadges, and later blamed them, and Schenck in particular, for bad advice which led him to give up his own company to work for M-G-M on a salary. His marriage to Natalie ended in divorce in 1932, largely because of his own personal problems and erratic behavior. She was given a large settlement, and later legally changed the name of their two sons to Talmadge. Keaton's bitterness had not diminished by 1960 when he wrote his autobiography—neither Natalie nor any of the Talmadges were mentioned by name. Interestingly, he thought his wife a frustrated actress. Although Natalie appeared in several of her sisters' pictures in bit roles, and was Keaton's leading lady in *Our Hospitality,* she never caught on in movies. Contrary to Keaton, friends said that Natalie was never envious of her sisters' success.

Norma Talmadge's golden period, both artistically and financially, opened with *Yes Or No?* in 1920. Shortly before, Schenck had negotiated a fabulous new releasing contract with Associated First National, an exhibitors' combine, which brought her $7,500 a week and a major share of the profits of her films.

Yes Or No? typified the women's pictures which would eventually earn as much as $350,000 each for her—a huge sum by 1920 standards. Norma played dual roles in two parallel stories. In one she was a neglected wife who leaves her wealthy husband for a cad (Lowell Sherman). He refuses to marry her, and in despair she commits suicide. In the other story Norma was the wife of a poor slum boy. She resists the efforts of a lecherous chauffeur (Gladden James) to seduce her, and is seemingly rewarded for her virtue when her husband invents a washing machine and becomes rich! The two plots were linked by having the sister of the poor girl become the society matron's maid. Norma was extremely effective in this maudlin drama, and wore a blond wig and beautiful gowns as the rich woman, gingham aprons and plain black dresses as the poor wife. Natalie Talmadge revealed a flair for comedy, and made a good team with Edward Brophy. (Brophy, in addition to his acting, was an assistant director on many Talmadge films, and later a writer for Buster Keaton; his wife, Anne, was Norma's secretary for several years).

Anita Loos did the screen play for *The Branded Woman* ('20). Norma married a wealthy man (Percy Marmont) but concealed the fact that her mother was a prostitute. Her husband discovers the truth when she is blackmailed, and leaves her, but they are reconciled by their small daughter.

Passion Flower ('21), also shown as *Love or Hate,* was a costume drama with Miss Talmadge as an exotic Castillian girl. Her hatred for her stepfather eventually turns into passionate love, which results in her mother's death. Norma had a stunning scene at the mother's grave when, overcome by guilt and grief, she realizes the enormity of her betrayal. Despite some trouble with the censors, *Passion Flower* was one of her favorite films. It was the first of several she did under the direction of the brilliant Herbert Brenon, an old friend of Joe Schenck. Although she blossomed under his tutelage, Norma complained later that he was temperamental and nervous, and easily enraged if anything went wrong on the set. Brenon also directed her in *The Sign on the Door* ('21), a drama of a married woman mixed up in the murder of a worthless idler, and *The Wonderful Thing* ('21) a Peg O' My Heart story of an American girl in a snobbish English country home. Norma Shearer had a bit in *The Sign on the Door,* but it wound up on the cutting room floor.

Love's Redemption ('21), directed by Albert Parker, cast Norma as a young Jamaican girl who married a boozy beachcomber (Harrison Ford) and reformed him. They return to his home in England, but gradually become disillusioned with the materialism and insincerity of civilization. When their marriage is threatened by his returning alcoholism, they go back to Jamaica

Norma and Constance Talmadge by poolside at Norma's Hollywood home (c. 1925).

Norma Talmadge (about 1926).

and find happiness in a simple life. Norma was too sophisticated and intelligent for the role of the native girl, and Ford over-acted badly.

In 1922 Norma scored one of her greatest successes in *Smilin' Through,* possibly the best and certainly the most popular film of her career. The old Jane Cowl-Jane Murfin play was made for her, a compendium of tragedy, sentiment, and ro-mantic mysticism. Expensively and handsomely mounted, *Smilin' Through* featured beautiful costumes and sets, and fine photogra-phy by Charles Rosher and J. Roy Hunt. Sidney Franklin was back to direct, and an exceptional cast included Harrison Ford,

Glenn Hunter, Wyndham Standing, Alec B. Francis, Gene Lockhart, and the lovely child actress, Miriam Battista.

Smilin' Through told of the tragic love of John Carteret and Moonyean, who is accidentally killed at the wedding ceremony by a rejected suitor. Forty years later her niece Kathleen, now Carteret's ward, wants to marry the nephew of her aunt's murderer. Carteret, an embittered old man grieving over the loss of Moonyean, has an uncontrollable hatred for the family of the man responsible for her death. His prejudice is overcome by true love, and he forgives and permits the marriage. The dead Moonyean reappeared in spiritual manifestations (via double exposures), and at the end a rejuvenated John joins his eternally young wife in the spirit world after death. Norma gave a touching performance in the dual roles of Moonyean and Kathleen. So popular was *Smilin' Through* that it was twice remade in talking pictures, first with Norma Shearer and later in a musical version starring Jeanette MacDonald.

Miss Talmadge then embarked upon a long series of incredibly popular pictures extending over the next five years. Encouraged by the returns of *Smilin' Through,* Schenck gave them lavish budgets and employed only the best of directors, writers, technicians and performers. Virtually all of Norma's films between 1922-27 were written by Frances Marion, a specialist in sentimental drama who had done the scenarios for many Mary Pickford movies. In Frank Lloyd, and later Frank Borzage, she found two sensitive directors, each with a remarkable talent for combining pictorial composition, fluid action and intimate characterization.

The Eternal Flame ('22) was an elaborate costume drama of the court of Louis XVIII, based on Honoré Balzac's "La Duchesse de Langeais." Norma was an amoral wife who teased and lured men—"the toast of Paris," as a title said—and cast them easily aside. When she meets the strong, silent General de Montriveau (Conway Tearle), a calculated flirtation develops into a soul-searing love. She trifles with him, and he makes her pay. One critic said Norma's performance ranged from "unassailable virtue to sly deviltry, blank innocence to cynical sophistication, tyrannical domination to abject submission, and from bored worldliness to spiritual regeneration." The highlight was a gorgeous court ball, impressively used by Frank Lloyd to heighten the tragedy of the Duchess and the General (although the bobbed and marcelled hair styles of the women extras were clearly in the prevalent flapper styles of the '20s). Conway Tearle was particularly fine as the General, and a large cast included Adolphe Menjou, Irving Cummings, Rosemary Theby, Wedgwood Nowell, and Juanita Hansen.

Eugene O'Brien was back to co-star with Norma in *The Voice from the Minaret* ('23), another enormous box-office bonanza. He played an English missionary who has a shipboard romance with Miss Talmadge, the wife of the Governor-General of India (Edwin Stevens). She follows him to Damascus, but his superior sends her back to her husband. Later they meet again in England, but O'Brien is saved from scandal when Stevens conveniently dies and paves the way for the lovers to marry.

Within the Law ('23) continued the cycle of Talmadge hits, with Norma in the Jane Cowl role in Bayard Veiller's 1912 Broadway success. Her performance as Mary Turner, a shopgirl who is framed for theft and sentenced to three years in prison, was a study in contrasts. After Mary's release she blackmails the crooks who wronged her, but there is a final retribution and happy ending as she marries the son of a wealthy department-store owner. Norma made no pretense at being glamorous in the early scenes, and was most effective as the drab, bewildered salesgirl. Later she was very beautiful and poised, and her gorgeous clothes added to the sophistication of her changed characterization. Jack Mulhall was the boy, but acting honors went to Lew Cody and Helen Ferguson.

Ashes of Vengeance ('23) was another spectacular costume drama, laid in sixteenth-century France, when Catherine de Medici permitted the weak-minded, knock-kneed Charles IX to imagine himself the ruler of the country. There was much exciting swordplay, and the inevitable lavish court ball at the Louvre with hundreds of dancing extras. The involved plot concerned a duke (Conway Tearle) who indentures himself to save the life of a Huguenot girl. Norma had an unsympathetic part as an arrogant noblewoman. Wallace Beery was amusing as the cowardly Duc de Tours, while Tearle, in contrast to his fine work in *The Eternal Flame*, hammed it up, posturing and stamping his foot in a thoroughly unworthy performance. Frank Lloyd directed. *Ashes of Vengeance* had a spectacular premiere at the New York Strand, with dozens of celebrities attending, and a pit orchestra performing a special score by Victor Schertzinger.

Norma was miscast as a tempestous Algerian dancing girl

in *Song of Love* ('23)—released in some areas as *Dust of Desire*. It was out-and-out melodrama about a French under-cover agent (Joseph Schildkraut) who tried to thwart an Arab uprising. To gain information he makes love to a rebel chieftan's daughter. There was an exciting attack on the desert garrison, and a contrived ending in which the warring factions are brought together and the lovers united. Norma was entrancing in brief but expensive native costumes, and Schildkraut was praised de-spite a lurid make-up that accentuated his effeminate appearance. *Song of Love* had many scenes of luxurious tents and desert caravans silhouetted against the evening skies, all obviously in-spired by Valentino's *The Sheik*. Frank Borzage was originally scheduled to direct, but was replaced by Chester M. Franklin, who became ill and was replaced by Frances Marion. Franklin did most of the action scenes, and Miss Marion, who had di-rected Mary Pickford in *The Love Light* ('21), did the romantic sequences.

Miss Talmadge returned to her sobs and smiles in *Secrets* ('24), one of her biggest and best-remembered hits. This senti-mental love story was told in flashback through an old woman

Noah Beery and Norma Talmadge in The Dove *(1928).*

looking at her diary, which is labeled "Secrets." Norma appears first as a happy young girl in crinolines and curls in her English home. Against her parents' objections she marries a young man (Eugene O'Brien) and goes with him to Wyoming, where they experience unbelievable hardships—hunger, an Indian attack on their cabin, and the death of their baby. Norma is then seen as a lady of wealth in her forties. Her husband has succeeded, but the marriage is threatened by his infatuation for another woman (Gertrude Astor). Finally, having condoned her husband's sins for forty years, the faithful wife is seen at his deathbed futilely praying for his recovery.

Norma's popularity crested with *Secrets,* and although she made several good pictures in the next few years, her career began to decline. *The Only Woman* ('24), directed by Sidney Olcott, had an absurd plot in which Norma marries a drunken young millionaire to save her father from disgrace. She manages to rehabilitate him, but only after such hardships as a shipwreck and the hero being kicked in the head by a horse! The ship scenes utilized the *Sultana,* the lavish yacht of banker E. H. Harriman, and required several weeks to shoot. Eugene O'Brien was again the male lead.

The Lady ('25) cast Norma as Polly Pearl, an English music-hall soubrette who marries a worthless man. He abandons her, and she is forced to give up her baby. Polly Pearl sinks lower and lower, becoming a prostitute in a cheap Marseilles café, and finally a tired old woman selling flowers in the London streets. A lifelong search for her son ends when she finds him wounded in a military hospital in France during World War I. As in *Secrets, The Lady* was also told in flashback. Norma was saucy in the short skirts of the soubrette, but more convincing as the aged mother. Tony Gaudio's photography of the London fog, the murky waterfront, and the gay music hall was magnificent. Frank Borzage again directed.

Graustark ('25) was a modernized version of the old popular classic by George Barr McCutcheon, handsomely mounted but short on action—and interminably long on passionate embraces. Miss Talmadge was the unlikely-named Princess Yetiva Guggenslocker of Graustark, who attracts the attention of a handsome adventurer (Eugene O'Brien) while traveling incognito on a train. He follows her to her kingdom and becomes involved in conspiracy and intrigue. Norma was stately and royal in her fabulous gowns, and suffered beautifully as the princess torn between love and duty. Director Dimitri Buchowetski played it straight, seemly unaware *Graustark* was in reality just a wonderful spoof.

Norma's only picture in 1926 was *Kiki,* an ill-advised and disastrous attempt at comedy—her first since the Vitagraph days ten years earlier. Norma played an impossible character, a Paris hoyden of fifteen, dressed in tam-o-shanter and short skirt. She falls in love with a theatrical producer (Ronald Colman), and to be near him tries to become an actress. After several labored situations, Colman comes to realize he loves the gamin, and Kiki develops into a real performer.

Miss Talmadge was not well suited to her part, and overdid the repetitious physical gyrations she apparently thought the role demanded. A long scene in which she feigned a cataleptic fit was tiresome and ludicrous, and another handicap was the slangy American titles (a frequent criticism of Talmadge films). *Kiki* was not all bad. As a hilariously inept chorus girl, Kiki falls through a bass drum in the orchestra. Undaunted, she climbs back on stage and takes a bow with the haughty star (Gertrude Astor) whose act she has ruined. Equally delightful was the sophisticated, slightly risqué comedy in Colman's apartment where Kiki manages to retain her virtue in the face of compromising temptations. Colman was very suave, and George K. Arthur was delightful as his long-suffering valet. *Kiki,* based on the old David Belasco play made famous by Lenore Ulric, suffered from a distressing lack of modernization—a mistake Mary Pickford would repeat in her talkie remake of 1931.

Early in the '20s Alla Nazimova had urged Norma Talmadge to play Alexander Dumas' tragic lady of the camelias, but her *Camille* ('27), done in modern dress, was but a faint recollection of the original. Norma's performance, while good and at times striking, was not in the traditional style of Duse, Bernhardt, or Rejane. Her choice of a director—Fred Niblo, of *Ben-Hur* fame—was unfortunate. Niblo placed little emphasis upon characterization, and Norma's Camille Gautier was shallow and poorly motivated. She was in sore need of a Sidney Franklin, Frank Borzage, or Clarence Brown.

Camille was such an extraordinarily lavish motion picture that it detracted from the plot and its characters—yet mercifully obscured some of the shortcomings. It had gorgeous sets by William Cameron Menzies, beautifully diffused photography and expensive costumes. The familiar story was unchanged—a wom-

Norma Talmadge and Gilbert Roland as they returned from Europe in 1929.

an of poor reputation sacrifices her love for a wealthy young man to save his family from scandal. He returns to her, only to find she is dying of tuberculosis. Norma gave the role of the father to Maurice Costello, partly out of gratitude for his help in the Vitagraph days, and although he gave a good performance it did nothing for his ailing career. Gilbert Roland was handsome as Armand, but rather wooden and too immaculately dressed.

Miss Talmadge's personal life had undergone various changes by the mid-'20s. After the completion of *Love's Redemption* in the fall of 1921, she moved her company from New York to Hollywood. Soon afterward, Constance Talmadge closed the studio on East 48th Street and followed her sister West. Norma's marriage to Joseph M. Schenck began to fail shortly after they moved to California, but the couple did not separate until 1927. They had a lavish eighteen-room house on Hollywood Boulevard, but Norma spent most of her time at an elaborate beach house in Santa Monica, next door to Bebe Daniels.

Norma's shadowy father, Fred Talmadge, drifted back into the lives of his famous daughters after an absence of many years. One story, told by Anita Loos, is that Peg Talmadge, while riding with her daughters in Central Park, spied her husband asleep on a bench. She stopped the car and introduced Norma and Constance to their father. Fred Talmadge appears to have worked as a property man at the Select Studios, and perhaps in other odd jobs which were found for him. He died in California in 1925, and *The New York Times* said in an obituary that he had been retired for four years. Interestingly, several fan magazines wove a tearful story of how Talmadge had died at the Chase Sanitarium in New York, with his daughters making a hurried trip from Hollywood to be at his deathbed.

Peg Talmadge never ceased in her devotion to her daughters, and until her death in 1933 looked after their business and professional interests (with the advice of Joseph M. Schenck). She garnered a circle of distinguished friends in the film capital, was widely quoted for her witty sayings, and became known for the helping hand which she gave many aspiring young actresses. In 1924, Mrs. Talmadge wrote—or was purported to have written —a biography of her three daughters, *The Talmadge Sisters,* much of which was devoted to sentimental philosophizing about love, marriage, and careers.

Soon after the release of *Camille* Norma was often seen in the company of her leading man, Gilbert Roland, an intense young Mexican whose father had been a toreador. Without acting experience, Roland had broken into movies on the strength of his Latin good looks with a bit opposite Clara Bow in *The Plastic Age* ('25). He was eight years younger than Norma. The Talmadge-Roland affair first made headlines in 1928 when they went on a Hawaiian vacation together, chaperoned by Norma's mother. There were persistent reports she would divorce Schenck and marry Roland. An ugly and completely unfounded rumor that Schenck had hired gangsters to kill or mutilate Roland circulated in Hollywood for years.

In 1927, Joe Schenck became president of United Artists Corporation, the Pickford-Fairbanks-Chaplin combine, and arranged to bring both Norma and Constance into the company upon the expiration of their First National contracts. In an interview at the time, Norma said she and director Roland West planned to do a picture at the UFA Studios in Berlin, for United Artists release, using the "exciting new techniques of the German film industry." It was a curious statement, as the German studios were rapidly declining, and most of the artists with the "exciting new techniques" of the early '20s—Lubitsch, DuPont, Pommer, Murnau—were already at work in Hollywood!

The UFA project did not materialize, and for her first United Artists release, Norma made *The Dove* ('28), based on Willard Mack's popular Broadway play. The locale was inexplicably transferred from Mexico to an imaginary Mediterranean country. Norma was badly miscast as a native girl who entertains by playing the guitar and singing in a gin mill owned by Harry Myers. Gilbert Roland was an American bartender who keeps Norma from being seduced by Noah Beery. The film was a tour-de-force for Beery, in the original Holbrook Blinn role, as a greedy, sensuous, cold-blooded revolutionary who had seized control of the country. Slow-moving and unrealistic, *The Dove* was hampered by poor titles in which Norma spoke such broken English slang as "You betcha my life!" Roland West directed.

Norma's last silent picture was *The Woman Disputed* ('28), based on Guy de Maupassant's "Boule de Suif." In this border romance of World War I, she played an adventuress who spurns a Russian officer (Arnold Kent) for a young Austrian (Gilbert Roland). When the Russian army captures Norma and many leading citizens, women, and children of the Austrian town, she makes a bargain with Kent. In exchange for the release of the captives, Norma becomes his mistress, and the film closes on this somber note.

Henry King's impressive battle scenes were imaginatively constructed and beautifully photographed (by Oliver T. Marsh). However, Schenck did not like King's version of *The Woman Disputed,* and thought it too slow and humorless. Several weeks after shooting had ended, he brought in Sam Taylor to direct considerable additional scenes, which were inserted in the last third of the film. Taylor's tampering did not help the pedestrian pace of the dreary picture.

When Charles Chaplin visited the set of *The Woman Disputed,* King and his assistant, Robert Florey, got the comedian to play a practical joke on Miss Talmadge. The scene in progress, laid in a dark street, called for a passer-by to stop and light her cigarette when she finds she has no match. As the light flared, Norma was startled to see Chaplin's grinning face. He flicked out the match, tossed it over his shoulder, and with a typical Chaplin gesture kicked it with his heel as it fell. Miss Talmadge barely managed to keep a straight face, and collapsed in laughter as King yelled "Cut!" The unpublicized bit was kept in the final picture, although Chaplin's comic kick of the match was edited out. In an elaborate ceremony Florey presented Charlie with a check for $7.50 for his work.

"Norma was such an easy person to work with," Robert Florey recalls. "She took direction so well. I never saw her temperamental, and she was always kind to the actors, extras, and crew—always on time, never posing or pretending to be

High Priced Harmony! Norma Talmadge, United Artists star, gives Joseph M. Schenck (left) head of United Artists Corporation, a sample of her "talkie" voice while Irving Berlin (right) gives her vocal support with the strains of one of his latest song hits. Photo snapped on arrival at Hollywood of Mr. Schenck after an extended business trip east in 1929.

an important star . . . just an extremely nice person."

Although the failure of *The Dove* and *The Woman Disputed* had been danger signals that her career was in trouble, Norma faced a major crisis with the arrival of talking pictures. Her first voice tests were disappointing, and for more than a year she wisely postponed her sound debut. Along with dozens of other stars caught in the frenzy of the new medium, she took daily lessons from voice coaches hastily recruited from Broadway.

Her first talkie, *New York Nights,* released late in 1929, was terrible. It was a hackneyed backstage triangle of an alcoholic songwriter, his faithful wife, and a lecherous gangster. Norma's voice was not bad, but lacked training. The film was static and largely shot with a single stationary camera. Except for a wild underworld party, it had no action. Lewis Milestone, the director, is said to have quit before its completion. Later, while he was at work on *All Quiet on the Western Front,* United Artists completely re-edited *New York Nights,* using some footage shot by another director.

After the bad reviews on *New York Nights* came out, Constance Talmadge was reported to have cabled her sister from Europe, "Get out now—and be thankful for the trust funds Mama set up!" Constance's own career had ended in the late '20s, and she wisely did not attempt a talking picture.

But Norma made one last effort, *Du Barry, Woman of Passion* ('30), based on the antique play which David Belasco wrote for Mrs. Leslie Carter in 1901. It was a stilted film with few dramatic moments, and suffered from poor acting and poor direction. Norma, as Madame DuBarry, behaved more like an ingenue, and was only passable in an unbelievable role. Time Magazine noted that Norma's voice had improved—"in her first dialogue effort she talked like an elocution pupil," it said. "This time she talks like an elocution teacher!" Time also hoped "this will be the last attempt to establish her as a great figure in sound pictures." The veteran William Farnum was incredibly hammy as an aging Henry XV, and Sam Taylor's confused direction robbed the mob scenes and glamorous royal fetes of their vitality with too many tight close-ups.

With the failure of *DuBarry, Woman of Passion,* Norma Talmadge was content to write an end to her acting career. She had earned a large fortune in movies—reportedly five million dollars during the last eight years she was on the screen.

It had been wisely invested in stocks and real estate—Schenck had once given her an eleven-story apartment building in Los Angeles as an anniversary present—and she retired a rich woman. Much of her time was spent traveling abroad, and at the posh resorts of Florida and Europe. She said later the greatest pleasure of her retirement was to be rid of the autograph pests, whom she had always detested.

Norma's romance with Gilbert Roland cooled, and she was soon being seen with comedian George Jessel. In 1932 she joined him in a vaudeville tour, and soon afterward a Florida court was told Miss Talmadge would guarantee a $100,000 divorce settlement which Jessel was making on his wife. Jessel later gave Norma an expensive house in Palm Beach, presumably in return for her financial help.

Miss Talmadge divorced Joseph M. Schenck in Juarez, Mexico, on April 14, 1934, alleging incompatibility. Although they had been separated for seven years, he had continued to guide her business affairs. Schenck publicly took the blame for the failure of their marriage, and said that after he became president of United Artists he was forced to be away from home for long periods of time. "I forgot to send my wife flowers . . . and neglected her in many ways," he told newspaper reporters. The settlement was not disclosed, but was rumored to be in excess of $500,000.

Nine days later Miss Talmadge and Jessel were married at Atlantic City, New Jersey, by Mayor Harry Bachrach. Both were noticeably nervous. Norma later appeared with Jessel on a syndicated radio program which did not succeed. Their marriage ended in divorce in 1939. Jessel blamed the break-up on malicious gossip and the frequent separations due to his work.

In 1946 Norma married Dr. Carvel James, a Las Vegas, Nevada, physician. In the later years of her life she suffered increasingly from arthritis, and was finally confined to a wheelchair. She maintained homes in Las Vegas, Palm Springs, and Tucson to take advantage of the warm sun. She died, at sixty, on December 24, 1957, and was buried at Hollywood Memorial Cemetery.

4
COMIC STRIPS ON THE SCREEN

*T*HE movies and the newspaper comic strip had their beginnings at approximately the same time and place. On April 23, 1896, Edison's wonderful invention had its commercial premiere at Koster & Bial's Music Hall on the northwest corner of 34th and Broadway in New York City. A few blocks away, and two months before, Richard F. Outcault, a staff artist for the New York *World,* gave birth to the comic strip by drawing "The Great Dog Show in M'Groogan's Avenue," starring the famous Yellow Kid.

It took the pioneer filmmakers a decade to realize that the comic strip was a source of material replete with distinctive characters established in public favor. In the ensuing half-century practically every major comic strip found its way to the screen as an animated cartoon, a one- or two-reel comedy, a serial, or a feature with live actors.

Winsor McCay's *Gertie the Dinosaur* ('09) was the first film based on a comic strip. As a minor and occasional character in "Little Nemo," a beautifully drawn and exquisitely colored strip dating from 1905, Gertie had attracted little attention. Then McCay, inspired by Emile Cohl's early French cartoons, made over 100,000 drawings of her for the first American animated cartoon, which he called *Gertie the Dinosaur*. McCay appeared, along with other leading comic-strip artists, in the film's prologue. He subsequently put Gertie in several more films. None was really popular, and when McCay found it impossible technically to duplicate the artistic intricacies of his original drawing on the screen, he abandoned movies altogether (except during World War I, when he made a few propaganda cartoons for the government).

Arthur Lake was Harold Teen and Mary Brian was Lillums in Harold
Teen *(1928), Mervyn LeRoy's silent version of the Carl Ed comic strip.
Lake would later play Dagwood Bumstead in another comic strip brought
to the screen, the* Blondie *series.*

In 1913 animated cartoons were made of Sidney Smith's
"Old Doc Yak" and George McManus' "Snookums." Smith,
best known as the creator of "The Gumps," personally supervised the animation of the *Old Doc Yak* films for the Selig
Polyscope Company. They were an animal series, with sketchy
plots and crude horseplay about anything at all—Santa Claus,
golf, a pair of impudent kittens. The series was not popular
and Smith decided to devote all his time to his newspaper strip.

The Gumps, Smith's most popular characters, were featured
in two-reel comedies Universal produced from 1923 to 1928.
They were long on slapstick and contrived comedy, and much
of their success was due to Joe Murphy, who bore an amazing
likeness to the chinless Andy Gump. Fay Tincher played Min—
and was much prettier than her comic strip counterpart—and

Jackie Morgan was Chester. *The Gumps* was a training ground for several comedy directors, including Erle C. Kenton, William Watson, and Norman Taurog, who won an Academy Award in 1930 for his direction of another comic strip, *Skippy*.

George McManus, the creator of Jiggs and Maggie, turned out other comic strips that became movies. "The Newlyweds," which first appeared in 1906, featured an enfant-terrible named Snookums, who came to the screen in 1913 in a series of cartoons called *Snookums*. Universal revived the strip in 1927 in a series of live two-reel comedies called *The Newlyweds*. Ethlyne Clair and Syd Saylor were the bungling young parents, and Sunny McKeen a beautiful Snookums. This series gave Gus Meins, later a stalwart Hal Roach director, his first opportunity.

McManus' "Let George Do It" strip, which dated back to 1908, inspired a series of short comedies produced by Universal under the same title in 1926. As in the comic strip, George, played by Arthur Lake, was a well meaning oaf who always did everything wrong.

Mitzi Green had the lead in Little Orphan Annie *(1932), the first version of Harold Gray's popular strip about a spunky orphan. Shown here with Buster Phelps.*

McManus, who later furnished comedy ideas for several of Larry Semon's Vitagraph silents, hit pay dirt as a comic-strip artist with "Bringing Up Father" in 1913. The popularity of newly rich Jiggs and his social climbing wife Maggie is still undiminished more than fifty years later.

Jiggs and Maggie first appeared on the screen in cartoons drawn for the International Film Service in 1916 by a pioneer animator, Frank Moser. After World War I they were used in a series of two-reel Pathé comedies. In 1928, at the height of the strip's newspaper popularity, M-G-M produced *Bringing Up Father,* a six-reel feature with script by Frances Marion and direction by Jack Conway. J. Farrell MacDonald played Jiggs, whom he greatly resembled, but Marie Dressler was miscast as Maggie. The picture was not a success, due primarily to the addition of maudlin situations not in the strip.

Jiggs and Maggie reappeared in the talkies in a group of slapstick features produced by Monogram (*Jiggs and Maggie in Court, Jackpot Jitters* and others). Joe Yule, father of Mickey Rooney, made an ideal Jiggs with his short stature and bandy legs, and the angular Renee Riano was perfect as Maggie. But the cheap production values doomed the films to the lower half of double bills. (Later, Yule and Miss Riano played Jiggs and Maggie in a skit for a touring tent show).

Richard F. Outcault, whose Yellow Kid of 1896 is recognized as the first modern comic strip, created another popular character six years later—Buster Brown. In 1914 Charles H. France began a series of *Buster Brown* cartoons for Edison. Universal revived the character in 1925 in two-reelers starring Arthur Trimble. The newspaper Buster was almost forgotten by then, but audiences enjoyed Tige, a dog whose left eye was ringed by a circle of black fur.

One of the earliest newspaper comic strips, "The Katzenjammer Kids," begun in 1897, did not get to the screen until 1917, when Gregory H. LaCava produced a series of cartoons for International Film Service. LaCava's series stuck faithfully to Rudolph Dirk's original, and Der Captain was unremittingly plagued by Hans und Fritz in such films as *Der Captain Is Examined for Insurance* and *Der Captain Goes A-Flivering.* The anti-German feeling of 1917-18 killed the series. A former newspaper cartoonist himself, LaCava soon left film animation and became one of Hollywood's best directors (*Stage Door, Gabriel Over the White House*). In 1938 M-G-M revived the

Kids in cartoons called simply *The Captain and the Kids.* Hans und Fritz made a surprising comeback in cartoons for television commercials in 1970.

George Herriman's "Krazy Kat" strip was an American classic. Its gentle ironies and fantasies gave it intellectual appeal, and in this it was unique. Several foredoomed attempts to translate it to the screen in animated form were made. In their cartoons of 1916-18 Frank Moser and Leon Searl wisely retained most of the strip's timeless characters—Ignatz Mouse, Offisa Bull Pup, Kristopher Kamel, etc. Nevertheless, the results bore little resemblance to the original. Bill Nolan's 1926-28 series for Winkler Pictures were just ordinary cat cartoons, and Charles Mintz's interminable series of 1930-38 possessed nothing of the original but the name. "Krazy Kat" was no more adaptable to the screen than Walt Kelly's "Pogo," another delightful intellectual comic strip, would be today.

Bill Nolan's *Happy Hooligan* cartoons (1913-17) were based on Opper's tramp with the tin-can hat, and competed in those years with *Mutt and Jeff,* an animated version of Bud Fisher's popular comic strip. Both became strong instruments of propaganda during World War I, and Mutt and Jeff, in particular, were constantly embroiled with German spies and the Kaiser. Walter Lantz later revived them in a short-lived cartoon series in 1930.

Several other comic strips found their way into two-reel comedies during the '20s. *The Hall Room Boys,* based on H. A. McGill's now forgotten strip, comprised the first films produced by Harry and Jack Cohn for their CBC Productions, later Columbia. Sid Smith and George Monberg, among others, played the knockabout pals, Percy and Ferdy, who were very much in the idiom of the later Three Stooges. Pathé made a series of cute comedies out of Berndt's *Smitty* with a gang of brash kids which included Billy Bruce, Jackie Combs, Betty Jane Graham and Donald Haines (of the enormous freckles). FBO's version of *Toots and Casper* was poorly received and was replaced by another comic-strip favorite, *Hairbreadth Harry,* which failed to live up to the promise of its title. Rube Goldberg's *Ike and Mike* (Universal, 1927-28) had little of interest except the comedy of Charley Dorety, a pathetic type with a Stan Laurel style. Ethlyn Gibson was rather appealing in the title role of *Winnie Winkle,* a popular series produced by Artclass under the experienced comedy direction of Ralph Ceder and Arvid E. Gillstrom. Plans to revive *Winnie Winkle* in television, with June Havoc in the lead, never materialized.

The quaint characters in Fontaine Fox's "Toonerville Trolley"—the Skipper, Aunt Eppie Hogg, the Powerful Katrinka, and the Terrible-Tempered Mr. Bangs—were first represented on the screen in a series of two-reelers released in 1921-22. *The Skipper's Scheme, Toonerville Tactics* and *Boos-Em Friends* were heavy-handed humor. Larry Darmour revived the strip in movies in 1927 with a group of charming kid comedies based on Fox's tough youngster with the derby hat, Mickey (Himself) McGuire. Mickey Rooney, then known as Mickey Yule, was ideally cast in the lead. These comedies never achieved the success of Hal Roach's *Our Gang,* and were discontinued in 1933 when Rooney outgrew the part. *The Toonerville Trolley* cartoons released by RKO Radio in 1936-37 were poorly animated and failed to transmit the charm of the newspaper strip.

Billy DeBeck's "Barney Google" comic strip was a national craze in the flapper era of the '20s. There was a popular song, "Barney Google With the Goo-Goo-Googly Eyes"; children played with dozens of Google toys and games; and the slang of the times included such Google-isms as "osky-wow-wow" and "the heebie-jeebies." Larry Darmour capitalized on the strip's popularity with a series of two-reelers in 1928-29 (*A Horse on Barney, Slide Sparky Slide*). Despite Ralph Ceder's talented direction, it was impossible to re-create the characters on the screen, particularly the lovable horse Spark Plug with his soulful eyes and patched blanket, and the films were never more than ordinary slapstick in a racetrack setting. Charles Mintz's cartoons for Columbia succeeded no better. After DeBeck's death Fred Lasswell, who took over the strip, introduced a new character— Snuffy Smith, a sawed-off, wise-cracking hillbilly, and in 1942 Monogram brought out *Private Snuffy Smith* and *Hillbilly Blitzkrieg,* with Bud Duncan as Snuffy. They were inane.

Ella Cinders ('26), based on the popular comic strip of Bill Conselman and Charley Plumb, gave Colleen Moore one of her best roles. She was just right as the small-town, spunky slavey who made good in Hollywood. For once the character in the movie *looked* like the one in the comic strip. The film retained most of the strip's other characters, especially Lotta Pill and Prissy Pill, Ella's trouble-making half-sisters, and deployed them before the intriguing background of the movie

Bill Elliott played Red Ryder in Republic's series based on the popular Western adventure comic strip. Here is Elliott (right) in Lone Texas Ranger *(1945).*

capital. Harry Langdon made a delightful guest appearance, and *Ella Cinders* was a huge box-office hit.

Mervyn LeRoy had done so well on the script of *Ella Cinders* that two years later First National let him direct a film version of Carl Ed's *Harold Teen.* Arthur Lake, who had played the bungling hero of *Let George Do It,* and later became firmly established as the amiable Dagwood Bumstead of *Blondie,* was an ideal Harold Teen, whom he greatly resembled. In 1934 Warner Brothers brought out a musical version of *Harold Teen,* with dancer Hal LeRoy in the lead, but it lacked the charm of the silent.

Russ Westover's "Tillie The Toiler," glamorizing the whitecollar working girl, began in the New York *American* in 1921. Six years later blonde Marion Davies portrayed the brunette Tillie in M-G-M's *Tillie the Toiler.* It was light farce and suited Miss Davies' talents. Matt Moore made a good foil as Mac, Tillie's long-suffering boyfriend. Fifteen years later Columbia made a silly little program picture, of the same title, with Kay Hughes and William Tracy in the leads. It was mediocre.

The best motion picture ever made from a comic strip appeared in 1930. In Paramount's *Skippy*, Percy Crosby's child characters were delightfully brought to life, and Jackie Cooper was a sensation in the title role. The alternation of comedy and pathos made it one of the year's most popular pictures, and it was nominated for an Academy Award. Norman Taurog got an Oscar for directing it. Jackie Cooper, who had been nominated for the best male performance of the year, was nosed out by Lionel Barrymore for *A Free Soul*.

A sequel, *Sooky*, based on another character in the Crosby strip, also did well financially but was an infinitely poorer picture. Jackie Coogan's brother Robert was cute in the title role, but lacked Jackie's acting talent. In 1938 some former associates of Walt Disney turned out a series of *Skippy* cartoons for United Artists. They were not successful, and the producers were soon in financial difficulties.

Although a popular comic strip since the early '20s, Harold Gray's "Little Orphan Annie" did not reach the screen until 1932. David O. Selznick used the spunky, tow-headed character as a starring role for Mitzi Green, who had attracted attention in *Skippy* and *Sooky*. Despite good direction by John S. Robertson, it did not succeed. Another version by Paramount in 1938, with Ann Gillis as Annie, did no better. Neither Miss Green nor Miss Gillis seemed to convey Annie's traditional resourcefulness. Two other comic strip kids that didn't make the grade were Ernie Bushmiller's *Nancy*, brought to the screen in cartoon form by Terry-Toons in 1942, and Jimmy Hatlo's *Little Iodine* ('46), with Jo Ann Marlowe as the troublesome brat.

Ham Fisher's perennial fight champion, Joe Palooka, was a natural for the movies. Stuart Erwin first essayed the role in *Palooka* ('34), with Jimmy Durante as the redoubtable Knobby Walsh, Joe's excitable manager. The Fisher strip had not yet reached the height of its popularity and *Palooka* was regarded as just another fight film. It was advertised with little reference to the strip. Warners attempted a series of two-reel slapstick comedies in 1936-37 which failed miserably. Ten years later Joe Kirkwood, a professional golfer with a striking physical resemblance to Palooka, took on the role in a series of Monogram features (*Joe Palooka—Champ, Gentleman Joe Palooka*). Leon Errol played Knobby Walsh, and after his death James Gleason assumed the part.

One of the strip's most hilarious characters, the indestructible

man-mountain from West Wokkington Falls—Humphrey Pennyworth—was introduced into the later films of Monogram's
Palooka series and did much to prolong its popularity. Robert
Coogan of *Sooky,* now grown and rotund, was the first Humphrey. He was replaced by Rufe Davis, a hillbilly singer who
really looked like Humphrey Pennyworth. Monogram's Palooka
series ended in 1951 with *Joe Palooka in the Triple Cross.*

Chic Young's comedy of married life, "Blondie," was an
overnight sensation and for many years ran a close race with
"Lil Abner" as the most popular newspaper comic strip. The
antics of shapely but dumb Blondie, and the bumbling of Dagwood, needed little adaptation for the screen. Columbia began
its series of features in 1938 with *Blondie* and released two a
year for the next thirteen years. Penny Singleton and Arthur
Lake were ideally cast in the leads, and most of the favorites of
the strip—Baby Dumpling, Cookie, Mr. Dithers, and the dog
Daisy and her raft of hilarious pups, appeared throughout the
series. The earlier films, directed by Frank R. Strayer, were the
best, and in later years the series became contrived and leaned
heavily on slapstick. *Blondie* was revived briefly, and unsuccessfully, in television, with Arthur Lake repeating his role of
Dagwood. Pamela Britton, a cute blonde from Broadway, was
Blondie.

To replace the *Blondie* series, Columbia in 1951 brought out
Gasoline Alley, based on Frank King's comic strip in which
"nothing ever happens." Nothing happened in the movie version
either, and after a second film, *Corky of Gasoline Alley,* the
series was dropped. Scotty Beckett made a good Corky, but
Jimmy Lydon was unconvincing as Skeezix.

As a comic strip, Al Capp's "Lil Abner" has long been a
national institution. A broad satire on American life—a fact
not recognized by some, or admitted by others—it has poked
fun at political and social mores for over twenty-five years. None
of the strip's hillbilly humor and charm, or its pungent satire,
was to be found in the film called *Lil Abner* ('40), produced by
Lou Ostrow, who created the Andy Hardy pictures for M-G-M.
The comic strip's characters were represented through the use
of grotesque make-up, and in some cases by masks, which
heightened the unreality of the plot. An unknown, Granville
Owen, who had Abner's physical attributes, was miscast in the
lead. Martha O'Driscoll was a ringer for Daisy Mae, and
Buster Keaton was hilarious as Lonesome Polecat, the deadpan

The Western comic strip character, Red Ryder, came to the screen several times. Here is Jim Bannon in the role of Red Ryder in The Fighting Redhead *(1950). Also Marin Sais, Emmett Lynn, and Billy Hammond (as Little Beaver).*

Indian. Several years later Columbia turned out a few poorly done Lil Abner cartoons.

After its success as a Broadway musical, *Lil Abner* came to the screen again in 1959. Except for one or two rousing numbers by a talented troupe of dancers, it was pure corn with a type of humor that went out with vaudeville. Once again, the use of grotesque make-up contributed to the unreality of the plot. Peter Packer, who created the role on Broadway, was as good as could be expected as Abner—his one and only screen appearance. The stand-out hit of Melvin Frank's expensive production was Stubby Kaye, a burlesque comedian, ideally cast as Marryin' Sam.

E. C. Segar's saga of the one-eyed sailor with the corncob pipe, "Popeye," first came to the screen as a Fleischer cartoon in 1933. Its brand of constant mayhem was a success with juvenile audiences, and the series persisted for over twenty-five years, and is constantly revived on television. The *Popeye* films were appallingly alike, with Popeye coming to the rescue of

Olive Oyl after a last-minute application of canned spinach. Segar, incidentally, once drew a comic strip entitled "Charlie Chaplin's Comic Capers" for the Chicago *Evening Post*. Although Chaplin had licensed the series, he was not pleased with it and soon withdrew the rights from Segar.

Otto Soglow's "The Little King" comic strip was first planned as a Buster Keaton feature in 1933, with Marshall Neilan directing. The project blew up in the face of a series of difficulties, and the film was never made. Soglow then sold the rights to RKO Radio's subsidiary, the Van Beuren Corporation, for a poorly conceived group of cartoons released in 1933-34 (*Jolly Good Felons, Sultan Pepper*). Marge's *Little Lulu*, which originated in the *Saturday Evening Post* before being syndicated in a newspaper strip, had a fair run as a Fleischer cartoon series for Paramount in the late '40s.

The adventure strips, such as "Terry and the Pirates" and "Smiling Jack," have been particularly suited to screen serials. Universal's *Tailspin Tommy* ('34) was the first of many newspaper strips which the company brought out as chapter plays— *Flash Gordon, Secret Agent X-9, Ace Drummond, Radio Patrol, Buck Rogers, Adventures of Smiling Jack, Tim Tyler's Luck, Don Winslow of the Navy, Red Barry, The Green Hornet*, and others. Later, in the '40s, Columbia used several strips as the basis of such mediocre serials as *Tex Granger, Mandrake the Magician, Brick Bradford, The Batman and Robin, The Phantom, Blackhawk, Bruce Gentry, Hop Harrigan*, and *Brenda Starr—Girl Reporter*. Columbia also brought out two *Superman* serials based on that enormously popular comic strip (and radio show) of a mild-mannered reporter who uses his amazing strength and ability to soar through space to combat crime. Later, *The Adventures of Superman* was a ludicrous television series. (*Superman* also appeared in 1942-43 in an animated cartoon series for Paramount).

Chester Gould's jut-jawed detective, Dick Tracy, was introduced to the movies in four Republic serials—*Dick Tracy, Dick Tracy Returns, Dick Tracy's G-Men* and *Dick Tracy Versus Crime, Inc.*—in 1937-41. The late Ralph Byrd was quite effective in the title role. After World War II, RKO Radio made a series of feature melodramas out of Gould's horrible villains —Cueball, Itchy, and Gruesome (appropriately played by Boris Karloff). Morgan Conway was Tracy, but was later replaced by Byrd. Byrd could not escape his identification with the role and played Tracy in a cheap television series in the early '50s. UPA had a short-lived group of Dick Tracy color cartoons in 1962.

"The Lone Ranger" originated as a radio serial and became a newspaper strip in 1935. Shortly thereafter Republic made two serials around the masked rider and his Indian friend, *The Lone Ranger* and *The Lone Ranger Rides Again*. It became a pioneer television program beginning in 1948, and later its producers brought out two features, *The Lone Ranger* ('56) and *The Lone Ranger and the Lost City of Gold* ('58) for Warner Brothers release. Clayton Moore was most often seen as the masked champion of justice, although John Hart, Lee Powell and Robert Livingston were others who played the role. Tonto was portrayed by two Indian actors, Chief Thundercloud and Jay Silverheels.

Another popular western strip hero, Fred Harman's "Red Ryder," was seen first in a Republic serial, *The Adventures of Red Ryder* ('40), with Don Barry in the lead. It then became a popular feature western series with Barry, Allan Lane, Bill Elliott and Jim Bannon appearing successively as Ryder.

Warners' *The Adventures of Jane Arden* ('39) retained little more than the title of the Monte Barrett-Russell E. Ross strip, although lovely Rosella Towne was an attractive foil for some very ordinary villains. Universal's *Jungle Jim* ('37) was a twelve-episode serial in which Grant Withers played the hero of the newspaper comic. In 1948 Johnny Weissmuller, too old to play Tarzan any longer, took over the role in an incredibly bad series of potboilers. Weissmuller dead-panned it through innumerable wrestling matches with alligators and encounters with pygmys, and played straight man to a boring chimpanzee. Much of the jungle footage consisted of badly matched stock shots. After torturing theater audiences for several years, *Jungle Jim* moved to television, again with Weissmuller.

Harold Foster's beautifully drawn "Prince Valiant" faithfully re-created the legends of King Arthur. But 20th Century-Fox's Cinemascope feature of 1954, despite lush settings and a top budget, was routine knighthood cinematics. Robert Wagner in the title role behaved like a high school boy in a bad wig.

Universal-International's *Up Front* ('51) capitalized on the Bill Mauldin cartoons of World War II. Little more than slapstick, it had none of the ironies of Mauldin's perceptive looks at the tragedy of war. A similar fate befell Bruce Bairnsfather's

The first version of Al Capp's Li'l Abner *starred Granville Owen as Abner and Martha O'Driscoll as Daisy Mae (RKO, 1940).*

"The Better 'Ole" drawings of World War I. Neither the British film of 1918 nor the Syd Chaplin feature of 1926 did justice to the original. *The Sad Sack* ('57), a Jerry Lewis training-camp comedy, had little identification with the wartime strip of a befuddled, always fouled-up draftee. *Dondi* ('61), based on Gus Edson's surprise comic-strip success, concerned an Italian war orphan smuggled into the United States by a group of GI's.

Several comic strips have evolved from motion pictures. All of Walt Disney's principal cartoon characters—Mickey Mouse, Donald Duck, Pluto, etc.—star in their own newspaper strips. After the success of his *Song of the South* ('46), Disney created a popular comic strip featuring the Uncle Remus tales of Joel Chandler Harris. Pat Sullivan's *Felix the Cat,* which originated in movies, was even better known to newspaper readers. Richard Hall's "Patsy" was patterned after Shirley Temple, and Martha Orr's "Apple Mary" was similar to the central characters in Frank Capra's *Lady for a Day* (and, in the remake version, *Pocketful of Miracles*). After the success of *Show Girl* ('28), starring Alice White, J. P. McEvoy developed a popular strip out of its characters which eventually became "Dixie Dugan." The cycle came full circle in 1943 when 20th Century-Fox starred Lois Andrews in a picture by that name. (Another McEvoy strip provided the basis for Paramount's *The Potters*, a W. C. Fields vehicle of 1927). A short-lived newspaper strip was inspired by Max Fleischer's *Betty Boop* cartoons—which, in turn, seemed to have been inspired by movie actress Helen Kane, the "Boop-Boop-a-Doop" girl. *Betty Boop* on the screen often contained guest appearances of such comic-strip characters as Swinnerton's "Little Jimmy," Carl Anderson's "Henry," Soglow's "The Little King," and others. Some other familiar screen characters, originally drawn from novels, that became comic strips were Tarzan, Charlie Chan, and King of the Royal Mounted.

Although no longer a subject for feature motion pictures, newspaper comic strips continue to find their way into television. *Dennis the Menace,* based on Hank Ketcham's mischievous little boy, was seen for years before Jay North outgrew the part. *Hazel,* starring Shirley Booth as Ted Key's laconic maid in the *Saturday Evening Post,* has been even more popular. As evidence of its influence, television has now begun to inspire comic strips— *I Love Lucy, Dragnet, Davy Crockett* and *Ben Casey,* among others. What is unquestionably today's most popular comic strip, Charles Schulz's "Peanuts," made its television debut in 1967 with a series of animated commercials for Ford Motor Company. It soon graduated to half-hour TV specials, which are frequently re-run, and in 1969 was expanded to a feature-length theatrical cartoon, *A Boy Named Charlie Brown.* Despite the appeal of Charlie Brown, the fussbudget Lucy, and the dog Snoopy, it did not hold up for 85 minutes of running time, and appealed only to children.

5

MARY PICKFORD'S
DIRECTORS

*A*T sixteen, during her first days at the brownstone
Biograph Studio on New York's 14th Street, Mary
Pickford discerned "a steady, brilliant flame of genius"
in D. W. Griffith. But she also found him "arrogant and
pompous" and quarreled with him.

Some of her early screen hits were directed by the eccentric
Edwin S. Porter, who introduced the principle of film editing
in his pioneer *Life of an American Fireman* and *The Great
Train Robbery*. Today she dismisses Porter as "a mechanic
forever tinkering with the camera . . . with not the slightest
interest in acting or the dramatic aspects of motion pictures."

Of her other directors, Miss Pickford thought Cecil B.
De Mille, who bested her in a battle of wills, to be "terrifying,"
and had a lifelong uneasiness in his presence. She was annoyed
by Sidney Olcott's pedestrian pace in movie making, unimpressed
by Thomas H. Ince, admired the ill-fated William Desmond
Taylor for his elegant manners, and believed Allan Dwan a
"man's director" better suited to the swashbuckling vehicles of
Douglas Fairbanks.

She disliked Ernst Lubitsch from the start—"a perfect
autocrat on the set"—and was horrified at his bad manners.
But she never had any bitterness toward him for the failure of
Rosita—"our association was just a mistake," she says—and is
proud to have started him on his meteoric rise in Hollywood.
In 1929 her sensitive performance in *Coquette,* an atypical Pickford role, won her an Academy Award, but she insists her director, Sam Taylor, had nothing to do with that.

Sentiment, friendship, and family ties have figured im-

Edwin S. Porter, director of the history-making The Great Train Robbery *in 1903, also directed Mary Pickford's first feature films.*

portantly in the selection of her directors. She gave a much-needed boost to Paul Powell, an old friend from the Griffith days who had bogged down in a series of commonplace films, by letting him direct *Pollyanna.* At the height of her success she entrusted two expensive pictures (*Through the Back Door* and *Little Lord Fauntleroy*) to her brother Jack, at a time when he had neither the experience nor the inclination to be a director. Earlier, she permitted her scenarist and close friend, Frances Marion, who had directed only one other movie, to direct her in *The Love Light,* which was a failure.

Among the twenty-seven directors who helped shape her spectacular career, the Pickford admiration is clearly reserved for the remarkable French emigré, Maurice Tourneur, and for several promising youngsters she helped push into the limelight

—Alfred E. Green, Sidney Franklin, and William Beaudine—
and most of all, for the mercurial and inventive Marshall
"Mickey" Neilan, director of her most popular films. However,
she has a deep respect for Griffith, De Mille and perhaps
Lubitsch, but it is colored by unforgettable personal conflicts.

The Pickford movies, particularly those made by her own
company after 1917, are invariably well but not brilliantly
directed. The distinctive, dominant Pickford personality inevitably overshadows the direction. *Secrets* is not among the
best work of Frank Borzage, *The Little American* and *Romance
of the Redwoods* are second-rate De Mille, and *Rosita* is an
anomaly among Lubitsch films—yet all have the mark of talent
and craftsmanship. Only Neilan, with his flare for comedy
devices so ideally suited to the Pickford requirements, seemed
able to give his direction a uniquely personal quality.

While the weight of her opinions and wishes as star, producer
and financier must have been strongly felt, Mary Pickford resists
the suggestion that she more or less directed her own pictures
(excluding from consideration those she did with Griffith,
De Mille and Lubitsch).

"I have always taken an active interest in my films from
beginning to end, from the script down to the editing and
titling," she says. "I tried to learn everything I could about
making motion pictures. But I *always* felt the need of a good
director, and I relied upon my directors. They were hired for
what they could contribute—new ideas and intelligent ways to
make my pictures better. They weren't expected to 'yes' me,
and I insisted they use their initiative and authority. Being my
own producer, I could have directed my own pictures, but I
never wanted to. I've had some of Hollywood's best directors,
and they didn't need anyone's help."

Sixty-one years have elapsed since Mary Pickford went to
work for D. W. Griffith at Biograph in 1909. Today, it is
difficult, if not impossible, properly to assess the Griffith-Pickford
relationship. Both have become legends, and legends have a way
of obscuring fact. Regrettably, the literature of the screen offers
little documentation. A definitive biography of Griffith, as well
as of Miss Pickford, has yet to appear, and her autobiography
(*Sunshine and Shadow*) offers only a few sketchy but candid
glimpses of the great director. She admits to trifling grievances
against Griffith, but is quick to temper her criticisms with
pronouncements of admiration for his genius. At their first

encounter she thought him hateful and boorish. Griffith seemed unimpressed by her Broadway engagements with David Belasco, told her she was too fat, called her acting wooden, and shocked her prudish sensibilities by asking her to dinner.

Other squabbles were to follow. Mary complained that the best roles went to Griffith's favorites among the Biograph actresses, and protested she was given the leftovers. He tried to make her jealous with unfavorable comparisons to Lillian Gish and Blanche Sweet, and on one occasion wounded her deeply by making fun of her dress. Once Griffith lost his temper when a scene was not going well and gave her a good shaking, where-upon Mary bit him as sister Lottie pulled his ears from behind. She says these quarrels usually resulted in her quitting and the contrite Griffith apologizing and begging her to stay. Her salary was always a source of controversy. When the company was boarding the train for California in 1910, she refused to go unless Griffith raised her ten dollars a week; Griffith called her bluff by threatening to take Gertrude Robinson in her place.

Despite these differences, Miss Pickford appears to have got along reasonably well with Griffith. They had stimulating arguments about acting—she felt he was inclined to let his cast overact—and he was impressed with her intelligent interest in the mechanics of movie making. "I used to sit for hours and watch him at work on the set," she said later. "It was fascinating to see Griffith direct, especially when he would come up with some exciting innovation. Sometimes he would say, 'What do you think, Pickford?'—and I felt complimented that he asked me. And yet, I believe he didn't really care what others thought."

Late in 1910 Miss Pickford broke away from Biograph and signed with the IMP Company. She now says the change was prompted by money—Carl Laemmle offered her $175 a week—but at the time she told a fan magazine that Griffith was making a machine of her. She complained he would tell her "every step to take, every gesture to make" and that it was difficult to add the slightest bit of personal interpretation to a role. "I was terribly afraid my acting was getting mechanical."

During the first eight months of 1911 Miss Pickford starred in a dozen pictures for IMP (*Their First Misunderstanding, Science, In the Sultan's Garden,* etc.). Her director was the brash young Thomas H. Ince, whose own career in movies had begun only the previous year. For Mary the IMP contract was a miserable experience. Her mother was upset at her secret

Famed movie director, D. W. Griffith.

marriage to her leading man, Owen Moore. Much of the shooting was done under primitive conditions in Cuba, where Laemmle had gone to evade the Motion Picture Patents Trust—and on the leanest of budgets. Ince and Moore did not get along, and Moore soon ran afoul of Cuban authorities after administering a beating to an Ince assistant, and had to be smuggled back to the United States.

Ince's talent was in the formulative stage and displayed none of the ingenuity that marked his later work as a producer. Miss Pickford is noticeably reticent to discuss Ince, and gives the impression she considered him of ordinary ability. She admits disappointment with the IMP films and says, "I never thought they were particularly good, but audiences seemed to enjoy them." (Years later, at the height of her fame, she was quite upset when they were repeatedly reissued to cash in on her popularity.) Although she may have been influenced at the time by Moore's distaste for the director, Miss Pickford and her second husband, Douglas Fairbanks, became close friends with

Ince and were mourners at his funeral.

With the expiration of the Laemmle contract, Miss Pickford worked briefly for Majestic Pictures—at $225 a week. It was an even more disastrous experience, as the new company was badly underfinanced and torn by internal dissension. George Loane Ticker, a promising young director at IMP, was assigned to direct, beginning with *The Courting of Mary* ('11). His career was cut short by his untimely death in 1921, soon after the release of his best picture, *The Miracle Man,* Lon Chaney's first major success. Although unaware that Miss Pickford had insisted upon it, Owen Moore was given an opportunity to direct several of her Majestic films. Their marriage was already headed for the rocks. Moore was drinking heavily, and they did not get along in this new relationship of star and director. He was abusive and sarcastic on the set, and openly resentful of her growing popularity. The Majestic films were incredibly poor, although *Little Red Riding Hood* ('12), with its fairy-tale background, brought hordes of children to the theaters. Moore's direction was inept, and he soon resumed acting.

In 1912 Mary abruptly returned to Griffith at Biograph— reportedly at her old salary, but with promises that her name would be billed. Griffith made a charming speech of welcome which was widely quoted in newspapers and trade publications. More than ever Miss Pickford found the Biograph actresses in an intense rivalry for the best parts, and she was soon faced with the competition of two fast-rising newcomers, Lillian Gish and Mae Marsh.

Her spasmodic differences with Griffith were renewed, and a major quarrel erupted when she refused to appear bare-legged and shoeless in *Man's Genesis*—she considered it unladylike— and was replaced by young Mae Marsh. In a fit of pique Griffith also gave the coveted lead in *The Sands of Dee,* which Mary had been promised, to Miss Marsh. On another occasion, during a noisy argument, Griffith gave her a "rude shove," causing her to trip and fall to the floor. Robert Harron talked her out of quitting, and Griffith later apologized.

Griffith did not take seriously her repeated threats to return to the stage, and warned that no manager would consider an actress who had been "tainted" by three years in the movies. Miss Pickford worried that her speaking voice was suffering. In the fall of 1912 she began casting around for a Broadway offer, and eventually David Belasco engaged her as the blind girl in his production of *A Good Little Devil*. Miss Pickford says that tears came to Griffith's eyes when she told him of her decision, but he wished her luck and later came to the opening of the play. Their last and best picture together was the charming *The New York Hat* ('12), written by the sixteen-year-old Anita Loos. At its completion Griffith again told her he sincerely believed her future lay in the movies, and that she was making a mistake.

In later years Mary Pickford and D. W. Griffith enjoyed a pleasant and more mature friendship based on mutual respect. Their association as partners in United Artists, formed in 1919 with Charlie Chaplin and Douglas Fairbanks, had its stormy moments, and she did not consider him a good businessman. "Griffith never had much sense about money," she says. "He would let his production costs get out of hand, and was haphazard in the financing and selling of his pictures. Some of them made money, but he didn't keep much of it."

Mary's notices were uniformly excellent when *A Good Little Devil* opened on Broadway, and she was much relieved when critics praised her diction. Long lines formed at the box office, and she was astonished at how widely known she had become through her movies. In the fall of 1913, shortly before the Rostand play was to resume after a summer layoff, Miss Pickford became ill and withdrew from the cast. Upon her recovery Adolph Zukor, whose Famous Players Company had made a deal to film *A Good Little Devil,* asked her to re-create her role of the blind Juliet. While the picture was still shooting the canny Zukor offered her a contract; after some haggling her salary was fixed at $500 a week, a goal she had set herself in the Biograph days.

Her director was the screen pioneer, Edwin S. Porter, a former machinist who became an early director-cameraman for the Edison Company. His intelligent application of the principle of film editing in *Life of an American Fireman* ('02) gave the motion picture exciting new dimensions, and he achieved even greater recognition with his historic *The Great Train Robbery* ('03), one of the first fictional films. Porter subsequently directed dozens of pictures for Edison, of which only a few (*The Dream of a Rarebit Fiend, The Kleptomaniac*) had more than ordinary merit. He was more interested in the technical aspects of motion pictures, and some of his work was influenced by the trick films of George Melies. In 1912 Adolph Zukor, after failing to lure Griffith from Biograph with a $50,000 offer, brought Porter into Famous Players as director-general. In this capacity Porter supervised the company's annual program of thirty to fifty films, and also personally directed the more expensive pictures with such stars as John Barrymore, Minnie Maddern Fiske, and House Peters.

A Good Little Devil was an incredibly bad movie, so much so that Zukor postponed its release several months, after Mary had scored in other pictures. David Belasco was engaged to work with Porter in a supervisory capacity, but he did not like the way the film was going and would have little to do with it. He did consent to appear in a prologue, shot largely for publicity purposes, in which he dreams of the play's characters coming to life (via double exposures).

Jack Pickford, Mary's playboy brother, a star in his own right but also co-director of Mary's Through the Back Door *and* Little Lord Fauntleroy.

Alfred E. Green, co-director of Mary Pickford's Through the Back Door *and* Little Lord Fauntleroy.

A third director, J. Searle Dawley, also appears to have had some hand in the production of *A Good Little Devil*. The peppery Dawley was an Edison refugee whom Porter brought to Famous Players as his executive assistant and director. Each evening Porter, Dawley, Daniel Frohman, Frank Meyer and other studio officials—and often Mary Pickford—would meet to discuss the progress of the various pictures in production. At one of these sessions Dawley (who had been temporarily assigned to work with Belasco) insisted that *A Good Little Devil* be photographed exactly as it had been presented on the stage, with the players going through the full text of their lines! The result was a painfuly dull, static film enlivened only by Mary Pickford's charming performance. Zukor was now certain she would be a big star and rushed her into *In the Bishop's Carriage* ('13), on which Porter and Dawley collaborated. Mary played a young girl who escapes from a poorhouse, enters upon a life of crime, but finally becomes a famous actress. It was followed two months later by *Caprice,* a sentimental love story based on Minnie Maddern Fiske's Broadway hit, directed by Dawley.

J. Searle Dawley had been actor, stock-company impresario, and playwright before coming to the Edison Company in 1907, where he directed more than three hundred films. Because of his stage experience, Dawley was originally hired to coach Porter, whose forte was action, in the rudiments of acting and characterization. He stayed on as Porter's assistant, and was soon writing and directing his own pictures. An ill-defined relationship existed between the two men. They collaborated in the direction of many pictures (including *Rescued from an Eagle's Nest,* in which D. W. Griffith made his debut as a screen actor). Porter was also a cameraman and photographed numerous films credited to Dawley. The latter appears to have directed some scenes for *A Good Little Devil,* although Porter was both the official director and cameraman. Over a period of years, at both Edison and Famous Players, Porter and Dawley worked together closely. Porter relied upon Dawley for suggestions and advice in the selection of story properties, and also in the development of what Dawley termed "emotional scenes."

Dawley continued as a leading director at Famous Players and other studios until the early '20s, when his career abruptly declined and soon came to an end. He is best known for sixteen pictures starring Marguerite Clark, Miss Pickford's principal rival as a sunshine girl (*Snow White, Uncle Tom's Cabin,* and the *Bab* series). Although he was not unaware of the importance of action in motion pictures, Dawley emphasized acting and characterization, and some of his published views in 1914 show a remarkable affinity for today's method theory of acting. He may have been thinking of Porter when, in the same article, he questioned that a cameraman could make a good director. "I have found," Dawley wrote, "that the mind of a cameraman is on a mechanical basis . . . and rarely on an artistic level." He could not understand Porter's incessant tinkering with the camera.

This criticism was not entirely applicable to Porter, but nowhere is Porter's unevenness of style more apparent than in *Hearts Adrift* and *Tess of the Storm Country,* Miss Pickford's next two pictures. *Hearts Adrift* ('14) was a melodramatic tale of a young girl and a married man shipwrecked on a desert island. Porter's composition of the exteriors brought out the natural beauty of the Pacific settings—"animated paintings," as one reviewer expressed it. He would spend hours trying to catch a certain effect—the sun's rays on the ocean or the rhythmic ebb and flow of the tide—and then rush indifferently through the dramatic sequences with his principals.

Porter offered even less guidance on *Tess of the Storm Country* ('14)—there is not a single close-up in the picture—and his direction wandered between technical impressiveness and an archaic lack of style more suited to his Edison antiques of ten years earlier. The "Porterian photography," as a tradepaper called it, helped obscure his deficiencies as a director. Porter's shots of the lonely fishing village are lovely, and the storm scenes are magnificently contrived—a tribute to his mechanical ability—but his handling of the plot and characters is confused and lacking in accent.

Mary Pickford succeeded in spite of Porter—*Hearts Adrift* and *Tess of the Storm Country* were enormous hits and the touchstones of her phenomenal popularity. Her principal recollection of Porter is his absorption in the technical details of filmmaking—"he was more of an inventor than a director," she says. "He knew very little about acting, and the cast got very little help from him." She recalls that he was experimenting at the time with three-dimensional movies.

Never fully at ease as a director or production executive, Porter retired from the studios in 1916 after completing a lavish series of dramas starring Pauline Frederick (*The Eternal City, Zaza*). His last several pictures were in collaboration with Hugh Ford, a gifted Broadway stage director and designer, who became increasingly responsible for the acting and characterization. (Late in 1914 Mary appeared under their direction in *Such a Little Queen*—while she thought it "a pleasant experience," she felt Ford was still limited by a "stagey" technique of direction and gave Porter only limited assistance.) To the end Porter continued as his own cameraman, even though he was in charge of all production at Famous Players. Later he headed the Simplex Projector Corporation and dabbled with talking pictures. His fortune vanished in the 1929 stock market crash, forcing him to work in a small machine shop in New York. Until his death in 1941, at seventy-one, Porter was more and more an eccentric recluse, forgotten by the industry he helped to create.

In 1914-15 Miss Pickford did nine pictures with James Kirkwood as her director. The flamboyant, hard-drinking Kirkwood was already on his way to becoming a legendary figure in show business. Aided by his distinguished good looks, he achieved some success on the stage opposite Margaret Anglin, Blanche Bates and others. In 1909 he became a leading man for D. W. Griffith at Biograph—where he and Miss Pickford became good friends—and three years later was made a director. Kirkwood had a lifelong admiration for Mary Pickford, and he claimed that they were once engaged to be married (presumably during their early days at Biograph). It is doubtful that a serious romance existed, as Mary soon wed Owen Moore, and Kirkwood married Gertrude Robinson, another Biograph performer.

Miss Pickford's films with Kirkwood had a wide range of story material that gave him an opportunity to demonstrate his versatility. The first, *The Eagle's Mate* ('14), was a drama of a wealthy girl kidnapped by a rough mountaineer. Kirkwood was also her leading man, as well as in *Behind the Scenes* ('14), in which Mary was a successful actress who gave up her career to be a poor farmer's wife. *Cinderella* ('14) was a disappointing rendition of the popular fairy tale. Mary was an astringent Nell

Mary Pickford in Little Lord Fauntleroy *(1921), directed by Alfred E. Green and Jack Pickford.*

This photo of Ernst Lubitsch (right) was taken on the day he arrived in Hollywood from Europe to direct Mary Pickford. Man at left is Robert Florey, then doing foreign publicity for Pickford and Fairbanks (August 1922).

Gwyn amid the costumed pageantry of *Mistress Nell,* a solemn Alaskan Indian half-breed in *Little Pal,* and a London slum beauty in the pseudo-religious *Dawn of a Tomorrow.* Two of her other Kirkwood films of 1915, *Fanchon the Cricket* and *Esmeralda,* were based on sentimental Broadway plays. The best picture of the Pickford-Kirkwood collaboration was *Rags* ('15), her first waif role. It had some wonderful sight gags (clearly derived from Mack Sennett) and occasional Chaplinesque overtones.

Kirkwood knew how to create a mood in Mary. If she had a sad scene to do, he would recall some disappointment or heartache in her life, and soon she would be weeping and ready for the camera. If she was to be gay or carefree, Kirkwood would come up with a warm memory of a happy event from her child-hood. Most of these details came to him from Mary's mother, Charlotte Pickford, who was constantly on the set. If Mary was to register fear, Kirkwood had only to predict some dire calamity in her future.

"I adored Jim Kirkwood," says Miss Pickford. "He was such fun, and a lot like Mickey Neilan. I suppose that is why he and Mickey were such pals. They worked hard, and they played hard—and they loved life. There will never be another pair like those two."

In common with Neilan, Kirkwood was never able to take his work seriously, either as actor or director. He was versatile and clever—and after *Rags* he could have gone on to be a top comedy director, but his career seemed to lack emphasis and direction. Quite possibly he never really liked the movies, and often told cronies at The Players that he "sneaked" into Bio-graph because he was broke and needed the $5 a day that Griffith was paying.

James Kirkwood continued to direct for several years, mostly for independent studios—he could work fast and keep within a budget—but his pictures had only moderate success. Among his films was a series of frothy comedies with Mary Miles Minter, a Pickford imitator. His last efforts as a director, *Bill Apperson's Son* and *In Wrong,* starred Mary's brother, Jack Pickford, and were produced in 1919 by a company owned and financed by the Pickford family. Out of friendship for Kirkwood, Mary probably used her influence to get him the assignments.

A resurgence of Kirkwood's acting career in the '20s brought him new success, beginning with the title role in Marshall Neilan's *Bob Hampton of Placer* ('21), and he appeared in numerous films over the next dozen years. He made occasional returns to the stage, scoring most strongly in Channing Pollock's *The Fool* in 1922. Kirkwood is reported to have lost $100,000 on a Broad-way production of *Edgar Allan Poe,* starring his second wife, screen actress Lila Lee. The 1929 stock market crash wiped out a million-dollar fortune, and after the mid-30s Kirkwood found it impossible to get a job. He lived out a precarious, alcoholic existence until his death, at eighty, in 1963.

"I recall Jim Kirkwood not so much for his illustriousness as for the fact that never in a lifetime have I seen an actor so gallant in adversity," said actor John Griggs. "He was ribald, raffishly funny, and he kept a fine perspective on the absurdities of show-business life."

In 1915 Mary Pickford made two films under the direction of Sidney Olcott, *Madame Butterfly* and *Poor Little Peppina* (released early the following year). An early screen actor, Olcott's reputation had been in the making since 1907 when he began directing for Kalem. He pioneered location shooting, making films in Ireland and Egypt, and in 1912 had turned out a highly successful although controversial drama of the Christ, *From the Manger to the Cross,* in Palestine. He was one of several top directors Zukor brought into Famous Players to handle an expanding production program.

Shooting on *Madame Butterfly* was barely underway before Miss Pickford and Olcott began to clash. She found him opinionated and "totally disinterested in anyone's ideas but his own," and when directing could be brusque and unreasonable. It was a marked change from the friendly Kirkwood set.

There were incessant delays as production ran behind schedule. Olcott was slow and a stickler for detail, and he and cameraman Hal Young often spent hours in planning the beautiful photographic compositions which distinguished the picture. Olcott was miffed when Miss Pickford complained to Samuel Goldwyn that the film had no action and suggested that Marshall Neilan, who was playing the male lead, had some good ideas for "pepping it up."

As the tragic Cho-Cho San, the Japanese girl who is deserted by her American husband, Mary was playing a role entirely different from the usual Pickford heroine. Her conception of the part and Olcott's were totally different—she favored a warm, sensitive portrayal, while Olcott thought her emotions should be rigorously suppressed in the traditional Oriental manner. Olcott had his way, and critics protested that her performance was cold and wooden.

She also felt the picture needed more contrast between the American boy and the Japanese girl, and suggested a scene of Pinkerton teaching Butterfly to play baseball be included—but Olcott would have none of it. Another tiff erupted over the costumes, and on one occasion she refused to wear the shoes which were provided, arguing that they were "not right."

The major quarrel which threatened to close down production on *Madame Butterfly* concerned Marshall Neilan. "Mickey was such a handsome, talented fellow, and I knew he would be a big star," says Miss Pickford, "but Olcott resented him and picked at him. Mickey had an Irish temper of his own and could always find ways to make Olcott look ridiculous.

"In one of the big climactic scenes of *Madame Butterfly,* Olcott kept Mickey's back to the camera, more or less ignoring him, when obviously Mickey, as Lieutenant Pinkerton, had to be an important part of the scene to make it hold together dramatically. I kept insisting Olcott feature him to better advantage. He refused, and we had a furious quarrel which resulted in Olcott stalking off the set.

"I was shaking with anger, and Mickey Neilan kept trying to calm me down. Finally, I called the company around me and proposed that we continue with the day's work until, I was sure, Mr. Zukor could replace Mr. Olcott. I said I would try, with the help of Mickey and the crew, to try and direct the scenes. Suddenly, Mr. Olcott swooped back on the set—he had been

Maurice Tourneur, the famous French director who directed Mary Pick-ford in Pride of the Clan *and* A Poor Little Rich Girl.

lurking behind the scenery—positively livid with rage. He assured me that no one but Sidney Olcott would ever direct any scenes for *Madame Butterfly*. Then it was my turn to walk off the set."

Adolph Zukor brought his troubled star and director together, and Miss Pickford says she and Olcott "came to an understanding about some things" and that he was "somewhat easier" to work with after that. *Madame Butterfly* was completed and acclaimed as an artistic success—but Mary's fans did not like her as a Japanese girl who commits suicide.

Several months later Olcott directed Miss Pickford in *Poor Little Peppina,* a comedy drama of an American girl who is kidnapped and raised in Italy and later returns to the United States seeking her parents. Mary says she agreed to work with Olcott again because Zukor asked her to—she does not recall why he was so insistent. "We got through *Poor Little Peppina* all right, but only because I would bite my lips and do as I was told to avoid making trouble. Zukor would pat me on the back and mollify me when I complained about Olcott, and I resolved never to work again with him." Until his retirement in 1928 Olcott continued to direct such top stars as Marion Davies, Gloria Swanson and Rudolph Valentino in a long series of box-office successes.

After the fiasco with Sidney Olcott, Miss Pickford appeared in three films directed by John B. O'Brien, all released in 1916— *The Foundling, The Eternal Grind,* and *Hulda from Holland*. O'Brien is undoubtedly the least known of her directors, and his name is now forgotten. He played juvenile leads with the Augustus Thomas stock company before joining Essanay in 1910 as an actor and assistant to Broncho Billy Anderson. After directing briefly at Universal, O'Brien joined the new Mutual Company and under the supervision of D. W. Griffith turned out numerous films with Lillian Gish, Blanche Sweet, Robert Harron, Mae Marsh, Wallace Reid, and other Griffith stars. After 1920 he did only a few cheap westerns and soon vanished from the studios.

The O'Brien films were followed by *Less Than the Dust* ('16), in which Miss Pickford played a native girl of India who was a thief. She admits it was "terrible" and says, "I don't think anyone liked it"—yet most of the published reviews were favorable. Her director, John Emerson, was a promising playwright and stock company director before entering the

Thomas H. Ince directed Mary Pickford in many of her Imp films in 1911. He later became a famous Hollywood producer.

movies as actor, writer and director for D. W. Griffith. Utilizing some engaging scripts by Anita Loos, whom he later married, Emerson directed a number of saucy comedies with Norma and Constance Talmadge and the budding Douglas Fairbanks (*His Picture in the Papers*). The fault of *Less Than the Dust* lay in an absurd script—not by Miss Loos—and its unsuitability to Miss Pickford. Although Mary enjoyed working with Emerson, he elected to return to the Fairbanks unit to direct the acrobatic star in a series of amusing comedy dramas (*The Americano, Wild and Woolly, Down to Earth*). In the '20s Emerson gave up directing to collaborate with Miss Loos on several Broadway plays, later returning to Hollywood as a writer and producer at MGM (*San Francisco*).

Mary Pickford's next two pictures, *Pride of the Clan* and

A Poor Little Rich Girl, released early in 1917, were directed by the brilliant Frenchman, Maurice Tourneur. Brought to America six years earlier by the Eclair Company, Tourneur was just beginning to come into recognition with an individualized, esthetic approach to film construction. In later years his stylized technique would win him a secure place in motion picture history with such artistic triumphs as *Victory, Treasure Island, The Last of the Mohicans, Prunella,* and *The Blue Bird.*

Miss Pickford calls her association with Tourneur "a delightful experience" and says he was "not at all temperamental . . . a most charming man, very serious and painstaking in his work." He helped her to realize the importance of visual values— settings, composition of scenes, and photography—but Mary could not be swayed from a long-held premise dating back to her Griffith days: a moving picture should *move!* She thought *Pride of the Clan* too much on the artistic side and lacking in action, and terms it "a disastrous failure." It did poorly at the box-office.

By contrast, *A Poor Little Rich Girl* was an enormous commercial success, and seldom, if ever, had Mary's legion of fans been more pleased. She played a very young girl, almost a child, who is mischievous and appealingly helpless. It was the first of a type of role which became, with various refinements, her stock in trade. Whereas the ill-fated *Pride of the Clan* had been wholly a Tourneur product, *A Poor Little Rich Girl* was truly a Pickford-Tourneur collaboration. His distinctive contribution was the imaginative, stylized direction of the dream and fantasy sequences, which took Mary into a world of unreality both charming and at times horrible and forboding. More than any other picture, except possibly his *Trilby* of the preceding year ('15), *A Poor Little Rich Girl* marked the beginnings of Tourneur's aesthetic technique which was to become his trademark.

For her part Miss Pickford, with the assistance of her talented scenarist, Frances Marion, brought humor and warmth to *A Poor Little Rich Girl*—and, most of all, the Pickford personality. She was wise enough to recognize the need for comedy and clever bits of business, and probably wished she had substituted funny gags in place of Tourneur's interminable, however beautiful, panoramas of the Maine coast in *Pride of the Clan.* Mary would spring these comedy touches without warning, and Tourneur would bring the camera to a stop, look bewildered and say, "Now, Mlle. Pickford, show me where in the script it says you are to do that."

Tourneur protested that most of the slapstick and clowning was irrelevant to the story. Although he did not think them funny, he permitted most of the Pickford-Marion additions to remain in the picture—possibly out of his great respect for her sense of film-making, especially about her own pictures. Mary began to worry that the gags weren't funny, that perhaps Tourneur was right, but her doubts were dispelled by a jubilant audience at the first showings of *A Poor Little Rich Girl.*

Ben Carré, the distinguished art director who was associated with Tourneur over a period of years, says Miss Pickford had a very good rapport with the French director. "I do not recall any friction between them," he says. "Tourneur was always open to suggestions for improving a scene, and he accepted many of her ideas. Tourneur was too self-critical to express satisfaction with what he had done. His usual reaction was that he should have done better."

Carré thinks Miss Pickford is probably right in an observation that Tourneur did not understand American film comedy. "At lunch time, when we talked about comedy, Tourneur never showed any interest. He found pie-throwing and other comedy clichés of the period rather disgusting," Carre remembers. "I doubt that he had a very strong sense of humor, either French or American. His thoughts were always with the artistic and the beautiful."

A minor conflict between Tourneur and Miss Pickford involved Carré. The actress had her own art director, but Tourneur refused to work with him and insisted Carré do the sets for *Pride of the Clan* and *A Poor Little Rich Girl.*

"My personal feeling is that Tourneur thoroughly enjoyed working with Mary Pickford," Ben Carré says. "For one thing, he preferred petite women and was more comfortable with them. Perhaps it made him feel more masterful." Carré thinks Tourneur was sorry not to have the opportunity to do other pictures with her, but Mary had already agreed to do two films to be directed by Cecil B. De Mille.

Tourneur remained in Hollywood until 1926, when he returned to France after a quarrel with Metro-Goldwyn-Mayer over the making of *The Mysterious Island.* He continued to direct in France and Germany until 1948. He lost a leg in a Paris automobile accident two years later, and died in 1961. Despite the brilliant virtuosity of his style Tourneur never directed a

Paul Powell, director of Mary Pickford in Pollyanna. *This photo was taken about 1914.*

truly distinguished motion picture. Unable to rid himself of the limitations of his early stage training, he could bring beautiful and unforgettable passages to some otherwise commonplace films. Shortly before his death he called himself "the Michelangelo of the movies." In retrospect, it seems to be an increasingly apt description.

Cecil B. De Mille was no stranger to Mary Pickford—nearly ten years earlier they had acted together in David Belasco's production of *The Warrens of Virginia* on Broadway. In the interim De Mille had gone to Hollywood and embarked upon a flashy career as a talented director. Nearly all of Mary's pictures had been made in New York. At Adolph Zukor's insistence she shifted to the West Coast for two films to be made under De Mille's guidance.

The extent to which Miss Pickford had begun to exercise a strong voice in the selection of her stories, cast and director, and in the progress of the actual shooting, was reflected in an ultimatum from De Mille that he would brook no interference from his new star. Fresh from his triumphs with a series of successful pictures with Geraldine Farrar, the opera star, De Mille had also reached a point in his career where he was accustomed to total authority.

Zukor in some manner prevailed upon Mary to place herself unreservedly in De Mille's hands, and she sent De Mille a telegram to that effect. At the time she was worried that some of her own comedy ideas in *A Poor Little Rich Girl,* to which Tourneur had objected, might have ruined the picture.

"I was absolutely terrified of Cecil B. De Mille," Miss Pickford says. "We made together what I consider to be two very fine pictures (*Romance of the Redwoods* and *The Little American*) with no real problems or controversy. I was quite honored to work with a man of De Mille's stature, but I never escaped, throughout all the years up to his death, the feeling of uneasiness with him. Even under the most delightful social conditions, I could not feel comfortable in his presence."

Mary admits she resented the complete control which De Mille exercised over *Romance of the Redwoods* and *The Little American*—and that she never forgot the mortifying telegram which Zukor persuaded her to send to De Mille. "But I lived up to my word to Adolph," she says. "If I didn't agree with the way Cecil was doing a scene, I didn't let him know it. I determined to give the very best performance possible, as I have always tried to do, so that he could have no criticism of me. I am glad to have had the opportunity of working with Cecil B. De Mille, but at the time it was like being in an iron cage. I determined to never again appear under his direction. I always had a great respect for Cecil and valued our friendship—but we were simply not professionally compatible."

De Mille wrote later that Mary was not difficult to work with—and that he gave her career a needed boost at a time when it was at a low ebb! The latter statement is grossly unfair, reflecting the depth of the De Mille ego, and one with which Miss Pickford rightfully disagrees. If *Less Than the Dust* and *Pride of the Clan* had been disappointing, Mary's personal popularity was of record proportions, and she had negotiated a lucrative new contract and the prestige of her own unit at Artcraft (a Famous Players subsidiary). Never had her career been in less need of De Mille's help.

In 1917, as part of the prerogatives afforded by her revised deal with Zukor, Mary Pickford insisted upon the brilliant, unpredictable Marshall "Mickey" Neilan as her director. In less than a year he turned out five of her best-remembered films —*Rebecca of Sunnybrook Farm, The Little Princess*, the superb *Stella Maris, Amarilly of Clothesline Alley*, and *M'liss*, each an extraordinary commercial success.

Her former leading man (in *Little Pal, Rags, A Girl of Yesterday* and *Madame Butterfly*) had forsaken acting to direct, first at Selig and then for Famous Players-Lasky, where he made a run of slick box-office hits with such stars as Blanche Sweet, Jack Pickford, Sessue Hayakawa, and Thomas Meighan. His magnetic personality, sharp wit and musical ability added to his charm, and at twenty-six he had acquired a reputation as a gifted, inventive director.

If any of his pictures can be said to have made Marshall Neilan, it was those he did with Mary Pickford. His emerging style—essentially an ability to clothe a basic plot in a stream of incident—was ideally suited to the Pickford requirements. Neilan was adept at devising gags and amusing bits of business, and he had a knack of producing revealing, subtle facets of characterization in his players. His personal rapport with Mary, born of mutual respect and a long, warm friendship, contributed materially to their collaboration. He brought a definition and stability to her screen character, at a time when she was perhaps confused by the differing Tourneur and De Mille experiences.

Mary has always felt that she gave her best performances under Neilan's direction. "He believed in creating a mood or emotion as a reaction to an external cause," she says, "and would invent all sorts of methods to produce the desired expressions and responses in me—things he would dream up in advance and then at the precise psychological moment unexpectedly blast them at me.

"I remember that in *The Little Princess*, in which I played a ten-year-old girl, the final fade-out called for me to change my expression from utter bewilderment to a slow birth of mirth— which was difficult to achieve convincingly because it is a far cry from the reaction of a child of ten to that of a young lady in her twenties. To accomplish this Mickey stuffed his pockets with silver dollars, and at the right moment started to recklessly toss them around the set. I was properly bewildered and then amused as I realized what he was up to—and the camera caught the whole transition of my emotions."

Neilan had an uncanny ability of remembering little bits of business, lines of conversation, quaint anecdotes, and interesting and amusing characters he had met—and using them, with refinements, in his films at the right place at the right time. He had a gift for compounding a gag, building laugh upon laugh— something he got from Mack Sennett, whom he much admired.

"We were doing *Daddy Long Legs,*" Mary recalls, "and there was a scene where Wesley Barry and I, as two rebellious orphans, had been thrown out of the orphanage without lunch because we were on strike against a steady diet of prunes. Wes and I decided to pray for food. The script called for a tramp,

Owen Moore, Mary Pickford's first husband and leading man, also directed some of her Majestic films (about 1912).

caught with a stolen lunch box, to throw it over the wall into our laps.

"Mickey immediately began figuring how to make it funnier. First, he had the lunch box hit Wes on the head. Wes looked up appealingly and said, 'Snappy service, Lord, but is such accuracy necessary?' Next, Mickey added a jug of cider, which we drank, becoming tipsy at once. By then he was in a passion of creative frenzy—I can still remember how his eyes popped with excitement—and he came up with a topper. A little fox terrier, which Neilan had seen the night before in a vaudeville act, was brought into the studio and added his bit of hilarity by lapping up the cider and leaning drunkenly against the wall, finally staggering the whole length of it on his hind legs. What the audience didn't know was that the dog, attired in a dinner jacket and trousers, did this nightly in his vaudeville act. We had a terrible time getting him to perform without the clothes!"

Neilan's versatility as a director, and Miss Pickford's as an actress, is well illustrated by the films they did together. *Rebecca of Sunnybrook Farm* added comedy and slapstick to Kate Douglas Wiggin's homey classic. *A Little Princess* was a melodrama of a young girl who lived in a dream world of imagined adventures and romances. *Stella Maris,* in which Mary played a dual role, was a somber drama with psychological overtones, culminating in murder and suicide. *Amarilly of Clothesline Alley* was about a sunshine girl from the wrong side of the tracks who rejected a wealthy suitor for a poor boy, and *M'liss,* based on the Bret Harte story, was little more than a western with some inventive comedy.

Later, Neilan would direct Mary in two more films, *Daddy Long Legs* ('19), based on Jean Webster's novel of an orphan who fell in love with her guardian, and *Dorothy Vernon of Haddon Hall* ('24), an elaborate costume drama of the England of Mary Tudor. Both of these pictures were made by Miss Pickford's own company, using her own money, and by then she was no longer tolerant of Neilan's frequent, costly absences from the set. "I would tell him, 'I would rather you put your hand in my pocketbook than steal the time and patience of my entire company, to say nothing of my own,'" she says. But Neilan would laugh and placate her with some inventive gag or bit of business.

"Mickey Neilan was a whimsical, genuine genius with many colorful, admirable facets," says Miss Pickford. "I don't think there will ever be another quite like him. If he had played his cards right, he could have been Hollywood's best and most successful director right up to his death—but Mickey was erratic. I didn't like some of the films he made after he left me, and I told him he was wasting his talent on those odd little pictures. I have always felt that I inspired Mickey—we were a good team."

With Marshall Neilan off to New York to direct a George M. Cohan feature (*Hit-the-Trail Holliday*), Mary Pickford made three delightful comedies in 1918—*How Could You Jean?*, *Johanna Enlists,* and *Captain Kidd, Jr.*—under the direction of William Desmond Taylor. In 1922 Taylor would be the victim of an unsolved murder case which wrecked the careers of two leading actresses, Mary Miles Minter and Mabel Normand, and brought pious outcries for moral reform in Hollywood.

While the details of his early life remain obscure, the Irish-born Taylor spent fifteen years on the stage in England and America, including a stint as leading man to Fanny Davenport. He acted for Ince's New York Motion Picture Company, and began directing in 1914 for Vitagraph and Balboa. Taylor was no stranger to the Pickford family. His first important work was as co-director (with Jacques Jaccard) on the thirty-episode serial, *The Diamond from the Sky* ('15), starring Mary's sister Lottie. (The producers had first offered Mary $4,000 a week to play the role, but she refused.) Taylor later piloted some of the shy comedies of Jack Pickford (*Tom Sawyer, The Varmint*), and Mary says she hired him because she liked his work with her brother.

Although he was a competent craftsman, Taylor's direction lacked style. He cannot be described as "brilliant" or "distinguished," the two adjectives so overworked in the sensational press accounts of the bizarre mystery. Taylor had a good grasp of characterization and at times could make good use of the camera. Given a good cast and script, he would usually turn out a well-constructed, entertaining picture.

"What I particularly remember about Bill Taylor were his beautiful manners," says Miss Pickford. "They were simply elegant, so natural and unaffected. He was a quiet, cultured man who read a lot—he would bring books to the set, some work on philosophy perhaps, and read aloud passages that interested him." She thinks he did a good job as her director, but believes he was helped by the detail of Frances Marion's scenarios.

Douglas Fairbanks and Mary Pickford teamed in The Taming of the Shrew *(1929).*

She cannot be drawn into discussing the Taylor murder, except to express her shock at the wild rumors that sprang up about him. "So many absurd things were told for the truth and widely believed," she says.

The World War I years of 1917-18 brought busy, exhausting days for Mary Pickford. In addition to starring in four pictures annually, she plunged tirelessly into war work—selling Liberty Bonds from coast to coast, visiting training camps and hospitals, appearing in government propaganda shorts (directed by Neilan), and even sponsoring a regiment of Hollywood volunteers. She and her mother were seriously ill in the widespread influenza epidemic. Mary had separated from Owen Moore, and despite fears that gossip might ruin her career she was often seen in company with Douglas Fairbanks.

The three Taylor films ended her contract with Artcraft, and in 1918 she organized a new, wholly self-financed company to distribute through the Associated First National exhibitors syndicate. An auspicious start was made with *Daddy Long Legs* ('19), one of the most successful pictures of her career. Marshall Neilan was back to direct, and at the last moment also replaced one of the leads (Albert Ray) who had fallen ill.

Miss Pickford was then directed in *The Hoodlum* and *Heart o' the Hills* (both '19) by the twenty-six-year-old Sidney A. Franklin. Beginning as an actor with Selig, he broke into directing with a series of kid comedies at Fox. Many of his early pictures were made in collaboration with an older brother, Chester M. Franklin. Shortly before the coveted Pickford assignments he attracted attention with several slickly directed dramas starring Norma Talmadge (*The Forbidden City, Probation Wife*), who recommended him to Miss Pickford.

Mary thought Franklin had promise, and was impressed by his ability to extract a good performance from an actress. "I was one of the first in Hollywood to advance the concept that certain directors are a woman's director, just as others are a man's director and do best with a male star," she says. "Many important people in the studios disagreed with me. Today it is a recognized fact, but back then no one seemed to think it counted for much."

Miss Pickford chided Franklin for not being more selective in his assignments—not long before he had done a Tom Mix western—and urged him to specialize in pictures with top female stars. "I told him he was wasting his talent in directing westerns, and to make use of his precious gift of bringing out a fine, sensitive performance from a woman," she says.

After the Pickford films, which were disappointing, Franklin was in increasing demand with such leading stars as Constance and Norma Talmadge, Greta Garbo, Norma Shearer, Luise Rainer, and Marion Davies (whom he could not make into a topflight dramatic actress). His pictures, such as *The Last of Mrs. Cheyney,* Garbo's *Wild Orchids, The Guardsman* (with Lunt and Fontanne), and *Reunion in Vienna,* became more and more sophisticated. He was occasionally guilty of unabashed sentimentality, such as in *The Dark Angel* and *Smilin' Through.* He made two versions of the latter—the silent with Norma Talmadge and a talkie remake starring Norma Shearer. In 1936, after completing *The Good Earth,* a rather unconventional

Franklin assignment, he abruptly gave up directing for a producer's berth at Metro-Goldwyn-Mayer. Franklin produced such fine films as *Mrs. Miniver, Madame Curie, Random Harvest,* and *Waterloo Bridge,* and was awarded the Irving G. Thalberg Award of the Academy of Motion Picture Arts and Sciences for "consistent high quality" of product. In 1956 he made a brief return to directing with a new version of *The Barretts of Wimpole Street,* which he had first done twenty-two years earlier. He retired soon after its completion.

Allan Dwan, who directed many of Douglas Fairbanks' pictures (*A Modern Musketeer, Robin Hood, The Iron Mask*), is Miss Pickford's idea of a man's director. In 1915 Dwan directed Mary in *A Girl of Yesterday,* best remembered for its exciting airplane stunts (by aviation pioneer Glenn Martin). Although she enjoyed working with him, she thinks Dwan was more at ease when handling a masculine personality. "The success of *Robin Hood* and his other Fairbanks movies illustrates what I mean by calling Allan Dwan a man's director," she says. "Allan was just right for Douglas, but possibly not for me." (Dwan is noncommittal, but wryly notes that he directed many of Gloria Swanson's best pictures.)

Miss Pickford's first release for United Artists, in which she was partnered with Chaplin, Fairbanks and Griffith, was *Pollyanna* ('20), a charming rendition of Eleanor H. Porter's saccharine story of a young girl who looked on the bright side of every adversity. Her director, Paul Powell, had given up a newspaper career to direct for Lubin in 1911. Later he was associated with D. W. Griffith, first as an actor and later as director for Griffith's Fine Arts unit, from which he had gone to Universal. Powell, an old friend of Miss Pickford, asked for a chance to do one of her films. She eventually permitted him to direct *Pollyanna,* which helped his reputation and got him a contract at Paramount. Despite some creditable movies, Powell never really caught on as a director, and his career ended soon after the advent of talking pictures.

Mary then played a drab London slavey in *Suds* ('20), an uneven jumble of Griffith pathos and Sennett slapstick that drew mixed reviews. She chose a relatively unknown director, John Francis Dillon—known in those days simply as Jack Dillon—who had acted and directed for a dozen companies, including a stint with the Mack Sennett menage at Keystone. Dillon also came from the official Pickford family, having directed both

William Beaudine, director of Mary Pickford in Little Annie Rooney *and* Sparrows. *This photo taken about 1924.*

Jack Pickford (*Burglar by Proxy*) and Jack's ill-fated young wife, Olive Thomas, who had accidentally swallowed poison while the couple were on vacation in Paris in 1920, (*Love's Prisoner, Follies Girl*). *Suds* gave his career a boost, and Dillon went on to direct such top stars as Colleen Moore, Richard Barthelmess, Corinne Griffith, and Clara Bow. A versatile, facile director, Dillon tended to take himself too seriously in later years, when his films began to lose their sparkle and warmth. He died on a hunting trip with Darryl F. Zanuck and William A. Wellman in the early '30s.

In 1920 Mary Pickford had the unusual experience of appearing under the direction of a woman, Frances Marion, her scenarist and close friend. The picture was *The Love Light*, a drama of a young Italian girl who discovers her supposedly

American husband is a German spy. It was one of her least popular pictures.

A former newspaper reporter and magazine illustrator, Frances Marion worked as a film extra before authoring *The Foundling*, one of Mary's early hits at Famous Players. A life-long friendship with the actress sprang up, and Miss Marion, a talented and prolific writer, scripted most of the classic Pickford movies. During World War I she went to France as a war correspondent, and soon after the Armistice married Fred Thomson, a Presbyterian minister and champion athlete who later became a popular screen cowboy.

Miss Pickford married Douglas Fairbanks on March 28, 1920, and soon afterward the two couples went on a joint honeymoon to Europe. During this trip Miss Marion showed the actress the scenario of *The Love Light*, which she had written

Mary Pickford in a scene from the 1922 version of Tess of the Storm Country, *directed by John S. Robertson.*

with Mary in mind. Miss Pickford was quite excited about it, and insisted that Miss Marion also direct the picture. *The Love Light* did not get into production for several months, and in the meantime Miss Marion made her debut as a director on *Just Around the Corner,* a film she did in New York for William Randolph Hearst. (For some unaccountable reason its release was delayed until after *The Love Light* came out.)

Mary says she had no qualms about working under Miss Marion's direction. "She knew what I expected and demanded in a director, and she knew my views on what made a good picture. Frances was very talented and imaginative."

Miss Marion persuaded Mary to make Fred Thomson her leading man. He was an inexperienced actor—*The Love Light* was his first picture—and his wife devoted much time to her husband's role. "At times I had the feeling we were making a Thomson film rather than a Pickford film," Mary adds. "Frances was very ambitious for Fred, and very much in love with him—and I think that explains everything."

Frances Marion feels she was qualified to direct through her experience as a writer. "I can scarcely recall a film made from one of my scenarios that I didn't sit alongside the director on the set during the entire shooting—to make the necessary changes in the script, or suggestions helpful to his direction," she says. "The training was invaluable. I had the experience of working on the cutting and the changes indicated by the many previews—not doing the physical work that directing involves, but just keeping an eye on procedure and calmly evaluating the scenes that were enacted before me."

The Love Light was not a popular Pickford movie. Audiences were weary of the overworked spy themes of World War I, and Mary was miscast in a somber and more mature role. Miss Marion was generally praised—"the direction is first class," said *The Moving Picture News,* but the same reviewer called the climactic shipwreck "phony" and "tame." Actually, it had been filmed in a raging surf, and assistant director Nat Deverich, who was doubling for Mary, nearly lost his life when trapped in an overturned fishing boat. He was rescued by Fred Thomson, Douglas Fairbanks (who was visiting the Monterey location) and several crew members. Cameraman Charles Rosher filmed the entire incident.

Although she continued to use Miss Marion as a writer, Mary Pickford did not engage her again as director. She says

Miss Marion had decided not to continue directing, and doesn't recall any discussion about her doing another Pickford film. Mary thought Miss Marion did a good job on *The Love Light,* but she now admits she would not have appeared again under a woman director. "With all due respect to Frances Marion, I simply felt I would do better with a male director," she adds.

Frances Marion says the reason she gave up directing was to push Fred Thomson's career as a cowboy star. Joseph P. Kennedy, father of President Kennedy, was interested in starring Thomson in a series of westerns for his FBO company. Miss Marion agreed to help get the project off the ground by supervising the initial pictures and supplying story ideas. After Thomson's death in 1928 she became an increasingly successful writer, scripting such famous M-G-M films as *The Big House, Anna Christie, Min and Bill, Dinner at Eight, Camille,* and dozens of others.

"Women can be good directors," Frances Marion said. "Ida Lupino has proved that—but there are too many factions in the studios that believe otherwise." She regrets that Hollywood quickly forgot the competent movies made before 1920 by such women directors as Lois Weber, Alice Blache, Ida May Park, Elsie Jane Wilson, Mrs. Sidney Drew, and later by Dorothy Arzner. Lillian Gish also tried her hand at directing, and so did several other early actresses—Cleo Ridgely, Grace Cunard, Helen Holmes and Mabel Normand. "It was a wonderful era of happy-go-lucky togetherness," Miss Marion says.

In 1921 Miss Pickford again surprised Hollywood by selecting another relatively unknown, Alfred E. Green, and her brother, Jack Pickford, to co-direct her in *Through the Back Door,* a charming comedy drama of a Belgian refugee.

Al Green entered the movies in 1912 as an actor in Selig's jungle dramas. Later he was an assistant to director Colin Campbell and had directed two-reel comedies. He was no stranger to the Pickfords, having been Mickey Neilan's assistant on *Daddy Long Legs.* Green had just directed several of Jack Pickford's films (*The Double-Dyed Deceiver, Just Out of College, The Man Who Had Everything*), and he and Jack were close friends, sharing a taste for good clothes and fast cars.

More surprising was the designation of Jack Pickford as co-director. Although he had been in movies since childhood, he had never directed. At the time he was restless and depressed over the death of his wife, the beautiful Olive Thomas. Miss

Mary Pickford in Coquette *(1929), directed by Sam Taylor. Matt Moore at left.*

Pickford says her brother had talked of becoming a director, and that she encouraged him, hoping that the change would not only improve his morale but open a new avenue to his career. But others believe Jack was indifferent to the idea.

Mary plainly had reservations about Jack's abilities as a director. She thought it best for him to share the responsibility with someone more experienced, and they quickly agreed upon Green. Although the two men were given equal billing as co-directors, they did not have equal authority. "It was understood from the start that Al Green was the senior director," Miss Pickford says, "and I never overruled him in the few instances when he and Johnny (Jack) disagreed. They were both on the set at all times. Johnny thought more in terms of gags and business, while Al was better with the acting and camera angles."

Charles Rosher, Mary's cameraman for more than twelve years, is more blunt about it: "Al Green did the directing. Jack would show up at the studio when he felt like it. He seldom took any active part other than suggesting a few gags."

Despite Jack Pickford's shortcomings as a director, he and Green were again teamed on Mary's next, *Little Lord Fauntleroy* ('21), one of her greatest hits. Upon its completion he resumed acting. Burdened by illness and personal problems, he was washed up in Hollywood when talking pictures came along. He died, at thirty-six, early in 1933 in the same Paris hospital where his first wife had died. Mary thinks Jack never recovered from the shock of Olive Thomas' death, although he subsequently married, and divorced, two other Ziegfeld beauties, Marilyn Miller and Mary Mulhern. "I have always believed Jack Pickford could have been a very fine director—or do just about anything in the theater or motion pictures that he wanted to do," says his sister. "He had so much talent and so many wonderful ideas."

On the other hand, *Through the Back Door* and *Little Lord Fauntleroy* made Alfred E. Green a big director overnight, and he received a flood of offers from other studios. In a long career spanning nearly fifty years he earned a reputation as a versatile, capable director of slick, commercial films. Green was responsible for the better silents of Wallace Reid, Thomas Meighan, and Colleen Moore. He moved easily into sound and guided such stars as George Arliss, John Barrymore, Douglas Fairbanks, Jr., Edward G. Robinson, and Bette Davis (in her Academy Award-winning performance in *Dangerous*). His biggest hit was *The Jolson Story* ('46). Green's career slumped off in the '50s, and he wound up directing *The Millionaire* and other television films prior to his death from arthritis in 1961. He never quite attained a top rank among Hollywood's better directors.

In 1922 Mary Pickford remade her early success, *Tess of the Storm Country*, this time under the direction of John S. Robertson. It proved to be infinitely better than Porter's version, a much more moving and dramatic film which delighted a whole new generation of Pickford fans. Robertson had been something of a Broadway matinee idol at one time, having appeared opposite Maude Adams in *L'Aiglon* and in many productions of Charles Frohman and Henry B. Harris. Entering movies in 1915 as an actor at Vitagraph, he quickly switched to directing and achieved recognition with a striking version of *Dr. Jekyll and Mr. Hyde* ('20), starring John Barrymore. Later he directed such favorites as Richard Barthelmess, Lillian and Dorothy Gish, Greta Garbo (*The Single Standard*), John Gilbert and Shirley Temple until his retirement in the mid-'30s. Robertson's warm personality and tasteful, intelligent direction made him popular with leading stars, and Miss Pickford was no exception. He died, aged 86, in 1964.

In 1922 Mary Pickford engaged Ernst Lubitsch, the brilliant German director of Pola Negri's *Passion,* to come to Hollywood to direct her in *Rosita*—by Mary's own admission the worst picture she ever made. This disappointing experience, in many respects a disaster for both star and director, began badly when Miss Pickford was publicly criticized for hiring Lubitsch. Anti-German feeling engendered by World War I still ran high in the United States.

Lubitsch came to America expecting to direct a film version of the opera *Faust,* with Mary as Marguerite. Robert Florey, then doing foreign publicity for Pickford and Fairbanks, was sent to the railway station to meet Lubitsch and his assistant, Henry Blanke (later a noted producer). Florey says Lubitsch talked of nothing but the sets for *Faust* and was anxious to get to the studio to confer with Sven Gade, the art director.

As soon as the amenities were over, Miss Pickford abruptly informed Lubitsch that *Faust* had been abandoned, and that instead he would direct her in *Dorothy Vernon of Haddon Hall,* a drama of Elizabethan England. Mary had been anxious to do Marguerite, but she now says her mother (Charlotte Pickford) "simply exploded when she found I wanted to play a young girl who kills her baby. She would not hear of my doing such a frightful role and warned it would ruin my career."

Lubitsch was furious at the fate of *Faust,* and aghast at the thought of doing *Dorothy Vernon,* which he considered trite and sentimental. He pretended not to understand the plot and to be confused by a multiplicity of characters, even though Miss Pickford had gone to considerable expense to have the script translated into German. Their daily conferences soon bogged down in his constant objections and complaints. "The fact was Lubitsch did not like *Dorothy Vernon* and had made up his mind not to do it," Mary says. She admits her own dissatisfaction with the scenario—"but Ernst was the problem; we could have licked the script difficulties." Finally, she postponed *Dorothy Vernon of Haddon Hall* and substituted *Rosita,* a costume drama in which she played a street singer of Seville who attracts the attention of the King of Spain.

Once shooting on *Rosita* had commenced, Miss Pickford got

along even less well with Lubitsch. He had little interest in her suggestions and would not brook any interference with his direction. Mary terms him "a perfect autocrat" and says that she went home from the studio each day and shed tears at the way the picture was going. Lubitsch's poor English may have handicapped his communication with her, although she feels it was not that bad, and that he used it as an excuse not to understand when they were differing on a point. She even hired an interpreter. Mary was also shocked at Lubitsch's personal manners and remembers he once ruined the wallpaper in her dressing room with his greasy, food-stained fingers. She says *Rosita* was completed by placing herself unreservedly in Lubitsch's hands and doing as he wished.

Rosita was not a popular picture—audiences did not like Mary in a more mature role that ineffectually combined a spirited Spanish girl and a Pickford Pollyanna. The reviews were mixed, but nowhere as bad as Mary seems to remember. Some of the comedy was quite sophisticated, and Lubitsch's direction, particularly of the crowd scenes, was generally praised. Many important critics felt that he handled Miss Pickford very well and brought a greater depth and sensitivity to her performance, despite her obvious miscasting. At the time Lubitsch confided to friends his fear that *Rosita* would bring his Hollywood career to a premature end, but he was soon engaged by Warner Brothers to direct the charming comedies of manners and morals (*The Marriage Circle, Lady Windermere's Fan*) which were the springboard of his enormous American success.

In 1923 Mary Pickford revived *Dorothy Vernon of Haddon Hall,* and her old friend and favorite director, Marshall Neilan, was assigned to the film. After Lubitsch, Mickey was like "a breath of fresh air," she says.

Neilan was then at the height of his career, having earned and squandered a fortune from a series of popular independent productions. He was broke, and Miss Pickford offered him $125,000 to direct *Dorothy Vernon.* Neilan was still late to the set and guilty of innumerable practical jokes, but there were none of the incidents which occurred on his own pictures when he would disappear for days at a time. He knew from experience that Mary would not stand for too much of his costly foolishness, and he also realized that he could not afford the adverse publicity of being fired from a Pickford film. Neilan was already involved in a fateful quarrel with Louis B. Mayer, M-G-M's powerful studio boss, which would eventually make it impossible for him to get a job in Hollywood.

Dorothy Vernon of Haddon Hall was a lavish costume drama enlivened by the Neilan bag of tricks, and was a huge commercial success. Mary again essayed a more mature portrayal as a petulant and headstrong young woman being forced into a worthless marriage.

Yielding to the incessant public demand, Miss Pickford returned to her waif roles in *Little Annie Rooney* ('25) and *Sparrows* ('26), both directed by William Beaudine. He was an old friend from the Biograph days, having been a handyman for Griffith. He had directed dozens of slapstick comedies for Mack Sennett and Al Christie, among others, before attracting attention with a series of features starring Wesley Barry (*Heroes of the Street, The Printer's Devil*). Mary says she hired Beaudine because of his knack for handling child performers—both *Little Annie Rooney* and *Sparrows* were kid pictures—and because he was a good comedy director.

William Beaudine had warm and revealing memories of Mary Pickford. "I met Mary in 1909 at the Biograph Studios," he recalled. "I was the property boy and Mary was the star. We were both working for peanuts. I was loaned to the Pickford Company by Warner Brothers, to whom I was under contract. They collected at least three times my salary—I guess that had something to do with the loan-out as Warners was in bad financial straits at the time. Mary had seen some of my Wesley Barry pictures, principally a good one called *Heroes of the Street,* and I think it was my knack with kids that sold me to her."

Beaudine admits his apprehension at working with Miss Pickford. "At first I was scared," he says. "The property boy-star relationship still persisted in my mind. I had the same feeling when I first directed Henry B. Walthall. I was very apologetic while giving Mary directions and almost afraid to ask for retakes. She must have sensed it, because about the third day of shooting on *Little Annie Rooney,* Mary took me aside and said: 'Bill, I am the producer, I am the star—do you want me to be the director too? If I hadn't thought you could do it, I wouldn't have hired you. Now, let's get back to work.' Needless to say, from that moment on I really *was* her director."

Beaudine says Miss Pickford was "wonderful" to work with. "She had great ideas for scenes and story construction. Her suggestions were invariably sound and, in my case, welcomed. She was a one-woman picture company!"

Little Annie Rooney was mostly broad comedy, with Mary as the leader of a gang of slum hoodlums who reform after her father is killed in a senseless fight. *Sparrows* was a more distinguished film, beautifully directed and photographed, which told of the hardships of a group of orphans on a Florida alligator farm. It had a Dickensian quality—an apt description by Edward Wagenknecht—that was marred by the intrusion of characteristic Pickford tricks.

The prestige of *Little Annie Rooney* and *Sparrows* put Beaudine in the top bracket of directors. For the next fifteen years he turned out dozens of features, mostly light comedies and melodramas, for virtually every studio in Hollywood. After 1940 he worked at Monogram, PRC, and other small independents, where even his quickies have been marked with professional craftsmanship. Beaudine remained active as director of the popular *Lassie* television series until shortly before his death in 1970. He was seventy-eight, and Hollywood's oldest active director.

In 1927 Mary Pickford made her last silent, *My Best Girl,* a comedy drama laid in a five-and-ten-cent store. It was also the last time she would appear as a sunshine girl, albeit a more mature one. *Photoplay* called it "the best picture Mary Pickford has made in years."

She had a new leading man, Buddy Rogers—ten years later he became her third husband—and a new director, Sam Taylor, who also directed the next three Pickford films, *Coquette* ('29), *Taming of the Shrew* ('29) and *Kiki* ('31).

Fresh out of Fordham University, Sam Taylor entered movies in 1916 as a writer on the popular Sis Hopkins and Ham & Bud comedies for Kalem. Later he was a scenarist at Vitagraph and a director of one-reel Century Comedies at Universal before joining Harold Lloyd's staff of talented gagmen in 1921. Lloyd soon promoted him to director, and Taylor was responsible for six of the comedian's classic silents—*Safety Last, Why Worry? Girl Shy, Hot Water,* and *The Freshman,* all in collaboration with Fred C. Newmeyer, and *For Heaven's Sake.* Lloyd recommended him to Miss Pickford for *My Best Girl,* and its sentimental story and abundance of gags were well suited to his talents.

At the urging of Lillian Gish, Mary selected *Coquette,* in which Helen Hayes had scored on Broadway, for her talking picture debut. It was a radical departure for Miss Pickford, a

Frank Borzage, director of Mary Pickford's Secrets *and many Norma Tal-madge hits, poses on the set of* Lucky Star *with Charles Farrell and Janet Gaynor.*

dramatic role of a mature Southern girl whose lover is killed by her father. Her voice was good, and she gave a striking, intelligent performance that won her an Academy Award.

Taylor was ambitious to do a serious picture and leave behind the slapstick comedies on which his reputation was based, and he welcomed the opportunity to direct Miss Pickford in *Coquette*. He was also trying to develop as a writer, and she permitted him to collaborate on the script. Taylor had never directed a talkie, but neither had most of Hollywood's directors, and the distinguished stage actress, Constance Collier, was brought in as a dialogue coach.

Miss Pickford was quite high on Taylor, both as a writer and director, and at the time apparently had no reservations about his ability to handle a dramatic theme. However, she now says Taylor's direction contributed little or nothing to her Academy Award-winning performance. She felt he was too shallow in his concept of the part and did not understand its motivations. "It was left up to me to make my role come alive, to get through to the audience's emotions," she says. "Mr. Taylor seemed to think the important thing was just to show me off in a sound movie—as though to say, 'Look, everyone, Mary Pickford can talk.' "

The making of *Coquette* was a difficult period for Miss Pickford. In addition to her anxieties over her talking picture debut and the unfamiliar problem of filming with sound, she was upset by a growing rift in her marriage with Douglas Fairbanks. She quarreled with Charles Rosher, her cameraman of many years' standing, and summarily dismissed him. *Coquette* was a gamble with her popularity—she was now a maturing thirty-six, no longer suitable for the waif roles—and her career was at a crucial point. For all these difficulties *Coquette* was excellent, and her sensitive portrayal was a great personal triumph.

Mary Pickford and Douglas Fairbanks then took the bold step of teaming as Katharina and Petruchio in a film version of Shakespeare's *Taming of the Shrew,* directed by Sam Taylor. The controversy as to whether it was a good or bad picture, or good or bad Shakespeare, has never been resolved. Miss Pickford has always thought it a poor picture, poor Shakespeare, and that she gave a poor and spiritless performance as the tempestuous Katharina. Fairbanks said later the idea to do the classic play came from Miss Pickford herself, Sam Taylor insisted it was Fairbanks', and Mary thinks it originated with Taylor. She says Fairbanks and Taylor were very enthusiastic about *Taming of the Shrew* and talked her into doing it against her better judgment.

Miss Pickford blames Sam Taylor for many of the film's shortcomings. She says he went into *Taming of the Shrew* deliberately intending to make a broad comedy tailored to the Pickford and Fairbanks screen personalities, rather than authentic Shakespeare. "I remember how furious I was when he remarked that the important thing was to keep the 'Pickford bag of tricks' in the film," she recalls. Mary thinks this approach weakened her characterization and sapped the vigor of her performance. She also believes Taylor erred in letting Fairbanks play Petruchio much in the offhand manner of d'Artagnan and Robin Hood, which robbed the part of the humor and warmth it demanded. But Miss Pickford apparently went along with Taylor and permitted the picture to be made the way it was.

Taylor had written a script of sorts for *Taming of the Shrew,* and more intelligent audiences were amused at the famous credit line, "additional dialogue by Sam Taylor"—of which, it turned out, there was very little. Mary was opposed to any such credit being given—"it was positively silly," she says—but was overruled by Fairbanks and Taylor himself. She feels it made a laughing stock of Taylor and had an adverse effect on his career. Taylor was undoubtedly hurt by the ridicule, and one magazine cartoon showed a bust of Shakespeare at the Library of Congress being replaced by a bust of Taylor!

The combination of Pickford and Fairbanks proved an irresistible lure, and if *Taming of the Shrew* was not classic Shakespeare, it was certainly box-office. Most audiences did not like the picture. It was too highbrow for the average moviegoer, who tired of the excessive dialogue, and it disappointed discriminating Shakespeare lovers. A poor word-of-mouth may have hurt the film, and returns from second runs were below expectations.

In fairness to Sam Taylor, *Taming of the Shrew* is not an entirely poor rendition of Shakespeare's play. He had tampered little with the dialogue, and he was not too insistent upon retaining the "Pickford bag of tricks." Mary's performance is not as poor or spiritless as she seems to think, but neither is it entirely divorced from her Pollyannaisms. Taylor apparently had much more difficulty in coaxing a good Petruchio from Douglas Fairbanks, despite the adaptability of the actor's physical qualities to the role. (Fairbanks was exceptionally difficult throughout the shooting of *Taming of the Shrew,* coming late to the set without knowing his lines, quarreling with Miss Pickford, and adamantly refusing Taylor's requests for retakes.) The acting in the minor roles is rather poor, suffering from excessive mannerisms and stilted dialogue delivery.

Taylor was undoubtedly responsible for an oversupply of slapstick, clearly out of the Mack Sennett custard pie school and not of the type of comedy usually associated with the play. For most audiences this clowning around was the best part of the picture. Taylor said later the addition of this low comedy was necessary to broaden the public appeal of the film, and denied that he ever intended to make a faithful version of the Shakespeare classic.

Sam Taylor's screen work, other than the Lloyd and Pickford

films, is of negligible value. Soon after the release of *My Best Girl* he was called in to complete John Barrymore's *Tempest,* a drama of the Russian revolution. Two previous directors, Viatchelav Tourjansky and Lewis Milestone, had given up in disgust. (It was the second fiasco of the brilliant Tourjansky's American career—earlier he had been fired in the midst of a Tim McCoy western at M-G-M). *Tempest* was dull and unbelievable, and marred by overly broad comedy and some incredibly hammy acting by John Barrymore and Louis Wolheim. Taylor was then scheduled to do *Lady of the Pavements* for D. W. Griffith, for which he had written the screen play, but Griffith eventually directed it himself. After *Taming of the Shrew,* Taylor directed Norma Talmadge in a mediocre costume drama, *DuBarry—Woman of Passion* ('30), which hastened the end of her career.

However disappointed Miss Pickford may have been with Taylor's handling of *Taming of the Shrew,* she once more retained him as her director—this time for *Kiki* ('31), based on the old Belasco play, for which Taylor also wrote the scenario. Mary was miscast as a mature hoyden, and her role called for her to sing and dance, which she did creditably. She says *Kiki* was "a misadventure"—and of Taylor only that she "decided not to use him again.". The parting was amicable.

Taylor's career was soon over. In 1931 he signed with Fox and directed three pictures—*Devil's Lottery* (with Elissa Landi), *Skyline,* and a fairly good Will Rogers vehicle, *Ambassador Bill.* After a very cheap and mediocre Slim Summerville-Zasu Pitts comedy for Universal, *Out All Night* ('33), he was idle for months. The following year Harold Lloyd took him back to direct *The Cat's-Paw,* but the spark of their earlier association was gone. In 1935 he directed Hal Roach's *Vagabond Lady,* a cute and sophisticated comedy with Robert Young and Evelyn Venable. It was his last assignment for nearly ten years. During World War II he reappeared briefly to direct Laurel & Hardy in a feature comedy, *Nothing but Trouble,* for M-G-M. His death in 1958 went virtually unnoticed.

In 1932 Mary Pickford began work on what would be her last picture, *Secrets.* She had tried unsuccessfully to film it two years earlier with Marshall Neilan as director. Everything went wrong—she was upset by her disintegrating marriage with Douglas Fairbanks, the script was poor and confused, her leading man (Kenneth MacKenna) photographed much too young, and Neilan was no longer so creative and imaginative. Miss Pickford abruptly shut down production with less than a third of the film completed, wrote off a $300,000 loss and burned the negative. No explanations were made to the press, and Neilan was assumed by many to have been responsible for the fiasco. It injected a note of bitterness into the Pickford-Neilan friendship which was never completely overcome.

For her second attempt at *Secrets* Miss Pickford hired Frank Borzage to direct. Winner of two Academy Awards (for *Seventh Heaven* and *Bad Girl*), he was much in demand, and Mary paid him a handsome fee for the assignment. She says she selected Borzage because of his success with sentimental drama and ability to coax a good performance from his female stars. Borzage was not well physically during much of the time *Secrets* was in production, but he worked conscientiously. Under his direction Miss Pickford gave her best performance since *Coquette*, but the picture was old-fashioned, maudlin, and depressing. Leslie Howard was badly miscast in the male lead.

Secrets went unnoticed and did poorly at the box office. Mary blamed the film's poor reception upon its untimely release at the height of the Depression in 1933. She now thinks a successful comedy might have prolonged her career.

Mary's decision to retire from the screen was not immediately made. Her brother Jack died in 1933, and her sister Lottie in 1936. She divorced Douglas Fairbanks in 1935, and soon afterward became ill and underwent extensive surgery. For a long time she was in no shape, physically or emotionally, to face up to the task of doing another picture. She read many scripts and stories which were brought to her, but none of them seemed right—she was now in her forties and no longer suited to romantic leads. Eventually she decided to make it a permanent retirement, bringing to a close a golden era in motion pictures.

6

COLLEEN MOORE

*T*O most persons Colleen Moore was the perfect flapper of the '20s.

She effectively combined in her screen character the madcap, pleasure-crazed, emancipated modern, and an innocent young woman caught up in the complexities of an era of flaming youth—a sort of naughty but nice jazz-age Cinderella who ended up on top without sacrificing her principles.

Her success was phenomenal. At one time she earned $12,500 a week—big money in those days—and her frothy comedies made huge profits. She set the styles in American glamor and fashion, and her severe Dutch-boy bob plagued a whole generation of little girls.

Essentially a natural comedienne and dancer, Colleen Moore was also a gifted dramatic actress, as her performances in *So Big* and *The Power and the Glory* will testify. Although her voice recorded well, her career was suddenly, inexplicably ended soon after talking pictures came. The vogue for flappers had waned, and she failed to re-establish herself in other roles. Whatever the reason for her decline—some said she was too rich to care—Colleen Moore left filmdom with a legacy of sixty pictures spiced with inventive comedy and touching pathos. She had a captivating personality which combined charm and Irish pluck to produce one of Hollywood's brightest and best-remembered stars.

Colleen Moore was born Kathleen Morrison in Port Huron, Michigan, on August 19, 1902. Her father was a well-to-do irrigation engineer and most of her childhood was spent in Tampa, Florida, although the family lived at various times in Atlanta, Detroit, and Hillsdale, Michigan. She studied piano from an early age at the Convent of the Holy Name in Tampa and at the Detroit Conservatory of Music. The impressionable

Colleen Moore. Marshall Neilan gave her major opportunities in his production of Dinty *and later in* The Lotus Eater. *Later, when Colleen was a big star, she hired Neilan to direct her in* Her Wild Oat. *Colleen also appeared in* Social Register, *one of Neilan's last films.*

youngster was hopelessly stage-struck from the age of four. After seeing a stock-company performance of *Uncle Tom's Cabin,* she began organizing backyard theatricals with the neighborhood children and her brother, Cleve, who was a year and a half younger. Movies were her special fascination. Something of a tomboy, she adored Grace Cunard's athletic adventures in the *Lucille Love* serials. Other early favorites were Mary Pickford, Ruth Roland, Marguerite Clayton, and, prophetically, the impish Mabel Normand.

Her first contact with motion pictures came during the summer of 1916 when she visited an uncle, Walter Howey, the colorful managing editor of the Chicago *American* and the prototype of the managing editor in Ben Hecht and Charles MacArthur's

The Front Page. He called the press agent at the Essanay Studios and arranged for her to be an extra. She worked only ten times, and spent most of her vacation sitting on the extras' bench.

Contrary to one of the movies' most persistent legends, D. W. Griffith did not "discover" Colleen Moore. The tale goes, set down in a dozen film texts, that when Griffith was dining at her uncle's home, the teenaged Colleen put on a maid's uniform and made a grand entrance bearing the pot roast. Griffith is supposed to have been so stunned by the beauty of the lovely child that he offered her a contract and shipped her off to California to be a dancing girl in *Intolerance.*

"There isn't a word of truth in it," Miss Moore says today with a chuckle. "I didn't meet Griffith until I was an established star, and as for *Intolerance,* it was completed before I went to Hollywood."

The facts of Colleen's discovery were much less dramatic. Griffith was a friend of her uncle and asked his help when Chicago censors tried to suppress the orgy sequences of *Intolerance.* Howey saw the picture, was enormously impressed, and used his influence to get it past the blue-nosed censors. When the appreciative Griffith asked what he could do in return, Howey said: "Well, I have this niece who wants to be an actress and . . ."

"My God," Griffith cried, "another movie-struck kid!"

But he arranged for her to be tested at the Essanay Studios, and about fifty feet of film were shot. There were apprehensions she might not photograph well—she has one blue eye and one brown eye—but it could not be detected on the screen. The test was dispatched to California where Griffith saw it and approved. Miss Moore was signed to a six-month contract with Griffith's Fine Arts Company at a salary of $50 a week. Chaperoned by her beloved grandmother, Mary Kelly, a remarkable Irish matriarch who regarded movies with a suspicious eye, she arrived in Hollywood late in 1916, only a few months after her fourteenth birthday.

Fine Arts was in financial hot water at the time, although Colleen did not find it out until some months later. To meet the needs of his distribution contract with Triangle (in which he was partnered with Thomas H. Ince and Mack Sennett), Griffith had set up several units turning out cheap program pictures. Production details were left to his story editor, Frank E. Woods, and a group of promising young directors, mostly Griffith protégés— Chester Withey, Edward Dillon, Tod Browning, Paul Powell,

Robert Harron at the time Colleen Moore appeared opposite him in her first two films, Bad Boy *and* An Old Fashioned Young Man *(Fine Arts-Triangle), 1917.*

Elmer Clifton, and Donald Crisp. With a fortune sunk in the unpopular *Intolerance,* Griffith was harassed with financial and legal problems which kept him absent from California for months at a time. In March, 1917, he sailed for England with Lillian Gish and her mother to make a propaganda picture for the Allies, *Hearts of the World.*

The Fine Arts studio was a collection of bungalows and barn-like structures at the intersection of Hollywood and Sunset boulevards, and Colleen and her grandmother rented a small house a half-block away. Another Fine Arts starlet, Carmel Myers, lived nearby, and the two would walk to work each morning, giggling and chattering about the handsome leading men. At the studio she met a number of other promising youngsters—Pauline Starke, Bessie Love, Alma Rubens, Mildred Harris (with whom she shared a tiny dressing room), as well as such established stars as Lillian and Dorothy Gish, Robert Harron, and Constance Talmadge.

Although a little informal acting instruction was given newcomers, Colleen learned by doing. "I just listened to the director, and watched the other players, and somehow I got by," she says. Two days after her arrival she caught the eye of director Chester Withey, who cast her with Robert Harron and Mildred Harris in *Bad Boy*. In this comedy drama of small-town life she played a visiting city girl with long curls. Withey then put her in *An Old-Fashioned Young Man*, a drama about a naïve young man who gets involved in big city politics. This time she played a vamp who tried to lure Robert Harron away from his country sweetheart (Mildred Harris). She had to wear high heels—her first— and stumbled around so badly that Withey had another girl double for her in the long shots.

Her third film for Fine Arts was *Hands Up!*, a melodramatic and thoroughly unbelievable western directed by Tod Browning and starring Wilfred Lucas and Monte Blue. Colleen had one big scene. Locked in the attic of a bandit hideout, she had to project adolescent terror as she beat on the door and cried for her father. Said *Photoplay:* "Colleen Moore, in her naïve ingenuousness, comes nearer to being a genuine child than any other actress in her teens." Miss Moore herself says: "Except for that one scene, I was terrible."

At the end of six months her contract was renewed, but in less than a month Fine Arts folded and the studio was shut down. Henry MacRae, general manager of Carl Laemmle's Bluebird Photoplays, gave her the small role of the French villainess in *The Savage,* filmed on location in the San Bernadino Mountains. Monroe Salisbury and Ruth Clifford had the leads.

Weeks of idleness followed, and Colleen made the rounds of the studios with a print of her big scene in *Hands Up!* Director Colin Campbell saw it and was impressed, and arranged for a contract with the Selig Company. For Selig she made *A Hoosier Romance* ('18), a comedy about a young girl whose father wanted her to marry a wealthy but eccentric old man, and *Little Orphant Annie* ('18), based loosely on the James Whitcomb Riley poem. Colleen played an impish Pickford gamin who encounters unbelievable hardships, and Tom Santschi, whom Miss Moore describes as "old enough to be my grandfather," had the male lead. (Santschi was thirty-nine at the time!). Then the Selig Company also went bankrupt. "I was a jinx," Colleen says.

By 1919 things were looking up for her. Thomas H. Ince gave her the lead opposite Charles Ray in two pictures: *The Busher*, a baseball comedy (John Gilbert was also in the cast), and *The Egg-Crate Wallop*, a breezy drama of a country bumpkin who outwitted a gang of crooked boxing promoters. She also obtained smaller roles in two films which Paul Powell, another Fine Arts alumnus, directed for Universal, *The Man in the Moonlight* and *Common Property*. Two other breaks were as leading lady to Tom Mix in *The Wilderness Trail* and *The Cyclone* at Fox. In the latter she was kidnapped by opium smugglers and secreted in Chinatown, but Tom, a Northwest Mountie, rode the trusty Tony up two flights of stairs and rescued her. It was great, action-packed hokum.

Colleen Moore and T. Roy Barnes in So Long Letty, *Christie-RC, 1920.*

In 1921, Colleen Moore co-starred with John Barrymore in The Lotus Eater, *directed by Marshall Neilan. She played Mavis, the innocent native girl.*

Miss Moore was anxious to play light comedy, and in 1920 she signed with Al Christie, whose slapstick shorts were gay and amusing, if less inventive than those of Mack Sennett. She appeared in Christie's *A Roman Scandal* and *Her Bridal Nightmare,* both two-reelers. The latter was a typical Christie situation comedy broadened into burlesque through an implausible but delightful chase. The slight story (by early screen actress Ora Carew) concerned a young bridegroom (Eugene Corey) whose wedding clothes are stolen by a sneaky rival. When he doesn't arrive at the church the heroine (Miss Moore) decides to commit suicide, with hilarious, unsuccessful results. The hero is arrested for being on the streets in his underwear, but borrows a uniform at the station and finally winds up married after a riotous chase of the villain.

Christie then starred Colleen in a feature version of the currently popular Broadway musical, *So Long Letty*. Its bounce and cute comedy were tailor-made for her talents, but she had real competition from the scene-stealing antics of T. Roy Barnes and Walter Hiers. For the first time the fan magazines called her a "flapper." Her dramatic loan-outs in 1920 were rather dismal. In *The Devil's Claim,* a lurid oriental melodrama starring Sessue Hayakawa, she was a Hindu princess. Colin Campbell's *When Dawn Came* was a cheap production with a confused pseudo-religious story.

The first real impetus to Miss Moore's career came when director Marshall ("Mickey") Neilan called her for *Dinty,* a film he was making with his child star discovery, Wesley Barry. The part was a small one—that of a courageous young Irish mother, little more than a girl, who must face the hardships of the world alone. "I knew the moment I saw Colleen that she was just right for the part," Neilan said later. He was sufficiently impressed to ask Christie to release her, and signed her to a year's contract at $750 weekly. Fresh from directing Mary Pickford in a half-dozen of her best films (*Rebecca of Sunnybrook Farm, Stella Maris, Daddy Long Legs*), Neilan saw in Colleen Moore a potential star of the same magnitude.

After *Dinty* Neilan loaned her to King Vidor for the feminine lead in *The Sky Pilot* ('21), based on Ralph Connor's novel of a frontier pastor. John Bowers, Kathleen Kirkham, and David Butler were others in the cast. The picture, one the youthful Vidor did for his own company, was beset by financial troubles from the start—his backer, a Los Angeles society woman, withdrew, and Vidor asked the cast and crew to go without salary until he could get a distributor's advance. There were delays and setbacks due to the weather; it snowed when summer scenes were to be filmed, and remained sunny and beautiful when the script called for snow. Miss Moore did well in a demanding role, but the highlight of the picture was a stunning cattle stampede.

Neilan then cast her opposite John Barrymore in *The Lotus Eater* ('21). She was lovely as Mavis, the native girl who loves the shipwrecked playboy (Barrymore), who yearns for an unfaithful wife at home. The peculiar problems attending the production of *The Lotus Eater* are described in the chapter on Marshall Neilan. Filmed at the old Biograph Studios in New York because Barrymore was unwilling to go to Hollywood, it was repeatedly delayed by the parties and drinking bouts of Neilan

and Barrymore. Miss Moore has no recollection of these difficulties, and says: "I was still an innocent kid in my teens, young
and naïve. My mother chaperoned me throughout the shooting
in New York, and later in Florida. I guess I never knew what
went on."

John Barrymore, she recalls, was the soul of kindness. "I
was scared to death when I met him, and no wonder, from all the
tales that were told about him. But he was sweet and kind and
gave me many useful suggestions about my acting. Sometimes he
would gently turn me so that the camera would catch me at the
best angle, and years later I heard that he did the same for
Katharine Hepburn in *A Bill of Divorcement*. I never heard him
say an unkind thing, or use a profane word. He was charming and
witty and ever so debonair, and I adored him." As *The Lotus
Eater* neared completion Barrymore asked her to appear with
him in his new Broadway play, but Neilan, fearing she would be
tied up for months, would not hear of it. As it turned out, the
play flopped and closed in a few weeks.

Miss Moore then did another Christie feature-length comedy, *His Nibs* ('21), in which she was a foil for the homespun
antics of Charles (Chic) Sale, who appeared in seven separate
roles. Next she played the lead in an independent production of
Irving Cummings called *Broken Hearts of Broadway* ('21), a
tear-jerker about a chorine who loved a wastrel. Alice Lake,
Creighton Hale, and Johnny Walker were others in the cast.

Marshall Neilan, who had abandoned his independent unit to
work for the reorganized Goldwyn Company, then persuaded
Samuel Goldwyn to sign Miss Moore for four pictures. Rupert
Hughes, the popular novelist, was also under contract to Goldwyn. He was charmed by Colleen, and certain that she would be a
big star. Hughes did the script for her first Goldwyn picture,
Come On Over ('22). She played Moyna, a young Irish girl who
waited impatiently for her lover (Ralph Graves) in the United
States to send for her. But he was a feckless soul with an inability
to keep a job—and an eye for a blonde Fifth Avenue model
(Kathleen O'Connor). Tired of waiting, Moyna makes the trip
on her own. The complications that followed were packed with
fun, but there was the inevitable happy ending. It was Colleen's
first association with director Alfred E. Green, who was later
responsible for some of her best-known hits.

Her second Goldwyn film, *The Wallflower* ('22), was directed, as well as written, by Rupert Hughes. It just missed being

a success. Miss Moore was less effective as a tragically unpopular wallflower who blossoms into an American beauty, with the usual consequences. Richard Dix was fine in the male lead, and a promising young actress, Laura LaPlante, scored in a supporting role.

The success of these two films brought Miss Moore many offers from other producers. Hodkinson teamed her with John Bowers in *Affinities* ('22), a commonplace story by Mary Roberts Rinehart on the home-versus-club theme—the reviewers accused Colleen of being too cute—and Universal put her op-

Colleen Moore, (about 1922) when she was studying ballet under Theodore Kosloff.

posite Cullen Landis in *Forsaking All Others* ('22), a tear-jerker about unrequited mother love.

Her third picture for Goldwyn, *Broken Chains* ('22), was a melodrama of a weak youth who finds strength in the hardships of the West. Colleen was a spunky frontier girl who helped make a man of the hero (Malcolm McGregor), but acting honors went to Ernest Torrence as a sadistic prospector. She then appeared opposite Warner Baxter in *The Ninety and Nine* ('22) for Vitagraph, a rehash of the hoary old railroad melodrama. Her last film under the Goldwyn contract was *Look Your Best* ('23), a clever comedy about a chorus girl who had trouble keeping thin. Rupert Hughes again directed from his own script.

By the end of 1922 Colleen Moore was firmly established as a talented actress, and her services were much in demand. She was named one of the Wampas baby stars that year, a gilt-edged selection that included Patsy Ruth Miller, Mary Philbin, Jacqueline Logan, Lois Wilson, Bessie Love, Claire Windsor, and Pauline Starke.

In 1923, after doing two quickies—*Slippy McGee*, directed by the promising Wesley Ruggles, and *April Showers*—she obtained, through her burgeoning friendship with William Randolph Hearst and Marion Davies, the leads in two Hearst-Cosmopolitan productions, *The Nth Commandment* and *Through the Dark*.

The Nth Commandment was a none too successful attempt to reunite the talents of novelist Fannie Hurst and director Frank Borzage, who had teamed on the striking *Humoresque* two years earlier. It was a maudlin tale of a brave little shopgirl (Miss Moore) who tried to keep her tenement home together after her husband (James Morrison) falls ill with tuberculosis. Robert E. Sherwood, reviewing it for the old *Life* magazine, named Colleen's performances as one of the ten best of 1923. *Through the Dark,* not released until the following year, was a Boston Blackie story with Forrest Stanley as the delightfully crooked hero. Colleen was the society girl whose faith in the thief made him go straight. *Through the Dark* was the first important picture directed by George W. Hill, a former Griffith cameraman who later directed such successes as *The Big House* and *Min and Bill.* Hill committed suicide while engaged in pre-production work on *The Good Earth.*

While working on *Slippy McGee*, Miss Moore had attended a dinner party at the swank Sunset Inn in Santa Monica, a favorite haunt of Charlie Chaplin and Rudolph Valentino, and had been introduced by Marshall Neilan to John McCormick, a handsome First National publicity man nine years her senior. A steady courtship developed, and she was soon referring to him in public as "my John."

McCormick had begun as an usher in a Seattle theater. Later he managed the Empress Theater in San Francisco, exploited *The Birth of a Nation* and *Tillie's Punctured Romance* in the Pacific Northwest, and worked as a publicist for producer Sol Lesser on the Jackie Coogan pictures. When a group of exhibitors bought into First National and reorganized it early in 1923, McCormick urged the company to include Colleen Moore among the stars it was developing to make up for the loss of Pickford, Chaplin, and Coogan. (Some of the others First National exploited into top box-office draws were Richard Barthelmess, Corinne Griffith, Milton Sills, comedians Harry Langdon and Johnny Hines, and cowboy Ken Maynard.)

Miss Moore's initial film under the First National banner was *The Huntress* ('23), a cheap western that seemed unable to decide if it was comedy or drama. Colleen played a white girl brought up by a band of Indians. When she learns she is white, she goes in search of a white husband—using Indian methods! The comedy potentials were never fully developed, due to a confused script, but there were some amusing moments when Colleen used her fists and frontier ingenuity to outwit a band of rascally adventurers. Cute in buckskins and braids, she got her paleface hero (Lloyd Hughes) in the final fade-out. Some of the shortcomings of *The Huntress* lay in the uninspired direction of Lynn F. Reynolds, whose previous work had been largely confined to Tom Mix westerns. A few years later, while entertaining guests in his home, Reynolds abruptly left the dinner table, walked into the bedroom and shot himself.

In her second film for First National, *Flaming Youth* ('23), Colleen Moore became a star of the first magnitude. She burst like a skyrocket upon the nation's delighted moviegoers as a sophisticated, jazz-mad flapper, an exponent of a new breed of young women with bobbed hair, rolled stockings, and a defiance of convention. Written by Samuel Hopkins Adams (under the pseudonym of Walter Fabian), *Flaming Youth* was a drama of an undisciplined young girl who discovers there is more to life than good times and the pursuit of pleasure. The story line was far from new, but it struck a novel note in laying some of the

Mervyn LeRoy was the youthful gagman on several of Colleen Moore's silent comedies, and later directed her in Oh Kay! *Here he and Colleen ham it up for a publicity shot made on the set of* Irene.

blame at the door of disinterested parents who had no control over their children. The movie exploited the wild parties, heavy drinking, and a midnight bathing scene (tastefully handled in silhouette).

For the rest of her career Colleen Moore would be the symbol of the restless youth of the '20s—the flapper. Her characterization set the pattern for a whole school of screen flappers—Clara Bow, Betty Bronson, Sue Carol, Olive Borden, Marjorie Beebe, and Joan Crawford. Colleen was not as bird-brained as Clara Bow, nor as wholesome as Betty Bronson, nor as hard as Joan Crawford. Her success lay in her ability to glamorize the naughty-but-nice concept of the flapper.

Colleen was only twenty-one years old when *Flaming Youth* was released, and had the world at her feet. "They called me an overnight star," she said recently. "But it really wasn't so sudden. I'd been working like a dog for six years."

John McCormick, who had been guiding and promoting her

career, married her during the shooting of *Flaming Youth,* on August 18, 1923, one day before her twenty-first birthday, one day after his thirtieth. McCormick was soon made producer of her pictures.

First National was quick to capitalize on the success of its new star and hurried *Painted People* ('24), which had been completed, into release. Although not strictly a flapper picture, it did expose some of the contemporary aspects of New York life in its story of a pair of tenement youngsters who climb the ladder of fame—she becoming an actress, he a playwright. It criticized sham society and the tinsel of the Broadway façade, but there was abundant comedy and a good cast including Ben Lyon and Anna Q. Nilsson.

Miss Moore was then rushed into *The Perfect Flapper* ('24), which was all the title implied. As Tommy Lou, a quiet mouse who decides to flap her way into male popularity, she was the life of several parties and a co-respondent as well. But there was a happy ending as she abandoned her jazzy ways for marriage with a young, old-fashioned and forgiving lawyer (Frank Mayo). Sydney Chaplin helped with some good comedy, and John Francis Dillon, who had been responsible for *Flaming Youth,* directed. *Flirting With Love* ('24) was another flapper vehicle, in which Colleen fell in love with a reformer (Conway Tearle) who preached against her wiles.

Colleen then sought to advance her career by means of an entirely different role, that of the selfless mother in Edna Ferber's *So Big.* It was a radical departure from her flappers, and although John McCormick encouraged her determination to do a dramatic part, First National officials were aghast. "I fought for *So Big,*" Colleen says, "because I wanted to prove that I could do something besides giddy flappers—not only to the public, but to myself."

As Selina Peake in *So Big,* Colleen Moore gave the finest performance of her career. It was a demanding and glamorless role that carried her from youth into maturity and old age—a challenge for the twenty-two-year-old actress. The somber story told of a schoolteacher in a Dutch farming community near Chicago in the 1880's. She married a poor farmer (John Bowers), who dies from poverty and overwork, leaving her with an infant son to whom she is selflessly devoted. She improves her farm, prospers, and sends the boy (Ben Lyon) to college. He becomes a successful architect, but is involved in a senseless affair with a married woman which threatens to ruin his career. The mother saves him and brings him back to the farm and the respectable life she had always planned for him. *So Big* was given a lavish production and boasted an exceptional cast—Wallace Beery, Ben Lyon, John Bowers, Jean Hersholt, Ford Sterling, Gladys Brockwell, and Phyllis Haver. Charles J. Brabin, a perceptive director whose work reflected the influence of Erich von Stroheim, directed.

Miss Moore did a stunning job of conveying the heartbreak of the rejected mother, and she was tender and poignant in the early scenes with her frustrated husband and with the infant son. The cute mannerisms of the flapper were completely absent, and her portrayal was restrained and mature. Although the critics had lavish praise for her performance, *So Big* was not popular with most audiences, who found it dreary and humorless.

Sally ('25) met all the requirements of Colleen's enormous legion of fans, an entrancing picture which proved her versatility as a comedienne and dancer. An adaptation of Florenz Ziegfeld's popular Broadway musical, it cast Colleen as a dishwasher in an East Side café who impersonates a notorious Russian dancer in an effort to win a rich young man (Lloyd Hughes). There were all sorts of amusing complications to the masquerade, but at the end Sally wins her millionaire and becomes a star in the Ziegfeld Follies. The rubber-legged Leon Errol re-created his Broadway role as an emigré count who works as a waiter, and his tender scenes with Colleen are memorable.

Miss Moore's dancing in *Sally* was a major contribution to the film. She had a natural talent for dancing and in the early '20s had trained in ballet under Theodore Kosloff (who De Mille tried unsuccessfully to make into a dramatic actor). Later she took lessons from Ernest Belcher, who had danced with Pavlova, and who arranged her dances in *Sally*. (Belcher's daughter is actress-dancer Marge Champion.) These numbers were executed to the music of Jerome Kern's delightful score. *Sally* fairly cried for sound.

Colleen's next, *The Desert Flower* ('25), was a railroad drama about a young girl, raised in a boxcar, who reforms a no-good tramp—who turns out to be a millionaire in disguise! There were some exciting railroad scenes and fresh and inventive comedy devised by a youthful gagman named Mervyn LeRoy. *Photoplay* observed that Colleen "is one of those girls who can be funny even when the villain still pursues her." Lloyd Hughes was again

John McCormick, Colleen Moore's first husband, about 1927, when he was producer of her films.

the leading man, and Irving Cummings directed.

She had a serious accident near the end of shooting on *The Desert Flower* when she fell backward from a moving handcar and broke her neck. For weeks she was encased in a high fracture collar while production was shut down. "The doctors were fearful I would have an immobile neck," she says, "but their worries were kept from me. Finally, the collar came off, and we were all relieved to find I could turn my head to either side." But moving her neck was painful, and for nearly ten years she slept in a leather neck-support.

First National's incessant demand for another flapper picture led to *We Moderns* ('25), based on Israel Zangwill's stage success. This time the revolt of flaming youth was set in England, and actual scenes were photographed in Buckingham Palace, Trafalgar Square, and Piccadilly Circus. Miss Moore was the toast of London and was frequently mobbed by enthusiastic fans. The climax of *We Moderns* was a wild party staged on a huge dirigible, and her famous Zeppelin dance preceded a spectacular mid-air collision with an airplane. Jack Mulhall took the male lead, and John Francis Dillon again directed, but the reviews were spotty.

Colleen then did *Irene* ('26), one of the great hits of her career. She played the shanty-Irish model in an exclusive New York gown shop partly owned by the young millionaire whom she marries (Lloyd Hughes). The highlight was a lavish fashion show photographed in the pioneer Technicolor two-color process. Colleen was lovely in the gorgeous Alice Blue Gown. Alfred E. Green, who had done so well with *Sally*, again directed. Harry Tierney's music from the Broadway original, with its entrancing "Alice Blue Gown" theme, was used by orchestras in the larger movie houses. (A handsome oil painting of Colleen in the Alice Blue Gown, by Leon Gordon, now hangs in her Chicago apartment).

Ella Cinders ('26), Colleen's next, was based on the popular newspaper comic strip and had a Hollywood setting. Miss Moore was the small-town slavey who makes good in the movies via the usual route of ruining a costly scene, a gimmick Harold Lloyd later used in *Movie Crazy*. The Hollywood sequences were particularly enjoyable, and Harry Langdon made a delightful, and all too brief, guest appearance. Colleen imitated Chaplin, Coo-

Colleen Moore was the cute slavey in Ella Cinders, *based on the comic strip, who goes to Hollywood and becomes a big star.*

gan, and also Lillian Gish, but she looked so wistful and lovely that the gag fell flat. She was the whole show in a picture packed with comedy. Lloyd Hughes played Ella's boyfriend, Waite Lifter. *Ella Cinders* was followed by *It Must Be Love* ('26), a trite story of a delicatessen-keeper's daughter who didn't want to marry a wealthy frankfurter manufacturer. It missed fire all around in spite of a good cast that included Jean Hersholt, Mary Brian, and Malcolm McGregor.

Set against the colorful backgrounds of the London tenderloin, *Twinkletoes* ('27) took Miss Moore back to drama in a poignant tale of a Limehouse waif who becomes a famous dancer. She achieved delicate shadings to a role of contrasts, subtly changing from a carefree gamin to a mature woman crushed through her love for a man married to another. Kenneth Harlan gave surprising depth to Chuck, the confused, braggart prizefighter. *Twinkletoes* did not repeat the fault of *So Big* by being too somber. There was much lively comedy, and the ballet scenes, some photographed in color, were charming. Charles J. Brabin directed.

By 1927, her tenth anniversary in movies, Colleen Moore was at the pinnacle of her career. Her success was a combination of talent, a unique personality, and a wholesome glamor. Her pictures—in spite of such tantalizing titles as *Flaming Youth, The Perfect Flapper,* and later, *Naughty but Nice*—with their unrealized promises of sex and sin—were family fare that paid off handsomely at the box office.

Her personal popularity was tremendous. First National's publicity department uncovered dozens of little girls who had been named for her. Her Dutch-boy bob, for many years her trademark, was widely copied. ("It was so easy to keep," she says. "I'd just shake my head and be ready to go—no curling and almost no combing.") She was the source for John Held, Jr.'s bird-brain flappers. Clothes and cosmetics bore her name, and there was the inevitable Colleen Moore doll. Her face was on sheet music and photoplay editions of *Flaming Youth* and *So Big,* and from all over the world came a flood of fan mail. She posed with visiting celebrities, such as Mayor Jimmy Walker of New York, and charmed them with her wit and intelligence.

With John McCormick's aid—he had risen rapidly to become head of First National's entire West Coast production—she attained the contractual right to select her own stories, scenarists, directors, and players. Miss Moore believed in the value of good writers, and some of Hollywood's best were employed on her pictures—June Mathis, Carey Wilson, Tom Geraghty, Willis Goldbeck. Her crew was mostly talented youngsters—cameramen Sid Hickox, Henry Freulich, and Ted McCord, film editor Alexander Hall (later a successful director), art director Harold Grieve, and directors Alfred Santell, William A. Seiter, Alfred E. Green, and Mervyn LeRoy. "We were just kids, having the time of our young lives," says Colleen nostalgically.

In their private life the McCormicks moved in a select Hollywood social circle. Her beautiful Bel-Air home, done in a Spanish motif, had an aviary, projection room, and guest houses, and was the scene of many lavish parties attended by such personalities as the Harold Lloyds, Bebe Daniels and Ben Lyon, Laura LaPlante and William A. Seiter, the George Fitzmaurices (Ouida Bergere), Joseph M. Schenck, Charles Brabin and Theda Bara, Gary Cooper, Corinne Griffith and Walter Morosco, the Lawrence Tibbettses, John Gilbert, Dorothy Mackaill and Lothar Mendes, the Henry Kings, Carey Wilson and Carmelita Geraghty, the Mervyn LeRoys (Edna Murphy), Joan Bennett, and many others. She was a frequent visitor to San Simeon as the guest of William Randolph Hearst and Marion Davies.

Colleen was always ready to find parts in her films for old friends and for those who had helped her in the struggling days. Julanne Johnston, leading lady to Douglas Fairbanks in *The Thief of Bagdad*, was in many of her pictures, as were Kathryn McGuire, Kate Price, Edythe Chapman, Maryon Aye, Eddie Phillips, Sam DeGrasse, Ena Gregory, Emile Chautard (who had directed her in *Forsaking All Others*) and many more. She also encouraged her brother, Cleve Moore, in his acting career. A handsome, poised young man with a shy smile, he did well in such films as *The Stolen Bride*, *Her Summer Hero*, and some of Colleen's films, including *We Moderns* and *Lilac Time*. He eventually gave up acting to manage a family plantation near Atlanta, Georgia, and died in 1961. (His first name was actually Cleeve, but shortened in spelling when he entered films).

Although Miss Moore tried to get away from flapper comedies, First National felt they were too lucrative to abandon. In *Orchids and Ermine* ('27) she was a dizzy telephone operator who meets a millionaire (Jack Mulhall). It was filled with insolent subtitles and contained many delightful scenes of New York—from atop a Fifth Avenue bus, around the old Plaza

Colleen Moore wore gorgeous clothes in Sally. *Seen here with Lloyd Hughes.*

Hotel, and of a less-gaudy Times Square of the '20s. Mickey Rooney played a midget who smoked cigars. Colleen did well under the direction of Alfred Santell, who was soon to distinguish himself with some of the better films of Richard Barthelmess. *Naughty but Nice* ('27) was more of the same—Colleen was a small-town girl who went to college and shocked the campus with her flapper ways. A very young Loretta Young was seen in a minor role.

Her Wild Oat ('27) was a modified cinderella-flapper theme in which Colleen inherited a lunch wagon, sold it and used the money to crash high society at a posh resort. Of course, she landed the inevitable millionaire (Larry Steers). Somewhat against their better judgment, Miss Moore and her husband assigned her old mentor, Marshall Neilan, to direct *Her Wild Oat*. His irresponsibility with a budget, heavy drinking, and arrogance with Hollywood studio officials was rapidly costing him his career. McCormick tried, with little success, to keep Neilan sober during the shooting of the picture, but there were costly delays due to horseplay and practical jokes on the set. Neilan would disappear for hours and even days at a time, and cutter Al Hall directed a few scenes to keep costs down. "There were times when I could have taken Mickey by the hair and knocked his head against the wall," Miss Moore says. "He was so exasperating, and yet, so charming and talented. I always forgave him." Neilan got $50,000 to direct *Her Wild Oat* at a time when he was broke and up to his ears in debt. He blew nearly $10,000 on lavish gifts and a party for the cast and crew, and three days later was again completely broke and living on borrowed money.

After doing *Happiness Ahead* ('28), a melodrama about a good girl who reforms a gangster (Edmund Lowe), Colleen tried to get the rights to *Peg O' My Heart*, Laurette Taylor's stage and screen success. Miss Taylor had hopes of doing a remake of the movie and would not sell (eventually they went to Marion Davies). Another vehicle with an Irish heroine, *Smiling Irish Eyes*, was purchased for her. Trouble developed on the terms of her contract, and before production could get underway she and McCormick walked out of the studio. Several weeks elapsed before First National capitulated and signed her to a handsome new agreement which included McCormick's continued services as producer.

Smiling Irish Eyes was indefinitely postponed—Colleen did not like the script—and instead she did *Oh Kay!* ('28), a honey of a comedy about a titled English lady who is shipwrecked, rescued by a rum-runner (Ford Sterling), and then masquerades as a housemaid to catch the penniless hero (Lawrence Gray). It was directed by Mervyn LeRoy, a slender lad in his twenties, and a refugee from vaudeville, who had been a gagman on the Moore films for three years. Much of the inventive comedy in *Sally, The Desert Flower, Irene* and *Ella Cinders* had stemmed from Le-Roy's fertile brain. Colleen had promised LeRoy a chance to direct, and he was originally slated to make his debut on *Smiling Irish Eyes*. When it was shelved Richard A. Rowland, a First National executive, let him direct *No Place To Go*, which starred Mary Astor and Lloyd Hughes. He followed it up with the highly successful college comedy, *Harold Teen*, with Arthur Lake as Carl Ed's comic-strip hero. *Oh Kay!* was LeRoy's third feature.

"I have never known a more genuine person than Colleen Moore," says Mervyn LeRoy. "Although surrounded by adulation, she was completely without pretense . . . I still think, as I did then, that she is one of the most wonderful persons I have ever known."

Part of Miss Moore's quarrel with First National had been her demand for dramatic, non-flapper roles. In *Lilac Time* ('28) she found a vehicle in which comedy and drama were so effectively combined that it is the picture by which she is best remembered. Essentially a poignant love story, *Lilac Time* capitalized upon the vogue for World War I films begun with *The Big Parade* and *Wings*. Colleen played Jeannine, a young peasant girl whose farm is near the French front and the airfields of the Royal Flying Corps. A tender romance with a daring aviator (Gary Cooper) grows out of a series of amusing misunderstandings, and there is a moving climax when Jeannine, believing her lover dead, finds him alive in an Army hospital.

As directed by George Fitzmaurice, *Lilac Time* tended to be maudlin and oversentimental, and lacked the sustained realism of war possessed by the Vidor and Wellman films. Elaborately mounted and beautifully photographed (by Sid Hickox), it contained many spectacular aerial dogfights and battle scenes. *Lilac Time* was immensely popular with audiences and a major advance in the fast-rising career of Gary Cooper.

While *Lilac Time* was in production, the revolution of sound rocked the motion picture industry, and it was not released until synchronized sound effects were added—the roar of airplane motors, sputtering machine guns and exploding shells—and a musical score built around Nathaniel Shilkret's theme song, "Jeannine, I Dream of Lilac Time."

During the latter part of 1928 Miss Moore completed two other silent pictures—*Synthetic Sin* and *Why Be Good?*—which were also released with added sound effects and a musical score. *Synthetic Sin* was about a nice girl from a small town who went to New York and "sinned" in order to become a great actress. Antonio Moreno was the leading man. *Why Be Good?*, Colleen's last silent, had her once more as the naughty-but-nice flapper who sacrifices pretty clothes and sugar daddies for an understanding young man (Neil Hamilton.). It was lively and a bit preachy, and Miss Moore was peppy in her dancing scenes in a speakeasy.

By early 1929 Colleen Moore had to face the challenge of the microphone. "I remember the day of the voice test so well," she says. "A young man from Western Electric, who couldn't

Colleen Moore and Gary Cooper in a scene from Lilac Time *(1928).*

have been twenty years old, was at the controls in the recording booth. All the First National executives were there, which didn't help my nervousness, and I hadn't the slightest idea of what I was supposed to do or say. Finally, they told me to recite a nursery rhyme!

"So I recited 'Mary had a little lamb'—just five words. My whole career hung on those five words and a teenage soundman!" She needn't have worried. Her voice recorded well.

Like all Hollywood studios, First National raided Broadway for dialogue coaches to help its stars make the transition from silent to talking pictures. The veteran actress, Constance Collier, was brought in to teach Miss Moore the rudiments of enunciation and delivery. Her approach was too pedantic, however, and Colleen did much better under the tutelage of the charming Laura Hope Crews.

She made her talkie debut in *Smiling Irish Eyes* ('29), the picture which had been planned and postponed two years before. The slight story was about a fair colleen in the old country who catches a greased pig at a county fair and uses the prize money to finance her boyfriend (James Hall) as a Broadway song-writer! Colleen sang several songs and handled her dialogue well despite an affected brogue. Says Miss Moore today: "*Smiling Irish Eyes* was the most mediocre picture imaginable." The reviewers shared her opinion, although *Photoplay* noted that Colleen "gains personality and charm in the talkies." She blames her inauspicious talkie debut, in addition to the poor choice of material, on the early difficulties of sound recording and the limitations imposed on dramatic action by immobile microphones and cameras.

Her second talkie, *Footlights and Fools*, was much better. The story, by Katharine Brush, concerned an ambitious American girl masquerading as a temperamental French musical comedy star. She wore beautiful gowns and a blond wig (although audiences had not liked her as a blonde in *Twinkletoes*), danced well, and displayed an improved and more versatile speaking voice. This time she was handicapped by an overdone French accent. Fredric March, newly recruited to the movies from the stage, had little to do as her wealthy admirer.

Footlights and Fools was Miss Moore's last picture for four years. With unbelievable suddenness her career came to a full stop. She seemed unable to adjust to sound, and the flapper, upon which her success was largely built, had become passe. Her marriage to John McCormick was breaking up, and they were divorced in September, 1930. (McCormick later became a successful talent agent in Hollywood, waged a long battle against alcohol, and became a leader in Alcoholics Anonymous. He died in 1960.) By mutual agreement she and Warner Brothers, which had purchased First National, tore up her contract.

"I'd had it," Colleen says today. "I realized it at the time, but the break-up of my marriage made it seem important to try and continue my career." Negotiations with other studios came to nothing, although she was reported at one time ready to sign with Pathe and again to have her own unit at United Artists.

In October, 1930, Miss Moore went to New York and shared an apartment with an old Hollywood chum, Virginia Valli. Arch Selwyn signed her to play on Broadway the lead in *On the Loose*, by Hollywood scriptwriter Benjamin Glazer. It proved to be a disastrous mess, and in six weeks on the road there were new lines each night, and eventually Ben Hecht was brought in to try and patch it up. Selwyn, who was also trying to entice Mary Pickford, Vilma Banky, and Rod LaRocque to Broadway, refused to let Miss Moore out of her contract. Although the play never reached New York, Colleen thinks Selwyn got his investment back from the tour.

She returned to California and signed with the West Coast impresario, Henry Duffy, to star in *The Church Mouse*, which Ruth Gordon had done on Broadway. It opened in San Francisco to good notices and moved to the Biltmore Theater in Los Angeles where a first-night audience was entranced. "They expected to see me fall flat on my face," Colleen says. Lionel Barrymore, Norma Shearer, and Irving Thalberg were among those who came backstage to congratulate her. However, Duffy abandoned plans to revive the play on Broadway.

Largely because of her work in *The Church Mouse*, Miss Moore was signed to a term contract by Metro-Goldwyn-Mayer at $2,500 a week, a fraction of what she had earned at First National. "I was so glad to get back to the studios I would have worked for nothing," she says.

Despite the interest of Irving Thalberg, MGM seemed unable to find a suitable role for her. She was announced for *Flesh*, starring Wallace Beery, but the part went to Karen Morley. Finally, she was loaned to Fox for the feminine lead opposite Spencer Tracy in *The Power and the Glory* ('33), which Jesse L. Lasky was producing. Tracy played an ambitious trackwalker who rises to the presidency of a railroad, and Miss Moore gave a compelling performance as the prim schoolteacher who marries him and commits suicide when he deserts her for another woman. Except in a few early scenes—particularly where she walks the track for Tracy while he is home studying—her performance had nothing in common with her cute silent roles. As the innocent-eyed Sally, bewildered by the changes which power brings to her husband, she fully realized the dramatic promise forecast in *So Big* nine years earlier.

The Power and the Glory was not a popular picture, however, and audiences were confused by its "narratage"—a trick of chopping the story's chronological sequence into parts, rearranging them arbitrarily, and issuing them through the mouth of a narrator or bystander. (The idea was not new, having had its literary inspiration in the novels of Joseph Conrad and the short stories of O. Henry.) William K. Howard's directorial technique was both praised and criticized, as was the spare script of Preston Sturges.

Colleen then appeared in *Success at Any Price* ('34) for RKO

Radio. Based on a downbeat play by John Howard Lawson, it bore some similarities to *The Power and the Glory*. She was the sweetheart of an East Side tough (Douglas Fairbanks, Jr.) who, through her influence and encouragement, gets a job with a Madison Avenue advertising agency. Through mean and mercenary tricks he becomes a powerful executive and throws her over for an expensive, faithless mistress (Genevieve Tobin).

M-G-M then offered her several roles similar to those in *The Power and the Glory* and *Success at Any Price*, which she declined to accept. At her request Louis B. Mayer tore up her contract.

In 1932 she married Alfred P. Scott, a Manhattan stockbroker, but the marriage ended in divorce two years later. While she was married to Scott and living in New York, Marshall Neilan asked her to star in *Social Register*, an independent film he was doing for a group headed by hotelman Jack Bergen. Neilan's career was at rock bottom, and he could no longer get a job in Hollywood. Miss Moore was not particularly eager to do the picture but she realized Neilan needed help. He also promised her a percentage of the profits, of which, it turned out, there were none. "*Social Register* was the picture I did for free," Colleen says. "I did it as a favor to Mickey in the hopes it would get him back on his feet."

On the strength of the Moore name, Bergen was able to negotiate a Columbia release, despite the dislike of Harry Cohn for Neilan. A fine cast was assembled—Pauline Frederick, Alexander Kirkland, Ross Alexander, Charles Winninger, Robert Benchley, and Margaret Livingston—and the picture was shot at the old Paramount studios in Astoria. Based on a play by John Emerson and Anita Loos which ran ninety-one performances on Broadway with Lenore Ulric in the lead, *Social Register* tells of an ambitious actress who is brutally snubbed when she tries to crash high society. The story was something out of Colleen's halcyon days at First National, but it no longer suited her, or the tenor of the changing times. Columbia made little attempt to properly exploit it, and *Social Register* got few bookings.

Colleen Moore's last screen appearance was as Hester Prynne in a cheap remake of *The Scarlet Letter* ('34) for Majestic Pictures. Her sensitive performance as Hawthorne's adulterous heroine was the only good thing in the picture. Handicapped by a shoestring budget, the film suffered from a bad script and poor technical values, and Robert G. Vignola's static, uninspired direction was more suited to the silent pictures in which he made his reputation twenty years before. The cast was sprinkled with a number of silent-screen favorites—William Farnum, Henry B. Walthall, Betty Blythe, Alan Hale, Flora Finch, and others. The mediocre quality of *The Scarlet Letter* made Miss Moore resolve to leave movies for good.

"My film career was an important phase of my life that came to a natural conclusion," she says. "Perhaps I should have terminated it once and for all when the talkies came along. I simply went on to other interests and new activities, which, with my family, have given me a lasting happiness. There are no regrets."

Miss Moore retired from movies with considerable wealth. "Colleen Moore rates as easily the smartest woman in the motion picture industry, not even excepting Mary Pickford," says Adela Rogers St. Johns, a long-time friend. Sergei Eisenstein, delighted with her naturalness and sense of humor, called her the only intelligent woman he met in Hollywood. (The Russian director of *Potemkin* thought Marlene Dietrich dull and Greta Garbo stupid.)

In 1937 Miss Moore married a widower, Homer P. Hargrave, a distinguished Chicago banker, financier, and founding partner of Merrill Lynch, Pierce, Fenner and Smith. It was a lasting and happy marriage. (Mr. Hargrave died in February, 1964.)

Her stepchildren and grandchildren are a source of great pride, and she is active in Republican politics in Cook County. She is on the board of the Chicago Art Institute and of Passavant Memorial Hospital. After her husband's death she lived in Rome for a year, and now goes to Europe every fall, and frequently to South America, Mexico, the Orient, and the South Seas. And to Hollywood to see old friends—King Vidor, Mervyn LeRoy, Jetta Goudal, Mary Pickford, and Buddy Rogers. The Colleen Moore pictures are still shown. The British Film Institute had a retrospective program of her films in London in 1962, and a year later Eastman House, to which she has given her memorabilia, had a showing of *Irene* (which she thinks stands up best of all her films). In 1968 she brought out her autobiography, and a year later a book of stock market advice for women.

The fabulous Colleen Moore Doll House has brought her almost as much fame as her motion pictures. Dolls and doll houses have always held a special fascination for her, and at one time she had a collection of 2,500 dolls from all over the world, most of which she later gave to orphanages.

Her hobby of building elaborate doll houses began early. The eighth and final one, begun in 1925, is an incredible fairyland castle to which more than seven hundred artists and craftsmen have contributed their skills. It is now on permanent loan to the Museum of Science and Industry in Chicago.

In 1935 she was persuaded to display the doll house at Macy's department store in New York, when a gold cornerstone was laid by former Governor Alfred E. Smith and Mrs. James Roosevelt, mother of FDR. It had been accorded a small corner in the luggage department, but by the second day the entire floor had been cleared to handle the thousands who queued up to see it. Later, Miss Moore took it on tour to dozens of American cities and donated the small admission charge—usually ten or fifteen cents—to medical charities, for which it earned a fortune.

The Colleen Moore Doll House must be seen to be appreciated. Costing $435,000 to build and furnish, it is a collection of exquisite miniatures. The castle itself, built to a scale of one inch to one foot, is nine feet square and its highest tower is twelve feet above the floor. It has running water in the kitchens and bathrooms, and electric lights the size of a grain of wheat. The doll house was designed by architect Howard Jackson, decorated by Harold W. Grieve (her former art director), and built under the supervision of Colleen's father, Charles Morrison, over the course of nine years.

The detail is incredible. Among more than a thousand separate items are such exquisite things as chairs cut from diamonds and emeralds, ivory in-lay floors, tiny books, and handwritten musical scores (by Gershwin, Berlin, and George M. Cohan) on a miniature grand piano that really plays. Many of these items have been bought at high prices in all parts of the world, and each is story in itself. Each room is built around a storybook theme, and Miss Moore is still at work searching out items for the library.

"As long as I live, the doll house will never be completed," she says.

7

CHAPLIN'S COLLABORATORS

*A*LTHOUGH Charlie Chaplin was the dominant force in the creation of his films, he was, like most comedians of the silent era, helped by a number of clever and ambitious young men who later became successful directors in their own right.

While Harold Lloyd and Buster Keaton accepted their collaborators as credited directors or co-directors, Chaplin's associates worked in virtual anonymity. Keaton has publicly expressed his appreciation to Clyde Bruckman, Edward F. Cline, and Edward Sedgwick. Harold Lloyd's best comedies were directed by Fred C. Newmeyer and Sam Taylor. Harry Langdon was indebted to the gifted Frank Capra, and much of Larry Semon's success came during his association with Norman Taurog. But Chaplin has consistently minimized the contributions of his assistants, and has said: "My films are my work and mine alone."

Through the years Chaplin surrounded himself with such promising talents as Monta Bell, Harry d'Abbadie d'Arrast, A. Edward Sutherland, Charles F. Riesner, and Robert Aldrich. At one critical stage of his career he even retained an established director, Robert Florey, to assist him on the ill-fated *Monsieur Verdoux*. Invariably these associations were relatively short and ended in bitterness and recriminations.

Significantly, Chaplin's dependence upon capable assistants was greatest during his ventures into drama—*A Woman of Paris, Monsieur Verdoux,* and *Limelight*—a realm in which his talent was uncertain. His assistants on his tramp comedies, an area in which he felt completely sure of himself, were, by and large, a court jesterate of yes men who merely catered to his ego—but who absorbed his comedy techniques for use later in their own careers.

Charlie Chaplin (right) poses with Jean de Limur (left), his assistant on A Woman of Paris *(1923), and Robert Florey (center), his collaborator on* Monsieur Verdoux *(1946). This was taken on the Chaplin lot when* The Pilgrim *was in work in 1923.*

Chaplin has always felt the need for an audience while at work in the studio. He was curious to know how he looked and liked to try out gags and story ideas on his assistants. As the years went by, he became less and less responsive to criticism, even resentful, although suggestions he received from others with derision would sometimes reappear as his own.

Although Chaplin would be the last to admit it, his awareness of his *technical* shortcomings may have prompted him to employ capable assistants. After more than a half-century in filmmaking he is still unlettered in the *mechanics* of putting a motion picture together, and he pretends to be contemptuous of what he calls "Hollywood chi-chi"—expressive camera angles and lighting, unusual pictorial composition, continuity in editing and crosscutting. His knowledge of such directorial techniques is virtually nil.

Largely on the strength of his essay into silent drama, *A*

Woman of Paris ('23), Chaplin has been called a great director. His lesser feature comedy, *The Circus,* was nominated for an Academy Award as the best directed picture of 1927-28. James Agee called his direction of *Modern Times* brilliant, and compared it with the best work of Dovzhenko.

As a director, Chaplin is inclined to overemphasize acting, even to the exclusion of technical construction, as King Vidor has pointed out. When he tries he *can* extract stunning performances from his players. Jackie Coogan in *The Kid* gave one of the finest interpretations of a child in screen history (particularly in his remarkable mimicking of Chaplin). Edna Purviance was striking in the difficult role of the demi-mondaine in *A Woman of Paris,* and Adolphe Menjou soared to new heights in the same film. There are moments of perception and tenderness in Georgia Hale's shallow part of the dance-hall girl in *The Gold Rush*— so oddly reminiscent of Mabel Normand—which clearly resulted from Chaplin's sensitive direction. He extracted a fine performance from Virginia Cherrill as the blind girl of *City Lights* under difficult circumstances (she was addicted to parties and good times and indifferent to acting). The performances of Marilyn Nash and even Martha Raye in *Monsieur Verdoux* are two of the few assets of that curious picture.

Except for his ability to direct actors, Chaplin's directorial techniques are minimal. Content, not technique, is his forte, a fact which many film students, who should know better, fail to recognize. Chaplin's directorial shortcomings are insignificant in the final evaluation of his films, for his total product in comedy, as an expression of social satire and the complexities in human relationships, is that of an unmatched, crystal clear genius.

Any discussion of Chaplin's associates must begin with Mack Sennett, who taught him the fundamentals of screen comedy, a contribution which Chaplin gradually refined into his own unique concepts. Sennett's personal on-the-set association with the young English comic was limited, and, except for the feature comedy *Tillie's Punctured Romance,* Chaplin was directed by Sennett in only eight Keystone comedies, all made in March, April, and May of 1914.

Chaplin worked first with Henry Lehrman, a brash ex-conductor of a horse-drawn streetcar who obtained his first job in movies with D. W. Griffith by representing himself as the American agent of France's film moguls, the Pathé Freres. Lehrman directed Chaplin in his first four Keystone comedies—*Making a*

Living, Kid Auto Races at Venice (in which Chaplin first used the famous tramp costume), *Mabel's Strange Predicament,* and *Between Showers.*

The Chaplin-Lehrman relationship was discordant from the beginning. Like all of Sennett's directors, Lehrman worked at top speed and had no time to explain the mechanics of filmmaking to the newcomer. Chaplin was confused by the shooting of scenes out of story sequence—a confusion he never overcame—and totally lacked an understanding of editing principles. Neither man liked the other, and Lehrman was often behind the practical jokes which the Keystone troupe constantly played on Chaplin.

The friction was so strong during the making of *Mabel's Strange Predicament* that Sennett had to step in and complete the picture. Lehrman denied this in later years and declared he had directed all of Chaplin's scenes and Sennett had merely handled a second unit with Mabel Normand. But after *Between Showers,* during which Chaplin and Lehrman barely spoke, Sennett personally directed his new star. Chaplin said later, in his autobiography, that he and Lehrman quarreled because Lehrman would not accept any individual bits of funny business, and insisted on routine chases. He also accused Lehrman of mutilating his best scenes in the cutting room.

George Nichols, a Keystone gagman and performer, occasionally filled in as director, and he was assigned to direct Chaplin in *His Favorite Pastime.* It was Nichols' only Chaplin film, and Sennett soon switched him to directing Ford Sterling, whom Nichols greatly admired.

Although he got along best with Sennett, it was soon obvious that Chaplin could not, or would not, take direction—not from Lehrman, Nichols, nor Sennett. He began a campaign to persuade Sennett to let him direct, and there were several stormy scenes between them, even though Chaplin had a grudging professional respect for the Keystone boss. Chaplin had begun to freely express his own comedy ideas and his emerging screen characterization did not fit into the conventional Keystone patterns. The basic problem was one of pace. Sennett had an inflexible rule that a gag be consummated in no more than twenty feet of film; Chaplin barely got going in a hundred.

Despite Chaplin's mushrooming success, Sennett was not yet ready to give in to his demands. He now assigned Mabel Normand, the dark-eyed darling of the Keystone lot, to direct Chaplin in *Mabel at the Wheel,* with herself as co-star. Miss Normand had already directed or co-directed several Keystone comedies. Barely twenty years of age, and possessed of a capricious temperament, childlike one moment and sophisticated the next, Mabel Normand had an inventive mind when it came to screen comedy, and had profited by her work in dozens of Sennett shorts. She had also appeared in more serious roles for Biograph.

Chaplin did not share Sennett's confidence in Miss Normand's abilities as a director, and the inevitable friction developed— Chaplin refused to follow instructions, and Mabel walked out. After threatening to fire Chaplin, Sennett patched things up and finished directing *Mabel at the Wheel* himself. But a question of prestige was involved, and Sennett finally saved face by prevailing upon Chaplin and Miss Normand to be co-directors. Much to everyone's surprise, the new arrangement worked.

Chaplin at first resented her as his co-director, but their relationship steadily improved, and they worked together effectively on a number of pictures—*Caught in a Cabaret, The Fatal Mallet, Mabel's Busy Day* and others. Miss Normand had disliked Chaplin when they first met and even refused to appear with him in *Making a Living* (the part went to Virginia Kirtely). But they gradually became friends and developed a close relationship that lasted until her death from drugs and tuberculosis in 1930. When Sennett was intractable, Mabel interceded, and since Sennett was in love with her, she usually had her way. Mabel developed a strong appreciation of Chaplin's talent and soon became his champion.

Paradoxically, it was Chaplin who most influenced Mabel Normand's own pictures later on. A wistful clowning that won her the title of "the female Chaplin" is to be seen in her portrayals in *Molly O, Susannah, The Extra Girl*, and other films.

Mabel Normand had no illusions about her talent as a director. As she told Robert Florey in 1922: "It would be pretense to say that the comedy chases in which I appeared with Charlie and Roscoe [Arbuckle] were directed by a director truly exercising his metier. The director, as we know him today, was then virtually non-existent. The films which I directed or appeared in were made without any directorial technique or photographic artistry. No one thought it necessary to explain to the cameraman what was wanted, and nearly all of the scenes were taken in long shots. Our pictures were a group effort, and our comedy evolved out of suggestions made by everyone in the cast and crew." In a sense, Chaplin shared her views, but he was already developing his own comedy style and resented any interference by the Sennett directors.

On directing Chaplin, Miss Normand said: "We reciprocated. I would direct Charlie in his scenes, and he would direct me in mine. We worked together in developing the comedy action, taking a basic idea and constantly adding new gags. Each day Charlie would come to the set brimming with new ideas, which he would act out for me. I would add my suggestions, and soon we were ready for a take. Some of our films took only a few hours to make, others occupied us for as much as several days."

Chaplin's association with Mabel Normand as co-director soon came to an end, although she continued to appear in many of his Keystone comedies. He demanded and got virtual autonomy, and both wrote and directed his own pictures. After he left Keystone he always worked alone.

Chaplin's success fattened his ego, and as he moved from Keystone to Essanay and then to Mutual, he gathered about him a court which included short, stout Henry Bergman, who literally adored the comedian; the laconic Albert Austin, another refugee from the Karno troupe; Sydney Chaplin, his half-brother, who came over from England as an actor and as Charlie's manager; and such performers as Leo White (the Count), Billy Armstrong, John Rand, Bud Jamison, and, on the distaff side, Edna Purviance. Frequently seen in bit roles in Chaplin films were two actors who later became highly successful directors: Lloyd Bacon (*42nd Street, Marked Women*) and Wesley Ruggles (*True Confession, Sing You Sinners*).

Bergman and Austin became permanent fixtures of the Chaplin retinue and functioned as assistant directors and performers. Bergman was often referred to as "Charlie's cast" because he frequently appeared in more than one role in the same film. He also became a successful Hollywood restaurant operator, and was Chaplin's faithful crony for thirty years. "I am his mascot, his trademark," he said shortly before his death from cancer in 1946.

Albert Austin was more talented and tried, with limited success, to be a comedy director. His best work was Jackie Coogan's *My Boy*, which he co-directed with Victor Heerman, and *Trouble,* both released in 1921, and some of Monty Banks' better comedies (*Keep Smiling*). Austin returned to Chaplin as assistant director on *City Lights*, did bit roles and extra work, and wound up as a studio gateman at Warner Brothers prior to his death several years ago.

Mabel Normand poses with Mack Sennett on the old Sennett lot (1914).

Chaplin's first important assistant was Charles F. (Chuck) Riesner, an ex-vaudevillian, lyric writer ("Goodbye Broadway, Hello France!"), and performer in Dillingham musicals. Riesner broke into movies as a gagman for Mack Sennett, and later starred in a series of dull one-reel comedies for Universal.

Riesner was a jovial man who had a natural flair for comedy, and his value to Chaplin lay in his ability to devise and prolong gags. Chaplin hired him as assistant director on *A Dog's Life* ('18), and Riesner remained with him through the completion of *The Gold Rush* ('25), except for the period when *A Woman of Paris* was in production. Riesner had screen credit as associate director on *The Kid, The Pilgrim, Shoulder Arms,* and *The Gold Rush,* and also played minor roles in several of those films. For a time he had a close personal relationship with Chaplin and was best man at the comedian's runaway marriage to Lita Grey. Chaplin was quite fond of Riesner's son, "Dinky" Dean, a talented child actor who appeared in *The Pilgrim,* and later starred in his own films in the Coogan genre (*A Prince of a King*). He is today a successful television writer.

When Sydney Chaplin signed with Warner Brothers in 1925 to star in a series of feature comedies, he asked that Chuck Riesner direct them. Several delightful pictures resulted. *The Better 'Ole* was a minor classic of slapstick comedy techniques, although it failed to reflect the ironies of Bruce Bairnsfather's pungent cartoons on World War I, on which it was loosely based. Sydney was perfectly cast as Old Bill, a sanguine British Tommy who accepted war philosophically and was constantly in hot water. Other Sydney Chaplin movies which Riesner directed included *The Man on the Box, Oh! What a Nurse, The Missing Link,* and *The Fortune Hunter.*

The quiet, gentlemanly Sydney was never able to overcome the handicap of being Charlie's brother. Riesner encouraged him to develop his own comedy style. Years before, in some English one-reelers, Sydney had tried to imitate Charlie, with disastrous results. The beginnings of Sydney's style were apparent in some of his early Keystone efforts (*The Submarine Pirate*), and in his appearances with Charlie, notably in *Shoulder Arms,* in which Sydney played two roles—the American sergeant and the Kaiser. But he never seemed able to fully cultivate his talent, and regrettably, his comedy was tainted with a vulgarity which he could not shake. Audiences were disappointed when Sydney failed to live up to the promise of the Chaplin name, and he vanished into obscurity in the early '30s. He died in Nice, aged eighty, in 1965.

Chuck Riesner subsequently directed Buster Keaton in *Steamboat Bill, Jr.* ('28), a hilarious comedy of a tough Mississippi riverboat captain and his milksop son. Although the story is officially credited to Carl Harbaugh, Keaton says it originated with Riesner. The highlight of *Steamboat Bill, Jr.* is a gag-ridden hurricane, jointly devised by Keaton and Riesner, which has become a comedy classic. Riesner often made good use of such mechanical stunts in his films. Later, at M-G-M, he guided such comedy talents as W. C. Fields, Karl Dane and George K. Arthur, Marie Dressler and Polly Moran (in their famous *Caught Short* and *Reducing*), Ed Wynn, Bert Lahr, Jimmy Durante, Jack Benny, the Marx Brothers (*The Big Store*), and Abbott and Costello (*Lost in a Harem*).

Riesner's flair was for broad comedy, and he had no facility for the subtle blending of humor and pathos, which is so necessary to good comedy direction. To some extent he shared Chaplin's fault of not always being able to distinguish what was artistic and what was vulgar in comedy. Although Riesner asserted in later years that Charlie Chaplin had greatly influenced his work, there is little evidence of it in the films he directed, though in *Harrigan's Kid* ('43), an average B-picture, are some touches that are reminiscent of *The Kid*. Riesner's talents were adaptable to talking pictures, but after 1945 he declined and became inactive after a few mediocre films. Riesner died in 1962 after being disabled for several years.

Chaplin's decision to make *A Woman of Paris* ('23), a straight dramatic picture in which he did not appear, except for an uncredited bit as the porter in the railway station, brought four new major talents into his studio—Monta Bell, Harry d'Abbadie d'Arrast, A. Edward Sutherland, and Jean de Limur.

A Woman of Paris was the culmination of Chaplin's long-felt desire to do something outside of comedy. He had grown ashamed of the little tramp and was already dreaming of appearing as Jesus Christ, or Napoleon. Although he called *A Woman of Paris* an attempt to make a serious actress of Edna Purviance, he made it for the sole purpose of impressing the public with his versatility.

The sordid story of *A Woman of Paris* concerns a French peasant girl who becomes the mistress of a worldly Parisian because she believes her fiancé has deserted her. Peggy Hopkins Joyce, the much-married showgirl, with whom Chaplin had a brief fling, had suggested the plot to Chaplin by telling him of her experiences with Henri Letellier, a wealthy French industrialist.

A Woman of Paris proved to be a milestone—largely as a model for sophisticated, intimate drama, and its subsequent refinement into the gay and witty comedies of manners which followed in the mid '20s. This genre is best exemplified by Ernst Lubitsch's *The Marriage Circle*, Malcolm St. Clair's *Grand*

Duchess and the Waiter, Monta Bell's *King on Main Street,* and the charming continental comedies of Adolphe Menjou directed by Harry d'Abbadie d'Arrast (*Serenade, Service for Ladies*). *A Woman of Paris* influenced a whole school of other directors, including Frank Tuttle, Lewis Milestone, Harry Beaumont, Victor Heerman, Roy Del Ruth, William A. Wellman, Herbert Brenon, Marshall Neilan, Dorothy Arzner, and Victor Schertzinger.

A Woman of Paris was also notable for its style in acting. Chaplin sought naturalness in acting and the *suggestion* of emotion, and eliminated all excessive gesturing and mugging. Adolphe Menjou, who stole the picture from Miss Purviance, says Chaplin would retire to the back of the set and direct from there, so as not to distract the actors. "Don't act—think!" Chaplin would say. "Don't sell it—remember the audience is only peeking at you."

Some film historians deny that *A Woman of Paris* was the source of the famed "touch" of Ernst Lubitsch. They point out that his *The Marriage Circle* was completed before the Chaplin film was previewed. However, Harry d'Arrast says that he and Chaplin gave Lubitsch a private screening of *A Woman of Paris* one evening at the Chaplin studio before *The Marriage Circle* went into production, and that the German director came away brimming with excitement. Although the Chaplin picture undoubtedly had its influence upon Lubitsch, it is the *content* of the two films that is similar, not their style. Lubitsch's technique is unique, and where Chaplin is crude in cinematic construction, Lubitsch is polished and definitive.

To assure authenticity of the French settings for *A Woman of Paris,* Chaplin hired two ex-French Army officers, Harry d'Abbadie d'Arrast and Jean de Limur, as technical directors, and at the suggestion of Thomas Meighan, took on A. Edward Sutherland as assistant director. He was a nephew of Meighan's wife (Frances Ring).

Chaplin's principal associate at that time was Monta Bell, who first came to him as a replacement for Carlyle Robinson in the publicity department. Bell had been a reporter for the Washington Post and was by way of being a frustrated actor, having toured for several seasons as a stock company juvenile. His first work for Chaplin was to ghost write *My Trip Abroad,* an account of the comedian's triumphal return to Europe in 1921. Chaplin dictated notes to Bell while en route on the four-day train trip from New York to Los Angeles. Although Chaplin got

$25,000 for the newspaper rights alone, Bell received only his small weekly salary. Despite his newness to motion pictures, Bell had a quick understanding of film content, an interest in new directorial techniques, and an appreciation of production values.

Probably at no time in his career did Chaplin rely on his associates for guidance so much as during the production of *A Woman of Paris*. Adolphe Menjou, who was on the set throughout the eight months of shooting, says Chaplin accepted major suggestions from Bell and minor ones from d'Arrast and de Limur. Chaplin bestowed the title of "Literary Editor" upon Bell, which probably accounts for some French film historians mistakenly identifying him as a cutter.

There was no written script for *A Woman of Paris* at any time. It was all in Chaplin's head, and he improvised as he went along, often coming up with the most bizarre ideas (like having Edna Purviance die in a leper colony in retribution for her sins) which Bell or d'Arrast would gently discourage. A continuity of sorts was written by Bell, on whom, as the picture progressed, Chaplin relied increasingly for usable suggestions. Bell had a knack for characterization and plot development, and for bits of "business," but it is not possible to say with any accuracy how much of his work, if any, is reflected in *A Woman of Paris*.

Oppressed by the constant demands of Chaplin's temperament and demanding ego, Bell left the comedian early in 1924. In later years he denied indebtedness to Chaplin, despite the fact that many of his early films are obvious refinements of the ideas and the style which originated in *A Woman of Paris*.

Adolphe Menjou brought Bell to the attention of Jack L. Warner, for whom Bell wrote and directed *Broadway After Dark* ('24), Menjou's first starring vehicle. This was followed by *How to Educate a Wife* ('24), also for Warners, and by Bell's striking success, Paramount's *The King on Main Street* ('25), which also starred Menjou. These sophisticated comedies of manners were clearly in the Chaplin-Lubitsch vein. A typical scene had Menjou as the bon-vivant bachelor in *Broadway After Dark* sitting in his tub sailing paper boats made from the love letters of various women.

Bell then moved over to M-G-M, where he became a great favorite of both Louis B. Mayer and Irving Thalberg, having been highly recommended by Thalberg's wife-to-be, Norma Shearer, and by producer Harry Rapf. One of his early assignments was to complete von Stroheim's *The Merry Widow,* after

Syd Chaplin, half-brother of Charlie, about 1917.

the German director had been removed because of a spat with the tempestuous Mae Murray. Stroheim later asserted that his crew, out of loyalty to himself, refused to work with Bell. Miss Murray told an improbable story of secretly doing some scenes of *The Merry Widow,* at midnight, with herself and cameraman Oliver T. Marsh as co-directors! But the truth was Stroheim was restored to the assignment (after apologizing to Miss Murray) before Bell could get much done.

At M-G-M Bell directed a series of uneven but generally successful pictures with such stars as John Gilbert, Greta Garbo, Norma Shearer, William Haines and others. Although he used the pseudo Chaplin-Lubitsch style occasionally, his technique varied widely from film to film. Perhaps his best picture was *The Snob* ('25), which had a Mennonite background and featured John Gilbert, Norma Shearer, and Conrad Nagel. *Lady of the Night* ('25) was a depressing drama about the rehabilitation of a delinquent girl, with Norma Shearer in a dual role. Bell's versatile direction had a quality similar to the later work of Josef von Sternberg. *Pretty Ladies* ('25) was a backstage drama of the Ziegfeld Follies, with sequences in color (and a young Joan Crawford in a bit). *Lights of Old Broadway* ('25) was a mediocre period piece with Marion Davies in a dual role. *Upstage* ('26) also had a show business background and was about a chorine (Norma Shearer) who could not find success. *After Midnight* ('27) was a maudlin story of a cigarette girl, played by Miss Shearer, who reformed a crook. *Man, Woman and Sin* ('27), a stark, unrelieved tragedy of infidelity and murder, starring John Gilbert and Jeanne Eagels, was brilliantly directed in a style clearly derived from *Variety* and other German films of the '20s.

Bell is best remembered as the director of Greta Garbo's first American picture, *The Torrent* ('26). One of her biographers says he was indifferent and rude to her and was more concerned with the performance of Ricardo Cortez, the leading man. Actually, Bell was patient and understanding, but found it difficult to communicate with Garbo because of her poor English. She was filled with resentment because her mentor, Mauritz Stiller, had not been assigned to the film. Stiller coached Garbo each evening in her scenes for the following day, and when Bell's conception of the scenes differed, she would be upset and confused. *The Torrent,* although a slow and somewhat stodgy movie, had a remarkable performance by Garbo.

Bell made an easy transition to talking pictures with M-G-M's *The Bellamy Trial* ('29), a stunning courtroom drama that made good use of early sound techniques. Leatrice Joy and Betty Bronson had the leads. Bell was then made production chief at Paramount's Astoria studio in New York. He supervised a number of early talkies (*Laughter, The Letter,* and Rouben Mamoulian's *Applause*) and personally directed *Young Man of Manhattan* ('30), a comedy drama with sparkling, sophisticated dialogue. He also began and directed much of *Behind the Make-Up* ('30), an arty backstage story with an inventive use of both sound and camera. For some reason Bell was replaced by Robert Milton before it was completed. These two pictures, so opposite in conception and execution, illustrate Bell's versatility.

His career at Paramount was soon over, and he then directed unimportant pictures at various studios—Lew Ayres in *East Is West* and *Up For Murder,* Nancy Carroll in *Personal Maid,* and John Gilbert in *Downstairs,* an arty and confused drama of the servant quarters. He made a brief return to sophisticated comedy with *The Worst Woman in Paris* ('34), starring Adolphe Menjou, but it went unnoticed.

Through Irving Thalberg's friendship Bell returned to M-G-M as a producer and did three films in 1934-35 (*Men in White, West Point of the Air,* and *Student Tour,* which was directed by Charles F. Riesner). His contract was not renewed, and six years of inactivity followed—his only work was when Alexander Korda sent him to India to check up on the production delays on Robert J. Flaherty's *Elephant Boy.* Bell then turned up on Paramount's staff and supervised several of Dorothy Lamour's jungle horrors. After 1942 Bell could not get a job in Hollywood—arthritis, marital troubles, and personal problems were partially at fault. His last work was as director of Monogram's *China's Little Devils* ('45), an odd war story which the producer, Grant Withers, is said to have completed. Soon afterward, Bell and Chaplin met at the funeral of Alfred Reeves, Chaplin's business manager, but did not speak to each other. Bell died destitute in 1955 at the Motion Picture Country Home and Hospital, all but forgotten.

Harry d'Abbadie d'Arrast arrived in Hollywood in 1922 at the urging of director George Fitzmaurice, whom he had met in France. He worked as a bit player and extra until Chaplin hired him, along with Jean de Limur, as a "French technical director" on *A Woman of Paris.*

D'Arrast was of the French nobility—his title was Marquis —and came from a wealthy and distinguished family which could be traced back to the Crusades. He had been well educated in Switzerland and Paris, and was a decorated hero of World War I—his right arm was badly shot up by the Germans in 1918. D'Arrast's continental charm appealed to Chaplin, who introduced him to the Marion Davies-William Randolph Hearst set. He was soon a familiar figure at San Simeon, and was on the Hearst yacht with Thomas H. Ince the weekend before Ince's sudden death. (Although completely unfounded in fact, reports persisted for years that Hearst had shot Ince.)

D'Arrast and de Limur enlivened the shooting of *A Woman of Paris* with prolonged and absurd arguments about minor points of decor—a deliberate game which began with Alphonse and Gaston politeness and worked up to threats of duels. Chaplin was vastly amused by this by-play.

However, d'Arrast was seriously interested in motion pictures and had an intelligent understanding of film problems. Chaplin soon made him an assistant director and for three years d'Arrast spent most of his waking hours—often up to eighteen a day—at Chaplin's side.

"Chaplin's influence on my work was total," d'Arrast says. "I knew nothing about pictures when I joined him, and he taught me to think in visual terms. He insisted I be with him when he cut his pictures. He so convinced me of the importance of cutting that when I became a director I insisted on the right to edit my own pictures."

D'Arrast was assistant director on *The Gold Rush*. It is difficult to determine the extent of his contribution to that picture, though it is known his suggestions helped strengthen the vital relationship of the tramp and the dance-hall girl. The veteran Chuck Riesner was also on hand to help with comedy values.

D'Arrast himself is quick to minimize his contributions to Chaplin's movies. "I remember being horrified when I read in an overfriendly French publication that I had inspired several of the Chaplin comedies," he says. "No, the Chaplin comedies are entirely Chaplin—and he is a very jealous author. Milt Gross, a talented and honest artist with whom I discussed all this, agrees with me that it was close to impossible to 'think' for Charlie."

While he was filming *A Woman of Paris* and *The Gold Rush* Chaplin was more receptive to the suggestions and ideas of associates than he would ever be again. "But our ideas had to be good," says d'Arrast, "and this rarely happened. Chaplin carried the ball all the time, and we were mostly used as punching bags to try ideas on. None of us yessed him, and he always listened to any criticism we might make. Later, as I got to know him better, I discovered the best criticism was silence—being a very sensitive artist, he knew something was wrong by the expression on our faces."

Although his relationship with Chaplin soon cooled, d'Arrast remained friends with the comedian for several years. In 1926 M-G-M hired d'Arrast to work with the Davies-Hearst unit, but he went for more than a year without an assignment. Adolphe Menjou then persuaded Paramount to let d'Arrast direct *Service for Ladies* ('27). This film, and two succeeding Menjou vehicles,

Gentlemen of Paris and *Serenade* were cut from the same cloth as Chaplin's *A Woman of Paris,* but with more emphasis upon sophistication and worldliness. Although he lacked Chaplin's ability to probe complex human relationships, d'Arrast was an intelligent, creative director much in the Lubitsch vein.

After directing *The Magnificent Flirt* ('28) with Florence Vidor for Paramount, d'Arrast did *Dry Martini* for Fox, another glossy comedy drama, which starred Albert Conti, a Menjou imitator. D'Arrast says Chaplin gave him many useful suggestions for both films. "I would tell him my story and it seemed to amuse Charlie after dinner to toss off ideas and work them up."

D'Arrast had a good deal of temperament—he was unkindly described as "nervous, somber, ugly, continually making faces and slightly hysterical"—and it began to hamper his career. A quarrel with Samuel Goldwyn erupted during the making of *Raffles* ('30), with Ronald Colman and Kay Francis, a delightful mystery comedy which demonstrated his ability to handle the new medium of sound. D'Arrast quit—or was fired—and the film was completed by George Fitzmaurice.

Monta Bell, then head of Paramount's eastern studio, assigned d'Arrast to direct *Laughter* ('30), with Nancy Carroll and Fredric March. Based on d'Arrast's own story of a young woman, married to an elderly millionaire, who cannot forget an early love, it turned out to be one of his two best pictures. *Laughter,* a bitter criticism of a money-dominated society, contained barbed, often insane, dialogue that helped make it a strikingly original film. It was almost wholly d'Arrast's work, although Donald Ogden Stewart wrote some additional dialogue. Chaplin was excited by *Laughter* and wired his congratulations, but it was too sophisticated to appeal to many audiences.

D'Arrast did not work again for three years. Then David O. Selznick let him direct Marcel Pagnol's *Topaze* ('33), the satiric but warm story of an eccentric French schoolmaster, beautifully portrayed by John Barrymore. It appeared on many lists of the ten best pictures of the year, and was named the best film of 1933 by the National Board of Review of Motion Pictures.

Topaze exactly suited d'Arrast's background and talents, and he effectively transferred Pagnol's irony and humanity to the screen. John Barrymore, eschewing the struttings and profiling of his Great Lover roles, actually *was* Topaze, the shabby, earnest, unworldly professor conscientiously trying to do right.

Eddie Sutherland at the time he was a leading man for Triangle-Keystone (circa 1916), later to become A. Edward Sutherland, the director.

Chaplin came to the preview of *Topaze* and was much impressed.

There had been problems during the filming of *Topaze*. D'Arrast had quarreled with Selznick, and the producer re-cut the picture. "Luckily," said d'Arrast, "I shoot very little film, and he wasn't able to make many changes." There had also been quarrels with the influential movie mogul, Joseph M. Schenck.

D'Arrast soon found that he could not get a job, and in desperation went to Spain and directed his wife, Eleanor Boardman, in an undistinguished film, *The Three-Cornered Hat*, which was not widely shown in the United States. It was his last picture. Except for the war years of 1940-46, which he spent in Hollywood in idleness, d'Arrast lived in Europe from 1934 to his death in 1968. He visited Hollywood once, however, in an unsuccessful attempt to interest Fox in filming *Cyrano de Bergerac*.

After World War II, d'Arrast lived for many years in the family home, a beautiful castle near Saint-Etienne de Baigorry in the Basses-Pyrenees. During the war it was occupied by ninety German soldiers, and its exquisite paintings and furnishings were vandalized. The castle was subsequently completely restored. In his last years d'Arrast lived in Paris and Nice. Eleanor Boardman, from whom he was estranged, has a home on the Marion Davies estate in Beverly Hills and works as an interior decorator.

D'Arrast was to become quite bitter toward Chaplin. He asked the comedian on several occasions to help finance pictures and secure United Artists distribution for them—but Chaplin refused. One of these consisted of the comic trials and tribulations of a great American war hero after his return home from World War I. "When I read the script to him Chaplin looked worried, scratched his head, and tried to find fault with the plot," d'Arrast says. "He finally agreed it was a fine idea, but said it was too much like his own work."

D'Arrast adds: "I suppose this serves to prove the influence of Chaplin on my own films. Never did I ask, 'What would Charlie do here?'—but I suppose I automatically followed his way of thinking. Instead of being pleased at this, Chaplin seemed annoyed and nearly accused me of plagiarism."

An amusing sidelight is the way d'Arrast proposed his story of the great American war hero to Jesse L. Lasky, then partnered with Mary Pickford in an independent company. "My character is a sort of Sergeant York played by Harpo Marx," he declared, unaware that Lasky was contemplating a project which ultimately became *Sergeant York.*

D'Arrast also says that in 1928 he thought of an original story about the friendship of a young Spanish boy and a bull born on his farm, and how, when the bull was finally taken to the arena, the boy jumps in to save the bull's life. Chaplin, who was in his bath when d'Arrast told him the story, was excited at its possibilities and offered to finance the production. The comedian withdrew when Benjamin Glazer, the scenarist, made the "mistake" of requesting a contract and cash advance. D'Arrast says he offered the story to every studio in Hollywood, and eventually saw it stolen, sold and resold—once to Robert J. Flaherty, once to Orson Welles (who shot footage for it in South America that was shelved by RKO Radio)—and finally made as *The Brave One* ('56), for the script of which the nonexistent Robert Rich (a pseudonym for Dalton Trumbo) received an Academy

Award. Trumbo was one of the "Unfriendly Ten," blacklisted for refusing to answer questions about his Communist sympathies before a Congressional investigating committee.

"My feeling about Chaplin is that he is a very great artist," says d'Arrast, "and that having collected a great amount of money from motion pictures, it was his moral duty to help the few real artists who had a small flame burning inside them and not to join in the Hollywood chorus that was trying to blow it out."

D'Arrast says that when he and Eleanor Boardman went to see Chaplin's sound reissue of *The Gold Rush,* with a narration spoken by the comedian, he remarked as they walked into the theater: "I bet Charlie has removed my name from the credits." Chaplin had.

Jean de Limur, Chaplin's other technical adviser on *A Woman of Paris,* arrived in Hollywood at the end of 1920. Before that he had been an officer in the French Army for ten years, and during World War I had earned ten decorations by shooting down seven German planes. An excellent horseman and good swordsman, de Limur fitted well into popular costume dramas, and appeared as an actor in many films with Douglas Fairbanks, Mary Pickford, Rudolph Valentino, Max Linder, and others. Following *A Woman of Paris,* he worked as assistant director on De Mille's *The Ten Commandments* ('23), spent several years in Europe as assistant to Rex Ingram on *The Arab, Mare Nostrum,* and *Black Orchids,* after which he rejoined De Mille as assistant director of *The King of Kings* ('27). De Limur became quite friendly with Jesse L. Lasky, and went to work for him at Paramount as a writer and director. He wrote quite a few films—including *Three Sinners, Magnificent Flirt,* and *Legion of the Condemned*—frequently in collaboration with Monta Bell or Harry d'Arrast. In 1929 he directed Jeanne Eagels in *The Letter,* which Monta Bell produced. He began another film with Jeanne Eagels, *Jealousy* ('29), but was replaced before its completion by Morton Blumenstock, a writer and ex-accountant at Paramount who wanted to direct. The two pictures fared badly and brought Miss Eagels' screen career to a close.

At the end of 1930 de Limur returned to Europe and directed *Mon Gosse de Pere,* an early French talkie that Adolphe Menjou did for Natan Brothers. During the next fifteen years de Limur directed a number of mediocre pictures in France and Italy (*Paprika, Le Pere LeBonnard, The Man Who Played With*

Fire) and worked with G. W. Pabst on the French version of
Don Quixote starring Feodor Chaliapin, who was de Limur's
father-in-law. His last effort was *Le Grande Meute,* filmed in
France in 1945. De Limur then left movies to become director of
public relations for the Simca motor car company.

De Limur, in his films, had neither taste nor imagination,
and he was indifferent to acting and directing techniques. He
had little conception of pictorial values or a definitive use of the
camera. The fact is, he simply did not have *"le cinema dans le
sang."* He made little or no contribution to Chaplin and seems
to have inherited nothing in return. Unlike most of the comedian's associates, de Limur has remained on good terms with
Chaplin.

A. Edward Sutherland, the assistant director of *A Woman
of Paris,* came to Chaplin after a varied career as a stage
juvenile, leading man in the Helen Holmes railroad serials, and
a Keystone cop. He was impatient with Chaplin's insistence upon
perfection—a kissing scene between Adolphe Menjou and Edna
Purviance was done 103 times—and bored with the long delays
when Chaplin was pondering a scene, playing the cello, doing
imitations, or moping in a corner. Chaplin often used Sutherland as a buffer in financial discussions with his players.

Sutherland, whose wives included actresses Marjorie Daw
and Louise Brooks, had a great respect for Chaplin's talents
and a perceptive insight into the Chaplin mystique. At the time
he was probably disappointed that he found so little in Chaplin
that could be applied later to his own films. He soon moved
to Paramount as a director, again via Thomas Meighan's good
offices, and there directed a series of grand slapstick silents
starring Wallace Beery and Raymond Hatton (the classic *Behind the Front, Fireman Save My Child*), some of the frothy
comedies of Richard Dix, Bebe Daniels, and Clara Bow, and
the amusing but less successful silents of W. C. Fields, including
a remake of *Tillie's Punctured Romance.* Later, he directed
many Bing Crosby musicals (*Too Much Harmony, Mississippi*),
and such diverse items as *Diamond Jim,* Eddie Cantor's *Palmy
Days,* Douglas Fairbanks in *Mr. Robinson Crusoe, The Boys
From Syracuse,* and Laurel and Hardy in *The Flying Deuces.*

During the '40s Sutherland turned unsuccessfully to drama,
slipped into cheap program pictures, and wound up directing
television police adventures. Although much of Sutherland's
best work was in light and often slapstick comedy, there is little

evidence that his training with Chaplin had more than a rudimentary influence.

Chaplin's assistants on *The Circus* ('28) and *City Lights* ('31) were drawn from his cronies—the ever-present Henry Bergman; Harry Crocker, a socialite columnist, part-time actor and man-about-town; and Albert Austin. On *Modern Times* ('36) he added the veteran vaudeville performer and early silent-film comic, Carter DeHaven. Dan James, Robert Meltzer, and Wheeler Dryden, Chaplin's half-brother, worked on *The Great Dictator* ('41).

In 1946, when he embarked upon *Monsieur Verdoux,* the story of a French bluebeard, Chaplin decided to employ as "Associate Director" Robert Florey, a talented director of twenty years' experience, who had been a close friend of Chaplin's ever since his arrival in Hollywood from France in 1921. Chaplin had helped Florey's career by his interest in *A Hollywood Extra,* an experimental film which Florey, Slavko Vorkapich and Gregg Toland turned out in 1927. A former assistant to King Vidor, Josef von Sternberg and others, Florey's career ran the gamut from the Marx Brothers' first picture, *The Cocoanuts,* and a little-appreciated horror film, *Murders in the Rue Morgue,* through a long series of program pictures to such successful films as *The Desert Song* and *God Is My Co-Pilot.*

While entertaining Florey at dinner, Charlie Chaplin had described his plans for *Monsieur Verdoux,* which was based on a sketchy plot by Orson Welles. Florey responded with a number of additional ideas and was surprised and flattered when Chaplin suggested he come to work on the film. The idea of working with the comedian intrigued Florey and he readily accepted.

The six months from April to September, 1946, when *Monsieur Verdoux* was in preparation and actual production, proved to be some of the most hectic in Florey's life. He quickly noticed that Chaplin had changed from the gay, charming Charlot of old, and was neither so amusing nor so creative. On the set he was difficult, obstinate, and frequently arrogant. His moods were unpredictable, and he would be angry or depressed one moment, clowning or playing the violin the next.

Florey told Chaplin the script was too macabre and urged him to lighten it with humor, eliminate several repetitive ideas, and convert some of the dialogue into action. Chaplin accepted many of Florey's suggestions, but obstinately retained the excessive dialogue. After thirty years of silence he had become

Director Harry d'Arrast and his actress wife, Eleanor Boardman, photographed on the Seine (Paris, 1933). d'Arrast was Chaplin's assistant on A Woman of Paris *and* The Gold Rush, *later a leading director in his own right.*

fascinated with talk, and several of his speeches were outright soliloquies.

The actual shooting took only twelve weeks—a record for Chaplin—possibly because the comedian was dismayed at the enormous jump in production costs since *The Great Dictator* was completed. Chaplin was almost totally ignorant of modern filmmaking technique, and the devices he had used in the simplicity of his silent comedies were not suited to the drama of *Monsieur Verdoux.* Modern camera angles were seldom used and actors were often photographed full figure—just as they had been in his Keystone days! "I act with my feet as much as my head," Chaplin told Florey. He had no use for trick shots and "Hollywood chi-chi," as he called it.

Florey tried to correct the production's technical deficiencies, but Chaplin frequently repulsed his suggestions. Close-ups were a particular problem—when Chaplin would consent to use them. He would order a close-up for himself, but refuse them for others in the scene, even when they were essential to proper cross-cutting and exchange of dialogue. He would jump from a long shot to a close-up without a transition. The differences in camera lens also baffled him. Florey, in virtual conspiracy with the cameramen (Curt Courant, Rollie Totheroh, and Wallace Chewning), managed surreptitiously to correct some of Chaplin's technically impossible or undesirable ideas. Chaplin seldom did his scenes the same way twice, and often moved the camera out of matching perspective, which made the editing extremely difficult.

Sometimes, after rejecting Florey's suggestions and filming a scene in a technically impractical manner, Chaplin would shoot it several takes later as Florey had suggested. It was his way of telling Florey and the crew that he was "master in my own house." For scenes in which he did not appear, Chaplin would occasionally stalk off the set saying, "Now, Robert, that I am gone, you can do the scene as you see it." It was his way of accepting, grudgingly, ideas which he knew to be desirable without admitting he approved of them, or had been wrong.

Since *Monsieur Verdoux* had a French background, Florey (a native of Paris) had expected to be useful in getting authentic atmosphere into the film. But Chaplin was not concerned with authenticity. He told Florey the story was a "universal" one which could be laid just as well in any country. One of Florey's major battles with Chaplin was getting him to eliminate obsolete apaches (Chaplin pronounced it as if they were American Indians) and the fin-de-siècle costuming from a café scene.

While Chaplin was resting at Catalina he had Florey shoot scenes of police raids, mob violence and destruction of property which Chaplin had thought of using as transitional sequences of unrest in Nazi Germany. Florey photographed them with his usual flair for effective composition and definition, but the results were so far removed from Chaplin's primitive techniques that they were scrapped and replaced with newsreel shots of Hitler and Mussolini.

Florey undoubtedly made some contribution to *Monsieur Verdoux*. Many location shots at Lake Arrowhead were Florey's, and he directed pick-up shots and some sequences in which Chaplin did not appear. He also made numerous contributions to the script, including such interesting touches as the last glass of rum Verdoux drinks before going to the guillotine, and the incident of the dummy of one of the victims found in the attic. Florey also wrote a continuity—an arrangement of scenes— which helped to facilitate shooting.

Chaplin entrusted Florey with the casting of the lesser roles, and it was Florey who hired William Frawley, Fritz Leiber, Arthur Hohl, Irving Bacon, John Harmon, Helen Heigh, and others. He also directed lengthy tests of Edna Purviance for the part of Marie Grosnay, a role eventually given to Isobel Elsom.

Although Florey succeeded in correcting some technical deficiencies, much of *Monsieur Verdoux* is in the out-dated style which Chaplin had used on *A Woman of Paris* twenty-three years earlier. It was embarrassingly old-fashioned and resembled, at best, a crude, self-conscious early talkie. The picture was a disaster at the box office, and pleased no one but leftists, Chaplin idolators, and a group of bemused intellectuals. United Artists soon removed it from general distribution.

Chaplin has consistently minimized Florey's contribution to *Monsieur Verdoux*. When the picture was previewed in Hollywood Florey was shocked to find the name of Wheeler Dryden, Chaplin's half-brother, listed as Associate Director *above* his own. Dryden had been only a second assistant director—Rex A. Bailey was first assistant—and most of his chores consisted of typing script changes and performing small errands. For the posters ordered in Paris for *Monsieur Verdoux* Chaplin directed that Florey be listed as *assistant* director, which was a clear violation of Florey's written contract. Chaplin also forbade any publicity about Florey's association with the film, and instructed Dryden not to give Florey any production stills which showed him with Chaplin. Florey has only a few snapshots taken with a small camera by Curt Courant. Though many of Florey's friends, including Hedda Hopper, urged him to sue Chaplin to correct the billing, he preferred not to do so. Chaplin and Florey have not seen or spoken to each other since the last day of shooting on *Monsieur Verdoux*.

Wheeler Dryden, Hannah Chaplin's son by an earlier marriage—if there ever was such a marriage—made no contributions to *Verdoux* or any other Chaplin picture. A bit player on the stage and in movies, he was in and out of the Chaplin studio for over thirty years. Charlie would find a job for him as actor or assistant director, but most often in such menial posts as errand boy, script typist, watchman, or handyman. At various times Dryden also worked at other studios as a writer, starred in a series of short subjects about famous musicians which James A. Fitzpatrick did in the '20s, and even did a stint as an animation cartoonist. In 1928 he directed Sydney Chaplin in *Skirts*, a soggy British comedy which Charlie is said to have financed,

Charlie Chaplin played a French bluebeard in Monsieur Verdoux *(1946)*.

but it did not help his career. Dryden's death several years ago went virtually unnoticed by even the theatrical press.

Limelight ('52), Chaplin's next picture, was far superior to *Verdoux*, partly because its English music hall setting was familiar ground to the comedian, partly because its photography, sets and editing were less crude. Comedy was incidental to the drama, but was well executed. *Limelight* clearly had auto-biographical overtones.

For this picture Chaplin hired an experienced, top-flight assistant director—Robert Aldrich. Although most of his work had been outside the major studios, Aldrich had assisted such outstanding directors as Lewis Milestone on *Arch of Triumph* and *The Red Pony,* Jean Renoir on *The Southerner,* William A. Wellman on *The Story of G. I. Joe,* and Robert Rossen on *Body and Soul.*

Aldrich is a thoughtful, perceptive man. Like Chaplin, he is a believer in motion picture content, but, unlike Chaplin, is addicted to the cinematic tricks which result in punchy, objective films. He saw in his assignment on *Limelight* an opportunity to discover what made Chaplin tick. It was an uneventful, and perhaps unproductive, relationship as far as Aldrich was concerned, although he brought a stability and leveling influence to the set.

Soon after the completion of *Limelight* Aldrich began directing on his own. His first important films were two large-scale westerns, *The Apache* and *Vera-Cruz*, both starring Burt Lancaster. He achieved greater recognition with *Kiss Me Deadly*, a mystery film directed in a pseudo-Welles style; with Clifford Odets' *The Big Knife*, an intensely bitter look at Hollywood; and with *Attack!*, an underrated war movie strongly influenced by the Milestone and Wellman techniques. More recently Aldrich has turned out *The Last Sunset*, a provocative Western with psychological undertones; *Sodom and Gomorrah*, a lavish but undistinguished Biblical spectacle made abroad; two horror fantasies, *What Ever Happened to Baby Jane?* and *Hush! Hush! Sweet Charlotte*, both with Bette Davis; and a shallow, sex-filled film about Hollywood, *The Legend of Lylah Clare*. A commando drama of World War II, *The Dirty Dozen*, and a story of lesbians, *The Killing of Sister George*, have been astonishing commercial successes. His work is uneven and has yet to fully justify the promise of his talent—despite the praise heaped upon him by liberal elements in film criticism. Aldrich has considerable individualism, partly because he produces his own films, yet frequently employs a most commonplace approach to film construction. He creates the feeling in perceptive viewers that he may one day do a truly fine motion picture.

Chaplin was also helped on *Limelight* by Eugene Lourie, an art director from French and English studios, whose planned efforts to blend settings, photography, and performers into an effective whole were not without success. Although this type of integrated pre-planning (popularized by the creative art directors William Cameron Menzies and Harry Horner) clashed with Chaplin's propensity for on-the-set improvisation, Lourie found the comedian had begun to be more aware of the relation between good production values and good films. Lourie's glossy sets for *Limelight* were in sharp contrast to the shoddy and unimaginative settings of Chaplin's other pictures. Lourie later became an unsuccessful director of science-fiction and monster dramas (*Beast from 20,000 Fathoms, Gorgo*), but soon returned to art direction. He now does detailed special effects, and his volcano eruption in *Krakatoa, East of Java* was nominated for an Academy Award in 1969.

Shortly after the release of *Limelight,* Chaplin moved with his family to Switzerland, and the old Chaplin Studios on LaBrea Avenue were eventually sold and used to make television films. The publicity of the Joan Barry paternity case, income-tax troubles, his heavily criticized association with left-wing and Communist organizations, problems with immigration authorities, the hostility of the American press, and the poor reception of *Monsieur Verdoux* and *Limelight* left Chaplin with a deep-seated bitterness toward the United States.

In 1957, Chaplin appeared in his last starring role in *A King in New York,* hurriedly filmed in Great Britain on a limited budget. An incredibly poor picture about the adventures of a deposed king, it was roasted by the critics and got few bookings. At sixty-eight, Chaplin was tired and cold, and his comedy devices were unimaginative and forced. The diminutive Jerry Epstein, who had worked on *Limelight,* was the assistant director. (Epstein subsequently became a successful producer in the British studios.) Chaplin is said to have been receptive to the suggestions of his cameraman, Georges Perinal, a top-flight director of photography responsible for many of Alexander Korda's better efforts.

As with art direction, Chaplin has never placed much value in good photography. He is indifferent to its potentials, due in part to his limited understanding of the technical operation of the camera. "I do not think Chaplin knows the camera has more than one lens," says Robert Florey. The photography of the Chaplin comedies has been generally poor, distinguished only by their clarity of focus. Chaplin's cameraman, Rollie Totheroh, worked exclusively for the comedian for more than forty years, beginning with *His New Job* at Essanay in 1915. Totheroh's work showed little, if any, technical improvement over the years. Ira H. Morgan, a favorite cameraman of Marion Davies, helped with the photography of *Modern Times.* Karl H. Struss, winner (with Charles Rosher) of an Academy award for his photography of Murnau's *Sunrise,* photographed *The Great Dictator* and *Limelight.* For *Monsieur Verdoux,* Chaplin hired Curtis Courant, a European refugee whom the California labor unions would not let work in Hollywood. Except for Struss and Perinal, Chaplin could have learned little from his cameraman, even had he the inclination to do so.

Except for Mack Sennett and D. W. Griffith, whose work Chaplin greatly admired—he saw *Intolerance* a dozen times during its initial run in Los Angeles—Chaplin has not been influenced by other directors. He admired Eisenstein and Dovzhenko, and is said to have appreciated the talents of King Vidor, Ernst Lubitsch, and Orson Welles. At one time or another he talked of doing a film in collaboration with each of these directors, but—fortunately, perhaps—none of these projects came into reality.

In 1926, impressed by Josef von Sternberg's *Salvation Hunters*, Chaplin hired Sternberg to direct Edna Purviance in *The Sea Gull*. Chaplin was still intent upon making an important dramatic actress of Miss Purviance, although she had not made a film since *A Woman of Paris* three years earlier. Sternberg found her extremely timid and withdrawn, and suffering from the incipient alcoholism which blighted her personality, but he was able to extract a satisfactory performance from her through long hours of patient coaching. However, the picture did not measure up to Chaplin's expectations, and Sternberg shot a second version. Still dissatisfied, Chaplin directed some additional scenes and then shelved everything, losing about $500,000. Robert Florey, who saw both Sternberg versions, says *The Sea Gull* was one of the director's best pictures and superior to most films then in release. "It was too sophisticated for Chaplin," Florey explains. "There was too much in it that he was incapable of understanding." One story is that Chaplin never released the picture because he was furious at Sternberg for previewing it without his permission. Sternberg said later he did not know why *The Sea Gull* was shelved. Chaplin did not bother with explanations, and curiously, Sternberg did not press Chaplin about the fate of the film. It was a carefully avoided subject, Sternberg said.

During the ten years following the release of *A King in New York*, Chaplin was periodically reported to be returning to the screen. A meeting with Premier Nikita Khrushchev in London led to rumors that he would do a film in the Soviet Union, but it never materialized. Late in 1965, the Italian film magnate Carlo Ponti startled industry circles with the announcement that Chaplin had been signed to write and direct *A Countess from Hong Kong*, a modern comedy starring Sophia Loren, Ponti's wife, and Marlon Brando.

Production began at the Pinewood Studios in London amid an enormous publicity campaign designed to rekindle the public image of Chaplin as a comedy genius. Glowing reports of his ability as a director appeared in countless news stories, and the seventy-seven-year-old comedian graciously granted dozens of interviews—but with the understanding that questions about his private life or political philosophies were taboo. Ponti shrewdly surrounded Chaplin with the finest in technical personnel, and the picture, filmed in Technicolor, was sumptuously mounted on a multi-million-dollar budget.

A Countess from Hong Kong proved a major disappointment, and the film was attacked by critics for its embarrassingly outmoded construction. It was repeatedly compared in style and content to the pseudo-sophisticated comedies which Hollywood turned out in the mid-30s. Even the Chaplin idolators could find nothing in it to praise, and a Paris reviewer acidly called it "a pitiful dud . . . made in the technique of 1925 . . . one of the oldest of the *old* waves." Chaplin replied that "he liked it" and predicted—erroneously—that the public would like it. Only the names of Loren and Brando saved it from being a box-office disaster. (As was expected, Chaplin and Brando did not get along, and Brando was openly critical of Chaplin's directorial technique—or lack of technique. He was quoted for his sarcastic references to Chaplin's "smashing *Limelight* set-ups.")

It is useless to speculate on what Chaplin might have accomplished by a closer association with such talents as Monta Bell, Harry d'Arrast, Robert Florey, or Robert Aldrich, or by employing *creative* cameramen, art directors, editors, and musicians. As far as the tramp comedies are concerned, they are as good as human genius can make them and require no apology. Even the cheap sets and outmoded photography are an asset, fitting in with the life-patterns of the "Little Fellow." But in the non-tramp comedies and the so-called dramas— *Monsieur Verdoux* and *Limelight*—Chaplin was in over his head. Sound advice and guidance, at least in the technical aspects of these pictures, could have minimized the errors and forestalled some of the loss of Chaplin's prestige. The gross mistake is that his career did not end with *The Great Dictator*.

In the last analysis, Chaplin and Chaplin alone is responsible for the great legacy which he has left to the world.

8

BASEBALL ON THE SCREEN

*T*HE first use of baseball as subject matter for a motion
picture was in 1898 when the Edison Company released
The Ball Game, a few disjointed shots of an amateur
team of Newark, New Jersey, playing an unidentified opponent.
This crude film was exhibited primarily in Edison's Kinetoscope
peepshows.

Another 1898 film which has survived, but whose title and
origins are now lost, showed U.S. Cavalrymen playing baseball
at a Spanish-American War training camp. The game ended
abruptly when a mischievous collie grabbed the ball and raced
away with the troopers in hot pursuit.

From these archaic beginnings the baseball movie evolved.
Despite the enormous popularity of the sport—more than
60,000,000 persons attended major and minor league games
in 1968—films about baseball have been indifferently received,
probably because they have been consistently stereotyped in
plot and characterization. With few exceptions they have been
box-office poison, and only one has been produced since 1957.

Baseball lacks impact on the screen. It has none of the
intense physical conflict of boxing or football, the fast action of
hockey, the personal danger of auto racing. Baseball's outstanding players have usually been average personalities with private
lives that offer little plot material. The screen biography of
Lou Gehrig (*The Pride of the Yankees*) packs punch only because of his impending death, and the film about Jim Piersall
(*Fear Strikes Out*) dramatizes his mental illness. Dizzy Dean's
offbeat personality provided the only distinction to the plodding
story of *The Pride of St. Louis.*

Baseball movies have been less about the game itself and
more concerned with contrived situations involving the protago-

The great John J. McGraw of the N.Y. Giants had a role in Edison's
One Touch of Nature *(1917). Here he is in the center. The hero (right)
is John Drew Bennett and the girl is Viola Cain.*

nists. Even this approach has its limitations. Since the World
Series bribery scandals of 1919 involving Shoeless Joe Jackson,
baseball has been clean and scrupulously regulated. It offers
few opportunities for villainy and deceit, and has none of the
colorful riffraff element that has been exploited in such boxing
pictures as *Champion* and *Requiem for a Heavyweight*. Neither
is the baseball film a plausible setting for a serious love story,
and the usual theme—baseball versus wife or sweetheart—becomes mired in tiresome sentimentality.

Although baseball had its beginnings when Abner Double-
day laid out the first diamond in Cooperstown, New York, in
1839, the National League was not founded until 1876, and
the American League until 1900. The pennant-winning teams
of the two leagues did not oppose each other in an annual World
Series contest until three years later.

Beginning with the Chicago-Detroit championship struggle

of 1908, Essanay filmed the entire World Series each year, condensing the action highlights into brisk one-reelers (later two reels). These highly profitable documentaries were advertised as "authorized World Series films," and both teams shared in the income. The contract was negotiated by G. M. Anderson, Essanay's production chief and star of the Broncho Billy Westerns.

A rabid baseball buff, Anderson incorporated leftover shots into two charming comedies which he wrote and directed, *Baseball Fan* ('08) and *Take Me Out to the Ballgame* ('10). These were among the earliest theatrical films to use actual big-league personalities in the cast. Selig took over production on these World Series specials in 1913 and gradually lengthened them to four reels. They were discontinued after World War I when newsreels began giving the Series detailed coverage.

In 1914 Selig inaugurated a popular series built around leading teams and players which used scenes of Spring training and portions of outstanding games. One release showed a riot by fans after an umpire's unpopular decision. Another followed the diamond heroes at their off-season occupations, revealing them as farmers, lumberjacks, trolley-car conductors, and bartenders—the era of fabulous salaries for baseball stars had not yet arrived!

Kalem briefly had a similar but less successful series, and also produced an annual baseball special featuring star players in dramatic stories laced with broad comedy. One of the best of these was Kenean Buel's *Home Run Baker's Double* ('14), with Frank "Home Run" Baker of the Philadelphia Athletics and Marguerite Courtot in a drama of mistaken identity.

Vitagraph's sporadic *Baseball Stars* series relied upon novelty, and the release of January 15, 1914, featured a hilarious game between a visiting Chinese team and the buxom Bloomer Girls (who won). An independent company, Winthrop Motion Pictures, earlier brought out an uneven series of one-reelers, each starring a famous diamond hero. *Christy Mathewson and the New York National League Team* ('07) did phenomenal business. Mathewson was a superb showman, and audiences were much impressed with his traditional grand entrance ten minutes before game time as he strode across the diamond in a long white automobile duster.

Most of the early theatrical baseball pictures were cut in predictable patterns of broad comedy and slapstick. Edison's

How the Office Boy Saw the Baseball Game ('07) recounted the
efforts of a sassy office boy to escape his dull job and see the
big game—only to discover his furious boss in the next seat!
Lubin's *How Jones Saw the Baseball Game* ('07) used practically the same plot. Thanhouser's *Baseball Bug* ('11) had a
small-town clerk, who imagines himself a pitching ace, be reduced to size when his disgusted wife hires four big league
players to expose his pretensions. Edison's dull comedian, Mr.
Bumptious, was seen in *Bumptious Plays Baseball* ('10), while
Biograph's *Play Ball on the Beach* ('06) featured a melee of
players enraged at a self-appointed umpire's bad decisions. Other
early baseball comedies included Vitagraph's *One Man Baseball*
('07), Lubin's *Baseball and Trouble* ('14), and Biograph's
Baseball, A Grand Old Game ('14).

Universal's "Baseball Bill" series of slapstick shorts starring
Smilin' Billy Mason effectively combined baseball comedy and
thrills. An early screen comedian with an infectious personality,
Mason was an excellent amateur player, and later did a vaudeville act as a one-man baseball team. The last-minute chase was
a standard ingredient of his 1916-17 series, whose titles included
*Baseball Bill, The Black Nine, Strike One! Flirting with Mar-
riage, Box of Tricks* and *Baseball Madness* (with a 17-year old
Gloria Swanson as leading lady).

Selig's charming "Mudville" baseball comedies of 1917
teamed Lee Morris and John Lancaster in some improbable
situations. One of the best was *The Bush Leaguer,* in which Morris is a losing pitcher for a country team. He takes lessons from
a hypnotist (William Hutchinson) and wins the next game by
hypnotizing his opponents into making all sorts of ridiculous
errors. In *Baseball at Mudville* a team of visiting toughs masquerades as the Milligan Bloomer Girls and wallops the local
stars, who are too gentlemanly to play rough ball. Lancaster and
his teammates throw courtesy aside when the opposing pitcher
accidentally loses his red wig. Two other films about a girls'
baseball team were Metro's *Fair and Warmer* ('19), with May
Allison as a fetching lady catcher, and *Baseball and Bloomers*
('19), a period comedy produced by physical culturist Bernarr
MacFadden.

The first picture in which Harold Lloyd used his famous
horn-rimmed glasses was *Over the Fence,* a baseball comedy of
1917. Lloyd and Snub Pollard were two clumsy tailors who
snip off the tail of a Prince Albert coat they are altering, dis-

cover two tickets to the ball game in the lining (of all places), and are soon involved in a variety of amusing antics on the diamond and in the stands. Bebe Daniels was the girl.

The portly Mack Swain was an unwilling baseball hero in *Home Run Ambrose,* one of a series he did for L-KO (the Henry Lehrman company) in 1917-18. In *Her First Game* ('17), one of Mr. and Mrs. Sidney Drew's delightful domestic comedies, Drew takes his wife to her first baseball game. She disrupts the entire grandstand with her bizarre reactions. The picture was actually filmed at the New York Polo Grounds, and Wally Pipp, the Yankee's flashy first baseman, had a role.

Mutual's *Love, Dynamite and Baseballs* ('16) had Jack Dillon as a big-league pitcher who gets involved with a fake count and a ring of crooks. They surrender to police when Dillon pitches baseballs loaded with dynamite at them. Priscilla

Rockcliffe Fellowes in Trifling with Honor *(1923).*

Dean is lovely as the girl.

Jaxon's *Play Ball* ('17) was one of the crude Pokes and Jabs series of comedies. Pokes, a hayseed clerk, goes to sleep at his desk and dreams of hitting a winning home run. The ball goes through the window of a neighboring office—and knocks out a safecracker!

Edison's *One Touch of Nature* ('17), based on a story by Peter B. Kyne, is a comedy drama about a young man (John Drew Bennett) who is a crack player on Yale's college baseball team. His wealthy father disinherits him when he marries a beautiful actress (Viola Cain), and the boy gets a job as a rookie with the New York Giants. The old man forgives his son when he wins the World Series! A rather portly John J. "Muggsy" McGraw and several Giants players had bit parts in the film.

Charles Ray's curious screen personality was ideally suited to two delightful baseball comedy dramas, *The Pinch Hitter* ('17) and *The Busher* ('19), both produced by Thomas H. Ince. The image Ray projected—a shy country boy incredibly naive and lost in daydreams—lacked the pep and spunk of Douglas Fairbanks and Harold Lloyd, but audiences of a predominantly rural United States identified with his unsophisticated efforts to make good.

In *The Pinch Hitter,* Ray played Joel Parker from Turkey Creek, Vermont—"the bashfullest critter in the country and sort of dummified," as a title put it. Looking not unlike Ichabod Crane, he enters Williamson College and promptly becomes the butt of all jokes. Ray gets on the baseball team as a mascot, becomes a pitcher through a fluke, and wins a spectacular victory and the hand of a pretty ice-cream-parlor proprietress (Sylvia Breamer). *The Pinch Hitter* was remade in 1926 with Glenn Hunter in the Ray role, and a young Constance Bennett as the waitress with whom Hunter falls in love.

In *The Busher,* Ray is a small-town pitching ace with thoughts of nothing but baseball. When a big league team is stranded by a railroad mishap, Ray and his team of local clodhoppers, ignorant of the identity of their opponents, trounce them in a game played to pass the time. Ray is offered a contract, and after the usual hazing and horseplay by his teammates, becomes a star pitcher. His head swells with fame, and he forgets the girl back home (Colleen Moore) for a flashy golddigger. Fired for insubordination and dissipation, he crawls home in disgrace, but redeems himself by pitching his old team to a ninth-inning victory. A big-league scout is conveniently present, but Ray chooses an idyllic country life with Miss Moore in preference to another try with the majors. The baseball scenes are brief and poorly done by director Jerome Storm. *The Busher* is a charming prototype of a Charles Ray vehicle—and for dozens of similar baseball pictures over the next two decades. The funniest thing in it is Ray's nervous, jerky wind-up and pitch.

Hal Roach's *The Battling Orioles* ('24) didn't have much baseball footage but it was good fun about a group of crotchety old men, all members of a champion team of 1874. They adopt the son of a deceased teammate with the intention of developing him into a star pitcher, but the boy (Glenn Tryon) is interested more in girls and good times. He is finally rescued by the oldsters, in a hilarious free-for-all, from a gang of crooks. *The New York Times* called *The Battling Orioles* "almost a Keystone."

Trifling With Honor ('23) was about an ex-crook (Rockcliffe Fellowes) who became a star player. In *The New Klondike* ('26), directed by Lewis Milestone, Thomas Meighan was a big-leaguer who gave up baseball to make a fortune in the Florida real estate boom. FBO's *Life's Greatest Game* ('25) was one of the few films to take a realistic look at baseball. It traces two generations of professional players, with Tom Santschi as the old-timer who tries to make his irresponsible son (Johnny Walker) a credit to the game. Maudlin and uninspired, it makes baseball more human by emphasizing the rank-and-file player rather than the big star. *Life's Greatest Game* was one of a series directed by Emory Johnson to glorify various occupations—the fireman (*The Third Alarm*), the postman (*The Mailman*), the railroader (*The Westbound Limited*), the policeman (*In the Name of the Law*), etc.

Baseball even got into the silent serials. *Play Ball* ('25) was a ten-episode chapter-play starring Pathé's popular new team, Allene Ray and Walter Miller. The story was attributed to John J. McGraw, manager of the New York Giants, but was actually the work of Frank Leon Smith, Pathé's veteran serial writer (who later admitted he knew nothing about baseball). Miller was a rookie who fell in love with the daughter (Miss Ray) of a millionaire who is being investigated by Miller's father, a United States Senator, for alleged connections with an enemy power. The hero uncovers a blackmail ring, clears the millionaire, and marries the girl. Baseball is interwoven into the story but has

Tom Mix in Stepping Fast *(1923). This Western had a baseball scene.*

little to do with the progress of the plot. A publicity tie with the Giants enabled director Spencer Gordon Bennet to shoot scenes at the Polo Grounds and at the team's spring training center at Sarasota, Florida, but he was not permitted to photograph the Giants in actual games with other National League teams.

It was inevitable that Ernest Lawrence Thayer's amusing ballad of an overconfident baseball hero, "Casey at the Bat," would find its way to the screen—not once, but five times. It had gained ill-deserved immortality from countless renditions in vaudeville and at other diverse functions by the leather-lunged De Wolf Hopper. He first declaimed it at a testimonial dinner for the New York Giants in 1888, and shortly before his death (in 1935) Hopper estimated he had recited the saga of Mighty Casey who struck out at least 10,000 times.

In 1899, the Edison Company used the title, *Casey at the Bat,* for a primitive baseball comedy. It was photographed on the back lawn of the Thomas A. Edison Estate in West Orange, New Jersey, and all scenes were taken from a single position facing the catcher. The plot—what there was of it—bore no relation to Thayer's poem. In 1913, Vitagraph used the story line of the Thayer ballad in a one-reel version of *Casey at the Bat*, with Harry T. Morey in the title role, and Norma Talmadge, Kate Price, and Harry Northrup in the supporting cast.

In 1915 De Wolf Hopper was signed by D. W. Griffith's Fine Arts Company to do a series of films for Triangle release, for which he was to be paid the sum of $83,000. After an ambitious start with an expensive picturization of Cervantes' *Don Quixote*, which proved a disastrous failure, Hopper appeared in a series of homespun American comedies. *Casey at the Bat* ('16) fleshed out the Thayer poem with some amusing baseball antics, but critics complained that Hopper, already in his fifties, was lifeless and unconvincing in the lead. Hopper's film career ended quietly in 1917, and he returned to the Broadway stage. As he said later, "I sank majestically beneath the oily waves of the cinema sea, and was never heard of again." A one-reeler entitled *Casey at the Bat* was copyrighted by John Franklin Meyer in 1920, but nothing is known of this picture.

Paramount's *Casey at the Bat* ('27), based on the Thayer poem, was an improbable but engaging look at the antic baseball of the '90s. Wallace Beery played "Mighty Casey," an uncouth junkman who became the town hero by belting out a homer for the local team every Sunday— and never striking out! Beery's insolent self-confidence at the plate was a delight. With a pitcher of beer in one hand and his bat—"the old waggin' tongue," as he called it—held casually in the other, he paid no attention to the throws until two strikes and three balls had been called. Beery would then knock the ball out of the park to clear the bases and win the game. Inevitably, the day came when Casey, framed by big city gamblers, struck out, but the picture made it clear there was a reason and that his prowess would return.

Casey at the Bat was larded with slapstick comedy—such broad situations as Beery losing his trousers in public, and having an encounter with Limburger cheese—provided by writer-director Monte Brice, a gagman for the highly successful Wallace Beery-Raymond Hatton comedies of the previous year (and later for Bob Hope and Bing Crosby). Hatton was originally scheduled for *Casey at the Bat*, but was replaced by Sterling Holloway. Ford Sterling, sporting an amusing array of false beards, made a delightful villain, and Zasu Pitts was Casey's long-suffering fiancée. The not always tasteful comedy tended to become tiresome, and was interrupted by a slim plot in which Casey is lured from Mudville to play for the New York Giants. The titles included such predictable things as "Pack up your other suit, Big Boy—New York's paging you. You'll forget Tanktown Tillie when you see those Broadway beauts!"

M-G-M's *Slide, Kelly, Slide*, ('27) was another story of the small- town hero who encountered problems in the major leagues. William Haines played a cocky, self-centered bushleaguer who demoralized his teammates. Enlivened with much good comedy, the picture was hoked up with a mawkish ending in which Haines wins the big game to give new hope to a dying boy (Junior Coghlan) in a hospital—soon to become a standard cliché of baseball movies. Harry Carey gave an admirably low-key performance as an aging catcher trying to compete in a young man's game, and the piquant Sally O'Neil is lovely as the girl. *Slide, Kelly, Slide* was partially filmed at New York's Yankee Stadium, and at spring training camps in Florida. The baseball scenes were imaginatively directed by Edward Sedgwick and accented by crisp editing. Sedgwick, a baseball buff, had earlier directed *Hit and Run* ('24), in which cowboy Hoot Gibson traded his chaps and spurs for a rookie's uniform—and uncovered a ring of crooked gamblers. Another western with baseball scenes was Tom Mix's *Stepping Fast* ('23).

Warner Brothers' *The Bush Leaguer* ('27) was intended as drama, but wound up a confusing mishmash of crooks, comedy, and baseball. Monte Blue was a young garage-owner and amateur ballplayer who rises through the bush leagues to the majors. In a predictable plot, he exposes a crooked gambling syndicate that tries to bribe him, wins the big game and the girl (Leila Hyams).

Comedy was the keynote of Richard Dix's *Warming Up* ('28), another yarn of a rube baseball star who gets a chance to pitch for the New York Yankees. He is mercilessly hazed by teammates, but determinedly competes with a scheming catcher (Philo McCullough) for the hand of the manager's pretty daughter (Jean Arthur). Dix goes into a slump after a spat with the girl, but pitches the Yankees to victory over Pittsburgh in a crucial World Series game after Jean signals from the stands that she will marry him. Brought out at the end of the silent era, *Warming Up* was hastily provided with sound effects. Synchronization was so poor the sound of the bat hitting the ball came two seconds late.

A few baseball scenes in Buster Keaton's *College* ('27) added to the charm of this rowdy romp. Buster played a brainy collegian whose girl (Ann Cornwall) becomes infatuated with a handsome super-athlete (Harold Goodwin). To win her back, Buster takes up sports with singularly unsuccessful results. He is maladroit at football, track and crew, and his try at baseball ends when the hitters run him down on the bases! When his rival locks the girl in a second-story room, Keaton's fury gives him the physical zeal to pole-vault through a high window, belt the villain, and escape with his admiring sweetheart. Another funny film of college baseball was *Around the Bases* ('26), one of Universal's popular series of short subjects, "The Collegians," with George Lewis and Dorothy Gulliver.

Paramount's *Fast Company* ('29) was the first talking picture about baseball. Based on Ring Lardner's "Elmer the Great," it had a cute story that lifted it a cut above the usual small-town-boy-in-the-major-leagues plot. Jack Oakie played Elmer Kane, the pride of Gentryville, a conceited hick who is a natural hitter. He is induced to sign with the Chicago Cubs by promises of favors from a beautiful actress (Evelyn Brent), whom he secretly admires. Elmer goes into a hitting slump when he finds she has been stringing him along, but recovers when Evelyn decides she really loves him. Skeets Gallagher was the deceitful manager, and Gwen Lee had a delightful bit as Miss Brent's dumb girl friend who is fired from the five-and-ten because she couldn't remember the prices!

In 1934 Warner Brothers remade the Lardner story under its original title, *Elmer the Great,* with Joe E. Brown as the mulish braggart with a strong back and a weak mind. The plot was fleshed out with a new twist—Elmer is framed by crooks in a gambling den and loses $5,000 when he thinks he is playing for fun. His teammates believe he is throwing the big game to pay off the debt, but Joe redeems himself by exposing the bribery ring—and winning the Series! Claire Dodd was the villainous actress, but this time Elmer's heart was with the girl back home (Patricia Ellis). Mervyn LeRoy directed.

The following year, Joe E. Brown starred in another Ring Lardner baseball comedy, *Alibi Ike* ('35), expertly directed by Ray Enright. Brown was again the cornfed rookie with a good excuse for everything, and the humor revolved around his preposterous alibis and explanations. Joe was the constant target of practical jokes by his fellow players—even the ancient gag where he is told on a Pullman to sleep with his pitching arm in the hammock provided for holding shoes! A conventional sub-plot about the inevitable crooked gamblers added nothing, and it was difficult to believe the beautiful and sophisticated Olivia de Havilland could fall for the doltish Brown.

Much of the success of *Elmer the Great* and *Alibi Ike* stemmed from Joe E. Brown's lifelong, fanatical interest in baseball, and his remarkable ability as an amateur player. His pantomime of the conceited pitcher on the mound became a comedy classic. After suspiciously examining the batter and warily eying the base runners, he would pitch in an exhausting wind-up . . . and stare in bewilderment as the ball sailed over the fence for a home run. Brown continually refined the act, and used it to delight thousands of American fighting men in the South Pacific during World War II.

Norman Taurog's *Hot Curves* ('30) was a maudlin account of the ups and downs of a Jewish lad who was a misfit in both baseball and his private life. Benny Rubin was likable and sympathetic, but not very convincing as a ball player who clowned around on the diamond.

Murder in the St. Louis Cardinals was the subject of M-G-M's unique mystery melodrama, *Death on the Diamond* ('34), directed by Edward Sedgwick. A star pitcher (Joseph Sawyer) is shot as he rounds third base. Another pitcher (Robert Livingston) is strangled in the locker room, and a Neanderthal catcher (Nat Pendleton) is done in by an arsenic-sprinkled hot-dog. In a suspenseful climax, an attempt is made on the life of a rookie (Robert Young) by secreting a tiny bomb in the pocket of his uniform. Sedgwick again provided brisk action scenes intelligently edited to catch the spirit of the game.

Few baseball movies were produced in the fifteen years between 1934 and 1949. *Swell-Head* ('35) concerned a boorish batting ace (Wallace Ford) who learns humility after he is beaned and blinded by a pitched ball. *It Happened in Flatbush* ('42) is a delightful comedy about a butter-fingered ball player (Lloyd Nolan) who is dismissed from the Brooklyn Dodgers, but later returns as manager and pilots the team to a World Series pennant. Although filmed on a low budget, it has exceptionally colorful game scenes, well directed by Ray McCarey, brother of the more famous Leo. *Ladies Day* ('43) was just a silly comedy about the marital mix-ups of an oafish pitcher (Eddie Albert). Frank Capra's *Meet John Doe* ('41) is not about baseball, but Gary Cooper played a big-league star who became a bum after injuring his arm in an extra-inning game.

Charlie Chase's *The Heckler* ('40) is a very funny two-reeler about baseball, and has become something of a classic among comedy shorts. Chase was one of those noisy pests who infest the grandstands and harass the players. Columbia remade it in 1946 as *Mr. Noisy,* with Shemp Howard, but it lacked the sparkle of Chase's original. Buster Keaton turned to baseball in *One Run Elmer,* part of a series of two-reelers he made for Educational in 1935, but it had none of the inventiveness of the comedian's silent classics.

A revival of baseball films was initiated by *It Happens Every Spring* ('49), a truly funny picture about an underpaid chemistry professor (Ray Milland) who develops a compound that makes wood repel rubber. A baseball treated with the stuff cannot be hit—it makes a sprightly detour around the bat (via Fred Sersen's special effects) and plops into the catcher's mitt. Milland daydreams of being a big-league star, and uses his discovery to become an overnight pitching sensation—all his games are no-

Ray Milland was the college professor turned big league star pitcher—thanks to a wacky invention in It Happens Every Spring *(1949). His teammates were Ted DeCorsia (left) and Paul Douglas (center).*

hitters. He is exposed when his roommate, Paul Douglas, a dumb slob of a catcher, mistakes the compound for hair tonic with amusing results. Jean Peters is a lovely foil for Milland's wacky professor. *It Happens Every Spring* profited from Lloyd Bacon's fast-paced direction, and the baseball scenes were well done.

Ray Milland also starred in another offbeat baseball comedy, *Rhubarb* ('51), in which an eccentric millionaire wills a major-league team and $30,000,000 to a pet cat named Rhubarb. The animal becomes a good-luck symbol to the Brooklyn Loons, and the team goes from the cellar to win the World Series. Rhubarb has all sorts of encounters with anti-cat relatives, bookies, and gangsters, and the Loons go into a slump when he is kidnapped (or catnapped) by crooks. Escaping his captors, Rhubarb streaks back to the stadium, aided by just about everyone in Brooklyn, and inspires the team to victory.

H. Allen Smith's popular book had knocked around Hollywood for years before director Arthur Lubin (of Francis the talking mule fame) became interested in its screen possibilities. *Rhubarb* was rejected by several studios, one of which wanted to change the cat to a dog, the baseball team to a football nine—and to make the animal talk! Lubin finally persuaded producer William Perlberg to let him do the story as written, although Smith later complained that "Paramount fouled it up engagingly." The author's principal complaint was that Rhubarb lost his personality—instead of being brazen and sassy, he was merely cute. *Rhubarb* had many authentic scenes shot at Ebbets Field in Brooklyn, but its one-joke theme became tiresome.

M-G-M's *Angels in the Outfield* ('51) has an even more absurd premise: an assortment of interdenominational angels are called down from heaven to help the Pittsburgh Pirates win the pennant! Donna Corcoran is a baseball-mad orphan whose prayers bring about heavenly intervention, and a pep talk by the Archangel Gabriel makes a believer of the Durocher-type manager (Paul Douglas). When Douglas promises to cut out fighting, drinking, and swearing, the Pirates go on a winning streak. At the crucial game with the Phillies the orphan sees an angel standing behind each Pirate player to thwart the forces of evil (personified by radio announcer Keenan Wynn), and at times the audience wondered if heaven was equal to the task of making champions of the Pirates. Clarence Brown, director of some of Garbo's better films (*Flesh and the Devil, Anna Karenina*), was understandingly uncomfortable with such silly material.

Baseball figures in two entertaining musicals, *Take Me Out to the Ball Game* ('49) and *Damn Yankees* ('58). The former is a spoof of the baseball of the turn of the century, and some antic comedy on the diamond helps its faltering script. Gene Kelly, Frank Sinatra, and Jules Munshin are obviously modeled on the Chicago Cubs' trio of triple-play specialists, Tinker to Evers to Chance, and even did a zany production number entitled "O'Brien to Ryan to Goldberg." It was all amusing fun, helped by Busby Berkeley's crisp direction and the able choreography of Kelly and Stanley Donen. Esther Williams is the girl, and she manages to find a convenient pool for her inevitable water ballet.

Damn Yankees takes the opposite tack from *Angels in the Outfield* and has the Devil guarantee success on the diamond. Ray Walston is the thoroughly modern Mephistopheles who agrees to make a big league idol of a frustrated middle-aged man (Robert Shafer) in return for his soul. Shafer is immediately transformed into a youthful triple-threat man, played by Tab Hunter, who leads his team through a sensational season. In a hilarious climax the Devil and his sexy assistant (Gwen Verdon) are thwarted when the hero exercises an escape option in his Faustian pact and returns to his former life. Designed as satire of the national game, *Damn Yankees* suffers from the intrusion of tasteless and out of place messages. Baseball players are made to seem dumb and oafish to sharpen the absurdity of a man selling his soul for anything as insignificant as baseball fame. On the wide-screen *Damn Yankees* is even more noisy and overblown.

The Big Leaguer ('53), a minor effort of the promising Robert Aldrich, was the best of several program pictures of the early '50s which marked the end of the baseball movies. Edward G. Robinson was miscast as an aging coach in the bush leagues whose baseball know-how helps a rebellious rookie (Jeff Richards) get into the majors. In *The Kid from Cleveland* ('49) George Brent is a sports announcer who rescues a delinquent boy (Russ Tamblyn) from a life of crime by getting him a job as a bat boy for the Cleveland Indians. Another drama of a bat boy who made good is in *The Kid from Left Field* ('53), in which Dan Dailey, a peanut vendor, connives to make his son into a star player. *Kill the Umpire* ('50) is an affectionate and frequently funny look at the training and trials of a big-league umpire. William Bendix was perfectly suited to the lead, and Una Merkel was fine as his long-suffering wife.

Harold Young's *Roogie's Bump* ('54), filmed in New York

Left to right: Richard Lane, Ruby Dee, Jackie Robinson, and Minor Watson in The Jackie Robinson Story *(1950). Lane played the manager of the Montreal team; Watson was Branch Rickey, owner of the Dodgers.*

on a shoestring budget, was a delightful sleeper about Little League baseball that became a staple of Saturday-morning kid shows for years. In *The Great American Pastime* ('56), Tom Ewell was a harried attorney conned into managing a Little League team. Another Little Leaguer story is *Safe at Home* ('62), in which a youngster runs away to the New York Yankees' spring-training camp to try and get Mickey Mantle and Roger Maris to attend a Little League banquet. Mantle and Maris were incredibly wooden and uncomfortable before the camera.

The best movies about baseball are a handful of romanticized biographies of big-league personalities. Despite their overdramatization and much outright factual error, they provide the screen's most authentic look at the world of baseball.

The story of Lou Gehrig, one of the great legends of baseball, inevitably found its way to the screen in Samuel Goldwyn's flawed production of *The Pride of the Yankees* ('42). A boy from the slums of New York, Gehrig became the idol of millions as a clean-up man and home-run king, only to die at thirty-eight of amyotrophic lateral sclerosis, an incurable, crippling disease. Ironically, the sportswriters had called him "The Iron Horse."

Surprisingly, *The Pride of the Yankees* has little to do with baseball, although such stalwarts as Babe Ruth, Bob Meusel, Bill Dickey, and Mark Koenig played themselves in it. Essentially, it is a tender but commonplace love story, heightened by a heart-breaking climax in which the ailing Gehrig bids good-bye to base-ball before 62,000 fans in Yankee Stadium. Gary Cooper's re-strained performance as Gehrig, while uncomfortable in the early scenes, won him a nomination for an Academy Award, and the picture itself was nominated as the best film of the year. (Curi-ously, Cooper detested baseball, and was reluctant to play Geh-rig.) Teresa Wright was fine as the gentle, courageous wife.

Except for his poignant death, Gehrig's life offered little dramatic material, and the overlong film was contrived of dull clichés, the most mawkish being Gehrig's promise to "hit a homer" for a dying boy in a hospital—something that had been used in *Slide, Kelly, Slide* fifteen years earlier. There was the usual last inning crisis when the Yankees were behind with two out and two on base; Gehrig disobeys manager Miller Huggins' instructions to walk by slamming out a home run—a situation that must have made the diminutive Huggins turn over in his grave! There was also a proliferation of noisy sportswriters, the eccentric Gehrig parents with hearts of gold, and a useless se-quence in which a rich snob at Columbia University tried to keep the poor but hard-working Lou from being pledged to a frater-nity.

The greatest fault of *The Pride of the Yankees* is its very lack of baseball scenes, and the few used are mostly long shots from the pressbox. Director Sam Wood missed an opportunity to capture on film the artistic grace and physical power of the ball player in action.

Although fleshed out with irrelevant sequences, including a dance routine by Veloz and Yolanda, *The Pride of the Yankees* was generally true to the facts of Gehrig's life. There was scant attention to his struggling years in the '20s, when he was over-shadowed by Babe Ruth, and the major deviation was a scene in which Gehrig is told by a doctor that he has a fatal malady. The general impression is that physicians at the Mayo Clinic did not immediately divulge to Gehrig the seriousness of his condition.

The intensely moving climax of Gehrig's farewell to baseball was blueprinted from newsreels of the actual event. The scene in which Cooper, as Gehrig, says, "Today I consider myself the luckiest man on the face of the earth," and trudges alone to the darkened locker room, symbolic of death, became a famous moment in motion-picture history. Fortunately, *The Pride of the Yankees* ended at this point and did not portray Gehrig's last two years as a parole commissioner for the City of New York.

In 1937 Lou Gehrig was signed as a screen actor by independent producer Sol Lesser. One report is that Lesser considered him for the lead in a Tarzan picture, but decided the ball player's legs were too beefy for the jungle hero. Instead, Gehrig appeared in a western entitled *Rawhide,* starring Smith Ballew, in which some baseball scenes were ingeniously included. Gehrig's acting was only passable.

The Babe Ruth Story ('48), the long-awaited screen biography of baseball's most famous player, was a major disappointment. What should have been an exciting and dramatic picture emerged under Roy Del Ruth's plodding direction as a dull tearjerker. It took incredible liberties with the facts of Ruth's life, and—like *The Pride of the Yankees*—relied upon maudlin clichés, and had few baseball scenes.

The major fault was the selection of William Bendix to portray Ruth. In a putty nose that yielded little resemblance, he played the baseball hero as an expressionless Neanderthal—and to add insult to injury, Bendix swung the bat as though beating a rug. His specious, unconvincing performance totally lacked the human qualities that distinguished Babe Ruth.

Del Ruth's priggish film, produced independently on a moderate budget for a small distributor (Allied Artists) in an effort to salvage his faltering career, seemed determined not to tarnish the idealism of the Babe Ruth legend. Its plot clichés are unbelievable. In one scene a hero-worshipping boy, a hopeless cripple, totters to his feet after Babe tosses a casual "Hi-ya, kid?" at him. At spring training Ruth slams a line drive that hits a ratty dog. Babe rushes the animal to a veterinarian for emergency surgery, only to have manager Miller Huggins fine him $5,000 for being absent without permission. There is the inevitable hospital scene where Ruth visits a boy who has lost the will to live, autographs a baseball, and promises to win the World Series. Most embarrassing is the endless sequence where Ruth visits the dying Huggins (Fred Lightner) in a hospital room to tell him of his marriage. While he prattles away about his new wife (Claire Trevor), Huggins quietly expires—probably from boredom.

Ruth then delivers a mawkish eulogy.

The unreality of *The Babe Ruth Story,* emphasized by the miscasting of Bendix, did a serious injustice to a genuinely human person and a genuine American hero. Ruth was neither a shallow dolt nor a plastic saint, and in his early years had got into all sorts of scrapes. The Ruth in *The Babe Ruth Story* is not the one his legion of admirers prefers to remember.

Babe Ruth appeared in several silent and talking baseball comedies and light dramas. His easy personality projected a bashful warmth, and although he made little attempt to act, Ruth was seldom uncomfortable before the camera.

In 1920, his first year with the New York Yankees after a meteoric career with the Boston Red Sox, Ruth starred in a low-budget comedy-drama entitled *Headin' Home.* It was produced by an independent company (Yankee Productions) and sold on a state rights basis. The financing came largely from Bauman and Kessel, the New York motion-picture impresarios who staked Mack Sennett and Thomas H. Ince in their early ventures. Ruth was to have received $50,000 for his appearance, but he later

Ronald Reagan (left) played Grover Cleveland Alexander in The Winning Team *(1952). Frank Lovejoy (right) was Rogers Hornsby.*

sued producers William Shea and Herbert H. Yudkin, alleging in his petition that he had been paid only $15,000.

The New York premiere of *Headin' Home* was held in the old Madison Square Garden, with Ruth and other Yankee stars making personal appearances. The film was geared for laughs— the titles were by sports humorist Bugs Baer—with Babe as an amiable rookie who played best when he got mad. The story, told in flashback by an old codger in the grandstand, had some similarities to Ruth's early life, but it skipped around and did not show how the hero got into the big leagues.

Also in 1920, Ruth sued Educational Pictures for $250,000 when it released two one-reel short subjects entitled *How Babe Ruth Hits a Home Run* and *Play Ball with Babe Ruth,* alleging his name and photographs had been used without permission. He also said the shorts were of poor quality and consisted only of newsreel shots of old games in which he had played. Educational countersued for $50,000, accusing Ruth of libel, and asserting it had bought the rights to the films from the copyright owners. A New York judge ruled Ruth was a public personage and could be photographed without his permission. Educational then withdrew its countersuit.

In 1926 producer Wid Gunning signed Babe Ruth to star in a charming baseball comedy, *Babe Comes Home,* released by First National. The story centered around a one-joke gimmick: Ruth is a big-league hitter whose batting eye is sharpened when he chews a wad of tobacco. When his sweetheart, a pretty laundress (Anna Q. Nilsson), makes him give up the nasty habit, he goes into a slump. Of course, she relents when the World Series is at stake, and with the cutplug restored to his jaw, Ruth slams out the crucial homer. *Babe Comes Home* was directed by Ted Wilde, a gagman for Harold Lloyd and a baseball buff—he had earlier co-directed *The Battling Orioles*—and his comedy and baseball action scenes were equally well done. First National said later that Ruth was paid more than his annual salary with the Yankees to star in *Babe Comes Home,* something in excess of $125,000, and that the picture lost money.

The following year Ruth appeared as himself in Harold Lloyd's *Speedy* ('27), which was also directed by Wilde. Lloyd was a breezy young man constantly in difficulty because of his obsession with baseball. While jerking sodas he keeps a box score by bending pretzels and doughnuts into numerals as the inning results are telephoned from the ballpark. Later, while driving a rickety taxicab, he daydreams of fame in the big leagues, and is astonished when Babe Ruth climbs into the back seat. He rushes Babe to Yankee Stadium in a hair-raising race through Manhattan traffic, arriving in time for Ruth to hit the winning home run in the World Series. Except for this climactic chase, baseball is incidental to *Speedy,* which is largely the story of the last horse-drawn trolley in New York. Wilde's direction was nominated for an Academy Award, the first year of the Oscar Derby.

In 1932 Babe Ruth starred in a series of one-reelers for Universal that mixed comedy and baseball instruction. He handled dialogue in a rather self-conscious manner, and the series was soon discontinued. Some of the titles were *Just Pals, Over the Fence, Perfect Control, Fancy Curves,* and *Slide, Babe, Slide.*

The Jackie Robinson Story recounts the problems of the first Negro to play major-league baseball. Robinson portrayed himself, and, although likable and photogenic, he was an actor only in the sense that he moved and talked. The quiet dignity and assured composure that marked his professional and private life was reflected in his performance, but this same reserve proved dramatically fatal.

Coming at a time when the Civil Rights movement was entering its first militant stages, *The Jackie Robinson Story* could have been a significant and powerful motion picture. Instead, it was inept and fumbling, and although arguing for tolerance and fair play toward the Negro, it took care not to offend political conservatives on the race issue. At best, the picture was well-intentioned in its efforts to illuminate some of the indignities of racial prejudice; at worst, mercenary in an obvious attempt to capitalize upon Robinson's athletic popularity.

The Jackie Robinson Story traced Robinson's California childhood, his success as an all-around college athlete, and his difficulties in finding a responsible job because of his color. He gets on a Negro baseball team, and some of the personal problems which he encounters in Jim Crow territory are painfully delineated. There is a memorable scene where Robinson, playing for Montreal, is razzed by organized racists, who throw a dead black cat on the field.

Initially a first baseman for the Brooklyn Dodgers, Robinson finds antagonism despite his abilities as a player. Minor Watson was fine as Branch Rickey, the Dodgers' colorful owner, who tells him that he must patiently "turn his cheek to the crowd," suffer the abuse of his teammates and opponents, and lead an ex-

emplary life. In retrospect, this seems an overtactful approach
that could only offend Negroes and integrationists. Actually, it
realistically reflected the calculated efforts which Rickey made
to bring a Negro player into the major leagues solely on the basis
of ability.

The baseball scenes in *The Jackie Robinson Story* were executed without imagination by director Alfred E. Green. Robinson's batting stance was tampered with to improve camera angles, a flaw readily detected by baseball buffs. Woven into the
story was Robinson's touching romance with his wife, and the
talented Negro actress Ruby Dee brought grace and dignity to
the role. Despite its hesitant approach to the issue of race in
athletics, *The Jackie Robinson Story* was a turning point (along
with Elia Kazan's *Pinky* and Joseph L. Mankiewicz's *No Way
Out*) in the screen's traditional bigoted portrayal of the Negro.

Several other film biographies of baseball idols have been
attempted with limited success. *The Pride of St. Louis* ('52)
chronicles the ups and downs of Jerome Herman "Dizzy" Dean,
with Dan Dailey as the Arkansas hillbilly who became a Cardinal
pitching ace. In keeping with Dizzy's irresponsible personality,
it was played strictly for laughs. The comedy pace was interrupted only by a contrived off-the-diamond triangle: the conflict
of Dizzy's love for his wife (Joanne Dru) and his love of baseball. *The Pride of St. Louis* climaxes with the arm injury that
forced Dean out of baseball in 1946, but he comes back as a successful radio and television "commertater," and the rest of the
film is a succession of corny Dizzyisms—such things as "he slud
into third base" and "the batter takes his stanch at the plate."
The baseball scenes were routine. Dean is said to have got
$100,000 for allowing 20th Century-Fox to film his story.

Ronald Reagan portrayed Grover Cleveland Alexander, the
pitching ace of the Philadelphia Phillies and the Chicago Cubs,
in *The Winning Team* ('52). Alexander's fame had crested
soon after World War I, and he was forgotten by all but baseball
buffs when this picture came out. Done in a conventional manner,
it depicts Alexander's progress from a telephone lineman to a
Midwestern bushleaguer in 1908. Three years later he sky-
rocketed to fame in a sensational first year with the Philadelphia
Phillies—28 won, 13 lost. His career folded when a bout of
alcoholism gave him double vision, but his wife (Doris Day) and
manager Rogers Hornsby (Frank Lovejoy) help him come back.
The picture ends with Alexander pitching the St. Louis Cardinals

to victory in the 1926 World Series. The baseball scenes are enlivened by the appearances of such big-leaguers as Jerry Priddy, Peanuts Lowrey, Hank Sauer, Irv Noren, George Metkovich, and Al Zarilla.

Monte Stratton, a Chicago White Sox pitcher who lost his right leg in a hunting accident in 1938, is the subject of M-G-M's *The Stratton Story* ('49). One of the better baseball biographies, it is a touching account of Stratton's efforts to resume baseball as a pitcher in the minor leagues (using an artificial limb). Van Johnson was originally set to play Stratton, but was replaced by James Stewart. The change was provident, for Stewart's performance in a difficult role is most convincing, particularly in the poignant scenes with June Allyson as his wife. Many humorous touches save *The Stratton Story* from becoming maudlin, and director Sam Wood's baseball scenes, in contrast to those he did for *The Pride of the Yankees,* are colorful and well staged. Baseball luminaries Bill Dickey and Jimmy Sykes played themselves. (In 1955 James Stewart again played a baseball star in Paramount's *Strategic Air Command* who gave up his career to fly for the Air Force).

Fear Strikes Out ('57) was the story of Jim Piersall, the erratic centerfielder of the Boston Red Sox, and his bout with mental illness. It traced, in clinical detail, Piersall's domination by an ambitious father, his early success in the major leagues, the antic clowning on the diamond that was symptomatic of a nervous breakdown and led to his being farmed out to Birmingham, his collapse and the tortured road back to sanity through psychiatric treatment.

The major flaw of *Fear Strikes Out* is the miscasting of Anthony Perkins as Piersall. Perkins lacked the masculinity the role demanded, although he effectively conveyed Piersall's instability and mental anguish. Acting honors went to Karl Malden as a blustery father who combines ignorant domination with genuine love and ambition for his son. Adam Williams is good as the psychiatrist, and Norma Moore was adequate as the bewildered wife. In many respects an uncomplimentary look at baseball, *Fear Strikes Out* also suffers from questionable psychiatric concepts, and a weak, unresolved ending. It was an inauspicious debut for director Robert Mulligan, fresh from live television, and gave little hint of the talent he was to display later in *To Kill a Mockingbird.*

Few other big-league baseball stars, past or present, offer a range of dramatic material needed for a screen biography. The major exception, Joe DiMaggio, with the enormous personal emotional impact of his unsuccessful marriage to the tragic Marilyn Monroe, is not likely to permit such a film during his lifetime. (In 1937 DiMaggio did a comedy sketch with Henry Armetta in a cheap musical, *Manhattan Merry-Go-Round*). Lesser possibilities: Joe Jackson, of the infamous Black Sox scandals of 1919, Ty Cobb, Ted Williams, Satchel Paige, Honus Wagner, Willie Mays, Tris Speaker, Walter Johnson, Mickey Mantle, Three-Fingered Brown.

9

MARSHALL NEILAN

*I*N his heyday in the 1920s as one of filmdom's most successful directors, Marshall (Mickey) Neilan lived on the scale
of an Indian sultan. His movies with Mary Pickford and
others brought him millions, which he squandered on fancy cars,
huge parties and beautiful actresses. The escapades of his spectacular private life blazed newspaper headlines from coast to
coast. Handsome, witty and possessed of instinctive charm, he
thumbed his nose at the studio gods—Mayer, Cohn, and De
Mille—and paid for his arrogance with a day when he could
not get a job.

Neilan was the Hollywood version of the Scott Fitzgerald
image in a fabulous period of bad booze and good times. "I can
stand anything but to be bored," he once said. This die-hard
gaiety remained his philosophy of living until he died alone at
sixty-seven, of cancer, in a charity hospital.

"He was an individualist, always searching for the humorous side of life, and always expressing himself in some dramatic
or unpredictable way," says Mary Pickford, whom Neilan directed in seven films.

Mickey was a genius who didn't grow up until it was too
late," said Colleen Moore, one of the stars he helped to make
famous. "He threw his career away," says Gloria Swanson, with
whom he was once in love. "Mickey had a pixy heart and wanted
only to play with life," says fellow director Allan Dwan. "Nothing was sacred or serious with him, and yet, he was the salt of
the earth."

Although critic Tamar Lane once compared him to von
Stroheim, Neilan never fully utilized his brilliant talents. Because he refused to take his work seriously, his pictures missed
greatness and are interesting now chiefly for the glimpses they

Marshall "Mickey" Neilan at the time he was an actor for American Pictures at Santa Barbara, Calif., 1912–1913.

provide of the days in which Americans lost their innocence.

Marshall Neilan was born in San Bernadino, California, on April 11, 1891. When his father, a civil engineer who built the first lumber roads into the San Bernadino Mountains, died soon afterward, his mother ran a boarding house, and subsequently worked in small hotels in and around San Francisco and Los Angeles. Her son, an only child, delivered milk and sold newspapers, and once, at six, earned a few dollars in a crowd scene at the Alcazar Theater of San Francisco.

He left school at eleven to become a messenger for the California Fruit Growers Association. Later, he was an office boy for the Santa Fe Railway, and a blacksmith's helper. His first contact with show business came when he stumbled on a job with the Belasco Stock Company in Los Angeles, with which he played a succession of boy's parts. An eight-year-old Fay Bainter was also in the cast.

Neilan was fascinated by machinery and mechanical things, and he returned to school in a futile attempt to prepare himself for admission to the Massachusetts Institute of Technology. After two years he ran away and bummed across the country, washing dishes and repairing automobiles, before the authorities returned him to his frantic mother. Then a family friend, Colonel Horace Peyton, a retired army officer, financed him for a year at the Harvard Military Academy of Los Angeles. Except for a brief term in a night business school some years later, that was the last of Neilan's meager education.

In 1905 he got a job playing bits with the Barney Bernard Stock Company in San Francisco, and was soon given the juvenile lead in *The Financier,* which toured the West. In the company was Lawrence Griffith, later and better known as David Wark Griffith.

When he tired of acting Neilan drifted around the California fruit fields, drove a stagecoach in the rugged Nevada mountains, and operated a hackstand at Van Nuys. One of his fares, the lovely Alice Joyce, was so impressed by his Irish good looks and personality that she urged him to try film acting.

Instead he became a salesman for the Simplex Motor Car Company and did so well he was made manager of its Los Angeles branch. Bored and restless, he threw it up to chauffeur for Oliver Morosco, then directing the stock company at the Burbank (Morosco) Theater. There Neilan smuggled drinks to the leading man—a handsome youngster named John Barrymore—shifted scenery, and played bit parts in such things as *The Heart of a Geisha, The Girl and the Judge,* and *Sherlock Holmes* (as Billy the page boy, a role taken abroad by Charlie Chaplin).

D. W. Griffith brought his Biograph troupe to California in the winter of 1909-10 and again the following year, when Neilan worked for him for several weeks as a chauffeur. Griffith urged Neilan to try the movies, and probably helped him get an acting job at the Kalem Studios in Santa Monica (at a salary of five dollars a day). After several bits, Neilan was soon promoted to male leads in Ruth Roland comedies. Some of the best of these 1911 split-reelers were *How Jim Proposed, The Romance of a Dry Town,* and *The Pasadena Peach.*

Early in 1912, at one of Griffith's lavish parties in Los Angeles, Neilan met Allan Dwan, a former Notre Dame football star and director of the American Film Company unit at La Mesa. Dwan soon induced Neilan to join his troupe, which included J. Warren Kerrigan as star, Jessalyn Van Trump and Pauline Bush as leading ladies, Jack Richardson as the heavy, George Periolat in comedy and character roles, and cowboys Pete, Carl, and Charlie Morrison.

Neilan usually played second leads or juveniles for American (better known as Flying A), and for a time was known as Steve Neilan. He was frequently cast as J. Warren Kerrigan's weak young brother, a characterization Neilan repeated over and over. His first film with American, *The Reward of Valor,* was released May 27, 1912.

Flying A, originally a Chicago company, had exhausted the settings of the La Mesa area in two years of filming and was seeking a site for a new studio. Neilan spent his free time junketing up and down the California coast on a high-powered motorcycle, and Dwan asked him to scout a location where "the ocean married the mountains, and cattle ranches and sophistication lived together." Neilan telephoned one day from Santa Barbara —he had found the spot.

For American's first studio at Santa Barbara, Dwan leased an ostrich farm on upper State Street, evicted the ostriches and moved in on July 6, 1912. Two days later he shot *The Greaser and the Weakling,* starring Jack Richardson, Jessalyn Van Trump, and Neilan.

Dwan made two 1,000-foot films each week, mostly westerns and action dramas, using scripts sent out from the Chicago offices of Flying A. Each picture was usually completed in a single morning, leaving most of the week free for beach parties or high jinks in Los Angeles. Whenever the troupe wanted a full week off, four films were ground out in four half-days of shooting. Neilan acted in approximately fifty films for American in 1912. Some of his best roles were in *The Stranger at Coyote, Father's Favorite, The Reformation of Sierra Smith, The Wanderer,* and *Nell of the Pampas.*

In November, Dwan was fired after a quarrel with J. Warren Kerrigan, who objected bitterly when Dwan organized a second unit with the handsome Wallace Reid as star. Neilan accompanied Dwan when the latter went to see Carl Laemmle about a directing job at Universal, and charmed Laemmle into giving Dwan a contract—a favor Dwan never forgot.

While waiting for Dwan to get his Universal unit organized—there was some delay due to financing—Neilan returned to Kalem and acted in a series of one-reel comedies with Ruth Roland and the popular comedian John E. Brennan. For some quixotic reason, Neilan often chose to be billed as "Horace Peyton," the name of his childhood benefactor. Among the best-remembered of these Kalem farces are *The Manicurist and the Mutt, The Fired Cook, The Hash-House Count, The Rube and the Boob,* and a very funny comedy poking fun at the notion of women policemen, *When Women Are Police!*

Allan Dwan then gave Neilan important roles in a series of two-reel dramas starring Wallace Reid, and in the spring of 1913 made Neilan and Reid co-directors. The team turned out *The Harvest of Flame,* but for some reason Reid was given sole credit as director. When Dwan took ill, Neilan finished *The Wall of Money,* another Reid vehicle.

D. W. Griffith brought his Biograph unit to California again in 1913, this time to the small town of Chatsworth, where *Judith of Bethulia,* his first four-reel film, was completed under conditions of great secrecy. Neilan was much taken with Gertrude Bambrick, a fifteen-year-old dancer whom Griffith was developing in ingenue roles. An intermittent courtship began under the watching eye of Mrs. Gish, mother of Lillian and Dorothy, with whom Miss Bambrick was living. When Griffith was ready to return to New York, Neilan asked him for an acting job with Biograph, confessing he was in love and wanted to be near the girl. A few weeks later Griffith wired him to come on to New York.

Neilan's association with Griffith at Biograph was short-lived, and he appeared in only two films, *Two Men on the Desert* and *Her Sentimental System,* both Blanche Sweet vehicles. Biograph was angered at Griffith for his reckless extravagance on *Judith of Bethulia,* and notified him he would henceforth supervise production but not direct. In October, 1913, Griffith resigned and joined the new firm of Majestic-Reliance (Mutual), but Neilan remained at Biograph.

The theatrical firm of Klaw & Erlanger had taken control of Biograph, intent upon converting its large library of stage properties to the screen. One of the first was William C. de Mille's *Classmates,* a drama of an unjustly court-martialed West Point cadet who cleared himself by bringing a guilty classmate back from the Amazon. James Kirkwood, who was directing,

Marshall Neilan, director of many Mary Pickford movies (about 1913).

cast Neilan in the meaty role of the villain. Henry B. Walthall, Blanche Sweet, and Lionel Barrymore had the leads. Neilan's performance was highly praised by the press. He then appeared in other Biograph pictures, including *The House of Discord,* with Blanche Sweet, Antonio Moreno, Dorothy Gish, Lionel Barrymore, and Jack Mulhall (in his first screen role), *The Wedding Gown,* with Gertrude Robinson (Mrs. James Kirkwood), *The Billionaire,* with Charles Mailes and Gertrude Bambrick, and *Men and Women,* opposite Blanche Sweet.

Alice Joyce introduced Neilan to several officials of Kalem, which was expanding in New York and on the Coast, and he soon charmed them into signing him as a director at the new Kalem Studio being built in Glendale, not far from the Mack Sennett fun factory. Neilan was only twenty-two.

Although Gertrude Bambrick had promised her mother to

wait a year before marrying Neilan, they eloped and were married in Hoboken, New Jersey, on December 21, 1913. Dorothy Gish and Robert Harron were bridesmaid and best man.

Neilan's first directorial work for Kalem was on the popular Roland-Brennan comedies. He had a flair for comedy and sight gags, and some of his work was as inventive as anything that came out of Keystone—small wonder, since he spent much of his free time with the riotous, uninhibited Sennett clowns. Neilan was soon writing his own scripts, many of which contained a part for himself. Cameraman Roy F. Overbaugh and his assistant, Victor Fleming (who much later directed *Gone with the Wind*), moved over from Flying A to handle the cameras. When studio production chief Pat Hardigan quit, Neilan brashly sent a wire to Kalem's president, Frank Marion, announcing he was taking over the studio. Marion was so impressed by his nerve that he let Neilan have the job.

Neilan soon noticed that audiences especially enjoyed the comedy of two minor performers—the massive Lloyd Hamilton and the diminutive Bud Duncan. He wisely shifted the emphasis to their slapstick antics, and the "Ham and Bud" tramp comedies earned a handsome profit for Kalem for several years. Ruth Roland, not yet the serial queen, was the leading lady, usually teamed with Neilan for just a hint of young romance to break the pace of the Hamilton-Duncan clowning. Some of these delightful comedies were *The Tattered Duke, Don't Monkey with the Buzz Saw, Si's Wonderful Mineral Spring,* and *Ham and the Villain Factory.*

At the expiration of his Kalem contract Neilan abruptly returned to New York. Allan Dwan urged Jesse L. Lasky to give Neilan the lead in *The Country Boy,* a picturization of the Cecil B. De Mille-Edgar Selwyn stage success. Fred A. Thomson directed, and Florence Dagmar was the girl. Neilan did well and was immediately assigned to an important role in Dwan's *The Commanding Officer,* an army drama with Donald Crisp, Alice Dovey, and Jack Pickford. He also appeared in Dwan's *May Blossom,* with Crisp and Gertrude Robinson.

Neilan had written a story, a drama of an Eskimo girl, with Mary Pickford in mind, and he and James Kirkwood took it to her. Neilan had met Pickford on one of Griffith's California junkets, and she prevailed upon Adolph Zukor to buy the story. Kirkwood was assigned the direction, and Neilan was given the choice plum of the male lead in *Little Pal* ('15), the first of several pictures in which he appeared as Miss Pickford's leading man.

Rags, a typical Pickford vehicle, gave Neilan an opportunity for comedy as a shy country boy. *A Girl of Yesterday,* directed by Allan Dwan, was enlivened by airplane stunts performed by Glenn Martin. In *Madame Butterfly,* Neilan was Lieutenant Pinkerton. Miss Pickford, as Cho-Cho San, did not get along well with the director, Sidney Olcott, and quarreled with Zukor over money. Neilan often drove Mary home in an old flivver. As they groused about Olcott, Neilan gave his ideas for directing the picture. Much impressed, Miss Pickford told Samuel Goldwyn: "You ought to make Mickey a director. He'd be worth at least $125 a week to you."

His popularity soared as a dashing hero of the Mexican War in *Mice and Men,* opposite Marguerite Clark. At this juncture of his career, when Neilan might have become a matinee idol, he abruptly went back to directing. Personal problems may have been the reason—or his characteristic restlessness.

In October, 1915, Neilan began directing and writing for Selig in California. His first assignment was a series of two-reel comedies, "The Chronicles of Bloom Center," which were built upon situations in a country town (*Landing the Hose Reel, The Come-Back of Percy, Spooks,* etc.). Early in 1916 he was transferred to Selig's Chicago studios, where he wrote and directed his first feature, *The Cycle of Fate,* a five-reeler starring Bessie Eyton and Wheeler Oakman. Director Colin Campbell then prevailed upon him to play the weak, arrogant young Southerner in *The Crisis,* an expensive Civil War drama filmed on location at Vicksburg, New Orleans, and Charleston.

Neilan directed and played the male lead in another Bessie Eyton vehicle, *The Prince Chap,* a costume drama partially filmed in New York. This was followed by an elaborate western, *The Country That God Forgot,* also written by Neilan, with Tom Santschi, Mary Charleson, George Fawcett, and Victoria Forde in the leads. The exteriors were shot on the Mojave Desert.

Although Neilan's work was well received by critics, he had not gotten on well at Selig. He disliked the Chicago studios and missed his Hollywood and New York cronies. Selig was noted for its penny-pinching, and Neilan had free-spending ideas. He had been promised the direction of *The Still Alarm,* a lavish fire-fighting drama, and did much research and planning on it. At the last moment it was reassigned, without explanation, to

Selig's senior director, Colin Campbell. When Neilan was asked to direct a series of Tom Mix westerns, he refused and Selig tore up his contract. Christmas of 1916 found him back in New York.

It was Blanche Sweet who induced Samuel Goldwyn to hire Neilan as her director at the Lasky Company at a salary of $125 a week. Neilan had first met this talented actress two years earlier at Biograph. She was a strong-willed young woman who danced in vaudeville before soaring to fame as the "Biograph blonde" under Griffith's tutelage. Miss Sweet got off to a slow start at Lasky, but soon became enormously popular.

The Lasky contract was the turning point in Neilan's career. A series of entertaining box-office successes with widely diverse themes established him as a versatile, imaginative, and talented director. Within a few months he turned out *Those Without Sin*, an absurd Civil War story in which the North was the villain, with Blanche Sweet and Tom Forman; *The Bottle Imp*, a psychological drama with satirical overtones starring Sessue Hayakawa; the pictorially beautiful *Tides of Barnegat*, a soap opera also starring Miss Sweet and Forman; *The Girl at Home*, with Jack Pickford and Vivian Martin; *The Silent Partner*, another Sweet-Forman vehicle written by the twenty-one-year-old Edmund Goulding; Gene Stratton Porter's *Freckles*, with Jack Pickford as the one-armed boy of the limberlost; and *The Jaguar's Claws*, with Hayakawa and Marjorie Daw (and Ramon Novarro as an extra).

Mary Pickford, who had become head of her own Artcraft unit, now insisted Neilan direct her in *Rebecca of Sunnybrook Farm* ('17). Her confidence was justified in a tender and charming picture of Kate Douglas Wiggin's sentimental novel. Eugene O'Brien, Marjorie Daw, Helen Jerome Eddy, and Wesley Barry headed a large cast.

Neilan quickly directed the four succeeding Pickford vehicles: *The Little Princess*, a drama of a young girl who imagines herself the heroine of fantastic adventures; *Stella Maris*, in which Miss Pickford played a dual role; *Amarilly of Clothesline Alley*, in which the sunshine girl from the wrong side of the tracks turns down the rich man and marries the poor boy; and *M'liss*, Bret Harte's drama of the West. In all of them the poor, hard-working gamin beset by unbelievable adversity finds the joy and happiness money cannot buy. Audiences ate them up.

Neilan said in later years that he "staggered" through the

Pickford movies, but probably at no time in his career did he show a greater enthusiasm for his work. Backed by Miss Pickford's confidence, he was able for the first time to exploit his own film-making ideas. The Pickford vehicles offered abundant opportunities for sight gags, ingenious bits of "business," and delicately conveyed ironies about human weaknesses. There were many children's parts, and Neilan had a knack of handling child performers. As much as anything, he brought his famous trademark of naturalness in acting styles, the indication of emotion by a gesture or a glance.

Mary Pickford has some delightful memories of Neilan:

"Mickey was one of the most delightful, aggravating, gifted and charming human beings I have ever known. There were times when I could have cheerfully throttled him—especially at his frequent failures to make an appearance on the set until after luncheon, keeping a large company waiting at considerable expense. To placate me he would manufacture some utterly implausible excuse—such as being called for jury duty! But so great was his talent that before the afternoon was over his genius would have brought forth an inspired scene.

"I would use the most insulting Irish language I could think of, telling him he was nothing but a bogtrotter, far-down shanty Irish, and a dirty scut!

"Mickey, who was a good actor, pretended to be shocked, and to shame me said, 'Tad (the endearing Irish name he always called me), what would the public think of their darling using such language?' And then he would pacify me with one of his creative gags that my fans still remember forty years later."

Neilan teased her about her constant vigilance in keeping production costs down, and would embarrass her by loudly proclaiming that Mary's great ambition was to be the richest woman in the cemetery.

"I can truthfully say that no director, not even the great D. W. Griffith or Cecil B. De Mille, could wring the performance from me that Mickey did," Miss Pickford says. "He invented all sorts of methods to produce the desired expressions and responses. He would dream up running gags long in advance and then at the psychological moment unexpectedly blast them at me. Mickey was an individualist, always searching for the humorous side of life, and expressing himself in some dramatic or unpredictable way."

With the outbreak of World War I, Neilan attempted to enlist but was rejected for poor eyesight. He volunteered his services to recruiting programs and Liberty Bond campaigns, directing many short propaganda films with such stars as Mary Pickford, Douglas Fairbanks, William S. Hart, and Charlie Chaplin.

At twenty-six, Neilan was the boy wonder of Hollywood. His salary had soared astronomically—Mary Pickford paid him $125,000 a picture—and he was wooed by every studio. Contemptuous of the pomposity of most movie moguls, he wanted to be free of them and produce independently.

After five straight Pickford films, he made several pictures that bore the stamp of his unique talent. *Hit-the-Trail Holliday* ('18), filmed in New York, poked fun at evangelist Billy Sunday.

A scene from The Stranger at Coyote *(American Pictures, 1912). J. Warren Kerrigan at left, Marshall Neilan in the sweater, and Cowboy Pete Morrison at right. One of Neilan's early acting experiences. Directed by Allan Dwan and filmed at American's studios in Santa Barbara.*

George M. Cohan was a bartender fighting prohibition. *Heart of the Wilds* ('18), a less successful drama of an eccentric French-Canadian trapper, had beautiful photography of Yellowstone Park by Walter Stradling. Elsie Ferguson, Thomas Meighan, and Matt Moore were the stars. *Out of a Clear Sky* ('18) was a sentimental tale with Marguerite Clark, Miss Pickford's number one rival as a sunshine girl, as a Belgian countess who marries a Tennessee hillbilly. Miss Clark was also starred in *Three Men and a Girl* ('19), a charming story of an embittered man (Richard Barthelmess) who falls in love with his landlord's daughter.

Neilan returned to direct Mary Pickford in *Daddy Long Legs* ('19), Jean Webster's delightful story of an orphan girl who grows into a sophisticated young woman and marries her wealthy guardian (Mahlon Hamilton). Things went less well on this film. Albert Ray, a promising young cousin of Charles Ray, took sick and Neilan elected to play his role. Though he gave a creditable performance, it was his last important acting experience for almost forty years.

In the fall of 1918 Neilan entered independent production with Harry Garson, a producer-director who was promoting Clara Kimball Young's career; Albert A. Kaufman, a young film executive; playwright Rupert Hughes; and Blanche Sweet. Their first picture was a propaganda drama called *The Unpardonable Sin,* but World War I was over before it could be released. Blanche Sweet returned to the screen, after a long illness, in a dual role. She was fine as an American girl who goes to Belgium to rescue a twin sister (also Miss Sweet) from the clutches of the invading Germans. Acting honors went to Wallace Beery as a brutal Prussian officer.

Neilan had troubles with *The Unpardonable Sin* from the outset. Financial difficulties delayed production, and even when his own money was involved Neilan would interrupt shooting for a party or a good time. He failed to find a distributor for the picture—audiences were tired of war movies—and had to peddle it on the state rights market and eventually sell it outright. Neilan had no hesitation in brazenly advertising *The Unpardonable Sin* as "*not* a war picture!"

Broke from his failure in independent production, Neilan signed to direct two Anita Stewart movies for Louis B. Mayer, the man who was to become his bitterest enemy. The one-time Russian junk dealer had prospered as a New England exhibitor and distributor. Hankering to become a producer, he lured the stunning Miss Stewart away from Vitagraph, after two years of costly litigation, with a campaign of attentions to her mother, a job for her husband (Rudolph Cameron), and the prestige of her own company (controlled by Mayer). Miss Stewart's early films for Mayer, directed by Lois Weber, had been disappointing.

Her Kingdom of Dreams, Neilan's first picture for Mayer, was shot while Mayer was in the East. Miss Stewart was a sunshine girl who pretended to be an adventuress. The second, *In Old Kentucky,* was barely underway when friction developed between Mayer and Neilan. Unaccustomed to interference, Neilan resented the producer's constant presence on the set, persistent interruptions and questions, and soon blew his top. Neilan scalded Mayer with the sarcastic venom reserved for the "money men" he so thoroughly despised. Mayer had a tough hide, but he did not forget Neilan's arrogance and rudeness.

Because of his annoyance with Mayer, Neilan disappeared for days at a time, and his assistant, Alfred E. Green, directed much of *In Old Kentucky,* including the exciting racing scenes. When the picture was released, it bore the odd credit: "Directed by Marshall Neilan and Staff." Anita Stewart was charming as the young girl who rides her horse to victory in the Kentucky Derby.

His difficulties with Mayer strengthened Neilan's resolve to get back into independent production, despite the failure of *The Unpardonable Sin.* He agreed to do several films for a new combine known as Associated Producers, which consisted of Thomas H. Ince, Allan Dwan, Mack Sennett, Maurice Tourneur, George Loane Tucker, and J. Parker Read. But the deal fell through. Finally, he negotiated a lucrative contract with First National, an exhibitors' group which provided major production financing.

Neilan's first for that company was *The River's End* ('20), an exciting drama of two look-alikes, a Mountie and the criminal he hunted. Lewis Stone played both roles. His second was *Don't Ever Marry* ('20), about a honeymooning couple (Matt Moore and Marjorie Daw) who try to keep their marriage secret from the girl's choleric father. Busy with plans for his next two pictures, Neilan hired Victor Heerman to complete *Don't Ever Marry.* The film is a typical example of the Neilan formula—to a basic situation add a wealth of incident and characterization.

This still was taken in the Kalem Studios in Edendale, California, in 1914. Some camera tests were being made. Director Marshall Neilan at left in derby. Behind the camera is Chief Cameraman Roy F. Overbaugh. *The other men are unidentified.*

Go and Get It ('20) was a science-fiction comedy drama which enabled Neilan to use his whole bag of tricks. A reporter is assigned to get the story of a mad scientist who transfers a murderer's brain to that of a huge chimpanzee. The hair-raising adventures which followed, including an aerial chase, delightfully satirized the films of Douglas Fairbanks. Pat O'Malley was the athletic hero, Agnes Ayres the rich heroine, and Bull Montana the ape.

While directing at Kalem in 1914, Neilan often bought tobacco and sandwiches at a nearby grocery store. The proprietor's son was a mass of freckles, red hair, and grin named Wesley Barry. Neilan soon realized the boy was a natural child actor ("All Wes needed was an intelligent explanation of the scene and he would deliver"). He used him in the Ham and Bud comedies, in Selig's "Bloom Center" series, and in many subsequent features, and came to look upon him as a son, especially after Wesley's own father died.

In 1920 Neilan starred Barry in the title role of *Dinty,* a charming comedy drama of a boy doing the things all kids do. It was a warm, moving picture with a performance by Colleen Moore, as the young Irish mother, that set her on the road to stardom. Once again the planning of another film caused Neilan to share the direction (with John W. McDermott, a writer and director of Christie comedies). *Dinty* was an enormous box-office success.

Bob Hampton of Placer ('21) was an ambitious, expensive western with James Kirkwood, Pat O'Malley, Marjorie Daw, and Wesley Barry in the leads, and was filmed on location at Fort Huachuca, Arizona. Its climactic battle sequences, utilizing hundreds of Indians and Army cavalrymen, were shot by cameraman Jacques Bizuel from a dirigible loaned by the Goodyear Rubber Company.

Bits of Life ('21), which Blanche Sweet believes was Neilan's favorite picture, comprised four separate stories. The first three were short—one had Lon Chaney as a mysterious hatchetman in San Francisco's Chinatown—while the fourth, written by Neilan, was a lengthy satire on *The Prisoner of Zenda.* Neilan's ironies were lost on audiences, and *Bits of Life* was one of his few commercial failures. One episode was directed by James Flood, with whom Neilan had worked at Biograph, and another was completed by Neilan's assistant, William Scully.

By 1921 Neilan was getting $125,000 a picture, plus a drawing account of $10,000 weekly against his share of the profits. He spent it on lavish parties with a huge guest list and gifts for all; he often distributed gold watches or expensive jewelry to the cast and crew of his pictures; he would take large numbers of friends, and people he scarcely knew, on trips to San Francisco, Tia Juana, or even New York. He was an easy touch for handouts and loans, which were never repaid, and shocked blasé waiters with extravagant tips. Automobiles were an obsession with him, and he spent thousands on custom-made cars. He was often seen, with a well-known actress, racing down Hollywood Boulevard, usually followed by a second car filled with madly playing musicians.

Neilan's love affairs, not always conducted with discretion, were the talk of Hollywood. His marriage with Gertrude Bambrick had not gone well. She withdrew three suits for divorce.

but a fourth was granted in 1921. They had one son, Marshall, Jr., now a television film editor. Miss Bambrick subsequently had a lasting marriage with Jack Alicoate, editor of *The Film Daily*.

Neilan's romance with Gloria Swanson was particularly torrid, and at one time or another his name was linked by the gossip columnists with those of Corinne Griffith, Marjorie Daw, Mary Miles Minter, Peggy Hopkins Joyce, Dorothy Mackaill, Alice Lake, Olive Borden, Sally O'Neil, and Anna May Wong.

He was often absent from the set days at a time. San Francisco and Catalina were the scenes of some of his biggest parties. On his return he would turn out scene after scene with his usual ease, making up for lost time. Pete Smith, his publicity director, recalled: "If Mickey didn't feel like directing, especially after a hard night on the town, he would arrive at the studio late, stall through the day and accomplish little. But the next day he would show up bright and early and shoot more scenes than any other director could do. When he wanted to, Mickey could show amazing speed in getting the picture into the can— but he didn't always want to."

The Neilan set was packed with cronies—James Kirkwood, Lew Cody, Jack Pickford, Norman Kerry, Matt Moore, Ford Sterling, Mack Sennett, Raymond Griffith, Sydney Chaplin, and occasionally Charlie Chaplin and John Barrymore. The incessant, often elaborate practical jokes held up production, but Neilan enjoyed them immensely. He and comedian Sammy Cohen once planted a cockroach in the soup at the posh Montmarte Restaurant in order to raise an indignant uproar.

Music was the only permanent love in Neilan's life. Although he could not read a note of music, he played the piano and organ beautifully. At one of his lavish Sunday-evening parties in 1922 he picked out an entrancing theme on his $10,000 pipe organ. Paul Whiteman and his pianist, Ferde Grofe, took it down and later added lyrics by Dorothy Terris to produce "Wonderful One," one of the most popular song hits of all time. Neilan got a lot of mileage out of "Wonderful One" through the years, assuring his current lady love it had been written for the day when she would come along. Neilan gave his interest in "Wonderful One" to Paul Whiteman. In later years, when he had fallen on hard times, the royalties would have kept him going.

Neilan's carousing with John Barrymore seems, in retrospect, typical of the way in which he wasted his youth and talent. They were much alike, each touched with unfulfilled genius, each possessing a capricious approach to life, a love for a good time, an incisive wit, a mania for practical jokes, a disrespect for the pompous, an amoral attitude toward women, and a prodigious capacity for liquor.

Their friendship began when Neilan was a teenage messenger smuggling drinks to Barrymore at the Morosco Theater in Burbank. Local bartenders had already marked the actor as an "86"—the progressive, quarrelsome drinker—and would not serve him. Neilan often traveled into the suburbs in quest of a bottle. For years Barrymore called him "Mercury"—for the speed with which he could produce a drink.

In 1920 Neilan purchased Albert Payson Terhune's *The Lotus Eater,* with Barrymore in mind as Jacques Lenoi, a millionaire's son raised at sea who did not see a woman until he was twenty-five! Barrymore was rather indifferent to the idea—he had made fifteen pictures, and except for *Dr. Jekyll and Mr. Hyde,* none had been particularly successful. He finally agreed to do it less from interest in the role than from an expectation of good times with Neilan during the filming.

The Lotus Eater was shot at the Biograph studio in the Bronx and in Florida because Barrymore refused to go to California. Major Edward Bowes, business manager for the company, tried vainly to keep Barrymore and Neilan on a shooting schedule. Shooting came to a frequent halt as Barrymore announced his intention to call upon his infant daughter Diana, and disappeared. Neilan would set off in pursuit, and often the pair did not return for days.

Much of the plot concerned the hero's experiences on a Pacific isle, dallying with a beautiful native girl (Colleen Moore). To get authentic tropical locales, Neilan scheduled several weeks of shooting in Florida. At Palm Beach, Barrymore and Neilan created disturbances in several of the better hotels. At Miami, Neilan insulted William Jennings Bryan when he phoned to ask if Neilan would be interested in a script Bryan had written. Thinking it was Barrymore playing a practical joke, Neilan shouted into the telephone: "Go back to bed, you crazy bastard, and leave me alone!"

Notwithstanding all this, *The Lotus Eater* was not a total loss. Barrymore did not merely mug, there were large doses of escapism, a sophisticated approach to sex and marriage, and beautiful photography, some of it from a dirigible again.

Neilan was indirectly involved in the sensational William Desmond Taylor murder case. Henry Peavey, Taylor's butler, told police only three movie personalities were frequent visitors to the murdered director's apartment—Mabel Normand, Mary Miles Minter, and Marshall Neilan. The night after the tragedy, Neilan and Miss Minter, with whom Taylor had been linked by the newspapers, talked of the strange case until dawn. Miss Minter was worried about some letters she had written Taylor. The following evening Mabel Normand, Gloria Swanson, Jack Pickford, and Frank Urson (Neilan's assistant) met at Neilan's home. He urged Miss Normand to tell the police all she knew. What, and how much, has never been made public. There are many rumors. One is that Taylor was killed after threatening to expose a narcotics ring which both supplied Normand with dope and blackmailed her. Taylor's murder remains officially unsolved.

Neilan's delightful filmization of Booth Tarkington's *Penrod* ('22) was released around the time of the Taylor scandal. Wesley Barry was tailor-made for the title role, and Neilan's ability to direct children and extract entertainment from their imaginative play was never more effectively utilized. Marjorie Daw and John Harron were the young lovers, and Lina Basquette was the vamp who teaches the kid the shimmy. Neilan was frequently absent during the production of *Penrod* and an assistant, Frank O'Connor, directed considerable portions of it. *Penrod* was a money-maker, but Neilan sold Wesley Barry's contract to Warner Brothers—he needed the cash.

He made two more pictures for First National—*Fools First,* in which a reformed gangster (Richard Dix) went to work in a bank, planned a daring robbery with his old gang, and at the last moment did an about-face; and *Minnie,* a comedy drama of a wallflower (Leatrice Joy). Neilan was so indifferent to *Minnie* that some of it was directed by Frank Urson.

James R. Grainger, Neilan's sales manager, said later that Neilan personally netted over a million dollars on eight of the ten films he did for First National release. Nevertheless, he was chronically broke and in debt. Pete Smith says that production on a film was sometimes completed only by using money advanced on Neilan's forthcoming pictures. Cast and crew often went without salary, once up to eight weeks, but Neilan always paid up in full. One picture—*No Drums Were Heard*—was never

This unusual scene was made on the set of a Ham And Bud *comedy at the Kalem Studios in Edendale in 1914. It shows Marshall Neilan directing a scene. The cameraman is* Victor Fleming, *in later years director of* Gone With the Wind. *Fleming was assistant to Chief Cameraman* Roy F. Overbaugh, *who made this still. The actors are unidentified.*

finished when banks shut off Neilan's credit.

It was largely these financial headaches that led Neilan to sign with the Goldwyn Company for $25,000 plus fifty per cent of the profits per picture, with Goldwyn doing all the financing. Frank J. Godsol, with whom Neilan had been associated on *The Lotus Eater,* gained control of the Goldwyn Company in 1922 after a long encounter with Samuel Goldwyn. Godsol had made an early fortune by selling phony pearls, had been indicted in France for embezzlement, and during World War I had been imprisoned as a result of a shady deal involving faulty war materials.

In the midst of these negotiations Neilan's on-again, off-again romance with Blanche Sweet culminated in marriage on June 8, 1922, in Chicago. The newspapers made more of Miss Sweet having bobbed her hair than of the ceremony.

Neilan's first picture for Goldwyn was *The Stranger's Banquet,* ('22), a long and confused treatise on capital and labor that had almost as many characters as *Intolerance.* It was difficult to know what Neilan was getting at, and except for a few left-wing reviewers, it was panned. He was often away from the set for days at a time during production, once while pursuing a short-lived affair with Peggy Hopkins Joyce. Eleanor Boardman, who made her debut in *The Stranger's Banquet,* recalls that the cast and crew waited two weeks after the starting date before Neilan made an appearance.

The Eternal Three ('23) was not much better. An unsavory story about a surgeon (Hobart Bosworth) whose pretty second wife (Claire Windsor) made time with his son (Raymond Griffith), it was cheap in theme and trite in execution. Neilan was accused of having written the continuity while on the way home from a Hollywood party. Frank Urson directed some of it.

Neilan's third film for Godsol, *The Rendezvous* ('23), was a contrived tale of an American soldier of World War I (Conrad Nagel) who falls in love with a Russian princess (Lucille Ricksen). Despite torrid love scenes, Sydney Chaplin's low comedy, and Neilan's satirization of the arty techniques of the postwar German directors, it was slow-moving and dull.

In 1922 Mary Pickford imported Ernst Lubitsch, the brilliant German creator of Pola Negri's *Passion,* to direct her in *Dorothy Vernon of Haddon Hall.* Handicapped by poor English, Lubitsch understood neither the script nor the character development. Miss Pickford shelved plans for the picture and appeared instead under Lubitsch's direction in *Rosita,* by her own admission one of the worst films ever made. The following year she revived *Dorothy Vernon of Haddon Hall* and engaged Marshall Neilan to direct. A lavish costume drama set in the England of Mary Stuart, it cost more than $1,000,000 to produce. Beautifully acted and photographed (by Charles Rosher), it was slickly but tastefully directed. Miss Pickford gave a sensitive, restrained performance. As on all Pickford films, Neilan was comparatively meticulous in the performance of his duties. *Dorothy Vernon of Haddon Hall* was a box-office bonanza.

For two years Neilan had been planning an ambitious production of *Tess of the d'Urbervilles,* Thomas Hardy's somber Victorian classic of philosophical realism, with Blanche Sweet in the title role. It was not the type of picture Neilan was accustomed to handling, requiring a deeper grasp of human motivations than he had conveyed in earlier films.

Before *Tess* was completed new problems were to arise for Neilan in the shape of his old enemy, Louis B. Mayer. In April, 1924, a complex transaction took place whereby Metro and the Goldwyn Company were merged as a subsidiary to Loew's, Incorporated. Under a fabulous financial arrangement the so-called "Mayer group" (Mayer, Irving Thalberg, and J. Robert Rubin) were brought in to run the studio. Neilan's contract, along with the other assets of the Goldwyn Company, were transferred to the new organization, which became Metro-Goldwyn-Mayer. Mayer was once again Neilan's boss.

Since their association on the Anita Stewart pictures Neilan had openly ridiculed Mayer. The producer was furious when *Photoplay* quoted Neilan as saying: "An empty taxi drove up to the studio today and Louis B. Mayer got out."

At the elaborate ceremonies inaugurating the new regime Neilan further insulted Mayer by walking out during Mayer's lengthy, sentimental address, accompanied by the cast and crew of *Tess* (then in the last stages of production). Neilan loudly and profanely complained Mayer was talking too much and that he didn't intend to waste his time listening to the speech. He and his unit then piled into waiting automobiles and roared noisily away.

Mayer soon had his innings. At a studio preview of *Tess of the d'Urbervilles* he ordered a happy ending substituted for Hardy's tragic climax. Instead of going to the gallows for the murder of her seducer, Tess was pardoned at the last minute and freed to return to the man she really loved. Neilan roundly abused Mayer in front of Harry Rapf and others, but Mayer was adamant, forcing Neilan to shoot a scene which accomplished the happy ending. At a sneak preview in San Francisco Neilan showed both endings and asked the audience for its preference. The vote was overwhelming in favor of the tragic ending, but Mayer was unimpressed and ordered the film released with the happy ending.

Not all the faults in *Tess of the d'Urbervilles* can be laid to Mayer. Neilan, to a certain degree, failed to grasp the complexities of the Hardy classic. The picture lacked definition and

Blanche Sweet at the time she was a Famous Players star (1915–17). This was several years before she married Mickey Neilan.

pace, and was largely saved by a fine, sensitive performance by Blanche Sweet (which, with *Anna Christie,* ranks as her best) and the beautiful photography by David J. Kesson. Many authentic English settings (filmed by Neilan, Kesson, and Frank Urson on a riotous European jaunt in 1922) were used, and the bleak towers of Stonehenge were particularly impressive.

To escape from Mayer, Neilan and Miss Sweet went abroad in 1924 to film exteriors for *The Sporting Venus,* a comedy about a titled Scottish lady who marries a commoner. The striking locales of the Earl of Airlee's Cortachy Castle in Kirriemuir were used. Neilan was on surer ground with this light farce, which reflected some of the sophistication popularized by Chaplin in *A Woman of Paris,* a picture Neilan much admired. Miss Sweet's vivacious Lady Gwendolyn was a welcome contrast to her somber Tess, and Ronald Colman, decked out in kilts, had little to do.

Neilan hastened to complete the two films still owing under his Goldwyn contract. The only thing that made his position tenable at M-G-M was his friendship with Irving Thalberg, who did what he could to ease the tension between Neilan and Mayer.

Plans for a top-budget production, *The Return of the Soldier,* to star Blanche Sweet, were scrapped, and instead Neilan did a cheap quickie, *The Great Love* ('25), with Viola Dana and Robert Agnew. Little is known about this picture, and it had few bookings and virtually no advertising or publicity. M-G-M may have deliberately withdrawn it from distribution.

Mike ('26), Neilan's last film at M-G-M, was a curious hodge-podge intended to showcase the talents of his latest discovery, Sally O'Neil. Born Virginia Louise Noonan in Bayonne, New Jersey, and known by the unlikely name of "Chotsie," she was fifteen years old when Neilan spotted her in a Hollywood hotel and induced M-G-M to sign her. She flowered under his direction, and her piquant, red-haired Irish beauty and flair for comedy were well used in many jazz-age comedies. She adored Neilan, and he was amused by her constant pranks. *Mike* was a railroading story which Neilan had originally written for Mary Pickford, but she rejected it as too similar to Colleen Moore's *The Desert Flower*. Mostly incident, but peppered with comedy and business from the Neilan bag of tricks, *Mike* made Sally O'Neil an overnight star. William Haines, Ford Sterling, and Charlie Murray were in the cast.

Neilan's troubles with Louis B. Mayer took a financial turn in a bitter controversy over the company's accounting practices. Entitled to 50 per cent of the profits of his films, Neilan objected to M-G-M's heavy charges for studio overhead, advertising, and publicity. He accused Mayer of double-dealing and initiated a lawsuit, but eventually, and reluctantly, settled for a fraction of what he considered was due him.

Freed of his M-G-M contract—but not of Mayer's hatred—Neilan reactivated his independent unit, and made *The Skyrocket* ('26), one of the very best films about Hollywood. The story was the familiar one of the little girl from the wrong side of the tracks who becomes a big star, but in picturing the luminaries of the screen world Neilan was utterly ruthless. Gloria Swanson was generally identified as the prototype of Sharon

Kimm, and many saw Neilan himself in Dvorak (Earle Williams), the star-maker director who thirsted after power and women. Only a thin veneer disguised the identities of Hollywood personalities represented by other characters. Peggy Hopkins Joyce, whose penchant for millionaire husbands was then much publicized, was the star. Neilan's earlier infatuation with her had cooled, and he was no longer amused by her, but he thought she was right for the part.

Neilan and Miss Joyce did not get along during the making of *The Skyrocket*. They had a bitter quarrel over her costumes in the earlier sequences—she wanted them made by Howard Greer, and Neilan insisted they be bought off the racks at a Salvation Army thrift shop. She was petulant and demanded, among other things, a chair with her name and "everything that Mary Pickford has!" Harold Grieve, Neilan's art director, remembers that Miss Joyce always carried a paper shoe box under her arm, in odd contrast to her chinchilla jacket and pearls. It contained a fabulous collection of jewelry and was never out of her sight.

Financed with the aid of Joseph P. Kennedy and P. A. Powers, *The Skyrocket* was released by Associated Exhibitors (later PDC and Pathé). Although an exhibitor combine to some extent, it lacked adequate sales facilities, and Neilan was irked at what he considered to be a poor promotional job. *The Skyrocket* barely made its heavy production cost. Rather than risk a second expensive picture, Neilan ended his contract with a cheap quickie, *Wild Oats Lane* ('26), an inconsequential crook drama with Robert Agnew and Viola Dana.

In 1925 Neilan had purchased the old Harry Garson studios in Edendale for $300,000, and spent thousands more remodeling it for his independent unit. Virtually every cent was borrowed, and Blanche Sweet is said to have put up $50,000 of the cost. The new studio had dozens of transplanted palm trees, a large swimming pool, and an expensive pipe organ in Neilan's private office.

With the prestige of *The Skyrocket*, Neilan negotiated a releasing arrangement with Paramount and turned out two successful pictures. The first, *Diplomacy* ('26), starring Blanche Sweet and Neil Hamilton, kidded the hoary old Sardou melodrama and was good lively fun. The second, *Everybody's Acting* ('26), was a honey of a comedy and one of Neilan's best films. Few vehicles were more suited to his talents than this Cinderella story of an orphan (Betty Bronson) raised backstage by Fathers Associated, five eccentric actors who bring her up (played in grand style by Raymond Hitchcock, Ford Sterling, Stuart Holmes, Henry B. Walthall, and Philo McCullough).

One of Neilan's backers was a gangling young Texas millionaire named Howard Hughes, whose interests were then evenly divided between airplanes, movies, and good times. Neilan had known his father, and had met young Hughes in 1925 and had introduced him to some of the Hollywood glamour girls. A round of fabulous parties followed. Hughes financed *Everybody's Acting,* which returned a 50 per cent profit. He was often on the set, morosely crouched in a corner, but soaking up Neilan's film-making techniques.

Hughes soon launched his own independent Caddo Produc-

Wesley Barry, the famous child star discovered by Marshall Neilan.

tions—with *Two Arabian Nights,* starring William Boyd and
Louis Wolheim—and announced he wanted to do an aviation
picture but had no story. Neilan came up with the idea, reportedly
no more than two typewritten pages, which Hughes purchased
and used as the basis for his multi-million-dollar *Hell's Angels.*
The story was one Neilan might have dredged up from his early
days with Allan Dwan at Flying A—the weak brother protected
by the strong brother, transported to World War I and the
pioneer Army Air Force.

Neilan was originally slated to direct *Hell's Angels,* but
more than a year elapsed before production began in 1927, and
his story had undergone alterations at the hands of Harry Behn
(scripter of *The Big Parade*), Howard Estabrook, and others.
Although Neilan helped with the casting and directed several
tests, he was replaced by Luther Reed as principal photography
commenced. Misunderstandings had arisen and cooled his friendship with Hughes.

Everybody's Acting was Neilan's last effort at independent
production for several years. His reputation for undependable-
ness made it increasingly difficult to secure financing, and he had
offended many in the Hollywood hierarchy besides Louis B.
Mayer. He earned the enmity of Cecil B. De Mille with a foolish
trailer, shown at an exhibitors' convention, which implied that
De Mille, who had left Paramount, was through. It aroused
indignation throughout the trade, and although Neilan publicly
apologized (at Adolph Zukor's insistence), De Mille did not
forget. Mayer, Harry Cohn, agent Myron Selznick, and others
virtually blacklisted Neilan.

Late in 1926 Neilan signed for three films at First National,
but at substantially less—about $50,000 a picture—than he had
been getting. *Venus of Venice* ('27), with Constance Talmadge,
was a witty and brisk little comedy about a light-fingered Italian
maid reformed by an American artist (Antonio Moreno). *Her
Wild Oat* ('27) was a comedy drama of a lunch-wagon waitress
(Colleen Moore) who used her savings in an attempt to enter
high society. Neilan was drinking heavily during its production,
and producer John McCormick found it necessary to keep him
under constant surveillance. First National did not renew his
contract after *Three-Ring Marriage,* a dull circus story with
Mary Astor, Lloyd Hughes, and Alice White.

Neilan then did *Take Me Home* ('28) for Paramount, a
comedy of backstage life with Bebe Daniels as a chorus girl who

loves an inept magician (Neil Hamilton). In 1928, at FBO, through the influence of Joseph P. Kennedy, he made his last two silents—*Taxi 13,* a cheap comedy about a superstitious cab driver (Chester Conklin), and *His Last Haul,* a maudlin quickie about a thief (Tom Moore) who reformed on Christmas Eve through the love of a child.

Neilan's career now took a sharp dip downward. The halycon days of the silent era were at an end, and the uncertainties of the talking picture made it necessary for stars, directors, and writers to prove their talents again. Neilan was frankly apprehensive. Several silent directors of repute—notably Herbert Brenon, Edwin Carewe, and Fred Niblo—were having difficulty adjusting to sound. Producers, beset by many new problems, were in no mood to indulge Neilan's indifference to budget, playboy temperament, and unreliability.

He tried unsuccessfully to persuade Howard Hughes to let him take over the direction of *Hell's Angels* (Hughes had scrapped Luther Reed's silent fragment to make a new talkie version, replacing the Nordic Greta Nissen with newcomer Jean Harlow). Hughes, aided by James Whale, was directing the film himself.

It was with one of the British companies, which, unable to get sound equipment and technicians in England, had taken the drastic step of coming to Hollywood to produce, that Neilan found an opportunity to write and direct his first talking picture. *Black Waters* ('29) was a lurid melodrama of the San Francisco waterfront featuring fog, a mystery ship, and a skulking fiend intent upon killing off the entire cast. Most of it was confined to the cabin of the ship, in deference to the immobility of the microphone. James Kirkwood, Neilan's old crony, was the crazed killer, and Mary Brian, Robert Ames, and John Loder were among the intended victims. Another figure from Neilan's past, Lloyd Hamilton, provided the comedy relief. Released by World Wide, an independent distributor, *Black Waters* was a mediocre film that had few bookings. Neilan then went to England to do another picture for the British & Dominions Company, *Wanted Men,* based on his own story. The deal fell through, and after some monumental high jinks in London, he returned to Hollywood.

Neilan's ability to bounce back was demonstrated when Maurice Revnes, a former associate, entrusted him with the direction of Pathé's *The Awful Truth,* a picturization of Arthur

Richman's hit play. It was the tonic Neilan needed, and he directed the dramatic story of love, marriage and divorce, enlivened by witty dialogue, in an extremely able and sophisticated style. Ina Claire was a delight in the lead.

Surprisingly, *The Awful Truth* did not put him back on top. He signed with RKO Radio and did *Tanned Legs,* a rowdy and exhilarating musical comedy with Ann Pennington's legs and June Clyde's knees, and *The Vagabond Lover,* an insipid effort to capitalize on the phenomenal popularity of crooner Rudy Vallee.

Neilan's career then came to an almost full stop. His downfall had been in the making for years. The palmy days were gone as Hollywood, characteristically, rejoiced in his comeuppance. He could not get a job.

"I was making $15,000 a week one year—the next I couldn't get fifteen cents," Neilan cried bitterly to the press. In 1930 he made only one picture, a dull cheapie called *Sweethearts on Parade,* which veteran producer Al Christie turned out for Columbia release. The next year he was reduced to directing three short subjects—it was all the work he could get. Mack Sennett let him do a two-reel comedy, *Ex-Sweeties,* and later he directed a couple of slapstick items with Guinn Williams, *Catch as Catch Can* and *War Mamas,* for Hal Roach.

In 1930 what promised to be a chance to re-establish himself turned into a bitter blow when Mary Pickford signed him to direct her in *Secrets.* Things went badly from the start—the script was confused and poorly suited to Miss Pickford, and she was upset with personal troubles in her marriage with Douglas Fairbanks. Abruptly, she stopped production and burned the negative. No explanations were made to the press, and Neilan was assumed to have been at fault. Frank Borzage was assigned to *Secrets* two years later and started all over with a different cast.

Bitter and depressed, Neilan took increasing refuge in the alcohol that was largely responsible for his troubles. His marriage to Blanche Sweet had come to an end in 1929, and her career was also in decline. She had hoped to repeat her role as Anna Christie in M-G-M's talkie remake, but the part went to Greta Garbo. Although Miss Sweet handled dialogue well and was extremely beautiful, she could not catch on in talking pictures. She appeared in several British and German films, and later did a stint on Broadway in the '30s, including a splendid performance in *The Petrified Forest* with Leslie Howard and

Marshall Neilan's piquant Irish discovery, Sally O'Neil.

Humphrey Bogart. Eventually she returned to California and did bit parts in movies, a radio serial, walk-ons in live television, and for a time was a saleslady in a Los Angeles department store.

Neilan's financial troubles grew acute. He had closed the Marshall Neilan Studios in Edendale after the completion of *Everybody's Acting,* and for some reason refused to rent it to other producers. It remained boarded up for years, deteriorating for lack of care, and eventually Neilan sold it for a fraction of what it had cost. In 1933 he filed as a bankrupt, listing $183,531 in debts, including $66,249 in unpaid income taxes. Four years later he again resorted to the bankruptcy courts.

After more than a year of idleness, Neilan went to New York in 1932 to try and promote a picture deal. Although virtually broke, he lived at the Marguery on Park Avenue and was seen in posh places handing out fives and tens—and then eating in the Automat. A publicity man, Ira Simmons, announced that Neilan would direct an independent film, and for months his office was a madhouse of fading movie queens and slipping male stars, all of whom, out of loyalty to old friends, Mickey was trying to cast in a picture that was never made.

A few months later he got financing, reportedly from Coca-Cola interests, for a film shot at the Sun Haven Studios in St. Petersburg, Florida. *Chloe* ('33) was embarrassingly bad, almost amateurish, with a ridiculous story laid in the Everglades. Olive Borden, debilitated by the alcoholism that led to her death, had the lead and frequently held up production with fits of temperament and illness. Philip Ober, Reed Howes, and Molly O'Day, sister of Sally O'Neil, were also in the cast. *Chloe* got only a few bookings on the state rights market.

Neilan then got together a New York group headed by hotelman Jack Bergen to do a screen version of Otto Soglow's comic strip, *The Little King*. Buster Keaton, whose career was also at a low ebb, came on from Hollywood to do the lead, and the company left for Havana for exteriors. With the hot weather (which melted the emulsion from the film), a revolution that broke out in Cuba, and Keaton's personal problems, the project was abandoned.

The Bergen group then bought *Social Register,* a play by Anita Loos and John Emerson that hadn't done too well on Broadway. A good script was prepared, after several false starts, which Neilan thought would be right for Colleen Moore. Although she had given a splendid performance as the tragic wife in William K. Howard's *The Power and the Glory* the previous year, Miss Moore had gone into eclipse, possibly because audiences could not forget her flapper roles of the silents, for which she was no longer suitable. She liked the script of *Social Register* and agreed to do the picture for a percentage of the profits. The cast included Pauline Frederick, Robert Benchley, Charles Winninger, Alexander Kirkland, and Ross Alexander. Another Hollywood expatriate lost in the shuffle of the talkies, William C. de Mille, was signed as associate producer. The picture was to be shot at the old Paramount Studios in Astoria, Long Island.

Realizing how crucial this venture was, Neilan, according to Colleen Moore, was "more mature and more responsible than at any time in his career. He was earnest in his work and did not waste time." But he frequently had to be sobered up after a night of heavy drinking before he could come to the set.

Bergen negotiated a Columbia release for *Social Register,* despite the hatred for Neilan of Harry Cohn, Columbia's fiery production chief. When the negative reached Columbia, Cohn sent it to the West Coast for further editing. When Neilan saw his picture again he felt the drastic changes had ruined it. *Social Register,* released in 1934, got few bookings, and Neilan was now seriously discouraged.

Nevertheless, the parties and good times continued and his suite at the Marguery was always filled with old cronies—James Kirkwood, Matt Moore, Ford Sterling—and young and not-so-young women. Neilan's idea of fun, in those days, was to bring, apparently by coincidence, all of his lady loves together at one time.

He returned to Hollywood and borrowed $1,500 from Charles Winninger "for living expenses" and immediately blew it on a gargantuan party for old friends at the Cocoanut Grove. Winninger was not invited, nor was he ever repaid.

Neilan soon wangled a job as a writer-director at Paramount. He wrote gags and directed a second unit for W. C. Fields' *Mississippi,* and persuaded Adolph Zukor to let him direct *The Lemon Drop Kid* ('34), a Damon Runyon story with Lee Tracy, Henry B. Walthall, William Frawley, and a young actress in whom Neilan had much confidence, Helen Mack. Once again he worked earnestly and even brought the picture in two days ahead of schedule. But the old Neilan spark was gone.

Paramount did not renew his contract and he went to Fox to direct Jane Withers in *Gentle Julia.* He was drinking heavily, and the film was reassigned to John G. Blystone. Winfield Sheehan kept him on the payroll and finally permitted him to direct another Jane Withers vehicle, *This Is the Life* ('35). It was very dull and reflected none of Neilan's early ability to handle child performers.

Months of unemployment followed. Irving Thalberg tried to bring him into M-G-M as a writer, but Louis B. Mayer would have none of it. Hal Roach offered Neilan a job directing two-reel comedies with Patsy Kelly and Thelma Todd, but nothing came of it. In 1936 he got a job with David O. Selznick's independent unit, and directed location scenes for *The Adventures of Tom Sawyer,* and worked with Budd Schulberg on the script of *Heartbreak Town,* which was never made. A flurry of publicity announced that Neilan would return to acting in the important role of the director in Selznick's *A Star Is Born.* It turned out to be a one-line bit, and even that was cut from the reissue version.

Neilan's last three films, made in 1937, were quickie musicals, *Sing While You're Able, Thanks for Listening,* and *Swing It, Professor,* starring Pinky Tomlin, for Ambassador (Melody) Pictures. They were not unentertaining, due to Pinky's shy comedy and distinctive song styling, but they did nothing to improve Neilan's prospects.

At forty-six, his remarkable career as actor, writer, and director was behind him. He tried, and failed, to get financing for an independent picture called *The Adventures of Davy Crockett, Boy Pioneer,* a sort of juvenile western in which he planned to star a fourteen-year-old child actor, Chad Kendall of Crystal Springs, Tennessee. Although Mary C. McCall, Jr. promised to write a script, no studio or distributor wanted any part of a Neilan project.

He worked for a few weeks as an agent for the John Zanft Agency, but too many doors in Hollywood were closed to him. When Sol Lesser hired Neilan to work on the script of *Fisherman's Wharf,* starring Bobby Breen, and sent him to San Francisco to film exteriors on the waterfront, he went on a bender and got fired.

In 1940 another old friend, Richard A. Rowland, gave him a few days' work directing a second unit for *Cheers for Miss Bishop.* The Screen Directors Guild made him an honorary member that year.

Alcoholism deepened his tragedy. Neilan was arrested several times for public drunkenness. Judge Milam Ryan fined him $50 (which he had to borrow) for drunken driving and put him on a two-year probation. He was sent to a police traffic school another time, and finally his driver's license was revoked. He could no longer afford the battered old flivver he drove and got around on buses and streetcars.

During World War II, largely through the friendship of Darryl F. Zanuck and Raymond Griffith, Neilan was put on the payroll at 20th Century-Fox, ostensibly as a writer. He was given an office and a regular paycheck, so he could eat. He turned in a few ideas, most of which went unread. For a time he worked in a defense factory, but could not hold the job because of his drinking.

As the years went by, Neilan lived in one room in run-down hotels on the wrong side of Beverly Hills, on borrowed money, never repaid. Occasionally he did extra work—he could have made a living from the extra work old friends would have thrown his way—but most often it was just an excuse to get inside the studio to put the touch on a former associate. Among the extras he would spot other once-famous directors who had fallen on hard times—Louis Gasnier, George Melford, Emile Chautard, and others.

Neilan spent much time with Mack Sennett and D. W. Griffith, drinking and recalling the golden days of Hollywood. He tried without success to sell scripts and story ideas. And he never ceased to believe there were better things ahead. Wesley Barry, now grown and trying for a career as a director, would bump into Neilan occasionally. "There was no bitterness in Mickey's feelings," he says. "He laughed and joked about the turn in his fortunes and was sure he would be on top again."

Neilan was always proud of Wesley Barry—years later he wrote in *The New York Times* that "no kid actor has ever slipped into the shoes of Wes Barry." Some of Neilan's other discoveries were Seena Owen, whom he encountered in the Kalem days and sent to Griffith (who gave her a lead in *Intolerance*), Sally O'Neil, Jerry Miley, Helen Lynch, Lucille Ricksen, and Dorothy Mackaill (whom Neilan picked from the chorus of the Ziegfeld Follies).

In 1956 Budd Schulberg suggested Neilan for the role of Senator Fuller in Elia Kazan's production of *A Face in the Crowd*, which was being filmed in New York at the old Biograph Studios, where Neilan had worked with John Barrymore thirty-six years before. Neilan was scared and nervous, but extremely eager, and Kazan was drawn to him, and found him a thoughtful and brilliant conversationalist on a great variety of subjects.

"I have never seen a man who had once been as big as Mickey behave with so little bitterness," Kazan says. "Or to put it positively, with so much generosity and genuine sweetness. He seemed to have no resentment or hatred in him. I guess he knew intuitively that show business is an up-and-down affair, and you have to take the bad with the good."

Kazan had no difficulties with Neilan as an actor, except that he had trouble remembering his lines. But everything Kazan said to him was understood, and Neilan's own ideas for the part were fine, Kazan thought. As Senator Fuller, Neilan was seen first as a bumbling, incompetent politician put into a position of power by machine politics—a stooge of the bosses, devoid of strength and inner warmth. Later, he is the same basic man, but now schooled in the techniques of vote-getting—glibly outgoing, glittering in open-handed friendliness. Neilan's shading of the part was admirable.

Soon afterward Budd Schulberg called him to play a role in his independent production, *Wind Across the Everglades,* to be shot on location in Florida. "I can play any part you want," said Neilan, "as long as you're making a silent picture." It was his way of telling Schulberg of the cancer that had been detected in his throat.

Neilan returned to California and was admitted to the Motion Picture Country Home and Hospital at Woodland Hills, where his condition steadily worsened. Toward the last a few friends from the old days—Mary Pickford, and Blanche Sweet and her husband, Raymond Hackett—came to see him, and were shocked at his appearance. With typical Neilan optimism he told Miss Pickford, "I'll beat it yet." At the end he was under heavy sedation and could not talk, and death came mercifully on October 27, 1958.

Catholic services were held at the Church of the Blessed Sacrament in Hollywood. His funeral was paid for by the Screen Directors Guild. To Mary Pickford he left a bundle of story ideas and half-completed scripts, with the request that she sell them and give the money to the hospital that cared for him in his last days.

Shortly before his death Neilan wrote his farewell instructions: no one was to accompany his remains to the cemetery. Instead, fifteen of his closest friends, including Mary Pickford, were to be invited to a wake at the Hollywood Knickerbocker Hotel immediately following the services.

Mary Pickford remembers: "Buddy [Rogers] and I ignored his request of not going to the cemetery. As we pulled away from the Church in our Rolls-Royce and on to Sunset Boulevard, it coughed and died, and we were stalled—something that never happened before. Finally, we gave up and took a taxi to the Knickerbocker as it was too late to go to the cemetery. I had the most weird sensation that Mickey was playing his last diabolical joke on me for disobeying his instructions! I could almost hear him saying to himself in glee, "Look at the Tad—

thought she was so elegant in her Rolls-Royce, but I outfoxed her!"

At the Knickerbocker there were refreshments and hors d'oeuvres, and, at the end of the bar where Neilan always sat, a card on the seat marked "Reserved for Mickey Neilan" and in front of his place, an open bottle of beer and a glass. Someone played "Wonderful One" and the musical numbers he had composed as the friends reminisced and discussed the many facets that went to make up the whimsical and genuine genius that was Mickey Neilan.

10

THE DOCTOR ON THE SCREEN

*F*EW groups have been so consistently distorted and maligned by Hollywood as the medical profession. From his earliest appearance in the curiosities of Georges Melies to the slick hospital dramas of modern television, the doctor has received an inaccurate and superficial presentation in motion pictures. He has been portrayed as the dedicated research scientist, the inhumane quack, the Lothario with pretty nurses and other men's wives, the flashy plastic surgeon and Park Avenue psychiatrist, the crazed creator of monsters, the bumbling country practitioner with a heart of gold, and the brilliant young intern who puts his stodgy superiors to professional shame. The glamour and fascination of medicine, as the public imagines it to be, makes good cinema, but bears little resemblance to the everyday life of the practicing physician.

Movies about doctors, nurses and hospitals have invariably been box-office successes—the most notable failure was Rosalind Russell's *Sister Kenny*. They have an enormous appeal for women, and as a result tend to be overdramatized and maudlin. From an informed, realistic medical viewpoint, however, only a few of these films have had anything of consequence to say.

The doctor got into movies quite early. He appeared in some of the crude Mutoscope and Kinetoscope peep shows around the turn of the century—such things as *The Doctor's Favorite Patient* and *The Downward Path*—and was featured in Melies' trick films, broadly caricatured but possessed of the air of mystery and importance doctors have immemorially enjoyed. He was satirized in such early comedies as Biograph's *Dr. Dippy's Sanitarium* and Lubin's *Dr. Curem's Patients,* and seen in contrast

Harold Lloyd was a breezy young medico in Doctor Jack *(1922).*

as a respected citizen in Edison's *The Greater Love* and Lubin's *The Doctor's Bride.*

The beloved country doctor was the protagonist of many silent movies, and it was not until the coming of talking pictures that the emphasis swung to the more sophisticated physician of the big city. One of D. W. Griffith's pioneer Biograph films was devoted to and called *The Country Doctor* ('09). The title was also used for the picture Rupert Julian directed in 1927 for Cecil B. De Mille's short-lived company—Rudolph Schildkraut was the country doctor who saved the life of the son of a rich man who had wronged him. Henry King's *The Country Doctor* ('36) was a sentimental account of the birth of the Dionne quintuplets. Jean Hersholt brought a quiet charm and amazing resemblance to the late Dr. Alan Roy Dafoe, the Canadian backwoods doctor who delivered the quints. The film skirted the controversial and sensational custody fight for the children, and Dr. Dafoe was sympathetically pictured. Authentic scenes of the five little girls were also used in two sequels,

Reunion ('36) and *Five of a Kind* ('38), which were much less successful.

The public's love and respect for the country practitioner precluded the intrusion of social values into films about him. This was particularly true of the *Dr. Christian* series, a group of medical soap operas released during 1939-41, featuring Jean Hersholt. Will Rogers brought his homey charms and a philosophical approach to human suffering in John Ford's *Doctor Bull* ('33), based on James Gould Cozzens' novel of a New England village medico who refuses to indulge his patients in their petty illnesses but becomes a hero when an epidemic strikes. Lew Ayres added considerable stature to the medical profession as a backwoods Pygmalion in *Johnny Belinda* ('48) who rehabilitated a pregnant deaf girl. Bing Crosby and Barry Fitzgerald traded the round collars of *Going My*

Ronald Colman was an unsuccessful country doctor in John Ford's Arrowsmith *(1931), based on the Sinclair Lewis novel. Beulah Bondi at left.*

Way? for the stethoscopes of *Welcome Stranger* ('47), more an attempt to capitalize on the success of the earlier film than to deal seriously with medicine.

The best country-doctor picture was RKO Radio's *A Man to Remember*. Filmed in fifteen days at a cost of only $119,000, this unpretentious B film proved to be one of the sleepers of 1938. It was Garson Kanin's first directorial effort, and Edward Ellis gave a beautifully low-key performance as the country practitioner who is too dour to be really popular, too kindly to collect his fees, and too conscientious to neglect his professional responsibilities.

Sir Luke Filder's famous painting, "The Doctor," has been faithfully reproduced in numerous movies, beginning with Edison's *The Doctor* in 1911. The scene of the sick child lying on two chairs, contemplated by the doctor as the worried parents hover in the background, was used again by Edison in *The Doctor's Duty* two years later. It turned up again in Rupert Julian's *The Country Doctor* in 1927. A year earlier a two-reel short told the story behind the painting, and in 1934 producer Al Christie built a one-reel musical around the painting, with an insipid title song sung rather touchingly by Helen Morgan. It was entitled, of course, *The Doctor*.

Doctors provide excellent situations for highly romanticized domestic dramas. In *The Prodigal Wife* ('18) Mary Boland was a surgeon's wife who left him because he was too poor! Lois Weber's *The Doctor and the Woman* ('18), based on Mary Roberts Rinehart's novel, was about a physician who neglected his work for a female vampire. In *Call of the Soul* ('19) Gladys Brockwell was a nurse seduced by a doctor and left with child—but he does the right thing and marries the girl after saving the son from a fatal illness. *The Love Auction* ('19) was about a married woman (Virginia Pearson) who was blackmailed by a doctor after having an affair with him. Frank Lloyd's *Dr. Mason's Temptation* ('15) was a soul-struggle of a doctor torn between duty and an infatuation with another man's wife.

The doctor-nurse-wife variant of the eternal triangle has been used in such fare as *Doctors' Women* ('29); *Wife, Doctor and Nurse* ('37), with Warner Baxter as the philandering physician; Frank Borzage's *Doctor's Wives* ('31); and *Between Two Women* ('37). The latter was scripted by Erich von Stroheim, although his name did not appear in the final credits, and the once-great director of *Greed,* according to the publicity, based his story on personal observations at the Los Angeles hospital at which his wife had been a patient.

Other domestic dramas with medical overtones included *I Take This Woman* ('40), *Wasted Lives* ('22), *I Married a Doctor* ('36), *The Doctor's Secret* ('29), and *The Doctor and the Girl* ('49), an absurd mish-mash of medicine, domesticity, and sociology. Robert Taylor was an unprincipled Park Avenue specialist in *Society Doctor* ('35), with more than a professional interest in his women patients. The role did little more than prepare him for his appearance as the dedicated young doctor in *Magnificent Obsession* ('36), which was remade in 1954 with Rock Hudson in the lead.

The doctor does not lend himself too well to comedy, although he has been broadly, and often viciously, caricatured since the earliest days of the movies. Max Linder, a hypochondriac with wide personal experience with doctors, poked fun at them in *Max-Médecin, Max, Victim of Quinquina,* and other early comedies. Mack Sennett's doctors were always ridiculous, and Stan Laurel had great fun with them in a take-off entitled *Dr. Pyckle and Mr. Pryde* ('25). Typical of the doctor in such slapstick comedies was James Finlayson in Laurel & Hardy's *Saps at Sea* ('40). Called to treat the ill Hardy, he comes dressed in morning clothes, misuses a head reflector, and makes his diagnosis with a ridiculous self-invention which explodes.

One of Harold Lloyd's best vehicles was *Doctor Jack* ('23), a spoof about a breezy young country doctor who believed in autosuggestion. Doctors delighted in Lloyd's unorthodox prescriptions: excitement for a bored society girl, the visit of a neglectful son to his ailing mother, curing a small boy by telling him the schoolhouse burned down. Stethoscopes became make-believe telephones, and temperatures were taken with sugar candy. If Lloyd satirized the pompousness of some doctors, he also showed that much of the art of medicine lies in inducing a sense of optimism and happiness.

Sophisticated light comedies have enabled a more respectful use of doctors in central roles. Strictly geared for laughs were such medical farces as *Every Girl Should Be Married* ('48), *Over the Moon* ('40), *The Doctor Takes a Wife* ('40), and *No Minor Vices* ('48). Fred MacMurray was a harried baby specialist in *The Lady Is Willing* ('42), as were Cary Grant in *Every Girl Should Be Married* and James Mason (in some

Paul Muni (right) played the title role in The Story of Louis Pasteur *(1935), for which he won an Academy Award. Donald Woods at left.*

curious casting) in *Caught* ('49), a peculiar mixture of comedy and drama. Peter Sellers made an odd-ball Hindu physician in *The Millionairess* ('61).

Doctors are frequent figures in action, western, and mystery films. *Dr. Jim* ('21) was a rollicking sea story about a doctor (Frank Mayo) who had a selfish wife. Thomas Mitchell gave an unforgettable performance as the drunken doctor of John Ford's *Stagecoach* ('39). Johnny Mack Brown was a convincing frontier doctor in *Flame of the West* ('45), as was Jeff Chandler in *The Great Sioux Uprising* ('53) and Charles Starrett in *The Medico of Painted Springs* ('41). Sean McClory etched a vivid picture of the incompetent Army doctor on the Indian frontier in John Ford's *Cheyenne Autumn* ('64), bitterly aware of his limitations.

Doctors have also been useful in mysteries—both to solve the crime and to commit it. Lionel Atwill was the physician sleuth of *Dr. X* ('32), while Macdonald Carey played a Times Square M.D. in *Dr. Broadway* ('42) who cleared up a murder mystery. *Green for Danger* ('42) was an intriguing melodrama of murder in a British operating room, with the surgeon (Leo Genn) as the prime suspect. In *Hush! Hush! Sweet Charlotte* ('65) Joseph Cotten was an unprincipled doctor in a small Southern town who helped drive Bette Davis into madness. And, of course, there is always the bumbling Dr. Watson of the Sherlock Holmes movies, invariably played for comic relief.

Although a "doctor" is an indispensable fixture of horror films, most producers designate them as "scientists." Even so, the practicing physician is seen in numerous pictures of this type —the often-made *Dr. Jekyll and Mr. Hyde,* the *Frankenstein* and *Dracula* films, and such items as *The Mad Doctor* ('41), *The Crime of Dr. Crespi* ('35), *Life Returns* ('34), and countless others.

The psychiatrist first made his appearance in movies in Eclair's *The Lunatics—Or Dr. Goudron's System,* imported into the United States in 1914. Based on a play by André de Lord, it upset American audiences with what purported to be authentic views of an insane asylum. The psychiatrist was a prominent character in many post-World War I German successes—notably *The Cabinet of Dr. Caligari* and both of Fritz Lang's *Dr. Mabuse* films, all of which contained interesting medical and psychiatric touches.

Gregory La Cava's *Private Worlds* ('35), the first of the modern psychiatric pictures, was a stimulating excursion into the social problems of mental illness. It was perhaps ten years ahead of its time, and it was not until 1945 that the psychiatric drama came into its own with the release of Alfred Hitchcock's *Spellbound*. Although essentially a Hitchcock chase, *Spellbound* was accurately documented and opened fascinating new vistas for screen drama. Neither Ingrid Bergman nor Gregory Peck made good psychiatrists—they seemed unable to diagnose or cope with their own mental problems—but Michael Chekov gave a realistic portrayal of a psychiatrist obviously modeled on Freud. A dream sequence designed by Salvador Dali was particularly impressive. Although adversely criticized in most medical circles, *Spellbound* presented an effective use of psychiatry and psychoanalysis as plot ingredients.

The Dark Mirror ('46) utilized Lew Ayres as a psychiatrist investigating the pathological complexes of twin sisters (played by Olivia De Havilland in a dual role)—one good and one evil. *The Doctor Takes a Wife* ('40) treated psychiatry in terms of comedy. Anatole Litvak's *The Snake Pit* ('48) was an exceptional film which attempted to show, honestly and thoughtfully, what happens when a person ceases to be an interesting neurotic and is locked in an institution. Leo Genn gave a restrained performance as the psychiatrist who helped Olivia De Havilland back to sanity. The accusing and terrifying theme of *The Snake Pit* made it unpopular with audiences, although mental-health leaders counted it a major force in an awakening of public interest to the low standards of psychiatric institutional care at the time.

Another medically accurate film dealing with psychiatry was *The Three Faces of Eve* ('57), in which Lee Cobb played a small town doctor exploring the multiple schizophrenia of Joanne Woodward. Vincente Minnelli's *The Cobweb* ('55) was about the personal and domestic problems of the psychiatric staff of a posh private sanitarium for wealthy neurotics. Other pictures dealing with psychiatrists and mental illness have included Joseph L. Mankiewicz's *Suddenly Last Summer* ('59), *The Couch* ('62), *The Caretakers* ('62), and Roger Kay's interesting remake of *Cabinet of Caligari* in a modern setting ('62).

The public health doctor was effectively, if belatedly, lauded in Elia Kazan's *Panic in the Streets* ('50), in which Richard Widmark tracked down a carrier of bubonic plague loose in New Orleans. A similar theme was featured in *The Killer That Stalked New York* ('50), with Evelyn Keyes as a smallpox carrier uncovered by a public health physician (Charles Korvin). The specialist in poliomyelitis got his due in *Young Lovers* ('50), a touching story about the psychological effect of the disease upon a young dancer, sensitively directed by Ida Lupino, and *Interrupted Melody* ('55), which emphasized the role of modern medicine in helping singer Marjorie Lawrence cope with the permanent crippling caused by polio. The prison doctor was featured in *My Six Convicts* ('52), the obstetrician in *Life Begins* ('32), the medical missionary and jungle doctor in *Grand Canary* ('34) and *The Spiral Road* ('62), the brain surgeon in *Dark Victory* ('39), and the plastic surgeon in *A Stolen Face* ('52), *Dark Passage* ('47), *The Scar* ('48), and *A Woman's Face* ('41). In the latter Joan Crawford was a hideously scarred woman who fell in love with the surgeon (Melvyn Douglas) who transformed her into a beauty.

The heroic role of the medical doctor in World War II received scant attention from Hollywood in its plethora of war films. Virtually the only picture about him was Cecil B. De Mille's

Edward G. Robinson had the lead in Dr. Ehrlich's Magic Bullet *(1940), the story of the discovery of a cure for syphilis.*

The Story of Dr. Wassell ('44). In a sensitive performance Gary Cooper portrayed Dr. Corydon Wassell, a small-town Arkansas physician who, as a Navy medical officer, successfully evacuated nine wounded men from Java to Australia after the Japanese invasion. De Mille could not resist giving this simple tale of simple heroism the bright and brassy trappings of a Technicolor epic, but it became an effective piece of screen propaganda. The World War II doctor was also seen in the British-made *Counterblast* ('50) and in a more humorous vein in *Mister Roberts* ('55). There were aspects of the military medico in *Captain Newman, U.S.A.* ('64), in which Gregory Peck was an Army psychiatrist trying to combat war neuroses, and in *The Men* ('50), with Everett Sloane as the doctor trying to rehabilitate multiple amputees in a military hospital. The refugee doctor was depicted in a disappointing version of Erich Maria Remarque's *Arch of Triumph* ('48). The wealth of medical detail in the novel was almost entirely lacking in this hackneyed film, and Charles Boyer was singularly unconvincing as the moody Dr. Ravic. The Army doctors in *M*A*S*H* ('70), a black comedy of Korea, are totally unrealistic.

The nurses of World War II were featured in *So Proudly We Hail* ('43) and *Cry Havoc* ('43), two dramas of the nurses on Bataan. The story of Edith Cavell, the British nurse accused of spying in Belgium and executed by the Germans during World War I, has been brought to the screen numerous times (*Nurse Edith Cavell, Dawn, The Woman the Germans Shot, Why Germany Must Pay, The Martyrdom of Nurse Cavell*), usually for propaganda purposes. Other dramas of nurses in the First World War were *The Mad Parade* ('31) and *War Nurse* ('30). Even the nurse of the Spanish-American War was glorified in Edison's *The Romance of a War Nurse* ('08).

Nursing has been depicted in dozens of movies including Biograph's *The Romance of a Trained Nurse* ('09), *The White Parade* ('34), *Registered Nurse* ('34), *Nurse From Brooklyn* ('37), *Prison Nurse* ('38), *The Nurse's Secret* ('41), and in a series of cheap mysteries starring Aline MacMahon (*Patient in Room 18, While the Patient Slept*). In *Nurse Marjorie* ('19) Mary Miles Minter was a rich society girl who scandalized her family by becoming a nurse—but she redeemed herself by marrying a wealthy doctor! Probably the best film about nursing was George Stevens' *Vigil in the Night* ('40), a somber story of a patient who died because of a nurse's dereliction of duty. Carole Lombard was wooden as the nurse, and Brian Aherne made a gloomy doctor.

The woman doctor was early portrayed on the screen by Bessie Barriscale in a frothy 1921 comedy entitled *Kitty Kelly, M.D.*, which made it clear medicine was not a profession for a woman. The lady medico appeared in a more serious vein in *Private Worlds* ('35), *Dr. Monica* ('34), and *Woman Doctor* ('39). *Girl in White* ('52) was the autobiography of Dr. Emily Dunning Barringer, the first woman doctor to intern at New York's Bellevue Hospital, played with appropriate enthusiasm by June Allyson. Its semi-documentary style vitiated what could have been a romantic account of interesting medical experiences. Mervyn Le Roy's *Strange Lady in Town* ('55) was about the resentment which a woman doctor (Greer Garson) encountered in a frontier town in New Mexico.

The medical student, played for comedy in the British-made *Doctor in the House* ('55), has been best depicted in John Berry's *Miss Susie Slagle's* ('45), in which Lillian Gish was the spinster who kept a boarding house for students of Johns Hopkins Medical School at Baltimore. Its humor and warmth

Rosalind Russell played the title role in Sister Kenny (1946), *the Australian nurse who fought medical prejudice to have her treatment for poliomyelitis accepted. Alexander Knox at right.*

was not repeated in the more modern and realistic view of the problems of the medical student contained in Stanley Kramer's *Not As a Stranger* ('55).

The drama and excitement of the metropolitan hospital have been reflected in some phenomenally popular films about interns and residents. *Young Dr. Kildare* ('38) began an engaging series in which a brash intern (Lew Ayres) was pitted against a brilliant but domineering head of a big city hospital (Lionel Barrymore). Doctors were amused at some of the clinical high jinks of Dr. Kildare, most particularly in his unorthodox methods of diagnosis and treatment, but audiences were delighted and trooped back to the theaters for years to see films which were appallingly alike. When Lew Ayres fell from public grace as a conscientious objector during World War II (he was later inducted into the Army), M-G-M substituted the bobby-sox idol, Van Johnson, in the lead, and the series continued with equal or greater success. The *Dr. Kildare* series, and its successor, the *Dr. Gillespie* pictures, had a great public relations value and did much to counteract the harmful effects of the medical exposés which Hollywood brought out from time to time.

Dr. Kildare was revived as an effective television series in the '60s with Richard Chamberlain, a charming and talented actor, in the title role, and the veteran Raymond Massey as Dr. Gillespie. Its widespread popularity was matched by a similar but less successful television series, *Ben Casey,* built around a surly resident in neurosurgery (excellently played by Vincent Edwards) whose bad manners hide a heart of gold. Both of these programs were finely constructed and succeeded where *Medic*, a realistic but short-lived medical television series of the '50s, starring Richard Boone, inexplicably failed (possibly because of its lack of romantic interest). The 1969-70 season brought a revival of medical television shows with *Marcus Welby, M.D.* (with Robert Young as a small-town general practitioner), *The Bold Ones,* and *Medical Center*. The latter, a Kildare-Casey retread, profited from an objective attention to clinical detail, and from a consistently fine performance by Chad Everett as the stubborn young resident.

The popularity of the *Dr. Kildare* and *Ben Casey* programs encouraged several feature films with interns and residents as protagonists. David Swift's *The Interns* ('62) and a sequel, John Rich's *The New Interns* ('64), were ineffectual soap-operas in which the interns were more occupied with sex than medicine. *The New Interns* had an absurd sex-orgy between interns and nurses (luridly publicized in the film's advertising) that did a great disservice to medicine and nursing.

Several pictures on medical history have added to the prestige of medicine, but have rather consistently failed at the box office. Two of the best were Warner Brothers' *The Story of Louis Pasteur* ('36) and *Dr. Ehrlich's Magic Bullet* ('40). The former traced the career of the conqueror of anthrax and father of the modern germ theory. Aided by Paul Muni's Academy Award performance, it was, despite some tinkering with truth, a faithful account of a medical triumph. *Dr. Ehrlich's Magic Bullet* touched on a hitherto forbidden theme—except in cheap exploitation films—of syphilis. The story of the discovery of 606, the arsenic compound used to treat the disease, was tactfully handled. The Hays office required that the script (by John Huston) reduce references to syphilis by name to twelve. Edward G. Robinson had the title role.

Madame Curie ('43), directed by Mervyn LeRoy, was a sensitive and restrained account of the discovery of radium with fine performances by Greer Garson and Walter Pidgeon as the French research physicians, Eve and Pierre Curie. John Huston's *Freud* ('62) was a partial biography of Sigmund Freud, the father of modern psychotherapy. It was talky and overlong, and hampered by the erratic performance of Montgomery Clift in the title role. The picture was limited to Freud's early experiments in Vienna with a disturbed young woman (Susannah York) and the failure of his colleagues to recognize the potentials of medical psychotherapy. *Freud* failed badly at the box office, and did no better when the producers reissued it as *The Secret Passion*. Paramount's *The Great Moment* ('44) was a confusing, but likeable, comedy-drama of the early use of ether by a Boston dentist, Dr. William T. G. Morton. As originally conceived by Preston Sturges, it essayed a dramatic interpretation, but studio officials were displeased and compelled him to cut nearly three reels. The emasculated result, consisting largely of contrived comedy episodes, was funny only to those who can enjoy laughter in a context of misery. Joel McCrea, Harry Carey, and Louis Jean Heydt were convincing doctors.

Other films utilizing medical history have included William Dieterle's *The White Angel* ('36), the story of Florence Nightingale in the Crimea (with an antiseptic Kay Francis failing in the lead); *Yellow Jack* ('38), an uninspired account of the conquest of yellow fever; and *The Prisoner of Shark Island* ('36), a biography of Dr. Samuel A. Mudd, the Maryland farmer-doctor sent to the Dry Tortugas for setting the broken leg of John Wilkes Booth after the assassination of Abraham Lincoln.

Joseph L. Mankiewicz has directed two strikingly different films about the medical profession, *No Way Out* ('50) and *People Will Talk* ('51). *No Way Out* was an intolerant attack on racial intolerance in the medical profession. A young Negro intern (Sidney Poitier), responsible for the death of a white patient, is persecuted by a pathological Negro-hater. It denigrated its values by proffering force and violence as the Negroes' "way out." *People Will Talk*, an adaptation of Curt Goetz's fine German film, *Dr. Med. Praetorious*, turned directly to the medical profession for an incisive look at doctors' manners, morals, and ethics. Cary Grant was an off-beat doctor whose advanced theories of medical art and science brought him the censure of his colleagues. Slickly written and directed, *People Will Talk* had many telling barbs, but was often tempered with

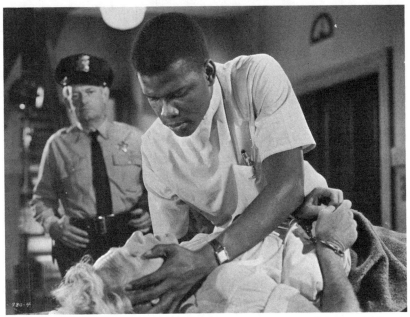

Sidney Poitier was the Negro intern who experienced racial prejudice in a big hospital in Joseph L. Mankiewicz's No Way Out *(1950).*

an understanding of the basic philosophies of medicine. It failed to be a realistic picture of the medical profession, partly because of its oversophistication, partly because of a profusion of eccentric characters, and was generally resented by responsible physicians.

Films attacking the medical profession appeared coincidentally with the world-wide economic depression of the early '30s, although such silent pictures as Lon Chaney's *The Penalty* ('20) and *A Blind Bargain* ('22) had hinted at professional incompetence and ethical shortcomings. Sinclair Lewis' *Arrowsmith* ('31) was the first really serious film about medicine to come out of Hollywood. Sensitively directed by John Ford, and superbly acted by Ronald Colman and Helen Hayes, it touched delicately on some of the professional, economic, and ethical problems of the American doctor by depicting the rise of a small-town physician and his conflict over whether to abandon his patients for a career in research.

In M-G-M's *Men in White* ('34) the medical profession experienced its first serious attack. As a play by Sidney Kingsley, *Men in White* had shocked blasé Broadway with its vicious picture of life in a large metropolitan hospital. Professional incompetence, questionable medical ethics, partisan hospital staff politics, emphasis upon the mercenary aspects of medicine, and implications of illegal abortion were combined to present medicine in a most unfavorable light. Although somewhat watered down in its screen version, *Men in White* was still a stinging indictment of the M.D., and drew a storm of protest from the medical profession. (Interestingly, it was banned by the Nazis in Germany as unfair to a dignified profession.) Cinematically, it was talky and slow-moving, due largely to the stagy techniques of its director, Richard Boleslawski. Clark Gable, then in the early stages of his career, was the young doctor who had to choose between marrying a wealthy society girl (Myrna Loy) and having an easy practice, or devoting himself to medical research. (Gable also played a doctor in two other films, *Strange Interlude* and *Homecoming*).

A Doctor's Diary ('37) was a derisive, savage attack on medical ethics, in which Sidney Blackmer, as a worldly surgeon, neglected a charity case in an emergency to pamper a wealthy patient. Robert Florey's *The Outcast* ('37) was about an unethical doctor who tried to rehabilitate himself. *Bedside* ('34), *Internes Can't Take Money* ('37), *Once a Doctor* ('37), *The Green Light* ('37), and *King's Row* ('41) also pictured some of the seamier sides of medicine and certain types of medical racketeering. Charles Coburn's incisive characterization of an incompetent, sadistic surgeon in *King's Row*—it was implied he operated without anesthesia—opened new avenues of criticism. This theme was also revived, although less brutally, in Republic's *Doctors Don't Tell* ('41), a well-made film which also pointed up the ethical responsibilities of physicians.

Cinematically, the best of the "exposés" was M-G-M's *The Citadel,* produced in Great Britain in 1938. It recounted the story of a young Scottish surgeon (Robert Donat) who sets up practice in a poor Welsh mining community. Discouraged by poverty and distrust, he moves to London's stylish Harley Street and embarks upon a career of fee-splitting and other hardened medical quackery. At the end he is read out of the profession by his peers. Except for the contrived ending, *The Citadel* faithfully followed Dr. A. J. Cronin's novel and was perceptively directed by King Vidor. It provided one of the few glimpses into the British medical profession.

In the mid-'40s American medicine received another stunning

blow in *Sister Kenny,* a screen biography of the Australian nurse whose controversial technique of treating poliomyelitis had led to open warfare with the medical profession. This hysterically partisan film cast organized medicine as a stupid, relentless menace incapable of accepting any medical advances which it did not itself develop. The picture was a curious mixture of interpretive fact, harmless fiction, and debatable propaganda. It was filled with distortions, implied rather than stated, the most repetitive being that doctors denounce Sister Kenny and her treatment. In actual fact the Kenny technique had become widely accepted as a *part* of the therapy for poliomyelitis; it was not accepted as the whole or only treatment. *Sister Kenny* smothered the fact that her results were no more than those usually obtained in recoveries and improvements by orthodox methods. Rosalind Russell, a close personal friend of the real Sister Kenny and a constant crusader and fund-raiser for her cause, played the title role, and is said to have badgered RKO Radio into producing *Sister Kenny* much against its wishes. Dudley Nichols' direction was no better than his confused and preachy script.

Probably the most damaging attack on medicine was contained in Stanley Kramer's *Not As a Stranger* ('55), based on Morton Thompson's runaway best-selling novel. There is almost nothing in the film to excite any sympathy for its protagonist, a young doctor who is idealistic about medicine and cynical about everything else, nor does it create any respect for medicine's professional attainments. Robert Mitchum was seen as an impoverished medical student who marries an unsophisticated, older nurse (Olivia De Havilland) solely for her savings to keep himself in school. After graduation from medical school he goes to a small town as an assistant to a country doctor (Charles Bickford) who knows he will die soon from coronary thrombosis. The picture exposes the audience to many clichés and stereotypes —the incompetent physician, neglect of penniless aged patients, the money-mad specialist (as played by Frank Sinatra), professional overconfidence, apathy and indifference to pain and suffering. Mitchum has an affair with a wealthy widow, tells his long-suffering wife to get out, and bungles an operation which would have saved the life of his benefactor. Thoroughly chastened, Mitchum stumbles back to his wife and practice, supposedly better qualified for his future as a country doctor.

Not As a Stranger was considerably less venomous than the

Robert Mitchum was the idealistic young doctor in Stanley Kramer's Not As a Stranger *(1955). At right is Charles Bickford as the older physician with whom Mitchum goes into practice.*

novel, yet many patently untrue things in the book were retained. The characterizations of the doctors were less venal, and Kramer emphasized the stress and exhaustion produced by the problems of daily practice. *Not As a Stranger* probably presented more of the minutiae of medicine than any preceding film, but this did not compensate for its highly debatable anti-medicine propaganda. Finally, casting Robert Mitchum as the ruthless, insensitive, but also idealistic young doctor was an unforgivable mistake. Kramer's picture, although it contains many good things in construction—such as the quick shifting from patient to patient to illustrate the scope of a small town practice—is largely a compendium of criticism of medicine, without any objective contrasting of its good points.

What do doctors themselves think of the manner in which they have been portrayed on the screen? The medical profession has resented the distortions of such films as *Men in White, Sister Kenny,* and *Not As a Stranger,* and the focusing upon the seamier sides of medicine in *The Citadel* and *King's Row.* Nevertheless, most doctors feel these excesses have been offset by the tributes of *A Man to Remember, Panic in the Streets,* and *The Snake Pit.* Most recognize that the *Dr. Kildare* and other medical television films, despite their overdramatization, have been exceptionally good for medicine. There has been a tendency to overemphasize the viciousness of the unethical or incompetent physician, and medicine has been given little credit in the movies for itself weeding out these undesirables. On the whole, however, the broadly caricatured doctor (as Frank Ferguson's obstetrician in *Caught*) is rare. For purposes of sensationalism, Hollywood also tends to make its doctors with an amoral streak —such films as *The Interns* and *The New Interns,* for instance, mistakenly create the impression that the hospital is one continual orgy of illicit sex between doctors and nurses and each other's wives.

Hollywood, usually attentive to such things, has tended to be careless about the authenticity of medical atmosphere and detail. Alan Ladd in *And Now—Tomorrow* ('44) made doctors chuckle when, as a young ear specialist, he injected Loretta Young with a self-developed and clinically untried drug to relieve her deafness. Barry Fitzgerald's supervision of his own appendectomy while under local anesthesia in *Welcome Stranger* was rightly regarded as ridiculous in the extreme. Probably more absurd was the Navy corpsman who removed an appendix from a sailor in *Destination Tokyo* ('43) by following a textbook and wirelessed instructions. Dr. Kildare, in the M-G-M feature series, constantly amused doctors by his grave snap diagnoses (always right, of course) and the pompous manner in which he imposed them upon the venerable Dr. Gillespie. The classic was in *Young Dr. Kildare* when Ayres, picked from a line of newly graduated medical students, diagnosed Gillespie's cancer after a dozen top specialists had failed to do so. The early Dr. Kildare films were also notorious for phony medical double talk.

Doctors were convulsed when Joel McCrea, as an ambulance intern, operated on the gangster (Lloyd Nolan), who had been shot in *Internes Can't Take Money,* with some tools from a nearby bar. Many plastic surgeons have watched open-mouthed at the antics of their screen counterparts. In *The Stolen Face* the surgeon (Paul Henreid) had no difficulty in duplicating the face of his lost love on a disfigured prostitute (Lizabeth Scott played both roles to simplify casting). The fallacy that faces can be duplicated has been a gimmick in numerous films. Paul

Henreid offended again in *The Scar*. After killing his double, a successful psychiatrist, he not only took over his lucrative psychiatric practice but had no difficulty in fooling his professional colleagues as well. Henreid destroyed credibility when he took a scalpel and duplicated a scar on his cheek—alas on the wrong side!

Considerable improvement in the accuracy of medical detail has been effected in recent years through standing committees of the American Medical Association and the Los Angeles County Medical Association. Practicing physicians not only review all scripts for authenticity, but are present on the set during actual shooting.

Most doctors feel Hollywood has yet to produce a truly accurate picture of the medical profession, and many doubt that such a film will ever be made. Occasionally an objective picture of the medical profession comes along, such as Philip P. Karlson's *The Young Doctors* ('61), a tender and moving story of an intelligent physician and his desire to be a good doctor—but such films are rare. Overdramatizing, the temptation to sensationalize, and a regrettable lack of understanding of medicine mitigate against such honest portrayals. Most of all, the success of the glamorized films of doctors at the box office will lead inevitably to their constant reproduction.

11

ROBERT FLOREY

OBERT FLOREY fell in love with the movies at twelve, when he witnessed a film company shooting scenes on the Place de l'Eglise in Paris. He was fascinated by the exciting things taking place in front of the crude camera—beautiful Gabrielle Robinne was being threatened by two swarthy villains, while the director impatiently shouted instructions through a small megaphone. From that moment in 1912 Florey had the cinema *dans le sang*—in the blood—and when he let it be known that he wanted to work in motion pictures, his disapproving professors warned that such thoughts could lead but to prison and perhaps the gallows!

Instead, his youthful enthusiasm eventually took him to Hollywood, where he became a talented and imaginative director of sixty-five features and more than three hundred television pictures. In the course of a long and remarkable film career dating from the early '20s, Florey has:

Collaborated with Charlie Chaplin in the direction of the controversial *Monsieur Verdoux*;

Directed two of the finest experimental, avant-garde films ever made—*A Hollywood Extra* and *The Loves of Zero*;

Written the screenplay of *Frankenstein,* the most famous horror movie of all time;

Directed the Marx Brothers in their sensational screen debut, *The Cocoanuts*;

Directed Bette Davis in her first starring vehicle, *Ex-Lady,* as well as the early talking pictures of Maurice Chevalier, Claudette Colbert, Edward G. Robinson, Kay Francis, Errol Flynn, Raimu, and Gertrude Lawrence; and

Led the march of responsible film directors into the challenging new medium of television.

In the Japanese garden of the old Metro Studio, 900 Cahuenga Blvd.,
Hollywood, Robert Florey (right) interviews Rex Ingram (left), director
of Valentino's famous The Four Horsemen of the Apocalypse. *Florey was*
then—1921—a writer for the French film magazine, Cinemagazine.

Florey's off-the-set career has been equally interesting. He
has been a confidant and biographer of Chaplin; press agent for
Douglas Fairbanks and Mary Pickford; a close friend and
manager of Rudolph Valentino; and the respected friend of
D. W. Griffith, Sacha Guitry, Tom Mix, René Clair, Mack
Sennett, Max Linder, Robert J. Flaherty, King Vidor, John
Huston, Josef von Sternberg, and a host of film personalities.

Robert Florey was born in Paris on September 14, 1900,
and educated in France and Switzerland. For a time he lived
near Robert Houdin's The Magician's Theatre, which had become the Melies Cinema, and there he watched Georges Melies
painting stage scenery or occasionally unreeling one of his early
curiosities—primitive trick films in which all sorts of absurd
things happened. He began to haunt the parks near his school
at Garches and Marnes la Coquette, outside Paris, where the

Eclipse, Gaumont, Pathé, Eclair, Aubert, and Film d'Art companies often shot exteriors. At seventeen Florey began writing sports news for a Geneva newspaper, but soon shifted to film news, movie reviews and interviews with screen personalities. Then, for Tombet-Films of Geneva, in 1919, he wrote, acted and served as assistant director on a number of one-reelers starring Walter Gfeller, the Swiss Chaplin. He was even permitted to direct one (*Isidore a la Deveine*).

Florey then became an assistant to Louis Feuillade, father of the French serial (*Judex, The Vampires*), at the down-at-the-heel Gaumont studio in Nice—the actors called it "the fly trap." The job meant that he was assistant director, property man, errand boy, cameraman's assistant and jack-of-all-trades. He was also one of the heavies who menaced the young leading man, René Clair, in Feuillade's twenty-four-episode *L'Orpheline* ('21). Each evening Feuillade would work out the script for the next day's shooting, and at dawn Florey would ride his bicycle to the director's villa. From his second-story bedroom Feuillade would shout down instructions—how many extras to hire, what props to rent, what sets to build, etc. By the time Feuillade arrived at the studio in mid-morning, Florey was expected to have assembled everything necessary for work to begin. At night, often in company with Clair and Louis Delluc, a young film critic who was just beginning to direct, Florey went to the local movie houses to watch the exciting techniques of Griffith and the American directors. The French movies of the time were still under the static influence of the Comédie Française.

While still in his teens Florey began writing for *Cinemagazine,* the first publication for movie fans in France. He was a tall (six feet four) gangling youngster and his enthusiasm and intelligent interest in motion pictures impressed the screen celebrities he interviewed. Max Linder, the French comedian, just back from the Essanay Studios in Chicago and an unsuccessful attempt to "replace Chaplin," urged him to try his luck in the United States, saying: "The future of the cinema is in America."

Jean Pascal, editor of *Cinemagazine,* promised to accept articles about Hollywood stars, and in the summer of 1921 Florey sailed from Cherbourg on the S.S. *Orbita.* When he arrived in Los Angeles he could not speak a word of English and mistook the picturesque Chinese and Mexican quarters for movie sets. A friendly French taxi driver directed him to the

William Fox Studios on Western Avenue, in the middle of a lemon grove. There then were no gatekeepers, and Florey, suitcase in hand, simply walked in with a group of cowboys. Inside, such stars as Shirley Mason, Tom Mix, William Russell, and Al St. John, the comic "Picratt" so popular in France, were at work.

Monte Cristo, starring John Gilbert, was just starting and Florey paused to watch. The atmosphere was so un-French and anachronistic—one Empire character was dressed as a Louis XIII musketeer—that Florey impulsively stepped before the grinding cameras and fervently protested in French.

Fortunately, the cameraman was Lucien Andriot, another French emigré (his sister was Josette Andriot, star of the famous *Protea* serials). He not only saved Florey from an unceremonious exit but persuaded the director, Emmett J. Flynn, to hire him as a French technical director. Joe Bordeaux, a French Canadian who was directing the Sunshine Comedies at Fox, took Florey to a boarding house on Sunset Boulevard. Other roomers included Bobby Dunn; Leo White (the "French Count" of the early Chaplins); Billy Armstrong, a refugee from the Karno troupe; the brother of comedian Slim Summerville; several stunt men; and a character who made and sold bathtub gin to the Prohibition-thirsty actors. Sennett comedian Eddie Gribbon was a neighbor.

Florey's first night in Hollywood ended with a visit to the drugstore at the corner of Hollywood and Vine, where he saw Wallace Reid browsing at the magazine rack, Mabel Normand eating ice cream, Lee Moran buying cigarettes, and Hank Mann losing nickels in a slot machine. Outside, Gloria Swanson buzzed by with director Clarence Brown in an expensive covered auto, and Priscilla Dean window-shopped with her husband, Wheeler Oakman. Up the street a George Walsh company was filming night scenes for a romantic drama. For the impressionable young Florey, his first twenty-four hours in Hollywood added up to an unforgettable, red-letter day.

In the course of the several delightful weeks he was technical director on *Monte Cristo,* he enjoyed a long location jaunt to Balboa, and became good friends with several compatriots who were working on the picture—notably Gaston Glass and Renee Adoree. Max Linder had returned to Hollywood for another try at American movies, and he often invited Florey to his home on fashionable Argyle Avenue. It was there that Florey first

*Alla Nazimova frolics with Robert Florey at Crystal Pier, California,
1921.*

met many of the Hollywood great—Alla Nazimova, Thomas
H. Ince, Leatrice Joy, Marguerite de la Motte, and Charlie
Chaplin, who lived next door. Chaplin was charmed by the
young Frenchman, and a close friendship which would last
twenty-five years sprang up.

After *Monte Cristo* was finished Florey got work as a gagman on the popular Sunshine Comedies at Fox. He wrote several
vehicles for Al St. John, which were full of sight gags and
slapstick in the Sennett manner. Occasionally he filled in as an
actor—in *Straight from the Farm* ('21) he was a rube sheriff—
an anomaly for the sophisticated Frenchman.

Late in 1921 Mary Pickford and Douglas Fairbanks made
him director of their foreign publicity. He took care of their

fan mail, wrote hundreds of articles for newspapers and magazines the world over (and a book about Doug), wrote the
French text for foreign programs and advertising, and prepared
the French titles for *Robin Hood*. Fairbanks induced Florey to
tutor him in French, and he often taught Doug French idioms
between mouthfuls of ham and eggs at breakfast at Pickfair.
"Douglas and I were so fond of Bob," Mary Pickford said
recently. "He was so charming and eager to please, and he
had such a capacity for hard work."

Meanwhile, Florey's articles for *Cinemagazine* were increasingly successful, and during 1921-22 he interviewed Fatty Arbuckle, Richard Barthelmess, Lon Chaney, D. W. Griffith,
Harold Lloyd, Charles Ray, and dozens of other personalities.
He paid special attention to the French colony in Hollywood,
and Max Linder, Maurice Tourneur, Renee Adoree, and Leon
Bary were just a few of the Parisians whose activities were
reported at length.

Paul Ivano, a cameraman, had introduced Florey to Nazimova, and she introduced him to Rudolph Valentino, the sensational twenty-five-year-old star of *The Four Horsemen of the
Apocalypse*. Florey and Valentino became fast friends. The
Italian star's companions at the time also included Jean de Limur,
a young Frenchman who was to become assistant to Chaplin
and De Mille and later director of Jeanne Eagels in *The Letter*
and *Jealousy,* and actors Douglas Gerrard and Mario Carillo.
They boxed, rode horses, played tennis, went on wild rides
along the Pacific Palisades in Rudy's white Fiat, and ate huge
dinners cooked by Valentino's German chef, Frederic.

After Valentino broke his contract with Paramount he accepted an offer of $3,000 a week to publicize Mineralava Cold
Cream, and early in 1923 invited Florey to handle publicity and
make a film record of his tour of the United States and Europe.
Valentino was also hopeful of appearing in *Quo Vadis?* in Italy
for Giuseppe Barattolo, and Florey was promised a job
as associate director. But the deal fell through when Paramount
threatened legal action.

When Florey returned to Hollywood he got several jobs as
assistant director, first to Louis J. Gasnier on Universal's *Wine*
('24), starring Clara Bow, and then to Alfred Santell at FBO
on *Parisian Nights* ('24), with Lou Tellegen and Elaine Ham-
merstein. And for Charles de Rochefort, the Pharaoh in De
Mille's silent *The Ten Commandments* ('23), Florey wrote a

one-act play entitled *L'Apache,* in which de Rochefort toured French Canada.

Florey's first American attempt at directing was *Fifty-Fifty* ('23), a two-reel comedy for Imperial Pictures, an independent company he and Paul Ivano set up. Maurice DeCanonge and Stella DeLanti played the leads. They couldn't find a distributor, and the little film had only a few showings in Los Angeles.

While working as an assistant director at FBO, Florey had made the acquaintance of Josef von Sternberg, an intense young man who was an assistant to director R. William Neill. Soon thereafter von Sternberg directed an unusual independent picture, *Salvation Hunters* ('24), which won him a contract at Metro-Goldwyn-Mayer. He asked Florey to assist him on his first picture at M-G-M, *Escape,* which starred Conrad Nagel and Renee Adoree. It was a sophisticated French comedy done in a manner later popularized by Preston Sturges. When it was previewed in Glendale, Florey and his companion, director Maurice Tourneur, were much impressed—but M-G-M executives found it "confused" and "too arty." It was shelved, but since the studio had $300,000 invested in the picture, much of it was later re-shot under the direction of Phil Rosen and finally released as *The Exquisite Sinner* ('25). Florey thought von Sternberg's version "a hundred times better" than Rosen's.

Von Sternberg soon lost his contract at M-G-M, after quarrels with Mae Murray and Louis B. Mayer, but Florey remained at the Culver City studio for several years, assisting such directors as John M. Stahl, Edmund Goulding, Christy Cabanne, Robert Z. Leonard and King Vidor, and later directing tests and second units. He frequently served as a French technical director. His association with King Vidor was particularly productive and gave Florey an opportunity to study the technique of the brilliant young director. They first met when Florey, along with most of M-G-M's assistant directors, was drafted to help in the battle scenes of *The Big Parade.* Vidor then appointed Florey as his assistant on *La Boheme,* an adaptation of the Murger-Puccini classic with John Gilbert and Lillian Gish as the tragic lovers, and on *Bardelys the Magnificent,* another French period piece also starring John Gilbert. Florey tried to secure authenticity in French costuming and design—by reference to the works of Schanne, Brugal, Champfleury and Delvan—but M-G-M's financial wizard, J. J. Cohn, thought his ideas too costly!

Another M-G-M executive, the late Bernard H. Hyman, then became interested in Florey as possible writer and director material, and assigned him to work with Albert Lewin on a scenario for a Mae Murray picture. Hyman also sent Florey to see Phil Goldstone, an independent producer at Tiffany whose financial economies and speed of production were the envy of the poverty-row studios. Goldstone was in greater need of a script than a director, and asked Florey and writer Houston Branch to do a scenario to be called *That Model from Paris—* in twenty-four hours! Goldstone had his script the next morning and immediately hired the sleepy Florey to write another.

However, Louis J. Gasnier fell ill while directing *That Model from Paris,* and Florey was drafted to complete it. During his first scenes as a director, a group of old friends—Mabel

Newly arrived in Hollywood from France, Robert Florey poses with Jack Pickford in 1922.

Normand, Fatty Arbuckle, Lew Cody, Monty Banks, and Al St. John—dropped by to kibitz.

Goldstone liked Florey's work and assigned him the direction of Tiffany's *One Hour of Love* ('26), a drama of the Yukon for which Florey also wrote the scenario. Jacqueline Logan and Robert Frazer headed the cast.

The second feature Florey directed was *The Romantic Age* ('27), for Columbia, an amusing comedy with Alberta Vaughn and Eugene O'Brien. While waiting for it to go into production Florey worked with Frank Borzage in preparations for *Seventh Heaven* at Fox. His knowledge of wartime Paris added much to the technical excellence of that picture.

Henry King, who had met Florey in Milan during the Valentino tour, then engaged him as assistant director on *The Magic Flame* ('27), a Ronald Colman—Vilma Banky vehicle, and on *The Woman Disputed* ('28), starring Norma Talmadge.

"I couldn't afford to be a director for the independent studios," Florey says. "Columbia and Tiffany paid me $175-$200 a picture—and that usually included editing it. A good first assistant at the majors got $250 a week, and was assured of months of employment." Nevertheless, Florey wanted to direct and couldn't resist doing *Face Value* ('27), a super-quickie with Fritzi Ridgeway, which he prefers to forget.

Florey had roughed out a scenario based on John Kendrick Bangs' imaginative novel, *A Houseboat on the Styx,* and at a Christmas party at Pickfair in 1927 fell to discussing it with Mary Pickford, Douglas Fairbanks, Charlie Chaplin, and Joseph M. Schenck, president of United Artists. The story brought together in hell such diverse personages as Napoleon, Julius Caesar, Sir Walter Raleigh, Hamlet, Darwin, Burns, Boswell, Homer, and Goliath!

As the evening wore on Schenck and Fairbanks became enthusiastic about its possibilities as a movie, and began to suggest a cast: Fairbanks as d'Artagnan; Chaplin as Hamlet; Mary Pickford as Mary Stuart; Norma Talmadge, Madame du Barry; John Barrymore, François Villon; Gloria Swanson, Cleopatra. Buster Keaton was put down for Julius Caesar! And at Florey's insistence, Ernst Lubitsch was pencilled in as Napoleon. Parts were thought up for Harold Lloyd, Constance Talmadge, Ronald Colman and Vilma Banky.

At three A.M. Florey was dispatched to rout out Emmett J. Flynn, who owned the screen rights, from an alcoholic slumber, and bring him to Pickfair. Flynn was engaged on the spot as director, with Florey as first assistant. In the cold light of dawn, and of an auditor's subsequent tally of probable production costs, *The Houseboat on the Styx* looked less and less promising. Two months later it was quietly dropped from United Artists' schedule. But it had been great fun planning it.

In 1927-28 Florey wrote and directed the four short experimental films which comprised the springboard of his successful directorial career. *The Life and Death of 9413—A Hollywood Extra,* the best of the four, cost $99. Slavko Vorkapich, an intense young painter who later became one of Hollywood's best montage artists, designed the sets and helped edit the picture. Gregg Toland, later the brilliant cameraman of *Citizen Kane,* shot the close-ups. For the title role Florey recruited Jules Raucourt, a former leading man for Gaby Deslys and Marguerite Clark, who considered all screen directors, except Murnau and Feyder, as turnips, and all actors hams. Another performer was the Rumanian, Voya George.

A Hollywood Extra, as Florey's film is best known, shows the influence of the great German films of the '20s. Vorkapich cleverly used such odds and ends as an Erector set, tin cans, cigar boxes, paper cubes and paper figures. Many scenes were photographed in Florey's kitchen, which he painted black, and Toland's garage. The idea for the picture came to Florey during a rendition of George Gershwin's "Rhapsody in Blue" and it was edited so that all movement is synchronized with that composition. (This is no longer true of the few heavily-mutilated versions still in existence).

The story of *A Hollywood Extra* is a blend of satire and fantasy. Mr. Jones, a would-be actor dreaming of glory in the movie studios, is given an audition with a casting director during which he is changed from an individual to a number— 9413—which is painted on his forehead. His lips move in a rhythmical gibberish. Mr. Blank, a handsome young leading man—number 15—is tested at the same time. He becomes a great success and the number on his forehead is replaced with a star. Mr. Jones' dreams fade in endless rounds of "no casting today." Finally he dies of starvation, and ascends to heaven, where an angel removes the offensive number from his face— an ending intended as a satire of Hollywood's traditional happy endings.

Florey showed *A Hollywood Extra* to Charlie Chaplin, who

Robert Florey (left) with Rudolph Valentino at the star's Whitley Heights home in Hollywood, January, 1922.

was so impressed that he invited Hollywood's top brass to a lavish dinner to see it. Among those present were D. W. Griffith, Jesse L. Lasky, King Vidor, Mary Pickford, Ernst Lubitsch, Norma Talmadge, Joseph M. Schenck, Lewis Milestone, Josef von Sternberg, Douglas Fairbanks, and Harry d'Arrast, all of whom shared Chaplin's enthusiasm. Schenck arranged for it to play at the new United Artists Theatre on Broadway, with a pit orchestra under Hugo Reisenfeld performing a score based on "Rhapsody in Blue." FBO later booked it into seven hundred theatres here and abroad.

Florey wrote and directed three more experimental fantasies: *The Loves of Zero, Johann the Coffin Maker,* and *Skyscraper Symphony.* All were made at a minimum cost and had backgrounds, costuming, and acting clearly deriving from *The Cabinet of Dr. Caligari* and other German films of the '20s. The best and most expensive of the three was *The Loves of Zero,* a modern version of the Harlequin and Colombine tale. Florey made an inventive use of the split screen, including the remarkable Machine Street sequence, in which the upper portion of the screen is filled with multiple exposures of whirling machinery and the lower portion showing the tiny figure of the lonely hero walking home. The decor was by William Cameron Menzies, the distinguished art director of *The Thief of Bagdad* and *The King of Kings*. Josef Marievsky, a dancer with the Chauve-Souris, Tamara Shavrova, and Anielka Elter headed the cast. In *Johann the Coffin Maker* an apache, prostitute, and soldier arose from their graves and told how they met their deaths. *Skyscraper Symphony*, which was made later, was largely a montage of New York scenes.

As a result of these avant-garde films John M. Stahl, production chief at Tiffany, asked Florey to direct a Ricardo Cortez vehicle (*Three Keys for a Door*), but before the contract could be signed Jesse L. Lasky invited him to join Paramount's New York studios where plans were being completed for the production of the company's first talking pictures.

Paramount had reopened its old Astoria Studio on Long Island, and one tiny, cavelike stage had been renovated in a not always successful effort to eliminate outside noise. The camera and crew were housed in a glass cage to keep motor noises from the microphone. Moving shots were not possible until some time later when a heavy padding (known as "the blimp") was devised to shield the camera. The set was like a furnace in summer and freezing cold in winter. Because of the sudden demand for talkies, the single stage was kept busy around the clock. Features were made during the week, tests at night, and shorts subjects on Saturday and Sunday.

Florey's first work in New York was to direct a test of Ethel Barrymore. The crude sound recording equipment was unkind to her voice, and neither Paramount nor Miss Barrymore was impressed. Florey turned out dozens of short subjects using such Broadway stars as Eddie Cantor, Lillian Roth, Fannie Brice, Mary Eaton, Maria Gambarelli, and Ann Pennington. Among other things, he directed a sound interview with Admiral Richard E. Byrd for use with the synchronized documentary *With Byrd at the South Pole*, and a one-reel skit with Madame Elinor Glyn, author of the spicy *Three Weeks* and *It*.

The first feature Florey directed was *Night Club* ('28), an inconsequential drama of New York night life with Fannie Brice, Ann Pennington and Bobbe Arnst (wife of Johnny Weissmuller). Much of it consisted of night-club and vaudeville acts, and it was not released until nearly a year after its completion. *Night Club* was generally double-billed with another Florey effort, *The Pusher-in-the-Face* ('28), an odd three-reel comedy written by F. Scott Fitzgerald (his first work as a scenarist). It was largely about a meek theatergoer who is annoyed by three noisy fat women sitting behind him. The cast included Raymond Hitchcock, Lester Allen, Estelle Taylor, a youthful Preston Foster, and Lillian Walker (the popular "Dimples" of the Vitagraph silents).

Florey's third talking feature was *The Hole in the Wall* ('29), a taut mystery melodrama about three crooks who use spiritualism to fleece a wealthy woman. The film introduced Edward G. Robinson and Claudette Colbert to talkies (both had appeared in the silents). Florey's assistant was Irving Rapper, later a top director at Warner Brothers (*The Corn is Green, The Glass Menagerie*). Florey then directed Maurice Chevalier in *Bonjour New York!*, a three-reeler for the French market in which the Paris music-hall idol was taken on a tour of Manhattan's tourist attractions. It was not shown in America, but was a big hit abroad, and marked the beginning of a lasting friendship between Chevalier and Florey.

By 1929 talking pictures were firmly established and Paramount's Astoria studio was operating at fever pitch. Walter Wanger and Monta Bell were supervising production, and Malcolm St. Clair, Millard Webb (director of John Barrymore's *The Sea Beast*), and Florey's old friend, Jean de Limur, had come on from Hollywood as directors. When Paramount engaged Rouben Mamoulian, the brilliant young Theatre Guild director, he spent several days watching Florey at work, and the two became good friends.

Paramount's decision to star the Marx Brothers in a film version of their stage hit, Irving Berlin's *The Cocoanuts* ('29), gave Florey one of the more important assignments of his career. Joseph Santley was called in to help with the lavish musical numbers. The Marxes—there were four of them then—clowned both on and off the set, and Harpo, who owned a villa at Cannes, persuaded Florey and his assistant, Jean Galeron, to give him French lessons.

At its Yonkers preview *The Cocoanuts* clocked over four hundred laughs in 140 minutes of running time, and the picture subsequently did record business. The Marx Brothers were

A young Robert Florey with boots, eyeshade, and megaphone directs Montagu Love, Robert Frazer, and William Austin in a scene from One Hour of Love *(1926). Note the three-piece orchestra for mood music.*

enormous successes. Florey's direction was fast, the gags well-timed, and the musical numbers were photographed from inventive overhead and oblique angles (an approach later refined by Busby Berkeley in the early Goldwyn and Warner musicals).

Florey's last picture at Astoria was a banal musical comedy-drama written by Gene Markey, *The Battle of Paris* ('29). Intended to showcase the talents of Gertrude Lawrence, it was a mishmash of music and drama, foredoomed by a poor script and inept casting, despite some good tunes by Cole Porter. Florey had asked not to be assigned to it. Because of the crowded schedule, it was necessary to work at night—from eight in the evening to five the next morning—and Florey spent part of each day at the site of a skyscraper being constructed on Lexington Avenue, near the Chrysler Building, shooting material for his experimental documentary, *Skyscraper Symphony*. After the completion of *The Battle of Paris* (which had some showings under the title *The Gay Lady*), Florey went for a vacation in Bermuda, and visited the sites where Herbert Brenon had directed Annette Kellerman in *Neptune's Daughter* in 1914.

Soon afterward Florey went abroad to direct films for Pierre Braunberger, a young Paris producer. *La Route Est Belle* ('30) was the first French-language film musical. It was shot at the British International Studios in Elstree because no studio in France was equipped for sound. Florey profited by the presence of an American cameraman, Charles Rosher, who had won an Academy Award for his photography (with Karl Struss) of Murnau's *Sunrise*. The beautiful Paris exteriors were shot silent by Georges Perinal. *La Route Est Belle* was a huge financial success, so much so that Braunberger used his profits to buy the Billancourt Studios.

L'Amour Chante ('30), Florey's second European picture, was filmed in French at Ufa's Neubabelsberg studios outside Berlin. It was a romantic comedy with Fernand Gravet and Josselyn Gael (then aged fourteen). Florey also directed a German version (*Komm' Zu Mir Zum Rendez Vous*), and a Spanish one (*El Profesor de mi Senora*), each with a different cast. His assistant on the three versions was Marc Allegret, later the brilliant director of *Children of Paradise*.

Florey then returned to the United States, but Braunberger immediately called him back to France to direct Sacha Guitry in *Le Blanc et le Noir* ('30), a moderately successful drama. This film introduced Raimu to the screen and also featured another young French performer, Fernandel, who was to win international recognition. Florey worked with Guitry on the script at the latter's home, and he was tremendously impressed with Guitry's ideas on filmmaking.

After his return to Hollywood in January, 1931, Florey was invited by Universal's scenario editor, Richard Schayer, to write a treatment of Mary Wollstonecraft Shelley's magnificent tale of terror, *Frankenstein*. Her story of a brilliant scientist, who brought to life a gruesome monster constructed from bodies stolen from graveyards and morgues, provided unusual opportunities for cinematic horror. Florey put into his script details from the macabre German silents and the Grand Guignol situations of the Théâtre de l'Epouvante. Many of the basic incidents of the picture—lacking in the novel—were born in Florey's imagination, notably: the unwitting substitution of a diseased brain in the monster; the half-insane hunchback assistant (vividly portrayed by Dwight Frye); and the stunning array of electrical equipment used so effectively during the storm when the monster comes to life. From the unique architecture of a Van der Kamp pastry shop across from his apartment on Ivar Street, Florey found the inspiration for the grotesque old mill where the monster is burned to death. His script, with dialogue written by Garrett Fort, was exactly what Universal had been seeking as a follow-up to its horror hit of 1930, *Dracula*.

Florey was promised the direction of *Frankenstein,* and in anticipation of the assignment he filmed two reels of tests of Bela Lugosi in make-up as the monster. The results were not satisfactory, and Lugosi was not enthusiastic about the role. Later it went to Boris Karloff, a bit player, whom Universal's make-up genius, Jack Pierce, transformed into the now-familiar monster.

At the last moment *Frankenstein* was handed to James Whale to direct. To assuage Florey's disappointment, Carl Laemmle, Jr. assigned him to write and direct an adaptation of Edgar Allan Poe's *Murders in the Rue Morgue* ('31). The script, written in collaboration with John Huston, was obviously influenced by *The Cabinet of Dr. Caligari.* There was an amusement-park background, a giant ape was substituted for the somnambulist, and there was an abundance of distorted rooftops and bizarre set-ups. The hero was a medical student, and the first appearance of Bela Lugosi as the mad physician and master of the ape, and his subsequent lecture in the tent, closely follows a similar sequence in *Caligari* with Werner Kraus and Conrad Veidt.

Murders in the Rue Morgue still sustains an atmosphere of terror and foreboding. The composition of its scenes, highlighted by Karl Freund's brilliant low-key photography, often exceeds in quality those of *Frankenstein.* Few horror films have featured such unrestrained savagery. The laboratory sequences were particularly grim, and the hero's discovery of his mother's corpse, stuffed head down in a chimney, was cut by many censors. The settings were impressive—many had served Lon Chaney's *Hunchback of Notre Dame* and *The Phantom of the Opera*— and a good cast included Sydney Fox and Leon Ames (then known as Leon Waycoff).

Florey spent the rest of 1931 collaborating with Garrett Fort on *The Werewolf of London* and *The Invisible Man*—his name did not appear on the release credits—and three other unproduced scripts. The following year he directed *The Man Called Back* for KBS-Tiffany. A drama which jumped from the South Seas to London, it starred Conrad Nagel, Doris Kenyon, John

Halliday, Reginald Owen, Mona Maris, and Mae Busch. He then did *Those We Love* ('32) for KBS-World Wide, another tearjerker with Mary Astor, Lilyan Tashman and Kenneth Mac-Kenna. Though dangerously ill throughout the shooting, Miss Tashman concealed her suffering beneath the gaiety which marked her charming personality. Her condition was hidden from her fans and friends, and she died soon after the preview of the picture.

The Man Called Back and *Those We Love* were sentimental love stories that did well at the box-office, particularly on the Warner circuit. Jack L. Warner, whom Florey had met at the Musso-Franks restaurant in Hollywood (where Chaplin held court), was sufficiently impressed to sign Florey to a term con-

A scene from Robert Florey's famous stylized experimental film, The Loves of Zero *(1927), designed by William Cameron Menzies. On ladder, Josef Marievsky. The girl is Tamara Shavrova.*

*Director Robert Florey and cameraman Fred H. Jackman, Jr. filming scenes
for* Oil for the Lamps of China *in Soochow, China (1934).*

tract. Florey was about to direct a Sherlock Holmes adventure,
A Study in Scarlet, for KBS-World Wide, for which he had
written a script based on Sir Arthur Conan Doyle's novel. He
relinquished the direction to his assistant, Edwin L. Marin, who
later became a successful director at M-G-M and other studios.

Girl Missing ('32) was Florey's first picture for Warners',
a breezy mystery that bore little resemblance to S. S. Van Dine's
The Blue Moon Murder Case, on which it was loosely based.
Ben Lyon and Mary Brian had the leads, and a frequent visitor
to the set was a young actor named Dick Powell, then much in
love with Miss Brian.

Florey received his next assignment at three o'clock in the
morning, when Darryl F. Zanuck called him to the Burbank
studio to discuss the script of *Ex-Lady.* The first scenes were shot
seven hours later. *Ex-Lady,* Bette Davis' first starring vehicle,
was very risqué in 1933 but dull by today's standards. It was

the story of a lady artist who liked to keep her affairs informal, but found that marriage was important when the right man came along. *Ex-Lady* was a big hit and made a star of Bette Davis—Florey had been interested in her talent for some time, and at Universal had urged Carl Laemmle, Jr. to give her the ingenue lead in *Murders in the Rue Morgue,* but the part went to Sydney Fox.

The House on 56th Street ('33) reunited Florey with Kay Francis, whom he had directed in *The Cocoanuts* four years earlier. She played a Floradora girl who marries well and later kills her former lover (Ricardo Cortez) when he tries to blackmail her. It was followed by two hospital dramas, *Bedside* ('33) with Warren William and Jean Muir, and *Registered Nurse* ('34) with Bebe Daniels and Lyle Talbot.

After *Smarty* ('34), an engaging little comedy tailored to the talents of Joan Blondell, Florey spent several weeks in the Orient filming backgrounds for Warners' *Oil for the Lamps of China.* Aware of the snarls of official red tape which had hindered George Hill in photographing authentic Chinese scenes for *The Good Earth,* Florey risked detention by working without authorization of the Nanking government. He and his cameraman, Fred H. Jackman, Jr., hid their cameras under newspapers and clothing, and worked from the interior of an ancient taxi. They got away with it, and with some excellent footage— including exciting shots of the sacred Festival of the Living Buddha, filmed in Hangchow in the midst of a menacing mob.

Florey and Emil Ludwig, the biographer, then tried to interest Warners in a picture based on the life of Napoleon. Florey was to direct, with Edward G. Robinson as the Little Corporal, Bette Davis as Josephine, and Reginald Owen as Talleyrand. But Robinson did not like the script, and the project was abandoned. Florey also badgered Jack L. Warner to let him direct a picture about Louis Pasteur, the conqueror of anthrax, but the assignment went to William Dieterle when Paul Muni was starred in *The Story of Louis Pasteur* two years later.

Florey then directed seven more films for Warners in 1934-35: *I Sell Anything,* with Pat O'Brien; *I Am a Thief,* with Ricardo Cortez and Mary Astor; *Woman in Red,* starring Barbara Stanwyck; *The Florentine Dagger,* with Donald Woods and Margaret Lindsay; *Going Highbrow,* a Guy Kibbee-Zasu Pitts comedy; *Don't Bet on Blondes,* with Warren William and William Gargan (and Errol Flynn in one of his first roles); and James Dunn in *The Pay-Off.* All were well made, slickly acted and directed. Pinch-hitting for the ailing Archie L. Mayo, Florey also guided Al Jolson and Ruby Keeler through portions of *Go Into Your Dance.* A major problem was keeping the nag-happy Jolson from rushing off to Santa Anita racetrack every afternoon.

After *The Pay-Off,* Florey left Warners. Universal wanted him for *Dracula's Daughter,* and Fox and Columbia made him offers, but he returned to Paramount, where in the next four years he directed seventeen features. The first, *Ship Cafe* ('35), was an unsuccessful attempt to further the American career of Carl Brisson, the popular Danish entertainer. Florey was then called in to shoot additional scenes of Marion Gering's confused production of *Rose of the Rancho,* a musical remake of the David Belasco classic, with Gladys Swarthout and John Boles.

Pictures with a Hollywood background have always appealed to Florey, and *The Preview Murder Mystery* ('35) and *Hollywood Boulevard* ('36) gave him ample opportunity to paint the behind-the-camera scenes of the film capital. He prevailed upon Paramount to offer the lead in *The Preview Murder Mystery* to his old friend, John Gilbert, whom he had met on his first day in Hollywood in 1921. Gilbert had not worked in a long time and was finding solace in alcohol. He refused the part when Paramount would not meet his price. The film was still shooting when Gilbert died, aged thirty-eight. Florey made a practice of giving work to former stars and directors, either in bit roles or as extras, and Conway Tearle, Bryant Washburn, Ian Keith, and Jack Mulhall were some of the silent favorites seen in *The Preview Murder Mystery.* For *Hollywood Boulevard,* a depressing story about a screen idol (John Halliday) who could no longer get a job, Florey assembled an even larger aggregation of the once-great: Francis X. Bushman, Maurice Costello, Eva Novak, Mae Marsh, Charles Ray, William Desmond, Neal Burns, Ruth Clifford, Jack Mulhall, and many others.

On all too many of his Paramount assignments Florey was hamstrung by poor scripts. His best effort was probably *The Outcast* ('36) an exceptionally fine drama of a discredited doctor (Warren William) who tries to start life anew. *Till We Meet Again* ('36), a World War I spy story with Herbert Marshall and Gertrude Michael was also well done. Another spy story, *Hotel Imperial* ('38), was a creditable remake of the Stiller-Negri silent. After two false starts as a top-budget attraction, first with Marlene Dietrich and then with Margaret Sullavan as star, it was rewritten to meet the requirements of a smaller budget. Florey was called in to replace Henry Hathaway as director, and Ray Milland and Isa Miranda, the Italian actress, inherited the leads.

Several of Florey's Paramount films were taut melodramas, a type of picture he does best. *The Magnificent Fraud* ('39) was a well-constructed tale of a French actor pursued to South America by police for a crime he did not commit. *Parole Fixer*

Robert Florey and his star, Barbara Stanwyck, on the set of Warner Brothers' The Woman in Red *(1934). Twenty-five years later Florey directed Miss Stanwyck in her* Barbara Stanwyck Theatre *television series.*

Robert Florey (right) with his French compatriots, famed directors Jean Renoir (left) and Rene Clair (center), in Beverly Hills, 1942.

('39) inaugurated a series of G-Men dramas based on the files of J. Edgar Hoover. *Death of a Champion* ('39) concerned a murder at a dog show. In *Disbarred* ('38) an unscrupulous attorney (Otto Kruger) used a lady lawyer as a front for his shady activities. *King of Gamblers* ('37) told of a respected publisher who secretly directed a gambling syndicate. *Daughter of Shanghai* and *Dangerous to Know,* two 1937 films, were helped by Florey's knowledge of the Orient, but failed to re-establish Anna May Wong as a top star. *This Way Please* ('37) was a pleasant musical starring Betty Grable as a theater usherette who became a star. *Mountain Music* ('37) was a silly hillbilly comedy capitalizing on the popularity of Bob Burns and Martha Raye. Florey's last film at Paramount, *Women Without Names* ('39), was a drama of a woman's prison, and one of Florey's best pictures. At its completion he married Virginia Dabney, an attractive Paramount actress. It has been an enduring and successful marriage.

Florey left Paramount, for the second time, in 1939, and directed three films for Columbia: *The Face Behind the Mask* ('40), an adult horror story with Peter Lorre and Evelyn Keyes (in a striking performance as a blind girl) ; *Meet Boston Blackie* ('40), which inaugurated that popular mystery series with Chester Morris as a reformed thief; and *Two in a Taxi* ('41), a dismal story of a miserable young taxi driver (Russell Hayden) and his efforts to earn enough money to buy a gas station.

In 1941 Florey returned to Warner Brothers for five years. His best pictures during this period were John Garfield's *Dangerously They Live* ('41), a Nazi spy drama; *The Desert Song* ('43), an expensive and colorful remake of the Sigmund Romberg operetta; and *God Is My Co-Pilot* ('44), starring Dennis Morgan and Raymond Massey. The latter was based on Colonel Robert Lee Scott's best-selling autobiography, and was an exciting drama of the Flying Tigers. A major box-office hit, it was voted the best film of World War II in a survey conducted by the Army Signal Corps.

Some of Florey's other films at Warners were less successful. *Lady Gangster* ('42), a Faye Emerson vehicle, was so bad that Florey asked that his name not appear on it, and it was credited to "Florian Roberts." *Danger Signal* ('46), another Faye Emerson picture, was a confused psychiatric drama, while *The Man from Frisco* ('44), made on loan-out to Republic, was a dull melodrama of the wartime shipyards.

Roger Touhy—The Last Gangster, which Florey directed for 20th Century-Fox in 1943, was an expertly handled biography of the notorious underworld character. In his usual quest for authenticity, Florey made the rounds of Chicago gangland haunts with police detectives and visited the scene of the St. Valentine's Day massacre. Using a stark documentary style —what Florey called *"The March of Time* technique"—he produced an intensely dramatic picture. The prison scenes were actually filmed at the Statesville federal prison, utilizing some 5,000 prisoners. The Hays Office objected to the brutal manner in which some of the crimes were depicted and snipped thirty-two minutes from an original running time of ninety-five minutes. The emasculated version, previewed at Statesville Prison, resulted in an historic lawsuit by Touhy, who charged his privacy had been invaded. The one-time gang leader lost.

Florey's last film at Warners, *The Beast with Five Fingers* ('46), was a minor classic of horror which escaped critical notice. Though hampered by a slow script and obvious special effects, it created a strong mood of terror. Its imaginative story was built around the hand of a brilliant pianist, which, amputated after death, became a living instrument of murder. In one of the most eerie scenes it ran rampant over the keys of a grand piano. Jack L. Warner was much pleased with it and told Florey, "The maker of *Frankenstein* would be jealous of this film." Had he forgotten Florey had written the screenplay of *Frankenstein*?

The story of Robert Florey's association with Charlie Chaplin on *Monsieur Verdoux* ('46) has already been detailed at length in an earlier chapter of this book ("Chaplin's Collaborators"). It was a bitter, disastrous experience that shattered a friendship of twenty-five years. Florey sincerely tried to be of help to Chaplin, particularly in correcting the technical deficiencies of his archaic style of directing—but, in retrospect, it seems all too apparent that the comedian came to resent Florey's suggestions. Chaplin jealously guarded his perquisite of being "the master in my own house," as he once expressed it to Florey.

From the first days when *Monsieur Verdoux* was in production, it was apparent that Chaplin was no longer the gay, carefree Charlot of old. The years of trial had taken their toll. "His thirty-five years of success and adulation, his disappointments and his deceptions, the constant attacks upon him . . . had changed his character," Florey said at the time. "All these experiences had transformed him from Charlie the lovable tramp to the cynical and disillusioned Monsieur Verdoux."

There were many at the Chaplin Studio who had been with the comedian for years—Katherine Hunter, his secretary for two decades; the amiable Rollie Totheroh, his cameraman since 1915; Frank Testera, the veteran studio electrician; and Sydney Chaplin and Wheeler Dryden, his half-brothers. There was a constant flow of visiting dignitaries to the set—Clifford Odets, Constance Collier, and the Russian writer Konstantin Simonov came on a single day. And his two sons by Lita Grey, Sydney and Charlie, Jr., of whom he was intensely proud, just released from the Army. And the still lovely Edna Purviance. "But I had the feeling that Charlie felt terribly alone," said Florey. Only when Chaplin's young wife Oona and the two babies came to the studio did his loneliness seem to vanish. "They were like a tableau by Renoir," Florey remembers.

Despite the stress of working with the intractable Chaplin, Florey insists that he enjoyed the *Monsieur Verdoux* experience. Soon after it was completed he wrote, "I hope that Chaplin will one day, whether it be in ten months or ten years, began to turn

Robert Florey on the set of the popular television show of 1954, The Loretta Young Show, *for which he received the Directors Guild nomination for the best directed TV program of the year. With his star, Loretta Young.*

his cameras again, according to his whim or inspiration . . . and to see, once again, one time more, in his element—Charlie. *Dear old Charlie!"*

Florey loved to poke around in the Chaplin Studio. In a small building housing the properties he found an amazing store of objects which had been used in the famous Chaplin comedies— a veritable Chaplin museum. Dozens of canes of all sizes and shapes were stacked in a corner. There were the outsized boxing gloves of *City Lights,* the roller skates of *Modern Times,* the gaslight which Charlie the policeman used to subdue the tough in *Easy Street,* the Army rifle and gas mask of *Shoulder Arms,* the miniature tank of *The Great Dictator,* the round minister's hat of *The Pilgrim,* and many other items, each recalling an unforgettable moment of laughter and pathos. It seemed as though nothing had been thrown away in thirty years. There was no trace of Chaplin's old scripts, marked with dozens of annotations and drawings in his own hand, and only a few of the ancient cameras were still about. File cases held hundreds of old photographs and posters. A few years later when the Chaplin Studio was sold—Charlie was living in Europe and could not get permission to re-enter the United States—much of this priceless memorabilia was thrown into the trash and lost forever.

After *Monsieur Verdoux,* Florey went to Mexico to direct *Tarzan and the Mermaids* ('47), the last of the jungle series to star Johnny Weissmuller. Then, at Universal-International, he wrote, with Robert Buckner, and directed *Rogues Regiment* ('48), a taut drama in which a tough American (Dick Powell) tracked down a high Nazi official after the war. *Outpost in Morocco* ('48) was a desert adventure in which George Raft was badly miscast. It was an independent production of Samuel Bischoff and Joseph Ermolieff for United Artists release. *The Crooked Way* and *Johnny One-Eye* were mildly entertaining melodramas which Florey did for Benedict J. Bogeaus-United Artists in 1949.

Florey's last feature movie was *The Vicious Years,* an exceptionally well-done independent film shot in twelve days for producer Anson Bond, which Film Classics released in 1950. It was about an almost savage youngster (Tommy Cook) in postwar Italy, and it drew splendid reviews. Said the Los Angeles Mirror: "If you didn't know it had been filmed on a Hollywood sound stage you'd think it came from a Rossellini or a DeSica, so superb is its shock realism."

Despite the excellent critical reception of *The Vicious Years,* the only offers Florey got were from small independents. After several months of idleness he decided to try television. His first tv show was *The Walt Disney Christmas Party* ('50).

One of the first movie directors to enter television, Florey has directed over 300 thirty-minute TV films, plus many hour-length dramas. These have included such top shows as *Four Star Theatre* (with Dick Powell, Charles Boyer and David Niven); *The Loretta Young Show; Disneyland; Wagon Train; The Barbara Stanwyck Show; Westinghouse-Desilu Playhouse; Michael Shayne; Zane Grey Theatre; Markham* (with Ray Milland); *Alcoa Theatre; The Untouchables; The Great Ad-

venture; and many others. He has been particularly effective in his bizarre mysteries for *Alfred Hitchcock Presents,* and in the science-fiction adventures of *Twilight Zone* and *The Outer Limits.*

In 1953 Florey received the first annual award of the Screen Directors Guild for the best directed television film of the year (*The Last Voyage,* starring Charles Boyer). He was nominated for the award in five subsequent years: in 1954 for *The Clara Schumann Story,* with Loretta Young; in 1955 for *The Executioner,* also with Miss Young; in 1956 for *The DeSantre Affair,* with Joseph Cotten and Joan Fontaine; in 1957 for *The Ruth Owens Story,* a "Wagon Train" adventure with Shelley Winters and Dean Stockwell; and in 1959 for *Innocent Assassin,* a "Desilu Playhouse" drama.

Ten years ago the French government made Florey a Knight of the Legion of Honor for his contributions to motion pictures. He has received four other decorations from France. In the late '30s and during World War II he helped many compatriots who had escaped from the heel of the Nazi invaders to find a new life in Hollywood, and he is today a frequent and gracious host to many distinguished Frenchmen visiting in California.

Florey has also written eight books about motion pictures, including two volumes on Chaplin, and biographies of Douglas Fairbanks, Pola Negri, and Adolphe Menjou. All are in French, and while none has been translated into English, several have appeared in German, Spanish, and Italian editions. His *Hollywood, Yesterday and Today,* published in 1948, is a remarkable combination of autobiography and nostalgic history of the motion picture. It is becoming increasingly scarce. Florey's latest book, *La Lanterne Magique,* published in Switzerland in 1966, recreates much of the golden days of Hollywood film history.

Florey has also attained wide recognition for his collection of antique French and European military curios and souvenirs, mostly of the period between the two Napoleons (1815-71). He also writes on this subject for specialized French publications.

Florey is philosophical about his long career in motion pictures. "My friends have always told me I was too independent," he says, "that I didn't like studio politics and didn't cater to the bigwigs. Perhaps it's true. But I never liked to ask favors. And if I felt like going to Mukden, or Tangiers, or Carthagena or Hongkong, I just went for a month, or even six months, even if it meant losing a job. I have always felt a director should see the world and learn—and feel free. So I have had my ups and downs. But I have loved this strange business of the movies."

As Cyrano says: *Ne pas monter bien haut peut-être . . . mais tout seul!*

12

THE INDIAN ON THE SCREEN

*M*OST contemporary Americans have so few opportunities to know Indians that many false notions about that admirable people abound.

The conception of the Indian as an insensitive lunatic who shot arrows at anything that moved, lived in a tepee, hunted buffalo, and said "ugh," stems largely from a half-century of irresponsible characterization in motion pictures. These screen caricatures have been so completely accepted that more realistic portrayals of Indian life in *Broken Arrow* and *Devil's Doorway* seem artificial and contrived.

Much of the tragedy of the Indian tribes—their betrayal and exploitation, their fighting spirit and great traditions broken, and their eventual confinement to government reservations as virtual prisoners—has been neglected in all but a few films. Hollywood has had little concern for historical accuracy or honest characterization, and most of the fundamental truths of the Indian—his remarkable heritage, his motivations to protest violently against his disintegration, and his desire to live in peace with the white man—have been obscured in a senseless defamation.

Because the screen Indian has been so confined to westerns, a type of film addressed to juvenile and unsophisticated minds, it is perhaps natural that a stereotyped Indian villain, or a stereotyped Hiawatha hero, should have been the major representations of the Indian. The intelligent appraisal and interpretation of the Indian in movies is a relatively recent phenomenon resulting, in part, from the current wave of racial consciousness.

Unfortunately, so many of these new representations of the Indian have been so oversympathetic as to arouse resentment

Warner Baxter and the lovely Dolores Del Rio as the ill-fated Indian lovers of Edwin Carewe's Ramona *(1928).*

among white audiences. Most of the whites in these films are made out to be knaves and liars, while the Indians are noble creatures merely trying to protect themselves. This approach has contributed no more to an understanding of the Indian than did the traditional stereotype of him as a red devil.

Many of the best movies about Indians are to be found among the early films of the silent era. Soon after the pattern of the Western melodrama was set by Edwin S. Porter's *The Great Train Robbery* ('03), and by the Broncho Billy pictures, the Indian began to appear as a central character in westerns. At first he was portrayed as a dignified hero of dramas of tribal life, which emphasized the loyalties of the tribe, dealt sentimentally with love and courtship, and frequently showed the Indian going to his death to avoid dishonor. Some of the best of these movies were Kalem's *The Navajo Blanket* ('14), Vitagraph's *An Indian Wife's Devotion* ('10), Ince's *Little Dove's Romance* ('13) and Selig's *An Indian's Gratitude* ('14).

The Red Man's Honor, filmed in France in 1912, was about a brave sentenced to die in one year for a murder he did not commit. He wanders the prairies and at the end of the year, although innocent, returns to his tribe and is executed—along with his sweetheart, who refuses to live without him. The bitter enmity between tribes was reflected in Bison's *The Winning of Wonega* ('11), in which an Indian girl is cast out by her people when she elopes with a young warrior from another tribe. Bison remade it the following year as *The Tribal Law,* with Margarita Fischer as the Hopi girl and Wallace Reid as the Apache brave, who flee to Mexico to escape tribal vengeance. Many of these early pictures were fantasies based on Indian legends and superstitions. Selig's *In the Long Ago* ('13), beautifully directed by Colin Campbell, told of an evil medicine man (Wheeler Oakman) who casts a lethargic spell on an Indian maid (Bessie Eyton). She is awakened only when her secret admirer (Tom Santschi) invokes an ancient charm. Another Selig film, *The Charmed Arrow* ('14), was about two Indian lovers (Mabel Van Buren and Joe King), each pledged to another, who were reincarnated by a medicine man's magic to find happiness in another generation. It had an ethereal quality, with many ghosts and scenes of the happy hunting grounds. Arrow's *Before the White Man Came* ('13) concerned an Indian girl who was believed to be in touch with the Great Spirit. When a spring is poisoned, her witchcraft is blamed, and the superstitious Indians burn her at the stake. Kalem's *The Legend of Scar Face* ('10) was a charming tale of a young brave, deformed and disfigured by a childhood encounter with a bear, who bathes in a magic lake and is miraculously restored—and, of course, marries the chief's daughter.

Many of David Wark Griffith's early Biograph films featured Indian themes and characters. His fifth picture as a director, *The Redman and the Child,* filmed in July, 1908, was a sticky and mercifully short tale of the effect of a child's innocence upon a savage. It was directed in the conventional style initiated by Porter, without any of the distinction which soon began to mark Griffith's work. His *The Mended Lute* ('09), a charming little Indian romance with James Kirkwood and Florence Lawrence as the lovers, was much better. The scenes of tribal life were surprisingly authentic, and genuine Indian costumes were used. Griffith's *The Mohawk's Way* ('10) was about a heartless white doctor who refused to treat a sick papoose. His wife secretly cures the child, and her kindness is repaid when the Indian mother saves her from death when savages attack the fort.

Indians were the protagonists in several other Griffith films between 1909 and 1913: *An Indian Runner's Romance, Song of the Wildwood Flute* (with Mary Pickford in buckskins), *Comata the Sioux, Leather Stocking, The Redman's View, The Chief's Daughter, Indian Brothers, A Squaw's Love* (with Mabel Normand as the Indian girl, very serious and very athletic), *A Pueblo Legend,* and *The Yaqui Cur.* Griffith's most sympathetic portrayal of Indians was in *Ramona* ('10), shot in California on the first of several location jaunts.

In 1911, also in California, Griffith began to use the Indian as the heavy—the enemy of the white man—without any inquiry into the red man's motivations. *The Last Drop of Water* and *Crossing the American Prairies in the Early Fifties,* precursors of James Cruze's *The Covered Wagon,* featured exciting Indian attacks on a wagon train, and *Fighting Blood,* a little known Griffith classic, was a brilliant depiction of an Indian raid on a settler's cabin. *The Massacre* ('12) was an ambitious and expensive production inspired by Custer's last stand, which, much to Griffith's chagrin, went generally unnoticed. This type of Griffith film reached its climax in *The Battle at Elderbush Gulch* ('14), his last two-reeler at Biograph.

The Indian fighting was savagely realistic in all of these pictures. Griffith delighted in showing redskins manhandling frontier women, holding up infants by their feet prior to scalping, and clubbing buckskin heroes with bloody tomahawks. In his later movies at Biograph, Griffith had little interest in the Indian as a personality, preferring to use him in stereotyped dimensions of menace. Real Indians were never used. Members of the Griffith stock company were repeatedly cast in the major roles, and white extras, dressed and painted like Indians, peopled the battle scenes. When Griffith began making features he lost his interest in Indian and Western themes, and, except for the climactic battle involving the Mohawks in *America* ('24), Indians were never again principal characters in a Griffith film.

Indians figured prominently in the pictures of all the pioneer companies. In 1909, Carl Laemmle inaugurated his trust-busting

IMP Company with a lavish one-reel version of Henry Wadsworth Longfellow's *Hiawatha,* supposedly filmed in authentic Minnesota locales under the direction of William Ranous. Gladys Hulette was Minnehaha, and Ranous also played the title role. In the same year Bison made its debut with *A True Indian's Heart,* starring Charles K. French. Some of Bison's biggest Indian hits were *Kit Carson* ('10), *Red Wing's Loyalty* ('10), and *At Old Fort Dearborn* ('12). Both of the latter were about an Indian girl who saves her white lover by informing him of an imminent attack by the redskins.

Selig used the Indian both as the stereotyped villain (*In Old Arizona, Totem Magic*) and as sympathetic heroes (*Curse of the Red Man, An Indian's Gratitude*). For some reason Indians were rarely seen, except in low-comedy roles, in Selig's popular westerns starring Tom Mix. Nowhere were screen Indians more ludicrous than in the films of the Edison Company. In *Captain John Smith and Pocahontas* ('08), for instance, obvious white actors smeared with brown make-up were dressed in long brown underwear and skullcaps to which ordinary

Loretta Young and Don Ameche as the Indian lovers of Henry King's Ramona *(1936).*

chicken feathers were attached! These travesties were perpetu-
ated in such Edison historical dramas as *Daniel Boone, or
Pioneer Days in America* ('07), *On the Western Frontier* ('09),
The Capture of Fort Ticonderoga ('11), and a series of westerns
built around the character of Buffalo Bill. Only occasionally, as
in *The Redman's Burden* ('12), did Edison essay a serious
approach to some of the Indian's problems.

The Lubin Company of Philadelphia brought some authenticity to its few Indian pictures by using popular Indian vaudeville
performers, including the famous Chief Standing Bear and his
troupe. Some of the best of the Lubin films were *The Falling
Arrow* ('07) and *The Heart of a Sioux* ('12), the latter a touching drama of an Indian girl who fell in love with her white
teacher at a reservation school. Pathé did many wagon-train
adventures in which Indians were seen attacking the whites, as in
Pioneers Crossing the Plains in '49 ('08) and *The Flaming
Arrows* ('11), and in more intimate Indian dramas, such as
The Message of the Arrow ('11), in which an Indian maid
betrays her people to save a white cowboy. Pathé's *The Prisoner
of the Mohicans* ('11) pitted good Indians against bad, with
a young brave rescuing a white girl kidnapped by an enemy
tribe. Beginning in 1910, Pathé's West Coast unit made many
creditable westerns in which Indians were portrayed in more
human terms. Two popular Indian players, James Young Deer
and his wife, Red Wing, were among the members of this company, which also included Bessie Eyton, Charles K. French, and
Jack Hoxie. Vitagraph, Thanhouser, American, Broncho, and
Essanay appear to have made little use of the Indian in their
films.

In terms of quantity, the Kalem Company was the acknowledged leader in Indian movies, turning out dozens between 1910
and 1915. Real Indians were frequently cast in the leads, the
most popular being Mona Darkfeather, a short and somewhat
stout Seminole. Kalem did an excellent series on the Seminoles
(*Love in the Everglades, An Indian Scout's Revenge, The
Seminoles' Vengeance*), using authentic locations in the Everglades and plots based on Seminole history and legend. Most of
the films in this series were directed by the talented Sidney Olcott
at Kalem's Jacksonville studios. Kalem's Indians were both good
and bad—he was played with reverence and respect in one picture, and seen as a bloodthirsty savage in the next. The plots
touched on all subjects: intermarriage between Indian and white

(*Red Hawk's Sacrifice*), relentless Indian vengeance (*His Indian Nemesis*), the attack on the settlers (*Raid of the Red Marauders*), the Indian falsely accused of crime by a white (*Arizona Bill*), the abduction of white children by Indians (*The Paleface Brave*), or the disintegration of Indian manhood by whiskey (*The Hopi Raiders*). Kalem also did good Indian historical dramas, as *The Indian Uprising at Santa Fe* ('12), which recreated the rebellion of Pueblo Indians against their Spanish oppressors, and *Wolfe, Or the Conquest of Quebec* ('14), which pictured the Indians who fought with the French against the English in 1763. Kalem's Indian dramas, designed for mass audience appeal, were uneven in quality and generally shallow in content, and a major handicap was the limited budget on which most were produced.

The major coup in Indian pictures was executed by Thomas H. Ince late in 1911 when he hired the Miller Brothers 101 Ranch Circus (then in winter quarters at Venice, California) and its entire entourage of Indians, cowboys, horses, cattle, costumes, and properties for $2,500 a week. This enabled Ince to turn out many excellent movies with Indian themes and characters, all filmed at Inceville, his new 18,000-acre studio near Santa Monica. His first film with the 101 Ranch Circus was *Across the Plains* ('12), a two-reeler starring William Eagleshirt, an impressive full-blooded Sioux. Some of Ince's better Indian dramas filmed during the next two years included *Battle of the Red Man, Past Redemption, Little Dove's Romance, Indian Massacre, Blazing the Trail, Heart of an Indian, The Lieutenant's Last Fight,* and *Monroe.*

Ann Little was an outlaw girl in *Past Redemption* ('12) who sold whiskey to the Indians, killed one in cold blood, and made it look as though the U.S. Cavalry was responsible. In *The Heart of an Indian* ('13) an Indian chief (J. Barney Sherry) stole a white baby to replace the dead papoose of his daughter (Ann Little). The child's mother follows him to the Indian village and pleads for the infant. Touched by the mother's love, the chief's daughter relinquishes the baby. Despite this, there is a tragic massacre of the Indians by the whites. *The Heart of an Indian* had many authentic touches in costume, facial decoration of the braves, the arrangement and construction of the Indian village, and an Indian burial with the body of the dead warrior laid out on the high stilted platform used by many of the Plains tribes, with the women weeping, wailing, and harming themselves. Ince's ambitious *Custer's Last Fight* ('12) re-created the Battle of the Little Big Horn, with Francis Ford as General Custer. For this expensive three-reeler Ince arranged with the government to use over a hundred reservation Sioux as extras. He found them difficult to direct—they would not follow instructions, showed little spirit in the battle scenes, and were self-conscious in front of the camera. Ince's problems mounted when the Sioux pilfered clothing and small properties, complained about the food, and wandered off to get drunk in a nearby saloon.

After 1915 producers lost interest in serious pictures about Indians and their problems, and more and more the Indian was relegated to an anonymous role of a rampaging red devil harassing the white hero. So effective was the redskin as a menace that audiences soon *preferred* him as a villain, and tended to be bored when he was presented in sympathetic terms. Of the few films utilizing Indian themes and characters between 1915 and 1922 the best were Cecil B. De Mille's two productions of *The Squaw Man;* Douglas Fairbanks' *The Half-Breed* and *The Mollycoddle;* Maurice Tourneur's fine production of *The Last of the Mohicans;* *The Hell Cat,* starring Geraldine Farrar; George Melford's *Behold My Wife;* and a charming little Universal three-reeler, *The Indian's Lament,* directed by Henry MacRae of serial fame.

Indians figured prominently in many of Douglas Fairbanks' peppy films. In his very first screen appearance, *The Lamb* ('15), he tangled with some Yaqui Indians and subdued them with jujitsu. In *The Half-Breed* ('16) Fairbanks was the Indian hero of an insignificant yarn concocted of action sequences which culminated in a spectacular forest fire. In *Wild and Woolly* ('17) he was an Eastern railroad clerk "just nuts about the West" who came to Arizona and became a glorified Indian fighter—against some of the most bizarre and nondescript redskins yet seen on the screen. It was played strictly for laughs. In *The Mollycoddle* ('20) Fairbanks was a foppish American, raised in England, who followed a pretty secret service agent (Ruth Renick) out West. Filmed on the Navajo reservations of Arizona, it featured real Indians, genuine costumes, ceremonial dancing and other tribal customs, and an exciting climax in which an avalanche wiped out an Indian village.

James Cruze's *The Covered Wagon* ('22), a major milestone in westerns despite its pedestrian pace, touched off a revival of interest in screen Indians. This pictorially magnificent film,

Chief Thundercloud, the famous Indian actor, played Tonto in Republic's 1938 serial, The Lone Ranger.

with its vast panoramas of prairie, mountain and sky, was shot on location at Snake Valley, Nevada, and Antelope Island, Utah. Although Cruze was cool to the idea, Jesse L. Lasky, Paramount's production chief, insisted on real Indians for the exciting attack on the wagon train. The responsibility for assembling and training five hundred Arapaho, Cheyenne, and Sioux for *The Covered Wagon* was assigned by the government to Colonel Tim McCoy, who was to play an important part in bringing about a realistic interpretation of the Indian in motion pictures.

McCoy was a handsome World War I hero, a striking personality who developed a fanatical interest in Indians in his early days as a Wyoming rancher. He soon became recognized as one of the foremost authorities on Indian culture and history —and especially on Indian sign language, to which he was introduced by the late General Hugh L. Scott, the last of the great

Indian fighters. McCoy's proficiency in sign language and Indian dialects led to his adoption by the Arapahoes, who named him High Eagle—"one who leads the coyote." Dressed in a feathered war bonnet and full ceremonial garb, he had competed in the Indian powwow at the Cody Stampede of 1921, winning first place against the best dancer of the Sioux, Chief Red Wolf. As adjutant-general of Wyoming and liaison officer with the U.S. Bureau of Indian Affairs, McCoy had been engaged for several years in improving the welfare of the reservation Indians and in promoting a greater public understanding of the redman.

McCoy's Indian charges gave him plenty of headaches during the filming of *The Covered Wagon*—much the same problems Thomas H. Ince had experienced ten years earlier. Although only the men were needed for the picture, whole families— squaws, children, grandparents, and multiple relatives—came along to the location, bringing cats, dogs, horses, and mountains of personal possessions. They lived in tents and native tepees, and broiled hunks of beef and buffalo over open fires. Some of the more resourceful added to their acting income by selling souvenirs to the crew and neighboring townspeople—and there were the usual difficulties with firewater and the appropriation of company property. Many of the older Indians had actually fought against the whites in the frontier wars—such as the aged Chief Broken Horn, whose squaw was a white woman he had kidnapped as a child from a wagon train.

The high respect of the Indians for Tim McCoy, and his ability to speak their dialects, helped him to solve many problems. "Anything he said was okay with the Indians," Katherine Hungerford, a visitor to the set, remembers. Some of the Indians had never seen a motion picture, but willingly followed directions. Colonel McCoy helped Cruze plan and stage the wagon-train attack and the remarkable buffalo hunt of *The Covered Wagon*. A splendid horseman, he also did some of the film's fine trick riding. Somewhat to Cruze's annoyance he was insistent upon authenticity in every detail of the Indian scenes. For the premiere of *The Covered Wagon* at the Egyptian Theatre in Hollywood McCoy reassembled twenty-five striking Indian chiefs and their squaws for a lavish stage prologue. The visiting Indians camped at the edge of town, and their cluster of tepees— colorfully decorated by Paramount's art department—quickly became a tourist attraction. Later, McCoy took the troupe to several Eastern theaters and to Europe for appearances at the

London Pavilion. After his return to California he served as technical adviser on other Indian films.

Although the success of *The Covered Wagon* materially broadened the scope of the western, the Indian continued, for the most part, in the role of a menace. Many historical westerns of the '20s featured exciting Indian battles, constructed with more imagination and detail than in the Cruze picture. John Ford's *The Iron Horse* ('24) utilized eight hundred Pawnee, Sioux, and Cherokee Indians in a spectacular attack on a trapped locomotive. Fighting Indians were authentically handled in *The Scarlet West* ('25) and Hoot Gibson's *The Flaming Frontier* ('26), two re-creations of Custer's tragedy, and in *A Daughter of the Sioux* ('25), Jackie Coogan's *The Bugle Call* ('27), James Cruze's *Pony Express* ('25), *The Devil Horse* ('26), Ken Maynard's *The Red Raiders* ('27), and two fine Fred Thomson westerns, *The Pioneer Scout* and *Kit Carson,* both released in 1928.

Paramount's *The Vanishing American* ('25) is perhaps the best motion picture about Indians ever made. The first third of it is a magnificent documented history of the Indian from the overthrow of cliff-dwellers to the coming of the Spanish Conquistadors. It then jumped to World War I and showed the Indian, though crowded back to rocky and infertile plains, and the victim of incompetent and criminal agents, being called upon to share his country's burden of conflict. His reward: the despoiling of his lands and crops while he was away on the battlefield. The irony of the Indian going off to fight for his oppressors was starkly depicted.

Though imaginatively directed by George B. Seitz in his first important assignment after graduation from serials, *The Vanishing American* suffered from the intrusion of a commonplace and sentimental story. The film tried to soothe both sides —white and red—and carefully made it clear that the Great White Fathers in Washington could not be blamed for the Indian's plight. At the end, in a burst of pure hokum, it made the Indian hero the great reconciler. Richard Dix's fine performance was the best of his career, and many real Indians appeared in leading roles. Seitz's handling of the Indian children was delightful.

Another Richard Dix vehicle, *Redskin* ('29), released at the very end of the silent era, was an infinitely poorer picture of reservation life. Dix was a misguided brave rejected by his tribe, but he redeems himself through acts of bravery and wins the beautiful Corn Blossom (Gladys Belmont). It suffered from director Victor Schertzinger's faulty grasp of Indian characterization, and emerged as a glossy conception of the redman's problems. Some glaring sequences in Technicolor's pioneer two-color process did little to create a sense of realism.

Irving Thalberg's decision to star Colonel Tim McCoy in a series of M-G-M westerns (1926-29) led to some very authentic Indian dramas. In some of these the redskin was less of a savage and more of a genuinely motivated individual fighting for his heritage. Many were filmed on the beautiful Wind River Reservation of Wyoming, seventy-five miles south of Jackson Hole National Park, and effectively utilized natural backgrounds, scenes of tribal life and customs, and the striking personalities of hundreds of Sioux, Shoshoni, and Arapaho Indians. Most of the Indians were old friends of McCoy, and bore such colorful names as Goes-In-Lodge, Afraid-of-His-Horse, Yellow Coyote, and Left Hand (who had fought against Custer at the Little Big Horn). *War Paint* ('26), shot against the majestic splendor of the Grand Tetons, was a minor classic built around the centuries-old feud between the Arapahoes and Shoshoni, and was notable for its realistic portrayal of the fighting habits of the two tribes. In *The Frontiersman* ('27), a drama of the Creek Indian Wars, McCoy rescued a pretty ward of Andrew Jackson who had been kidnapped by Indians. Others in this fine series were *Winners of the Wilderness* ('27), with Joan Crawford as leading lady, *Spoilers of the West* ('27), and *Wyoming* ('28). The talented direction of W. S. Van Dyke quickly earned him more important assignments (*White Shadows in the South Seas, Trader Horn*).

Despite the popularity of the series, Metro-Goldwyn-Mayer soon switched McCoy to less expensive, routine westerns. However, just before the advent of sound McCoy did two more excellent Indian films for M-G-M, *Sioux Blood* and *The Overland Telegraph,* both directed by John D. Waters. After leaving M-G-M, McCoy appeared in Universal's first talking serial, *The Indians Are Coming* ('30), one of the best chapter plays ever filmed. Most of its exciting Indian scenes were culled from Hoot Gibson's *The Flaming Frontier* of 1926. McCoy continued as a popular cowboy star for another ten years, but he made no more Indian movies, except for bit roles as a cavalry officer in *Around the World in 80 Days* ('56) and *Run of the*

Arrow ('57). In the 1950s he did an interesting television series
on Indian lore, and also starred in Nick Grinde's *Injun Talk*
('56), a color documentary explaining the origins of Indian
sign language. Sponsored by the Standard Oil Company, it was
also photographed on the Wind River Reservation.

Serials were long a source of employment for Indian performers, but they were also guilty of careless and irresponsible
interpretations of the redman. Pearl White's *The Perils of
Pauline* ('14) had a slew of rascally red villains—who can
forget her scampering down a steep mountainside trying to out-
race huge boulders loosed by a band of howling and obviously
phony Indians? After being shot by Pearl or the hero (Crane
Wilbur), the redskins didn't always stay dead—while still on
camera they would suddenly bounce up to see what was going on.
In both *Hands Up* ('18) and *White Eagle* ('22) Ruth Roland
was kidnapped by Indians who mistook her for a supernatural
goddess.

In 1922 Universal began making its excellent historical
chapter plays in which Indians were sometimes, but not always,
portrayed with some regard for their actual problems. The
white man's invasion of their hunting grounds, the violation of
peace treaties, and senseless atrocities by white settlers were
emphasized as the reasons for Indians taking to the warpath.
The best of these Universal serials were *In the Days of Buffalo
Bill* ('22), *The Oregon Trail* ('23), and *In the Days of Daniel
Boone* ('23), the latter a drama of the French and Indian War.
Universal remade these serials over and over in the ensuing
twenty-five years, often using the same stock shots culled from
the original silents. There was less and less attention to authentic
Indian characterization.

Other serials with Indian themes included Pathé's *Way of
a Man* ('24) and *Hawk of the Hills* ('27), both starring Allene
Ray; Mascot's *Last of the Mohicans* ('32) and *Fighting With
Kit Carson* ('33), Universal's *Battling With Buffalo Bill* ('31),
Heroes of the West ('32) and *Flaming Frontiers* ('38), RKO
Radio's *The Last Frontier* ('32), and Columbia's *Great Ad-
ventures of Wild Bill Hickok* ('38). Such later and inane efforts
as *Son of Geronimo, Cody of the Pony Express,* and *The Scarlet
Horseman* (with Paul Guilfoyle as a mysterious Indian Robin
Hood), produced during the last days of the serial in the early
'50s, contained the most ridiculous Indians yet seen on the
screen. Clumsy and obese white actors, often with Brooklyn

James Stewart is surrounded by hostile Apaches in Broken Arrow *(1950).*
Iron Eyes Cody is the Indian at left of Stewart.

accents, were ludicrous in phony wigs and warpaint.

Talking pictures brought a decline in Indian films which
persisted until the release of Cecil B. De Mille's *The Plainsman*
('36), starring Gary Cooper and Jean Arthur. This spectacular
picture re-created a vogue for dramas of Indian warfare which
remains unabated. De Mille's glossy battle scenes were not always true to the fighting habits of the Plains Indians, but they
were some of the most exciting ever put on the screen. More
than 1,200 Montana Cheyennes, hired away from the inertia
of W.P.A. jobs at $3.50 a day, lent a genuine note to *The
Plainsman*. Cheyenne tribal leaders were unhappy over some
of the scenes, especially the climactic battle in which a handful
of U.S. Cavalrymen held off hordes of howling redskins. De
Mille asserted the incident was based on fact, and produced
Army records showing that forty-eight troopers had outfought
eight hundred Cheyennes at Brecher's Island, Colorado, on
September 18, 1868. Paul Harvey as Yellow Hand, the Cheyenne chief killed in hand-to-hand combat with Buffalo Bill Cody
(James Ellison), was straight out of the "ugh" school of Indian

representation, but Anthony Quinn was superb as a rebellious young brave.

In sharp contrast to *The Plainsman*'s superficial approach to Indian motivation and characterization was Henry King's fine production of *Ramona* ('36). Based on Helen Hunt Jackson's quiet classic of an Indian girl in the San Jacinto Mountains of California (circa 1870), it provided a bitter disquisition on the traditional white methods of dealing with Indians. The story told of Ramona, rejected by a wealthy Spanish don when her Indian parentage became known, and her love for Alesandro, a poverty-stricken Indian farmer. The couple are driven from their farm by white usurpers, and eventually Alesandro is killed when he steals a horse to fetch medicine for his sick child. The disturbing social undertones were camouflaged in a contrived ending that left unresolved the problems of racial prejudice and discrimination.

Ramona has a long, successful history in movies. In 1910 D. W. Griffith paid $100 for the screen rights to the popular novel and gave it a sensitive production. Photographed against authentic California backgrounds, it cast Mary Pickford and Henry B. Walthall as the tragic lovers. Six years later Donald Crisp directed a second version with Adda Gleason and Monroe Salisbury. Edwin Carewe's silent of 1928 was also released with synchronized sound effects and a musical score. Dolores Del Rio and Warner Baxter had the leads. Henry King's talking version was the best of the four, but suffered from poor casting— Loretta Young was too sophisticated for the simple Indian girl, and Don Ameche too ill at ease in a fright-wig. All of the *Ramona* films were notable for their pictorial composition, effectively capturing scenic landscapes and authentic vignettes of Indian life—the Indian horse race, the wedding breakfast, the colorful native fiesta.

Where *Ramona*, with its sympathetic handling of the problems of its Indian protagonists, failed with audiences, *The Plainsman* and its limitations succeeded. The secret was clearly in the mass appeal of exciting battle scenes, and in the public preference for the Indian as a vicious, bloodthirsty killer. An endless succession of films cut from the cloth of *The Plainsman* followed in the next thirty years. Despite their similarities, and now-familiar clichés in plot and characterization, the popularity of these movies shows no sign of declining. A few descriptive titles: *Ambush, Apache Trail, When the Redskins Rode, War-*

path, Fort Defiance, The Command, Escort West, Ambush at Tomahawk Gap, The Battle of Rogue River, Fort Massacre, Blood Arrow, Frontier Uprising, Fort Apache, Buckskin Frontier, Last of the Comanches, Charge at Feather River, White Feather.

The decline of cheap series westerns in the post World War II era, the rise of the big star horse opera, and the vogue for espousing minorities qua minorities, have all contributed to the rehabilitation of the Indian in movies (he also fits nicely into the new color and widescreen processes). It was inevitable that Hollywood, in the maturity of its social questing, should come belatedly to the Indian.

The first picture in this objective trend was Delmer Daves' fine production of *Broken Arrow* ('49). Instead of blood-lusting savages endlessly whooping it up, the Indians were a proud, dignified race of warriors with their own culture, code of honor, and *justifiable* hatred of the white man. While some of *Broken Arrow*'s ethnology was questionable, it so effectively pleaded the cause of the Indian as to justify a special award from the Association on American Indian Affairs.

Based on Elliott Arnold's *Blood Brother,* the picture was a sympathetic portrayal of Cochise, an able strategist and wise statesman of the Chiracahua Apaches. First viewed through white eyes, the film builds up a fearsome picture of Indian terrorism around an Arizona outpost. James Stewart schools himself in Apache lore and language and goes out to reason with Cochise (Jeff Chandler). His long ride into the Indian country contains some of the most sustained suspense yet seen on the screen. Stewart and Cochise nurse a precarious understanding between whites and reds, and both fight venal renegades of either side. Despite many setbacks, their mutual respect and cooperation blooms into an uneasy treaty.

Broken Arrow further stimulated the flood of pro-Indian films, and the oppressed but valiant redman, usually personified by a dignified chief, became as much of a stereotype as the villainous savage had been. All the injustices to his race were charged to greedy, brutal, and insensitive whites—and to an impersonal government that ignored its responsibilities to the Indian.

Across the Wide Missouri ('51) told of a rascally trapper (Clark Gable) who married a proud Indian maiden so he could plunder the Blackfoot tribal lands. *Pony Soldier* ('52) was the true story of hungry Canadian Cree Indians who crossed the American border to hunt buffalo, and how they were persecuted by the United States government. *The Savage* ('52) considered the predicament of a white boy adopted by Sioux Indians. Grown to manhood as a handsome chief named Warbonnet (Charlton Heston), he must face torn loyalties when conflict with the whites breaks out. Howard Hawks' *The Big Sky* ('52) espoused the thesis that white culture destroyed the physical and moral integrity of primitive tribal life (though not as bitterly as did A. B. Guthrie's novel). Anthony Mann's *Devil's Doorway* ('50), which was widely acclaimed in Indian circles, had Robert Taylor, as an educated Shoshoni, who attempted to obtain justice for his tribe against usurping sheep raiders (there were some vague similarities to the life of Chief Joseph of the Nez Percé.) *Slaughter Trail* ('51) depicted the inability of the Navajos to persuade white authorities to punish three white bandits for the senseless murder of two Indians. The meanings of justice, as seen through white and red eyes, were clearly delineated. Samuel Fuller's *Run of the Arrow* ('57) suggested the white man should not condemn the Sioux for his excessive brutality because it was an integral part of his way of life.

Robert Aldrich's *Apache* ('54) inaugurated a wave of films that treated the Indian *over*sympathetically. It told the story of Massai (Burt Lancaster), who refused to join Geronimo in a peace contract with the U.S. Army. Shipped off to Florida with the old chief and his warriors, he escaped and made his way back to Arizona. The Army was eventually content to leave him alone when Massai was found plowing corn and enjoying the fruits of matrimony with a Hollywood-type squaw named Nalinle (Jean Peters). Despite its cloying ending, *Apache* was authentic in its Indian detail and contained many fine touches. Particularly effective was Massai's bewilderment as he wanders through the bustling streets of St. Louis in 1886, eying for the first time such strange sights as a woman's bustle, fire wagons, a player piano, and a cigar-store wooden Indian.

As the pendulum swung to the pro-Indian extreme, this unreal concept of the redman became offensive to intelligent whites and responsible Indians alike. Hollywood paid scant attention to their protests and plunged deeper into the depths of distortion.

Some of the more offensive films were *Chief Crazy Horse* ('55), *The Great Sioux Uprising* ('53), *The Battle of Apache Pass* ('52), *Seminole* ('53), *Smoke Signal* ('55) and *Taza, Son of Cochise* ('54). All of these were produced by Universal-International, whose pictures became more progressively unreal by the overuse of colorful, beautifully tailored costumes, an ethereal interpretation of Indian superstition, and the persistent casting of unsuitable matinee idols in principal roles. Not all the art of modern make-up and hairdressing could keep Jeff Chandler, Victor Mature, and Rock Hudson from resembling the Cleveland Indians more than the redmen they were supposed to portray. By the late '50s the oversympathetic Indian films began to diminish and within a few years virtually disappeared from the theaters. Once again, the Indian resumed his traditional role of menace.

One of the reasons the Indian has been poorly represented in motion pictures is that he has never been dealt with apart from his physical conflict with the whites (except for a few archaic efforts by Griffith and others in the early silents). The actual, real problems of the Indian—his unremitting struggle against starvation, his difficulties in assimilating into white civilization, his physical deterioration, his social discrimination, and the lingering effects of Indian superstition and custom—have seldom been treated more than casually on the screen.

As Oliver LaFarge, the Pulitzer Prize-winning Indian author of *Laughing Boy,* has said: "The Indians are one of our very smallest minorities. They are having an extremely hard time, and in much of the West they have to contend with violent racial prejudice. That prejudice, and the more widespread feeling that Indians are quaint and strange, but not quite human, are fed by the motion picture. This adds greatly to the obstacles which the unfortunate Indian is struggling to overcome."

The only social problem of the Indian treated on the screen in even semi-realistic terms has been the intermarriage of a white man and an Indian woman—with the apparently inescapable conclusion that such liaisons must end in unhappiness and tragedy. In many early silents the squaw was seen as a stupid but devoted half-savage whose only purpose was to provide hard labor and physical companionship for a lonely cowboy. Her eventual abandonment by her white husband, usually for a white woman, was freely condoned—a retribution for crossing the racial barriers. The burden of punishment and criticism always fell upon the squaw, and seldom if ever upon the guilty white man (except for fleeting twinges of conscience).

In D. W. Griffith's *Comata, the Sioux* ('08) a white cowboy entices an Indian princess (Florence Lawrence) away from her warrior suitor (James Kirkwood). The cowboy tires of her soon after the marriage and begins to court a cultured white woman. She rejects him when she learns of his Indian wife. In Lubin's *Heart of a Sioux* ('10) a white teacher at a reservation school marries a pretty Indian pupil, but has no qualms about abandoning her for his white fiancée back East. Selig's *Kit Carson's Wooing* ('11) told how a chief's daughter saved the frontier hero from death at the hands of the Indians. He marries her, but soon goes away on the pretext that he must help his own people. At the forest settlement he is welcomed by a beautiful white woman, and his Indian wife is obviously forgotten. Kalem's *Indian Blood* ('14) revolved around a tribe that tortured and killed an Indian girl who had been cast off by her white husband (who is ashamed that he married an Indian). Another

Jeff Chandler as Cochise in Delmer Daves' Broken Arrow.

Kalem drama of 1914, *Red Hawk's Sacrifice,* showed a white gambler viciously killing his Indian wife when he suspects her of trying to elope with her former suitor. He is unmoved when he learns the warrior was only saving the wife from an attack by a wild bear.

The Desert's Sting ('14) had a novel twist. Jeanie Mac-Pherson was an Indian girl whose white husband (Wilfred Lucas) tries to leave her for an educated white woman (Bess Meredyth). He dies in a fight with the Indian girl's former love (Charles Inslee), and the two women—white and Indian, both mourning for Lucas—go off together to do missionary work among the Apaches! In *The Flower of No Man's Land* ('16) Viola Dana was an Indian girl who marries a Metropolitan Opera singer who has come West to regain his health! He returns to New York without her, but she follows and discovers he has a wife and child. Everything ends happily—the faithless singer is conveniently killed, the Indian girl returns to Arizona and finds she is really white (having been kidnapped by Indians as a child), which paves the way for marriage with a white miner who has always loved her! The abused squaw did not always accept her betrayal with resignation. In Reginald Barker's *The Hell Cat* ('16), Geraldine Farrar knifed her unfaithful squaw-man after trying to kill the white woman he loved.

The most famous of these pictures was Cecil B. De Mille's *The Squaw Man* ('14), adapted from a 1905 stage play by Edwin Milton Royle. It told of a noble British officer who loved another man's wife. He went West to forget, married a dull-witted Indian girl and fathered her child. When the English lady's husband died she came to America to find her lover. Realizing she stands in the way of her husband's happiness, the Indian wife obligingly shoots herself—a Madam Butterfly in buckskins.

De Mille was so fascinated with this theme that he twice remade *The Squaw Man.* In his history-making version of 1914 (his debut as a movie director) De Mille used an attractive Indian actress named Red Wing, who had been a popular favorite in early Pathé and Bison films. Dustin Farnum was the British officer and Winifred Kingston the titled Englishwoman. In 1918 De Mille made a new version with Ann Little as Naturich, Elliott Dexter as the squawman, and Katherine McDonald as Lady Diana. De Mille's 1931 talking version of *The Squaw Man* was the poorest of the three. Lupe Velez was so much a dull squaw the audience could hardly keep awake until her welcome suicide freed Warner Baxter and Eleanor Boardman for matrimony. There was the inevitable sequel, *The Squaw Man's Son* ('17), directed by Edward J. LeSaint. Reared as an Englishman, the squaw man's half-breed son (Wallace Reid) goes back to the West, falls in love with an Indian maid (Anita King), whom he marries when his own wife (Dorothy Davenport) dies of drugs!

A more adequate characterization of the Indian wife of the white man has been given in more recent films, but Hollywood frequently seems obliged to apologize for the situation. Debra Paget, as the doll-like Sonseeahray in *Broken Arrow,* wearing brown-colored contact lenses over her blue eyes, took a bullet intended for James Stewart and died in his arms. In *Across the Wide Missouri* Clark Gable's Indian wife (Maria Elena Marques) was cut down by a Blackfoot arrow. In *Far Horizons* a fatherly Andrew Jackson told Sacagawea of the Shoshoni—Donna Reed in beautifully tailored buckskins—that she could never find happiness in the world of Lewis and Clark. (The imposition of an implied romance between Sacagawea and Lewis was a gross distortion of history). Similar things happened in *Run of the Arrow, White Feather* and *The Prairie.* Only rarely has Hollywood suggested that Indian and white can intermarry without retribution, as in the happy ending imposed on the tragic romance of Teal Eye and Boone in *The Big Sky,* and in *The Indian Fighter* and *The Wild North.* There were sympathies for the Indian wife of *Behold My Wife* (which appeared in 1921 with Julia Swayne Gordon, and again in a talking version in 1935 with Sylvia Sidney), who was taken from the reservation and plumped down in the midst of the English aristocracy to which her white husband belonged. After several reels of illustrating that the red and white twain would never meet, a contrived happy ending decided it might yet be possible!

The love of a redman for a white woman has been an almost totally forbidden theme in movies, a further reflection of unspoken racial prejudice. In Kalem's *Paleface Brave* ('14) the half-breed hero was rejected by a white girl and finally returned to his Indian sweetheart (Mona Darkfeather). In *Where the Trail Divides* ('14) Winifred Kingston was a white girl who married an Indian, who is pictured as cruel and uncivilized. She divorces him and marries an unscrupulous lawyer (Robert Edeson), and together they fleece the Indian of his rich oil lands.

In both *The Vanishing American* and *Redskin* Richard Dix loved
a white woman, but was prevented from marriage by racial
prejudice. Rod LaRocque was a college-educated Indian in *Braveheart* ('26) who falls in love with a white girl. He shoulders the
blame for a crime committed by her brother, but realizes even
this sacrifice cannot bring them together. In *Red Clay* ('27)
William Desmond was a rich, college-trained Indian chief, as
well as a war hero, but not all these qualifications could overcome
prejudice to win him the pretty white girl he loved. Robert
Taylor's love for a white woman lawyer (Paula Raymond) in
Devil's Doorway was reluctantly reciprocated, but his death in-
tervened to prevent marriage. In *Massacre* ('34), it was made
pointedly clear that Ann Dvorak, the girl friend of the Indian
hero (Richard Barthelmess), who was brought up and educated
by whites, was in reality an Indian.

But Hollywood never hesitated to tackle the problem of the
captured white woman defiled by Indians. One of the earliest
was Thanhouser's *The Forest Rose* ('12), in which Marguerite
Snow was rescued from her red captors by a white admirer.
She tells him marriage with him, or any white man, is no longer
possible. John Ford gave the subject a more realistic treatment
in *The Searchers* ('56), in which John Wayne tried to kill a
white girl (Natalie Wood) who rejected her people for the
Comanches. *The Charge at Feather River* ('53), *White Feather*
('55), *Trooper Hook,* ('57) and *Duel at Diabolo* ('66) upheld
the view that a white woman raped by Indians was unfit for
further association with a white man. In *Comanche Station* ('60)
Randolph Scott played a cowboy who had searched for ten
years for his wife carried off by Indians—but worried that he
could not bring himself to accept her back. There was a touching
scene in John Ford's *Two Rode Together* ('61), in which Mae
Marsh, as an old white woman kidnapped by Indians thirty years
earlier, tells her rescuers why she cannot, and should not, leave
the tribe. To their credit, many early silents (*A Tale of the
Desert, The Waif of the Plains, The Loyalty of a Savage*)
showed Indians treating captured white women with kindness
and respect, and displaying love for white children stolen from
wagon trains and settlements.

The prejudice against the Indian has been constantly reflected in films which intimate or express outright the superiority
of the white race over the red. *Tomahawk* ('51) restated the
old frontier maxim, as did the many movies about Custer's last

stand, that the only good Indian is a dead one. Buck Jones, as the Indian hero of *White Eagle* ('32), found immeasurable relief and a white bride when his white parentage was proved. In *Reprisal* ('56) Guy Madison was an Indian who passed as white in order to own land. John Wayne in *Hondo* ('53) was a half-breed who concealed his Indian heritage. *The Half-Breed* ('52) depicted the half-breed as weak and unreliable. Edward Dmytryk's *Broken Lance* ('54) dramatized the half-breed problem by emphasizing the rejection of Katy Jurado, a wealthy rancher's Indian wife, by both society and her stepsons. She counters hostility with love to convince her own half-breed son (Robert Wagner) of the futility of violence and revenge. A similar theme was used in *Flaming Star* ('61)—when a half-breed mother (Dolores Del Rio) is wounded in an Indian attack, bitter whites will not let a doctor attend her.

John Huston's striking production, *The Unforgiven* ('60), showed how a family and friendships nearly disintegrate when it is learned an adopted daughter (Audrey Hepburn) is actually an Indian. They rally to fight off a band of warriors who come to reclaim her. Gene Autry's *The Last Roundup* ('47) was an outspoken indictment of racial prejudice against Indians in a twentieth-century setting—an entire town bands together to cheat a group of poorly educated Indians out of valuable farm lands and water rights. This crime is apparently justified by otherwise respectable and honest citizens because the victims are Indians.

All of the white injustices to the Indian are crystalized in *Tell Them Willie Boy Is Here* ('70), written and directed by the controversial Abraham Polonsky. A complex, often brilliant film, it uses hostility toward the Indian to mirror the primitivism and inequities of the American culture. Robert Blake plays Willie Boy, a Paiute Indian who is hunted down by a white peaceofficer (Robert Redford) after he kills the father of his girl (Katharine Ross). Although realizing the white man's guilt in his relations with the Indian, Redford permits himself to be used by the forces of law-and-order as an instrument of revenge. Willie Boy becomes as much a victim of uncompromising racism as the bullets which take his life. *Tell Them Willie Boy Is Here* is set at the turn of the century, but is essentially a timely film of modern confrontation between two antagonistic levels of society. Although handicapped by its relentless bitterness, it is of major significance among motion pictures about Indians. It was Polonsky's first work as a director in twenty years after

Burt Lancaster as Jim Thorpe and the Indian football team of Carlisle Indian Institute in Jim Thorpe—All American *(1951).*

being blacklisted in the McCarthy era. He had directed only one other film, the overpraised *Force of Evil* ('48), with John Garfield.

Few films have seriously attempted to account for the redman's hostility to the white. It has usually been motiveless, or ascribed to a savage's amorality or primitive pleasure in killing, and only rarely to retaliation for outrages committed by whites. Kalem's *His Indian Nemesis* ('14) told of a warrior who tracked down and killed the white murderer of his squaw. Fox's *Gold and the Woman* ('16) pictured the revenge of Indians upon whites who drove them off their gold-rich lands. Broncho's *Yellow Flame* ('14) was about an Indian framed by a group of U.S. Cavalrymen for a murder he did not commit. Finally freed from prison, where he contracted tuberculosis, he seeks out the guilty troopers and kills them. George B. Seitz's *The Last Frontier* ('26) had Indians attacking buffalo hunters in a desperate effort to keep the herds, their principal source of food, from being slaughtered. Columbia's *Ride Out For Revenge* ('58) showed the Cheyennes going on the warpath when a peace treaty is broken and they are ordered to a government reservation. John Ford's *Cheyenne Autumn* ('65) was a sensitive account of the attempt of the Cheyennes, starved and oppressed in an Oklahoma reservation, to return to their home in the Dakotas.

On the other hand, white revenge for Indian atrocities was a common theme. King Vidor's *Northwest Passage* ('40), one of the most vicious anti-Indian films ever made, was built around the deliberate massacre of an Indian village in which men, women, and children are ruthlessly killed. The only motive was to avenge a white man whom the Indians had tortured to death. The sadistic cavalry officer, neither understanding Indians nor caring to understand them, has been so overworked as to become a cliché in movies. *Fort Apache, The Yellow Tomahawk, Only the Valiant, Fort Massacre, Two Flags West, Oregon Passage, Fort Bowie,* and *Cheyenne Autumn* are only a few of more recent pictures with this tendentious approach. The Army *had* neurotic Indian-hating officers, but it also had many understanding leaders who sought to bring peace between the races. Lew Ayres gave a good interpretation of one in *New Mexico* ('51), and so did Errol Flynn as General Custer in *They Died With Their Boots On* ('42). Raoul Walsh's *A Distant Trumpet* ('64) showed responsible cavalry officers protesting the sending of the Apaches to Florida.

Actual life on an Indian reservation has been infrequently and usually unrealistically treated. *Laughing Boy* ('34), although filmed in the natural settings of the Navajo reservations of New Mexico and Arizona, was not true to Oliver LaFarge's delightful novel. The superficial characterizations only occasionally captured the charm of these people, and Ramon Novarro and Lupe Velez were badly miscast as the Indian lovers. In *Massacre* ('34), Richard Barthelmess played a brash college-educated Indian who returned to the reservation to find his people dying under the oppression of a rascally Indian agent (Dudley Digges). After a series of tragedies, including the rape of a fifteen-year-old girl by a white man, Barthelmess leads the tribe in a return to pagan rites and a fateful massacre. In the end he goes before a Senate investigating committee to demand better treatment for the Indians. *Johnny Tiger* ('66) had a contrasting theme of a young Seminole Chief, educated by whites, who renounced his people.

Navajo ('51) is perhaps the best film about life on an Indian reservation as it exists today. Hall Bartlett's fine picture, filmed at a cost of $100,000 on the Navajo Reservation in northern Arizona, had no war whoops, feathers, or ceremonial dances. Instead, it offered a sensitive insight into the thoughts and emotions of a seven-year-old Indian boy (appealingly played by Francis Tee Hee) who strongly felt the tugs of his Indian heritage as he tried to adjust to the white man's world. Despite a contrived ending, *Navajo* is a superb film with almost documentary quality. Because of the beautiful exteriors in the Canyon of Death and the Great Rock Canyon, the camera work of Virgil E. Miller, who spent much of his career photographing Hoot Gibson and Charlie Chan, was nominated for an Academy Award.

The incompetent and often criminal Indian agent has been the stereotyped villain in dozens of Hollywood westerns, of which *The Vanishing American, Fort Apache, The Law Rides Again, Taza, Son of Cochise,* and Walt Disney's *Smith* are but a few. To portray the other side, *Walk the Proud Land* ('56) was a delightful little picture about John P. Clum, the progressive Apache agent whose contributions to the advancement of Indian education and to the preservation of Indian culture did so much to establish good relations between the races. Audie Murphy was a quiet prototype for many white Indian agents who have sought progress for the redman.

In its quest for new characters for screen biographies, Hollywood has found much excellent material in leading Indian personalities of American history. Regrettably, few of these have been handled with either taste or authenticity. *Sitting Bull* ('54), the story of the Hunkpapa Sioux who inspired the massacre of Custer at the Little Big Horn, is appreciated by Indians for its sympathetic treatment of the redman and authenticity in costuming and language, but it took broad liberties with history and was disfigured by poor production values. The film erroneously pictured General Custer (Douglas Kennedy) as an Indian-hating martinet whose dishonesty left Sitting Bull with no honorable course but war. No attempt was made to trace the fabulous career of Sitting Bull; and his last tragic years, with their full measure of heartbreak and death, were ignored. J. Carrol Naish portrayed the title role with dignity, but it was hard to forget that he also played Sitting Bull strictly for laughs in M-G-M's musical comedy, *Annie Get Your Gun* ('50).

Chief Crazy Horse ('54), starring Victor Mature, was a confused account of the reckless Oglala warrior who led the charges against Custer at the Little Big Horn. The picture tended to give Crazy Horse too much credit for the strategy of that battle—there has been a tendency to belittle Sitting Bull in recent years. He was seen as a neurotic whose decisions were dictated by visions, ethereal choirs singing in his ears, and visitations from long-dead ancestors. While superstition was a vital force in the Plains Indians, the lurid approach to it in *Chief Crazy Horse* only helped strengthen the public impression of the Indian as a lunatic. Historical fact was also sacrificed in a contrived story built around the lingering illness of Crazy Horse's squaw, Black Shawl, played by the late Suzan Ball in always clean costumes quite unlike those of real life.

    Broken Arrow made Cochise, the great leader of the Chiracahua Apaches, so dignified that he resembled a Harvard graduate more than an illiterate savage. (Michael Ansara repeated this defect in the later television series of the same title). *The Battle of Apache Pass* ('53) retained the characters of *Broken Arrow*, but none of its virtues. In *Conquest of Cochise* ('53) the venerable Apache chief was a flabby individual more concerned

J. Carroll Naish in the title role of Sitting Bull *(1954). The high stilted burial platform was used by many of the Plains Indians.*

with a pretty Indian maiden than the welfare of his people.

Paul H. Sloane's *Geronimo* ('39) was a fragmentary biography of the fighting Apache chief (played by Chief Thundercloud), who was pictured as extremely vicious and bloodthirsty. There was little attempt at historical accuracy—Geronimo is seen being captured when he tried to kill a white trader—and the action sequences were lifted from a half-dozen old Paramount westerns dating back to the silents. *Walk the Proud Land* was a more comprehensive account of Geronimo's capture and early days on a government reservation. Jay Silverheels, the Indian actor, played him with more gentleness and resignation. *I Killed Geronimo* ('50) was a mediocre and extremely cheap western in which the rebel chief died in a fist-fight. Arnold H. Laven's *Geronimo* ('62) traced the hardships of the Apaches on the San Carlos Reservation in Arizona, and the double-dealing of unscrupulous Indian agents which led them to an ill-fated escape into Mexico. Geronimo was portrayed as intelligent and keenly aware of the social problems of his people. There is a contrived ending in which he forcibly brings the plight of his people to the attention of a visiting delegation from Congress. The major fault of *Geronimo* was its ridiculous miscasting—Chuck Connors, with his beaming Irish face was totally unreal in the lead, and Kamala Devi, as his squaw, was equally unconvincing because of her stunning, exotic beauty.

Some other Indian leaders who have been inadequately portrayed in movies were Broken Hand (*White Feather*), Yellow Hand (*Buffalo Bill* and *The Plainsman*), Tecumseh (*Brave Warrior*), and Acoma (*New Mexico*).

Jim Thorpe—All American ('51) sympathetically told the story of the famous Indian athlete whose dazzling feats in college track, baseball, and football won him international acclaim, and who, because he played a summer of semi-pro baseball, was stripped of his medals in the 1912 Olympics. The picture was ambiguous as to whether Thorpe (Burt Lancaster) was an embittered victim of circumstances or unstable by nature. It showed his fall from the heights of sports fame to an unsuccessful job as a barker at a Los Angeles dance marathon, but mercifully did not trace his tragic final years as a Hollywood bit player, itinerant factory worker, and alcoholic, often dependent upon public relief for support of his family. Delbert Mann's *The Outsider* ('61) was the biography of Private Ira Hamilton Hayes, a young Pima Indian who was one of the Marines to help raise the American flag on the heights of Iwo Jima. Brought to fame by a famous news photograph of the event, he is confused by the wave of public hero worship, and broods that he is undeserving of these honors. After failing in a mission to Washington to secure water for his tribe, Hayes turns to liquor and eventually dies of alcoholism. Although the picture blamed war and other external factors for Hayes' downfall, rather than his own weakness, it did try to show some of his limited educational and cultural opportunities as an Indian. Tony Curtis did well in the lead, but the picture was singularly unsuccessful.

There has been little differentiation in Hollywood films between the Plains Indians and the Eastern Indians of the pre-Revolutionary War Frontier. James Fenimore Cooper's pedestrian novels have been indifferently transferred to the screen, and the Indian characters—particularly Chingachgook and the villainous Magua—have been largely stereotypes. However, Wallace Beery was particularly impressive as Magua, the renegade Huron chief, in the 1920 version of *The Last of the Mohicans,* directed by Maurice Tourneur and Clarence Brown. Chingachgook is invariably subordinated to the white hero, Natty Bumpo (or Hawkeye), with no interest in the origins of his friendship for a white man. Some other films which have treated the white-Indian conflict on the Eastern frontier have included D. W. Griffith's *America* ('24), Cecil B. De Mille's *Unconquered* ('47), Walt Disney's *Light in the Forest* ('58), *Rachel and the Stranger* ('48), and such potboilers as *Fort Ti* ('53), *Allegheny Uprising* ('39), *Brave Warrior* ('52), *Iroquois Trail* ('50), and *Mohawk* ('56). Most of these movies did indicate, however, that some of the Eastern tribes were peaceful and worked with the white settlers.

The all-Indian drama has rarely been seen on the screen since the early silent days. Henry Wadsworth Longfellow's venerable classic, *Hiawatha,* has had several tellings, ranging from Laemmle's 1909 version to Allied Artists' sentimental account of 1952. None retained the supernatural and magical elements of the poem, and most were ordinary accounts of warfare between the Ojibway and Dakota tribes and the efforts of Hiawatha to bring peace.

An all-Indian cast was employed in actual locales in an unusual and virtually unnoticed film of 1930, *The Silent Enemy.* It was a semi-amateur effort documenting the life of the Indians of the Hudson Bay country before the coming of Columbus.

Sal Mineo and Dolores Del Rio as the young Indian brave and his mother in John Ford's Cheyenne Autumn *(1964).*

The Silent Enemy drew its inspiration from Cooper-Schoedsack's *Grass* ('25), and depicted the Indians' year-round struggle against famine. Much of the footage was devoted to the tribe's search for an elusive herd of caribou in the barren tundra of the Far North. Some wonderful primitive rituals and exciting details of wild animal life were shown. *The Silent Enemy* was directed by H. P. Carver and photographed by Marcel A. LePicard, a former Griffith cameraman.

What do Indians themselves think of the way their race has been portrayed on the screen? Formal protests against misrepresentations of the redmen in movies were voiced by Indian groups as early as 1911. Representatives of sixty-two tribes, assembled at Claremore, Oklahoma, in 1958 were still repeating the same criticisms. Jesse Stevens, an Arizona Apache, summed it up: "The producers should hire some of us to show them how real Indians act. It's just a farce that . . . one white guy always manages to kill off a bunch of Indians. I was in an Alan Ladd picture once and got bumped off just like (finger-snap) that!"

While the basic criticisms go deeper, the thing the Indians most strongly resent is the depiction of the redman as an inadequate fighter. A study conducted by the late Stanley Vestal, biographer of Sitting Bull, concluded that in real life Indian casualties seldom ran more than two or three per cent, and that the Plains Indians killed five white men for every Indian killed, and wounded four white men for every Indian wounded. Contrary to the many films which show disreputable Indian agents selling obsolete Civil War guns and bullets to the redskins (as in *The Plainsman*), most Indians had good repeating rifles and used them well. Vestal quotes American officers on the poor quality of marksmanship in the Army: "Most soldiers couldn't hit the side of a barn."

The techniques of Indian fighting as seen on the screen have provoked much complaint from informed tribal leaders and Indian historians—particularly against the cliché of the chief sitting on the crest of the hill ordering his warriors into the fight in a long military line. Actually, there was no military discipline, and Indians charged, as General Mills has put it, "in herds and flocks like buffalo." Usually a group of warriors who knew and trusted each other rode out together to the battle scene, at which each attacked or sat it out according to his individual preference. Given a good horse, an Indian would show exceptional bravery. Unlike the impression conveyed by motion pictures, his acts were carefully and coldly calculated, and not the result of mass hysteria, unbridled savagery, and conspicuous recklessness.

Indians also object to the overemphasis which movies have given the drunken Indian. Most Indians, especially the warrior bands of the Plains, did not touch liquor. While there is evidence that alcohol played a part in the debilitation of some tribes, the ratio of alcoholics among redmen is smaller than for the whites. Selig's *A Romance of the Rio Grande* ('11) was about how liquor robbed an Indian chief of his responsibilities to the tribe. Another Selig film of 1911, *The Curse of the Redman,* told of an intelligent Indian who was sent East to study medicine, but returned to the reservation a hopeless drunkard. Firewater was used to incite the Indians to the warpath in Kalem's *Hopi Raiders* ('14) and Ince's *Past Redemption* ('12). Edison's *The Redman's Burden* ('12) showed Indians selling their pitiful possessions to buy whiskey. In *The Lass of the Lumberlands,* a Helen Holmes serial of 1916, Indians were cheated of valuable forest lands while drunk. More recently, the Indian attack in Fritz Lang's *Western Union* ('41) was laid to firewater, and Audie

Murphy's mother in *Drums Along the River* ('54) was murdered by a drunken Indian. Many other films showed Indians made into undisciplined savages by whiskey.

The dialogue given Indians on the screen is not characteristic of these loquacious and humorous people. Indians *love* to talk and are not at all the silent "ugh" type of creatures seen in many movies. Recently such informed technical advisers as Iron Eyes Cody, Nippo Strongheart, and Rodd Redwing have brought authentic Indian dialects and colorful sign language to the screen. In *Across the Wide Missouri* Indians spoke only in their native Blackfoot tongue—which, unfortunately, was interpreted in fractured French by the Canadian trapper (Adolphe Menjou).

Other principal objections of Indians to Hollywood's portrayal of them include: inadequate comprehension of Indian customs and culture; failure to show the redman's accomplishments, especially in modern times; neglect of contemporary Indian leaders as subjects of screen biographies; misrepresentation of the family life of the Indian, and the failure to show his strong love for his wife and children; the failure to use the Indian in appropriate vehicles simply as a character, and without reference to the fact that he is Indian; a consistent lack of intelligence in the characterization of Indians (except to emphasize his cunning as a villain); and the overdrawn farcical Indian— Buster Keaton in *The Paleface* ('21), and the absurd redskins of Douglas Fairbanks' *Wild and Woolly,* the Bob Hope western comedies, Abbott & Costello's *Ride 'Em Cowboy,* and countless others. Historical and geographical inaccuracies also offend. Essanay's *Life of Buffalo Bill* ('14) was such a picture. Although actually filmed in South Dakota, and purporting to show the battles of War Bonnet Creek, Wounded Knee, and the Badlands, it was so historically inaccurate—and so viciously anti-Indian— as to provoke a storm of criticism. Yet, it was shown at the White House and praised by Woodrow Wilson.

Hollywood's failure to use native Indian actors and actresses in important roles has aroused resentment. White performers are seldom convincing Indians—for example, Don Ameche in *Ramona,* or Sal Mineo as the pretty-boy warrior of *Cheyenne Autumn.* In the latter picture, however, several other established stars (Gilbert Roland, Dolores Del Rio, Ricardo Montalban, Victor Jory) enhanced its drama with thoroughly believable Indian characterizations.

A sizable number of Indian performers find steady work in

Iron Eyes Cody portrays Blackfish, a powerful Delaware tribesman in Walt Disney's full-length, live-action Technicolor production The Light in the Forest. *(Copyright Walt Disney Productions, Inc.).*

movies and television films, but few play leading roles. One of the best-known Indian actors is Iron Eyes Cody, a handsome and dignified Cherokee whose career dates back to *The Covered Wagon.* He never seems to age, and like Tim McCoy, a long-time friend, is proficient in Indian dialects, sign language, archery, costumes, hairdress, chants, war dances, and tribal history. Much of this knowledge comes from his father, Thomas Long Plume, who toured the United States with a Wild West show. In addition to hundreds of appearances as an actor, Cody has served as Indian technical advisor on such films as *Fort Osage, Light in the Forest, Warbonnet, Fort Defiance,* and *Westward Ho! The Wagons.* Two of his best performances were as Crazy Horse in *Sitting Bull* and again as the Indian chief in *The Great Sioux Massacre.*

Chief John Big Tree, a full-blooded Seneca (not an Iroquois as *Time* Magazine once reported), was for many years the dean of Hollywood's Indian colony. From 1915 to 1940 he graced numerous westerns, including John Ford's *The Iron Horse* and *Stagecoach,* and many of Tim McCoy's historical dramas at M-G-M. He was tall (six foot two) and dignified and accepted no role which he felt would reflect unduly upon his race. He came out of retirement in the late 1940s to appear in *She Wore a Yellow Ribbon* and *Devil's Doorway*; in the former he had a memorable bit as Pony That Walks, an old chief who is weary of conflict but can no longer keep his hot-blooded young warriors from the warpath. One of his most striking roles was as the taciturn but gentle Blue Back in *Drums Along the Mohawk.* He died at ninety-two (although claiming to be ten years older), in 1967 on the Onondaga Indian Reservation near his ancestral home at Nedrow, New York. Big Tree's greater claim to fame is that he posed in 1912 for the rare Indian-head nickel that is no longer minted.

Princess Red Wing (Lillian St. Cyr), the Naturich of De Mille's original *The Squaw Man,* was the screen's first Indian star. A Winnebago, she graduated from the Carlisle Indian Institute in 1902, and five years later made her first movie, *The Falling Arrow,* for the Lubin Company of Philadelphia. Later she appeared with Chief Standing Bear in his famous "Pioneer Days" stage spectacle at the New York Hippodrome. Some of her early films included Griffith's *The Mended Lute,* Kalem's *The White Squaw,* and the lead in *Red Wing's Gratitude,* shot at the Vitagraph Studios in Brooklyn. She played in many western dramas for the old New York Motion Picture Company and went with it to California, where it became the Bison Company under Thomas H. Ince. Her biggest hits for Bison were *The Flight of Red Wing* and *An Apache Father's Revenge.* Pathé starred Red Wing and her husband, James Young Deer, in a series of Indian westerns filmed at Edendale (just a block from the Mack Sennett Studios), of which *Back to the Prairie* is best known. Others in her unit were Lewis Stone, Art Acord, Hoot Gibson, Jack Hoxie, and a very young Bebe Daniels. Her role of the Indian wife in *The Squaw Man,* in which she gave a beautifully restrained performance, led to other important assignments—as the Indian mother in Donald Crisp's *Ramona* and opposite Tom Mix in *In the Days of the Thundering Herd.* When her career declined, she toured in vaudeville, lectured on Indian culture in public schools, and in more recent years has been engaged in designing war bonnets and Indian costumes for the theatrical trade. She now lives in New York City and is active in the Friends or Quakers, who have done so much to improve the welfare of the American Indian.

Some of the better-known Indian actors are Jay Silverheels, a Mohawk who won fame as Tonto in the *Lone Ranger* series of television and theatrical films; Rodd Redwing, a Chickasaw, who also teaches fast gunplay to the stars; John War Eagle, a Sioux; Silvermoon Cody, a Cherokee and brother to Iron Eyes; Winona (Connie) Buck, a Sioux who appeared in the *Brave Eagle* television series; Edith Mills, a Maricopa; Foster Hood, a Shawnee; Lee Bass, a Sauk and Fox; Lenmana Guerin, a Shoshone; Keena Nomkeena, a Hopi; Edward Little, Jr., a Sioux; Chris Gallerito, an Apache; Vi Ingraham, a Yakima; and Vincent St. Cyr, a Winnebago. Other Hollywood Indian performers bear such colorful names as Raven Gray Eagle, X-Brand, Big Little Owl, George Little Buffalo, and Dusty Iron Wing.

Charles Stevens, who died in 1964, was a grandson of Geronimo. He made his screen debut in D. W. Griffith's *The Birth of a Nation* ('15), and was seen in all of the films of Douglas Fairbanks, to whom he was much attached. One of his best roles was as the scheming South American militarist in Fairbanks' *The Americano* (1917). Chief Thunder Cloud (Scott T. Williams) was a full-blooded Indian who traced his lineage to Chief Pontiac, the legendary chief of the Ottawas in pre-Revolutionary days. He was the first Indian to enlist in World War I, and appeared in films, vaudeville, rodeos, and in radio from 1920 to 1960. Thunder Cloud created the role of Tonto in the *Lone Ranger* radio series (1936-39), and also played the title role in Paul H. Sloane's *Geronimo* ('39). He died in 1967.

Other Indian film personalities of the past were Chief Standing Bear, James Young Deer, Nasja Manhammer (the wonderful Navajo boy of *The Vanishing American*), Chief Thunder Bird, Greg White Spear, Mona Darkfeather, Princess Noola, White Horse, Edith Mills, Princess Whyneema, William Eagleshirt, Chief Yowlache (a Yakima whose screen career spanned forty years), Princess Leaping Deer (a beautiful Sioux who was leading lady to cowboy star Jack Hoxie), and Dark Cloud, an impressive Algonquin who starred in two fine Indian silents,

The Penitents ('15) and *John Ermine of the Yellowstone* ('17).

Few Indian actors and actresses have achieved any real measure of screen fame. Will Rogers had Cherokee blood, as did Monte Blue and Linda Darnell (which helped her as the Indian wife in *Buffalo Bill*); Jean Acker, briefly the wife of Rudolph Valentino, was part Cherokee and appeared to good effect as the Indian girl in *Braveheart*. The successful silent film director, Edwin Carewe, was also of Indian lineage—his grandmother was a full-blooded Chickasaw—which may have accounted for his sympathetic handling of the 1928 *Ramona*.

The Indian actor's attitude is best summed up by one member of the Hollywood Indian colony: "Indian actors understand about the Indian's portrayal on the screen, but, like any other race, we would prefer having historic truths shown, and would like to see ourselves depicted in a kindlier manner than in most wild and woolly westerns."

APPENDIX

THE FILMS OF NORMA TALMADGE

Between 1910 and 1915 Norma Talmadge appeared in approximately 250 films for Vitagraph, mostly one- and two-reelers. Some of her better known Vitagraph pictures are:

1910: *The Household Pest, The Dixie Mother, Heart O' the Hill, Mother by Proxy, The Love of Chrysanthemus.*

1911: *Paola and Francesca, In Neighboring Kingdoms, Mrs. 'Enery 'Awkins, Her Hero, Nellie the Model, The Convict's Child, Forgotten, The Child Crusoes, The Wildcat, The Thumb Print, Her Sister's Children, A Broken Spell, Sky Pilot, The General's Daughter, A Tale of Two Cities.*

1912: *The First Violin, The Troublesome Stepdaughters, Mr. Butler Butles, The Lovesick Maidens of Cuddleton, Fortunes of a Composer, Omens and Oracles, Mrs. Carter's Necklace, The Midget's Revenge, Mr. Bolter's Sweetheart, Captain Barnacles' Messmate, Captain Barnacles' Waif, Captain Barnacles-Reformer; O'Hara, Squatter and Philosopher; The Extension Table; O'Hara Helps Cupid.*

1913: *Casey at the Bat, The Silver Cigarette Case, Wanted—A Strong Hand, He Fell in Love With His Mother-In-Law, Plot and Counterplot, Lady and Her Maid, Sleuthing, 'Arriet's Baby, Country Barber, O'Hara As Guardian Angel, An Old Man's Love Story, The Tables Turned, Just Show People, Extremities, His Official Appointment, Under the Daisies, The Doctor's Secret, O'Hara's Godchild, Solitaires, Father's Hatband, Fanny's Conspiracy, His Silver Bachelorhood, An Elopement At Home, The Honorable Algernon, His Little Page, Officer John Donovan, The Sacrifice of Kathleen, Counsel for the Defense, The Blue Rose, The Other Woman.*

1914: *Sawdust and Salome, The Vavasour Ball, The Helpful Sisterhood, Cupid Versus Money, The Right of Way, Under False Colors, John Rance—Gentleman, Goodbye Summer, The Curing of Myra May, Sunshine and Shadow, A Daughter of Israel, Miser Murphy's Wedding Present, Old Reliable, The Hero, Fogg's Millions, The Hidden Letters, Memories in Men's Souls, Politics and the Press, The Mill of Life, A Loan Shark King, The Peacemaker, Etta of the Footlights, Dorothy Danesbridge—Militant, A Wayward Daughter, A Question of Clothes.*

1915: *Elsa's Brother, Janet of the Chorus, A Daughter's Strange Inheritance, The Barrier of Faith.*

Norma Talmadge's starring films are listed below. The director's name is in italics, and other names are those of cast members.

THE BATTLE CRY OF PEACE. Vitagraph, 1915. *Wilfrid North.* Charles Richman, James Morrison, Harry S. Northrup, Mary Maurice, James Lackaye, L. Roger Lytton.

THE CROWN PRINCE'S DOUBLE. Vitagraph, 1915. *Van Dyke Brooke.* Maurice Costello, Thomas Mills, Isabella Hart.

CAPTIVATING MARY CARSTAIRS. National, 1915. *Bruce M. Mitchell.* Allan Forrest, Bruce M. Mitchell, Jack Livingston, Constance Talmadge.

THE MISSING LINKS. Fine Arts-Triangle, 1916. *Lloyd Ingraham.* Robert Harron, Elmer Clifton, Thomas Jefferson, Constance Talmadge.

MARTHA'S VINDICATION. Fine Arts-Triangle, 1916. *Sidney A. Franklin* and *Chester M. Franklin.* Tully Marshall, Seena Owen, Ralph Lewis, Roberta Lee, William L. Hinckley, Georgie Stone.

THE CHILDREN IN THE HOUSE. Fine Arts-Triangle, 1916. *Sidney A. Franklin* and *Chester M. Franklin.* Eugene Pallette, Jewel Carmen, W. E. Lawrence, Francis Carpenter, Violet Radcliffe.

GOING STRAIGHT. Fine Arts-Triangle, 1916. *Sidney A. Franklin* and *Chester M. Franklin.* Eugene Pallette, Ralph Lewis, Georgie Stone, Kate Toncray. (Shown in Europe as CORRUPTION)

THE DEVIL'S NEEDLE. Fine Arts-Triangle, 1916. *Chester Withey.* Tully Marshall, Marguerite Marsh.

THE SOCIAL SECRETARY. Fine Arts-Triangle, 1916. *John Emerson.* Gladden James, Erich von Stroheim, Helen Weer, Herbert Frank, Nathaniel Sack.

FIFTY-FIFTY. Fine Arts-Triangle, 1916. *Allan Dwan.* J. W. Johnston, Marie Chambers.

PANTHEA. Select, 1917. *Allan Dwan.* Earle Foxe, George Fawcett, Winifred Harris, Richard Rosson, Erich von Stroheim, Charles Frankman, Murdock McQuarrie.

THE LAW OF COMPENSATION. Select, 1917. *Julius Steger* and *Joseph A. Golden.* Chester Barnett, Edwin Maxwell, John Charley.

POPPY. Select, 1917. *Edward Jose.* Eugene O'Brien, Margaret Whistler, Murdock McQuarrie.

THE MOTH. Select, 1917. *Edward Jose.* Eugene O'Brien, Adolphe Menjou, Donald Hall, Lorna Volare.

THE SECRET OF THE STORM COUNTRY. Select, 1917. *Charles Miller.* Niles Welch, Herbert Frank, Lorna Volare.

GHOSTS OF YESTERDAY. Select, 1918. *Charles Miller.* Eugene O'Brien, Stuart Holmes, Henry J. Herbert, Ida Darling.

BY RIGHT OF PURCHASE. Select, 1918. *Charles Miller.* Eugene O'Brien, Hedda Hopper.

DELUXE ANNIE. Select, 1918. *Roland West.* Eugene O'Brien, Frank Mills, Edward Davis, Fred R. Stanton, Joseph Burke, Edna Hunter.

THE SAFETY CURTAIN. Select, 1918. *Sidney A. Franklin.* Eugene O'Brien, Anders Randolf, Lillian Hall, Edwin J. Gilbert.

HER ONLY WAY. Select, 1918. *Sidney A. Franklin.* Eugene O'Brien, Jobyna Howland, Louis Stearns.

THE FORBIDDEN CITY. Select, 1918. *Sidney A. Franklin.* Thomas Meighan, L. Roger Lytton.

THE HEART OF WETONA. Select, 1918. *Sidney A. Franklin.* Thomas Meighan, Gladden James, F. A. Turner.

THE PROBATION WIFE. Select, 1919. *Sidney A. Franklin.* Thomas Meighan, Alec B. Francis, Florence Billings, Walter McEwen, Amelia Summerville.

THE NEW MOON. Select, 1919. *Chester Withey.* Pedro DcCordoba, Stuart Holmes, Charles Gerard, Marguerite Clayton, Mathilde Brundage.

THE WAY OF A WOMAN. Select, 1919. *Robert Z. Leonard.* Conway Tearle, Stuart Holmes, May McAvoy, Jobyna Howland, George LeGuere.

ISLE OF CONQUEST. Select, 1919. *Edward Jose.* Charles Gerard, Natalie Talmadge, Joseph W. Smiley, Claire Whitney.

SHE LOVES AND LIES. Select, 1920. *Chester Withey.* Conway Tearle, Ida Darling, Phillips Tead.

A DAUGHTER OF TWO WORLDS. First National, 1920. *James Young.* Gilbert Rooney, Winifred Harris, Frank Sheridan, Ned Burton.

THE WOMAN GIVES. First National, 1920. *R. William Neill.* Edmund Lowe, John Halliday, Edward Kepler, Lucille Lee Stewart.

YES OR NO? First National, 1920. *R. William Neill.* Lowell Sherman, Gladden James, Rockcliffe Fellowes, Natalie Talmadge, Edward Brophy.

THE BRANDED WOMAN. First National, 1920. *Albert Parker.* Percy Marmont, George Fawcett, Gaston Glass, Edna Murphy, Vincent Serrano.

PASSION FLOWER. First National, 1921. *Herbert Brenon.* Harrison Ford, Eulalie Jensen, Natalie Talmadge, Robert Agnew, Alfred Hickman, Courtenay Foote.

THE SIGN ON THE DOOR. First National, 1921. *Herbert Brenon.* Lew Cody, Robert Agnew, Charles Richman.

THE WONDERFUL THING. First National, 1921. *Herbert Brenon.* Harrison Ford, Robert Agnew, Julia Hoyt.

LOVE'S REDEMPTION. First National, 1921. *Albert Parker.* Harrison Ford, Montagu Love, Ida Waterman.

SMILIN' THROUGH. First National, 1922. *Sidney A. Franklin.* Harrison Ford, Wyndham Standing, Glenn Hunter, Alec B. Francis, Gene Lockhart, Miriam Battista.

THE ETERNAL FLAME. First National, 1922. *Frank Lloyd.* Conway Tearle, Adolphe Menjou, Irving Cummings, Kate Lester, Juanita Hansen, Wedgwood Nowell, Otis Harlan, Rosemary Theby, Thomas Ricketts.

THE VOICE FROM THE MINARET. First National, 1923. *Frank Lloyd.* Eugene O'Brien, Edwin Stevens, Carl Gerard, Winter Hall, Claire DuBrey.

WITHIN THE LAW. First National, 1923. *Frank Lloyd.* Lew Cody, Jack

Mulhall, Eileen Percy, Ward Crane, Helen Ferguson, Joseph Kilgour.

ASHES OF VENGEANCE. First National, 1923. *Frank Lloyd*. Conway Tearle, Wallace Beery, Courtenay Foote, Claire McDowell, Betty Francisco, Joseph Crowell, Winter Hall, Mary McAllister, Andre Beranger, Ann Cornwall.

SONG OF LOVE. First National, 1923. *Frances Marion* and *Chester M. Franklin*. Joseph Schildkraut, Arthur Edmund Carewe, Mabel Wayne, Albert Frisco, Hector V. Sarno.

SECRETS. First National, 1924. *Frank Borzage*. Eugene O'Brien, Claire McDowell, Gertrude Astor, Alice Day, Emily Fitzroy, Donald Keith, Doris Lloyd, Dick Sutherland, Winter Hall.

THE ONLY WOMAN. First National, 1924. *Sidney Olcott*. Eugene O'Brien, Kathryn Bennett, Winter Hall, E. H. Calvert, Stella di Lanti, Brooks Benedict.

THE LADY. First National, 1925. *Frank Borzage*. Wallace MacDonald, George Hackathorne, Brandon Hurst, Doris Lloyd, Walter Long, Emily Fitzroy.

GRAUSTARK. First National, 1925. *Dimitri Buchowetski*. Eugene O'Brien, Wanda Hawley, Roy D'Arcy, Frank Currier, Winter Hall, Albert Gran, Marc McDermott.

KIKI. First National, 1926. *Clarence Brown*. Ronald Colman, George K. Arthur, Mack Swain, Gertrude Astor, Frank Darro, Marc McDermott, Eugenie Besserer.

CAMILLE. First National, 1927. *Fred Niblo*. Gilbert Roland, Maurice Costello, Lilyan Tashman, Alec B. Francis, Helen Jerome Eddy, Albert Conti, Michael Visaroff.

THE DOVE. United Artists, 1928. *Roland West*. Gilbert Roland, Noah Beery, Alice White, Harry Myers, Michael Vavitch, Walter Daniels.

THE WOMAN DISPUTED. United Artists, 1928. *Henry King* and *Sam Taylor*. Gilbert Roland, Arnold Kent, Gladys Brockwell, Michael Vavitch, Gustav von Seyffertitz.

NEW YORK NIGHTS. United Artists, 1929. *Lewis Milestone*. Gilbert Roland, John Wray, Lilyan Tashman, Mary Doran, Roscoe Karns, Jean Harlow.

DUBARRY—WOMAN OF PASSION. United Artists, 1930. *Sam Taylor*. Conrad Nagel, William Farnum, Hobart Bosworth, Alison Skipworth, Henry Kolker, E. Alyn Warren, Edgar Norton, Ullrich Haupt.

THE FILMS OF ROBERT FLOREY

Listed below are the feature films directed by Robert Florey. The italicized name after the title is that of the producer and/or distributor. The date is the year of release. The names after the date are those of the principal players.

This listing does not include the many one- and two-reel shorts Florey made for Paramount in 1928–29, nor the four experimental films mentioned in the article. Florey also directed scenes in films credited to other directors, notably *Go Into Your Dance, Rose of the Rancho, Bombers Moon, Escape in the Desert,* and backgrounds for *Anna Christie.*

No attempt is made to list the more than 300 television films made between 1950 and 1965.

FIFTY-FIFTY. *Imperial.* 1923. A two-reeler. Maurice DeCanonge, Stella DeLanti, Richard Blaydon.

ONE HOUR OF LOVE. *Tiffany.* 1926. Jacqueline Logan, Robert Frazer, Mildred Harris Chaplin.

THE ROMANTIC AGE. *Columbia.* 1927. Alberta Vaughn, Eugene O'-Brien, Stanley Taylor.

FACE VALUE. *Sterling.* 1927. Fritzi Ridgeway, Jack Mower, Gene Gowing.

NIGHT CLUB. *Paramount.* 1928. Fannie Brice, Ann Pennington, Bobbe Arnst.

THE PUSHER-IN-THE FACE. *Paramount.* 1928. A three-reeler. Lester Allen, Raymond Hitchcock, Estelle Taylor.

HOLE IN THE WALL. *Paramount.* 1929. Claudette Colbert, Edward G. Robinson, David Newell.

BONJOUR, NEW YORK! *Paramount.* 1929. A three-reeler. Maurice Chevalier. French dialogue.

THE COCOANUTS. *Paramount.* 1929. The Marx Brothers, Kay Francis, Mary Eaton. Co-directed with Joseph Santley.

THE BATTLE OF PARIS. *Paramount.* 1929. Gertrude Lawrence, Charlie Ruggles, Arthur Treacher. Also released under the title THE GAY LADY.

LA ROUTE EST BELLE. *Braunberger.* 1930. Andre Bauge, Leon Bary, Laurette Fleury. French dialogue, filmed in Great Britain.

L'AMOUR CHANTE. *Braunberger.* 1930. Fernand Gravet, Pierre Bertin, Yolande Laffon. French dialogue, filmed in Berlin.

KOMM' ZU MIR ZUM RENDEZVOUS. *Braunberger.* 1930. German version of L'AMOUR CHANTE, filmed in Berlin in cooperation with Harmonie Films.

EL PROFESOR DE MI SENORA. *Braunberger.* 1930. Spanish version of L'AMOUR CHANTE, filmed in Berlin in cooperation with Cinaes-Madrid. Florelle, Valentin Parera.

LE BLANC ET LE NOIR. *Braunberger.* 1930. Sacha Guitry, Raimu, Fernandel, Suzanne Dantes. French dialogue, filmed in Paris.

MURDERS IN THE RUE MORGUE. *Universal.* 1931. Bela Lugosi, Sydney Fox, Leon Ames.

MAN CALLED BACK. *KBS-Tiffany.* 1932. Conrad Nagel, Doris Kenyon, John Halliday.

THOSE WE LOVE. *KBS-World Wide.* 1932. Mary Astor, Lilyan Tashman, Kenneth MacKenna.

GIRL MISSING. *Warner Brothers.* 1932. Ben Lyon, Mary Brian, Peggy Shannon.

EX-LADY. *Warner Brothers.* 1933. Bette Davis, Gene Raymond, Claire Dodd.

HOUSE ON 56TH STREET. *Warner Brothers.* 1933. Kay Francis, Gene Raymond, Ricardo Cortez.

BEDSIDE. *Warner Brothers.* 1933. Warren William, Jean Muir, Allen Jenkins.

REGISTERED NURSE. *Warner Brothers.* 1934. Bebe Daniels, Lyle Talbot, John Halliday.

SMARTY. *Warner Brothers.* 1934. Joan Blondell, Warren William, Edward Everett Horton.

I SELL ANYTHING. *Warner Brothers.* 1934. Pat O'Brien, Ann Dvorak, Claire Dodd.

I AM A THIEF. *Warner Brothers.* 1934. Mary Astor, Ricardo Cortez, Dudley Digges.

WOMAN IN RED. *Warner Brothers.* 1934. Barbara Stanwyck, Gene Raymond, Genevieve Tobin.

FLORENTINE DAGGER. *Warner Brothers.* 1935. Donald Woods, Margaret Lindsay, C. Aubrey Smith.

GOING HIGHBROW. *Warner Brothers.* 1935. Guy Kibbee, Zasu Pitts, Judy Canova.

DON'T BET ON BLONDES. *Warner Brothers.* 1935. Warren William, Claire Dodd, William Gargan, Errol Flynn.

THE PAY-OFF. *Warner Brothers.* 1935. James Dunn, Claire Dodd, Patricia Ellis.

SHIP CAFE. *Paramount.* 1935. Carl Brisson, Arline Judge, Mady Christians.

PREVIEW MURDER MYSTERY. *Paramount.* 1935. Reginald Denny, Gail Patrick, Frances Drake.

TILL WE MEET AGAIN. *Paramount.* 1936. Herbert Marshall, Gertrude Michael, Rod LaRocque.

HOLLYWOOD BOULEVARD. *Paramount.* 1936. Robert Cummings, John Halliday, Marsha Hunt.

THE OUTCAST. *Paramount-Cohen.* 1936. Warren William, Karen Morley.

KING OF GAMBLERS. *Paramount.* 1937. Lloyd Nolan, Claire Trevor.

MOUNTAIN MUSIC. *Paramount.* 1937. Bob Burns, Martha Raye.

THIS WAY PLEASE. *Paramount.* 1937. Betty Grable, Jackie Coogan, Fibber McGee and Molly.

DAUGHTER OF SHANGHAI. *Paramount.* 1937. Anna May Wong, Charles Bickford, Buster Crabbe.

DANGEROUS TO KNOW. *Paramount.* 1937. Anna May Wong, Akim Tamiroff.

KING OF ALCATRAZ. *Paramount.* 1938. Lloyd Nolan, Gail Patrick, Harry Carey.

DISBARRED. *Paramount.* 1938. Robert Preston, Gail Patrick, Otto Kruger.

HOTEL IMPERIAL. *Paramount.* 1938. Ray Milland, Isa Miranda.

MAGNIFICENT FRAUD. *Paramount.* 1939. Lloyd Nolan, Patricia Morison, Akim Tamiroff.

PAROLE FIXER. *Paramount.* 1939. Robert Paige, Gertrude Michael, Anthony Quinn.

DEATH OF A CHAMPION. *Paramount.* 1939. Robert Paige, Donald O'Connor, Virginia Dale.

WOMEN WITHOUT NAMES. *Paramount.* 1939. Ellen Drew, Robert Paige, Virginia Dabney.

FACE BEHIND THE MASK. *Columbia.* 1940. Peter Lorre, Evelyn Keyes.

MEET BOSTON BLACKIE. *Columbia.* 1940. Chester Morris, Rochelle Hudson.

TWO IN A TAXI. *Columbia.* 1941. Anita Louise, Russell Hayden, Dick Purcell.

DANGEROUSLY THEY LIVE. *Warner Brothers.* 1941. John Garfield, Raymond Massey, Nancy Coleman.

LADY GANGSTER. *Warner Brothers.* 1942. Faye Emerson, Jackie Gleason. Directed under the name of "Florian Roberts."

DESERT SONG. *Warner Brothers.* 1943. Dennis Morgan, Irene Manning, Faye Emerson.

ROGER TOUHY—GANGSTER. *20th Century-Fox.* 1943. Preston Foster, Victor McLaglen.

MAN FROM FRISCO. *Republic.* 1944. Michael O'Shea, Anne Shirley, Dan Duryea.

GOD IS MY CO-PILOT. *Warner Brothers.* 1944. Dennis Morgan, Raymond Massey, Andrea King.

DANGER SIGNAL. *Warner Brothers.* 1945. Faye Emerson, Zachary Scott.

BEAST WITH FIVE FINGERS. *Warner Brothers.* 1946. Peter Lorre, Andrea King, Robert Alda.

MONSIEUR VERDOUX. *Chaplin-United Artists.* 1946. Charlie Chaplin, Martha Raye. Associate Director to Charles S. Chaplin.

TARZAN AND THE MERMAIDS. *Lesser-RKO Radio.* 1947. Johnny Weissmuller, Brenda Joyce.

ROGUES REGIMENT. *Universal-International.* 1948. Dick Powell, Marta Toren.

OUTPOST IN MOROCCO. *Moroccan-United Artists.* 1948. George Raft, Akim Tamiroff, Marie Windsor.

CROOKED WAY. *Bogeaus-United Artists.* 1949. John Payne, Ellen Drew, Sonny Tufts.

JOHNNY ONE-EYE. *Bogeaus-United Artists.* 1949. Pat O'Brien, Wayne Morris.

VICIOUS YEARS. *Emerald-Film Classics.* 1950. Tommy Cook, Gar Moore, Russ Tamblyn.

THE FILMS OF MARSHALL NEILAN

This listing of films directed by Marshall Neilan does not include the shorts he did for Universal, Kalem and Selig, 1914–16, nor the two-reel comedies for Mack Sennett and Hal Roach in the early '30s.

THE CYCLE OF FATE. *Selig-Polyscope*. 1916. Bessie Eyton, Wheeler Oakman, Edith Johnson.

THE PRINCE CHAP. *Selig-Polyscope*. 1916. Bessie Eyton, George Fawcett, Camille D'Arcy.

COUNTRY THAT GOD FORGOT. *Selig-Polyscope*. 1916. Tom Santschi, Mary Charleson, George Fawcett.

THOSE WITHOUT SIN. *Lasky*. 1917. Blanche Sweet, Tom Forman, James Neill.

THE BOTTLE IMP. *Lasky*. 1917. Sessue Hayakawa, Margaret Loomis, James Neill.

TIDES OF BARNEGAT. *Lasky*. 1917. Blanche Sweet, Elliott Dexter, Tom Forman, Harrison Ford.

THE GIRL AT HOME. *Lasky*. 1917. Jack Pickford, Vivian Martin, James Neill.

SILENT PARTNER. *Lasky*. 1917. Blanche Sweet, Tom Forman, Thomas Meighan.

FRECKLES. *Lasky*. 1917. Jack Pickford, Hobart Bosworth, Louise Huff.

JAGUAR'S CLAWS. *Lasky*. 1917. Sessue Hayakawa, Tom Moore, Tom Forman, Marjorie Daw.

REBECCA OF SUNNYBROOK FARM. *Artcraft*. 1917. Mary Pickford, Eugene O'Brien, Marjorie Daw, Wesley Barry.

THE LITTLE PRINCESS. *Artcraft*. 1917. Mary Pickford, Norman Kerry, Zasu Pitts, Theodore Roberts.

STELLA MARIS. *Artcraft*. 1918. Mary Pickford, Conway Tearle.

AMARILLY OF CLOTHESLINE ALLEY. *Artcraft*. 1918. Mary Pickford, Norman Kerry, Wesley Barry.

M'LISS. *Artcraft*. 1918. Mary Pickford, Thomas Meighan, Monte Blue, Theodore Roberts.

HIT-THE-TRAIL HOLLIDAY. *Artcraft*. 1918. George M. Cohan, Richard Barthelmess, Marguerite Clayton.

HEART OF THE WILDS. *Artcraft*. 1918. Elsie Ferguson, Matt Moore, Thomas Meighan.

OUT OF A CLEAR SKY. *Famous Players-Lasky*. 1918. Marguerite Clark, Thomas Meighan, Bobby Connelly.

THREE MEN AND A GIRL. *Famous Players-Lasky*. 1919. Marguerite Clark, Richard Barthelmess, Percy Marmont.

DADDY LONG LEGS. *First National*. 1919. Mary Pickford, Mahlon Hamilton, Marshall Neilan, Wesley Barry.

THE UNPARDONABLE SIN. *Garson-Neilan-Equity*. 1919. Blanche Sweet, Wallace Beery, Holbrook Blinn, Wesley Barry.

HER KINGDOM OF DREAMS. *First National*. 1920. Anita Stewart, Mahlon Hamilton, Anna Q. Nilsson, Tom Santschi.

IN OLD KENTUCKY. *First National*. 1920. Anita Stewart, Mahlon Hamilton, E. J. Connelly.

THE RIVER'S END. *First National*. 1920. Lewis Stone, Marjorie Daw, Jane Novak.

DON'T EVER MARRY. *First National.* 1920. Marjorie Daw, Matt Moore, Wesley Barry. Co-directed with Victor Heerman.

GO AND GET IT. *First National.* 1920. Agnes Ayres, Pat O'Malley, Wesley Barry.

DINTY. *First National.* 1920. Wesley Barry, Colleen Moore, Marjorie Daw. Co-directed with John W. McDermott.

BOB HAMPTON OF PLACER. *First National.* 1921. James Kirkwood, Pat O'Malley, Marjorie Daw, Wesley Barry.

BITS OF LIFE. *First National.* 1921. Lon Chaney, Dorothy Mackaill, John Bowers, Anna May Wong. Co-directed with James Flood and William Scully.

THE LOTUS EATER. *First National.* 1921. John Barrymore, Colleen Moore, Anna Q. Nilsson, Dorothy Mackaill.

PENROD. *First National.* 1922. Wesley Barry, Marjorie Daw, John Harron. Co-directed with Frank O'Connor.

FOOLS FIRST. *First National.* 1922. Richard Dix, Raymond Griffith, Claire Windsor.

MINNIE. *First National.* 1922. Leatrice Joy, Raymond Griffith, Matt Moore. Co-directed with Frank Urson.

STRANGER'S BANQUET. *Goldwyn.* 1923. Claire Windsor, Ford Sterling, Eleanor Boardman, Stuart Holmes.

ETERNAL THREE. *Goldwyn.* 1923. Claire Windsor, Raymond Griffith, Hobart Bosworth, Bessie Love. Co-directed with Frank Urson.

THE RENDEZVOUS. *Goldwyn.* 1923. Conrad Nagel, Syd Chaplin, Lucille Ricksen.

DOROTHY VERNON OF HADDON HALL. *United Artists.* 1924. Mary Pickford, Allan Forrest, Estelle Taylor.

TESS OF THE D'URBERVILLES. *Metro-Goldwyn.* 1925. Blanche Sweet, Conrad Nagel, Stuart Holmes.

SPORTING VENUS. *Metro-Goldwyn.* 1925. Blanche Sweet, Ronald Colman, Lew Cody.

THE GREAT LOVE. *M-G-M.* 1925. Viola Dana, Robert Agnew.

MIKE. *M-G-M.* 1926. Sally O'Neil, William Haines, Ford Sterling, Charlie Murray.

THE SKYROCKET. *Associated Exhibitors.* 1926. Peggy Hopkins Joyce, Owen Moore, Lilyan Tashman, Earle Williams.

WILD OATS LANE. *PDC.* 1926. Viola Dana, Robert Agnew, Jerry Miley.

DIPLOMACY. *Paramount.* 1926. Blanche Sweet, Neil Hamilton, Matt Moore.

EVERYBODY'S ACTING. *Paramount.* 1926. Betty Bronson, Ford Sterling, Louise Dresser, Lawrence Gray.

VENUS OF VENICE. *First National.* 1927. Constance Talmadge, Antonio Moreno, Julanne Johnston.

HER WILD OAT. *First National.* 1927. Colleen Moore, Larry Kent, Julanne Johnston.

THREE-RING MARRIAGE. *First National.* 1928. Mary Astor, Lloyd

Hughes, Alice White.

TAKE ME HOME. *Paramount.* 1928. Bebe Daniels, Neil Hamilton, Joe E. Brown, Lilyan Tashman.

TAXI 13. *FBO.* 1928. Chester Conklin, Martha Sleeper, Jerry Miley.

HIS LAST HAUL. *FBO.* 1928. Seena Owen, Tom Moore.

BLACK WATERS. *World Wide.* 1929. Mary Brian, James Kirkwood, Robert Ames, John Loder.

THE AWFUL TRUTH. *Pathé.* 1929. Ina Claire, Henry Daniell, Paul Harvey.

TANNED LEGS. *RKO Radio.* 1929. Ann Pennington, Arthur Lake, June Clyde.

THE VAGABOND LOVER. *RKO Radio.* 1929. Rudy Vallee, Sally Blane, Marie Dressler.

SWEETHEARTS ON PARADE. *Columbia.* 1930. Alice White, Lloyd Hughes, Marie Prevost.

CHLOE. *Pinnacle.* 1934. Olive Borden, Reed Howes, Molly O'Day, Philip Ober.

SOCIAL REGISTER. *Columbia.* 1934. Colleen Moore, Pauline Frederick, Charles Winninger, Alexander Kirkland.

THE LEMON DROP KID. *Paramount.* 1934. Lee Tracy, Helen Mack, William Frawley.

THIS IS THE LIFE. *20th Century-Fox.* 1935. Jane Withers, Sally Blane, Sidney Toler.

SING WHILE YOU'RE ABLE. *Ambassador.* 1937. Pinky Tomlin, Toby Wing, Bert Roach.

THANKS FOR LISTENING. *Ambassador.* 1937. Pinky Tomlin, Maxine Doyle, Aileen Pringle.

SWING IT, PROFESSOR. *Ambassador.* 1937. Pinky Tomlin, Paula Stone, Milburn Stone.

THE FILMS OF COLLEEN MOORE

BAD BOY. *Fine Arts-Triangle.* 1917. Robert Harron, Mildred Harris, James Morrison. Director, Chester Withey.

AN OLD-FASHIONED YOUNG MAN. *Fine Arts-Triangle.* 1917. Robert Harron, Mildred Harris, Alma Rubens. Director, Chester Withey.

HANDS UP! *Fine Arts-Triangle.* 1917. Wilfred Lucas, Monte Blue. Director, Tod Browning.

THE SAVAGE. *Bluebird-Universal.* 1918. Monroe Salisbury, Ruth Clifford. Director, Rupert Julian.

A HOOSIER ROMANCE. *Selig-Mutual.* 1918. Frank Hayes, Thomas Jefferson. Director, Colin Campbell.

LITTLE ORPHANT ANNIE. *Selig-Mutual.* 1918. Tom Santschi, Eugenie Besserer. Director, Colin Campbell.

THE BUSHER. *Ince-Paramount.* 1919. Charles Ray, John Gilbert, Margaret Livingston. Director, Jerome Storm.

WILDERNESS TRAIL. *Fox.* 1919. Tom Mix, William Ellingford. Director, Edward J. LeSaint.

MAN IN THE MOONLIGHT. *Universal.* 1919. Monroe Salisbury, William Stowell. Director, Paul Powell.

THE EGG-CRATE WALLOP. *Ince-Paramount.* 1919. Charles Ray, J. P. Lockney, Jack Connolly. Director, Jerome Storm.

COMMON PROPERTY. *Universal.* 1919. Robert Anderson, Frank Leigh, Richard Cummings. Director, Paul Powell.

THE CYCLONE. *Fox.* 1920. Tom Mix, William Ellingford, Henry Herbert. Director, Clifford J. Smith.

A ROMAN SCANDAL. *Christie.* 1920. Earle Rodney. Director, Al E. Christie. A two-reeler.

HER BRIDAL NIGHTMARE. *Christie.* 1920. Eugene Corey. Director, Al E. Christie. A two-reeler.

THE DEVIL'S CLAIM. *Haworth-Robertson-Cole.* 1920. Sessue Hayakawa, Rhea Mitchell, Wilson Hummel. Director, Charles Swickard.

SO LONG LETTY. *Christie-Robertson-Cole.* 1920. T. Roy Barnes, Walter Hiers, Grace Darmond. Director, Al E. Christie.

WHEN DAWN CAME. *Hugh Dierker-Producers Security Corporation.* 1920. Lee Shumway, William Conklin. Director, Colin Campbell.

DINTY. *Neilan-First National.* 1920. Wesley Barry, Pat O'Malley, Marjorie Daw. Directors, Marshall Neilan and John W. McDermott.

THE SKY PILOT. *Curtis-First National.* 1921. John Bowers, David Butler, Kathleen Kirkham. Director, King Vidor.

THE LOTUS EATER. *Neilan-First National.* 1921. John Barrymore, Anna Q. Nilsson, Dorothy Mackaill. Director, Marshall Neilan.

HIS NIBS. *Christie-Exceptional.* 1921. Charles (Chic) Sale, Lydia Yeamans Titus. Director, Al E. Christie.

BROKEN HEARTS OF BROADWAY. *Cummings-Select.* 1921. Alice Lake, Johnny Walker, Creighton Hale. Director, Irving Cummings.

COME ON OVER. *Goldwyn.* 1922. Ralph Graves, J. Farrell MacDonald, Kate Price. Director, Alfred E. Green.

THE WALLFLOWER. *Goldwyn.* 1922. Richard Dix, Laura LaPlante. Director, Rupert Hughes.

AFFINITIES. *Hodkinson.* 1922. John Bowers. Director, Ward Lascelle,

FORSAKING ALL OTHERS. *Universal.* 1922. Cullen Landis, June Elvidge, Sam DeGrasse. Director, Emile Chautard.

BROKEN CHAINS. *Goldwyn.* 1922. Malcolm McGregor, Claire Windsor, Ernest Torrence. Director, Allen Holubar.

THE NINETY AND NINE. *Vitagraph.* 1922. Warner Baxter, Lucille Lee Stewart. Director, David Smith.

LOOK YOUR BEST. *Goldwyn.* 1923. Antonio Moreno, Earle Meltcalf. Director, Rupert Hughes.

SLIPPY MCGEE. *Morosco-First National.* 1923. Wheeler Oakman, Sam DeGrasse, Lloyd Whitlock. Director, Wesley Ruggles.

THE NTH COMMANDMENT. *Cosmopolitan-Paramount*. 1923. James Morrison, Eddie Phillips. Director, Frank Borzage.

APRIL SHOWERS. *Schulberg-Preferred*. 1923. Kenneth Harlan, Ruth Clifford. Director, Tom Forman.

THROUGH THE DARK. *Cosmopolitan-Goldwyn*. 1923. Forrest Stanley, Carmelita Geraghty. Director, George W. Hill.

THE HUNTRESS. *First National*. 1923. Lloyd Hughes, Lila Leslie, Snitz Edwards. Director, Lynn F. Reynolds.

FLAMING YOUTH. *First National*. 1923. Milton Sills, Ben Lyon, Elliott Dexter. Director, John Francis Dillon.

PAINTED PEOPLE. *First National*. 1924. Ben Lyon, Anna Q. Nilsson. Director, Clarence G. Badger.

THE PERFECT FLAPPER. *First National*. 1924. Frank Mayo, Sydney Chaplin, Phyllis Haver. Director, John Francis Dillon.

FLIRTING WITH LOVE. *First National*. 1924. Conway Tearle, Winifred Bryson. Director, John Francis Dillon.

SO BIG. *First National*. 1924. Wallace Beery, Ben Lyon, John Bowers. Director, Charles J. Brabin.

SALLY. *First National*. 1925. Lloyd Hughes, Leon Errol, Ray Hallor. Director, Alfred E. Green.

THE DESERT FLOWER. *First National*. 1925. Lloyd Hughes, Kate Price. Director, Irving Cummings.

WE MODERNS. *First National*. 1925. Jack Mulhall, Claude Gillingwater. Director, John Francis Dillon.

IRENE. *First National*. 1926. Lloyd Hughes, George K. Arthur, Eva Novak. Director, Alfred E. Green.

ELLA CINDERS. *First National*. 1926. Lloyd Hughes, Harry Langdon, Jed Prouty. Director, Alfred E. Green.

IT MUST BE LOVE. *First National*. 1926. Malcolm McGregor, Mary Brian, Jean Hersholt. Director, Alfred E. Green.

TWINKLETOES. *First National*. 1927. Kenneth Harlan, Warner Oland, Gladys Brockwell. Director, Charles J. Brabin.

ORCHIDS AND ERMINE. *First National*. 1927. Jack Mulhall, Mickey Rooney, Hedda Hopper. Director, Alfred Santell.

NAUGHTY BUT NICE. *First National*. 1927. Donald Reed, Loretta Young, Kathryn McGuire. Director, Millard Webb.

HER WILD OAT. *First National*. 1927. Larry Kent, Julanne Johnston. Director, Marshall Neilan.

HAPPINESS AHEAD. *First National*. 1928. Edmund Lowe, Lilyan Tashman, Diane Ellis. Director, William A. Seiter.

OH KAY! *First National*. 1928. Lawrence Gray, Claude King, Ford Sterling, Alan Hale. Director, Mervyn LeRoy.

LILAC TIME. *First National*. Gary Cooper, Arthur Lake, Kathryn McGuire. Director, George Fitzmaurice.

SYNTHETIC SIN. *First National*. 1928. Antonio Moreno, Montagu Love, Kathryn McGuire. Director, William A. Seiter.

WHY BE GOOD? *First National*. 1929. Neil Hamilton, John Sainpolis. Director, William A. Seiter.

SMILING IRISH EYES. *First National*. 1929. James Hall, Claude Gillingwater. Director, William A. Seiter.

FOOTLIGHTS AND FOOLS. *First National*. 1929. Fredric March, Raymond Hackett. Director, William A. Seiter.

THE POWER AND THE GLORY. *Fox*. 1933. Spencer Tracy, Helen Vinson, Ralph Morgan. Director, William K. Howard.

SUCCESS AT ANY PRICE. *RKO Radio*. 1934. Douglas Fairbanks, Jr., Genevieve Tobin, Frank Morgan. Director, J. Walter Ruben.

SOCIAL REGISTER. *Associated Film Productions-Columbia*. 1934. Pauline Frederick, Charles Winninger. Director, Marshall Neilan.

THE SCARLET LETTER. *Majestic*. 1934. Hardie Albright, Henry B. Walthall, Alan Hale. Director, Robert G. Vignola.

INDEX OF NAMES

411

INDEX OF FILMS